The Intermediate Spanish market increasingly demands interactive anc online instructional materials that align with the goals of the course. the participants surveyed said they would use an interactive e-book and felt that it would enhance the learning experience of their students.

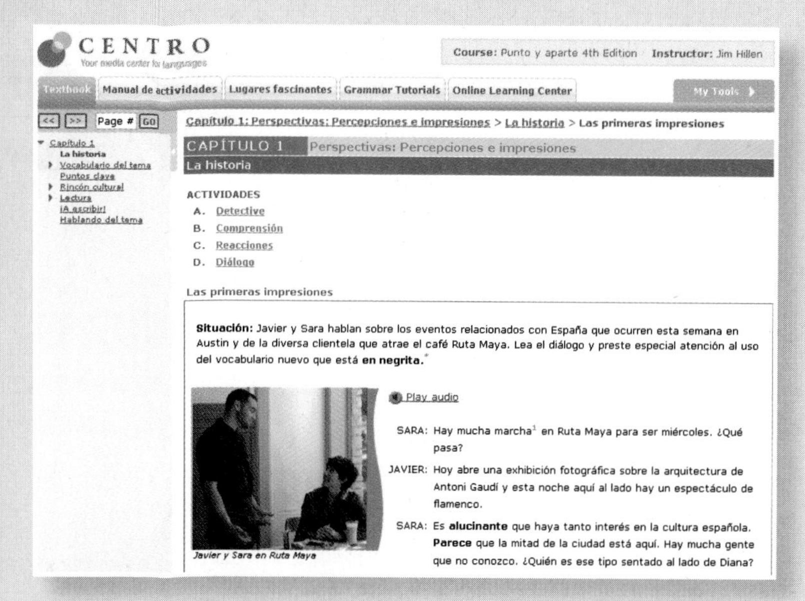

The Digital Edition of *Punto y aparte* contains presentation and practice, including embedded audio, video, and voice recording so that students can easily complete their paired communicative exercises online. A robust gradebook makes this the ideal course management system for both students and instructors.

58% of Intermediate Spanish instructors consider a high-quality video program to be an essential element of the Intermediate Spanish course.

For the Fourth Edition of *Punto y aparte*, McGraw-Hill, using footage provided by BBC Motion Gallery, has produced a stunning video that enhances the cultural content of the program by bringing to life all of the places featured in the **Lugares fascinantes** readings.

If you would like to participate in any of the McGraw-Hill research initiatives, please contact us at **www.mhhe.com/faculty-research.**

Punto y aparte

FOURTH EDITION

Spanish in Review • Moving Toward Fluency

Sharon Foerster

Anne Lambright
Trinity College

Published by McGraw-Hill, an imprint of The McGraw-Hill Companies, Inc., 1221 Avenue of the Americas, New York, NY 10020.

This book is printed on recycled, acid-free paper containing 10% postconsumer waste.

1 2 3 4 5 6 7 8 9 0 WVR/WVR 0

Student Edition
ISBN: 978-0-07-338530-3
MHID: 0-07-338530-1

Instructor's Edition (not for resale)
ISBN: 978-0-07-735021-5
MHID: 0-07-735021-9

Vice President, Editorial: *Michael Ryan*
Editorial Director: *William R. Glass*
Sponsoring Editor: *Katherine K. Crouch*
Director of Development: *Scott Tinetti*
Developmental Editors: *Connie Anderson and Max Ehrsam*
Executive Marketing Manager: *Stacy Best Ruel*
Marketing Manager: *Jorge Arbujas*
Editorial Coordinator: *Erin Blaze*
Production Editor: *Brett Coker*
Production Service: *Alice Bowman, Matrix Productions, Inc.*
Manuscript Editor: *Margaret Hines*
Designers: *Andrei Pasternak and Jenny El-Shamy*
Illustrator: *Rémy Simard*
Photo Researcher: *Kim Adams*
Production Supervisor: *Louis Swaim*
Media Project Manager: *Thomas Brierly*
Composition: *10/12 Palatino by Aptara®, Inc.*
Printing: *45# New Era Matte by Worldcolor*
Cover Image: © *Thorsten/fotolia*

Credits: The credits section for this book begins on page C-1 and is considered an extension of the copyright page.

Library of Congress Cataloging-in-Publication Data

Foerster, Sharon.
Punto y aparte / Sharon Foerster, Anne Lambright.—4th student ed.
p. cm.
Spanish and English.
Includes bibliographical references and index.
ISBN-13: 978-0-07-338530-3 (alk. paper)
ISBN-10: 0-07-338530-1 (alk. paper)
1. Spanish language—Textbooks for foreign speakers—English. I. Lambright, Anne. II. Title.
III. Title: Punto.
PC4129.E5F64 2010
468.2′421—dc22

2009047485

Dedication

This book is dedicated to our bilingual children:
Shaanti, Jonathan, Corazón, Isis, Paloma, Guillermo Bey II, and Maya.

About the Authors

Sharon Wilson Foerster retired from the University of Texas at Austin in 2001, where she had been the Coordinator of Lower Division Courses in the Department of Spanish and Portuguese, directing the first- and second-year Spanish language program and training graduate assistant instructors. She continues to teach Spanish in the Summer Language School at Middlebury College in Vermont. She received her Ph.D. in Intercultural Communications from the University of Texas in 1981. Before joining the faculty at the University of Texas, she was Director of the Center for Cross-Cultural Study in Seville, Spain, for four years. She continues her involvement in study abroad through her work as Director of the Spanish Teaching Institute and as Academic Advisor for Academic Programs International. She is the co-author of *Lecturas literarias: Moving Toward Linguistic and Cultural Fluency Through Literature* (2007), *Metas comunicativas para maestros* (1999), *Metas comunicativas para negocios* (1998), *In viaggio: Moving Toward Fluency in Italian* (2003), *Supplementary Materials to accompany Puntos de partida,* Sixth Edition (2004), *Metas: Spanish in Review, Moving Toward Fluency* (2008), *Pause-café: Moving Toward Fluency in French* (2009), and *Pasaporte: Spanish for Advanced Beginners* (2009).

Anne Lambright is Associate Professor of Language and Culture Studies in the Hispanic Studies Program at Trinity College in Hartford, Connecticut. She earned her Ph.D. in Latin American literature from the University of Texas at Austin. Her research and teaching focus on contemporary Latin American literature, Andean literature and culture, **indigenismo,** and Latin American women's writing, topics on which she has published several articles and books. She is the author of *Creating the Hybrid Intellectual: Subject, Space and the Feminine in the Narrative of José Arguedas* (2007), and co-editor of *Unfolding the City: Women Write the City in Latin America* (2007), with Elisabeth Guerrero. In addition, she is the co-author of *Metas: Spanish in Review, Moving Toward Fluency.*

Contents

CAPÍTULO 6 167

Hacia el porvenir:

Un mundo más verde y conectado

Explicación gramatical: 194

Los puntos clave

Referencia de gramática: 232

Los otros puntos gramaticales

To the Instructor

Are your students simply learning ***about*** *language or are they learning to* ***use*** *language?*

This simple question is fundamental to a key objective of the intermediate Spanish course: to help students improve their communicative skills in Spanish. Yet instructors often struggle to achieve this goal. While their course materials may provide a review of grammatical rules, they do not always provide ample opportunities for students to develop their language use. By the time students have reached their second year of language study, their needs as learners are beginning to shift. While second-year students need to continue refining their knowledge of grammatical rules, learning to use those functions in real-life in a variety of communicative scenarios is equally important.

Punto y aparte: Spanish in Review, Moving Toward Fluency places communicative goals at the forefront of the course so that students are encouraged to look at grammar in a different way. Grammar becomes the tool that allows students to express themselves with increasing fluency and accuracy. As such, students begin to see how mastery of specific grammar points is necessary for communicating most effectively. The activities in *Punto y aparte* require that students use language in meaningful contexts, such as expressing feelings, opinions, and speculations. They also use multiple communicative functions simultaneously (such as description and narrating in the past), which is closer to the real-life scenarios in which they will use their developing language skills.

A Unique Approach

The idea for the first edition of *Punto y aparte* came in response to a commonly expressed need at the intermediate level. Experienced instructors know that after relatively quick progress through the novice and lower-intermediate levels of proficiency, students are commonly faced with the phenomenon of the "second-year plateau." They often become frustrated and lose the necessary motivation to continue on into the high-intermediate and advanced levels. Thus, the goal was to identify learning strategies that would motivate students and help them move forward in the language acquisition process. By focusing on seven core communicative functions and the grammatical structures that support them, *Punto y aparte* helps students develop the ability and confidence to communicate and to think critically about language and culture. Since this is not the typical linear march through grammar one structure at a time, students are able to begin using language in a more authentic and natural way. As the title suggests, *Punto y aparte** puts students on a successful path from simple utterances to more extensive discourse, from sentence-level to paragraph-length expression.

***

A Visual System for Mastering the Functions

How does the *Punto y aparte* program empower your students to communicate with confidence in Spanish? *Punto y aparte* continually draws students' attention to seven communicative functions via marginal icons that appear continuously throughout every section of the book.

Descripción

Comparación

Narración en el pasado

Reacciones y recomendaciones

*In Spanish, **punto y aparte** is the expression used to indicate the beginning of a new paragraph.

Hablar de los gustos

Hacer hipótesis

Hablar del futuro

Each chapter highlights a separate communicative function and explicitly links it with the grammatical structures students will need for that function. At the same time, from the very beginning, all seven communicative functions are recycled constantly and often used simultaneously, as they are in natural language production. For example, after reading an anecdote in the past tense, a natural follow-up would be offering advice, thus the communicative value of the subjunctive becomes obvious. This also means that students don't run the risk of forgetting the structures they mastered in the previous chapters, because they *continue* to use them throughout the book.

Tools for Monitoring Accuracy

Three aspects of the *Punto y aparte* program help students improve their grammatical accuracy:

- **Diagnostic Tests:** After each communicative function is presented, an activity called **Prueba diagnóstica** helps students and instructors to identify the problem areas that need to be reviewed.
- **Grammar Explanations:** Students can find clear and thorough grammar explanations of any formal rule that they need to review in the "green pages" that appear after **Capítulo 6** in the main text. Each grammar structure comes with a self-correcting practice activity (**¡A practicar!**), whose answers can be found in **Apéndice 1.**
- **Extensive practice:** The student *Manual* allows for extensive practice of the grammar structures presented in the green pages. In every chapter of the *Manual,* there are verb charts to practice all tenses and moods, as well as **Los otros puntos clave,** which allows students to practice all of the structures, regardless of which chapter they are working on.

Windows into Spanish-Speaking Cultures

The cultural content of *Punto y aparte* enriches students' experience of language learning and introduces them to people and places outside their realm of experience.

- **Lugares fascinantes** sections cover four specific places within each of the six major geographical regions of the Spanish-speaking world. New to the Fourth Edition is a magnificent video program, produced by McGraw-Hill with footage provided by BBC Motion Gallery that corresponds to these **Lugares fascinantes.** The vibrant cultural segments of the **Lugares fascinantes** video program are presented as video blogs made by two traveling videographers who are sharing their travel experiences with friends and family. These videos are available online in CENTRO, and instructors may also request a complimentary DVD.
- **Un artista hispano** presents an artist who is from each featured region. In the new edition, the artists include, among others, the visionary Spanish architect Antoni Gaudí and the famous contemporary comic strip artist Maitena Burendarena from Argentina.
- **La música…** sections, new to the Fourth Edition, introduce songs written by musicians from the featured regions, along with accompanying comprehension and discussion questions. Students may listen to songs on the CD or in CENTRO, and instructors may request a complimentary copy of the CD.

Active Learning through Reading

Punto y aparte encourages students to become more active learners of Spanish as they read, teaching them useful skills that they can transfer into all of their encounters with the language. In each **Lectura** reading, three icons appear at intervals in the margins.

- The **Vocabulario** icon invites students to speculate on the meaning of a term by having them look at the context as well as the word itself.
- The **Visualizar** icon asks students to try visualizing what is being described.
- The **Verificar** icon accompanies three questions that appear within the text. Here, students are encouraged to step back from the reading briefly to monitor their comprehension: **¿Quién(es)? ¿Dónde? ¿Qué pasó?**

The Fourth Edition contains five new readings, based on reviewer suggestions. These include a wider variety of genres and a more representative cross-section of the Spanish-speaking world:

- **Capítulo 2:** "Entrevista: Benito Zambrano, director de *Habana Blues*" (interview)
- **Capítulo 3:** "Peregrina," the tragic, true story of Alma Reed and the Yucatán governor Felipe Carrillo Puerto (historical account)
- **Capítulo 4:** "Chile: Las tribus urbanas, rostros que buscan una identidad" (human interest article)
- **Capítulo 5:** "El candidato" (short story by Colombian writer José Cardona-López)
- **Capítulo 6:** "Los portadores de sueños" (poem by Nicaraguan author Giaconda Belli)

For those who would like more readings, the companion reader *Lecturas literarias* is also available.

What's New in the Fourth Edition?

Digital Resources

- **Interactive eBook:** The textbook is now available as an interactive eBook, which integrates all the multimedia content seamlessly into each chapter: the new video and audio components as well as recordings of the **La historia** dialogues and the active chapter vocabulary.
- **CENTRO:** McGraw-Hill has partnered with Quia, the leading developer of online tools for foreign-language instruction and learning, to create CENTRO **(www.mhcentro.com).** CENTRO is a comprehensive learning management system that allows you to manage your course with robust communication tools, record-keeping that can be imported to Blackboard and other CMS platforms, integration of instructor resources such as the Instructor's Manual and the Testing Program, as well as the ability to customize or add your own content.
- ***Lugares fascinantes* video program:** The new videos are presented in a video blog format and provide stunningly beautiful footage (provided by BBC Motion Gallery) of each of the twenty-four locations featured in the **Lugares fascinantes** readings, along with engaging and informative narration. Each chapter of the *Manual* contains an activity to accompany the video. The video is available in CENTRO and on a complimentary DVD for instructors.
- **Music CD:** The *Estampillas musicales* CD allows students to listen to songs featured in the new **La música...** section of each chapter.
- **Spanish Grammar Tutorials:** Animated online grammar tutorials allow students to brush up on a wide range of Spanish grammar points on their own.

Print Components

The Fourth Edition of the *Punto y aparte* main text contains the following new features, which respond to concerns expressed by reviewers:

- **Dialogues:** New **La historia** dialogues bring the dialogues up to date and provide excellent models of natural language exchanges. Audio recordings of these dialogues are available on the Online Learning Center and on CENTRO.
- **Sequencing of Grammar:** Past tenses are introduced a chapter earlier, in **Capítulo 2,** to allow for more practice of this challenging aspect of Spanish grammar.
- **Lugares fascinantes:** These sections contain a new feature called **¡Viaje conmigo a... !,** which includes a film still from the new video. An accompanying activity in the *Manual* invites students to give their personal reaction to the places they see in the video. The video is available in CENTRO and on a complimentary DVD for instructors.
- **La música...:** This new feature of the **Rincón cultural** section introduces students to music from each of the six Spanish-speaking regions covered in *Punto y aparte.* A short introduction to the featured musical genre is followed by pre- and post-listening activities, which include the full lyrics to each song. Students may listen to songs on the CD or in CENTRO, and instructors may request a complimentary copy of the CD.
- **Readings:** Five new **Lectura** readings include a wider variety of genres and a more representative cross-section of the Spanish-speaking world.
- **Communicative activities:** The last section of each chapter, **Hablando del tema,** has been expanded to allow for better synthesis of the chapter material in a communicative context.

- **Icons:** Clearer icons help students understand the application of the seven communicative functions throughout each chapter.
- **Photos:** Brand-new photos of the five friends give the book a modern, up-to-date look.

Instructor Resources

The following new or expanded instructor resources are available online on CENTRO and on the *Online Learning Center* (Instructor Edition). For password information, please contact your local McGraw-Hill sales representative.

- **Testing Program:** The tests and quizzes that were previously located in the Instructor's Manual have been consolidated and expanded in a separate Testing Program, which is available online.
- **Image Bank:** Designed to stimulate conversation in the classroom and to expose students to more visual images of the Spanish-speaking world, this online resource contains photos from the twenty-one Spanish-speaking countries.
- **Cultural PowerPoint™ Presentations:** These presentations contain beautiful images and allow instructors to do cultural presentations on all Spanish-speaking countries. Extensive notes on the images appear on each slide to facilitate presentation.

Guided Tour of **Punto y aparte**

Chapter Opener

Each chapter-opening page includes a piece of fine art, discussion questions that instructors can use as an advance organizer to move students into the chapter themes, and bulleted points listing the communicative functions, central themes, and country or region of focus for the chapter.

La historia

Each **La historia** section presents a new dialogue between some of the five friends. Words that represent active vocabulary (those found in the **Vocabulario del tema** listing) appear in boldface. Following the dialogue are activities designed to introduce students to the themes presented in the dialogue and the rest of the chapter. Each new dialogue can be read as a sequel to the original dialogue from the last edition, but it can also stand on its own. The animation to the dialogue from the previous edition is available on the Online Learning Center.

Vocabulario del tema

This section begins with a list of vocabulary items arranged thematically and/or semantically for easier association and reference.

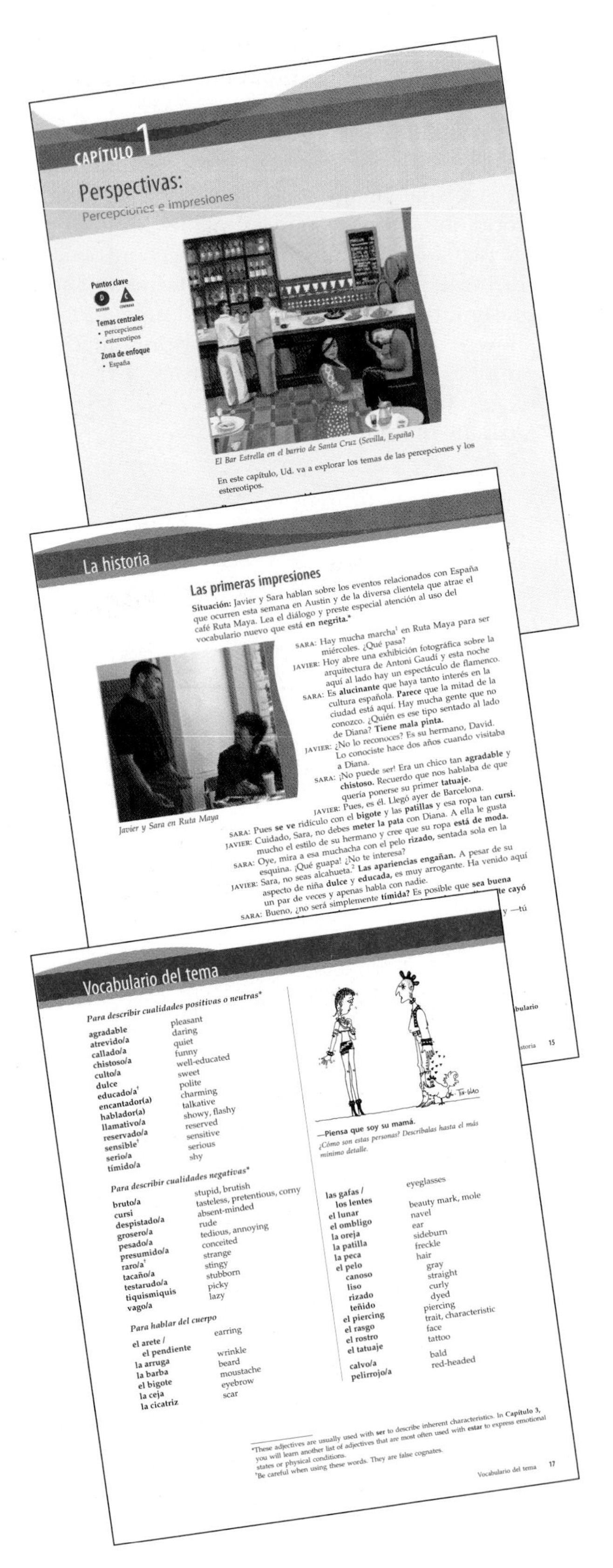

CAPÍTULO 1

Perspectivas:

Percepciones e impresiones

Puntos clave

Temas centrales
- percepciones
- estereotipos

Zona de enfoque
- España

El Bar Estrella en el barrio de Santa Cruz (Sevilla, España)

En este capítulo, Ud. va a explorar los temas de las percepciones y los estereotipos.

La historia

Las primeras impresiones

Situación: Javier y Sara hablan sobre los eventos relacionados con España que ocurren esta semana en Austin y de la diversa clientela que atrae el café Ruta Maya. Lea el diálogo y preste especial atención al uso del vocabulario nuevo que está **en negrita.**

SARA: Hay mucha marcha[1] en Ruta Maya para ser miércoles. ¿Qué pasa?

JAVIER: Hoy abre una exhibición fotográfica sobre la arquitectura de Antoni Gaudí y esta noche aquí al lado hay un espectáculo de flamenco.

SARA: Es **alucinante** que haya tanto interés en la cultura española. **Parece** que la mitad de la ciudad está aquí. Hay mucha gente que no conozco. ¿Quién es ese tipo sentado al lado de Diana? **Tiene mala pinta.**

JAVIER: ¿No lo reconoces? Es su hermano, David. Lo conociste hace dos años cuando visitaba a Diana.

SARA: ¡No puede ser! Era un chico tan **agradable** y **chistoso.** Recuerdo que nos hablaba de que quería ponerse su primer **tatuaje.**

JAVIER: Pues, es él. Llegó ayer de Barcelona.

SARA: Pues **se ve** ridículo con el **bigote** y las **patillas** y esa ropa tan **cursi.**

JAVIER: Cuidado, Sara, no debes **meter la pata** con Diana. A ella le gusta mucho el estilo de su hermano y cree que su ropa **está de moda.**

SARA: Oye, mira a esa muchacha con el pelo **rizado,** sentada sola en la esquina. ¡Qué guapa! ¿No te interesa?

JAVIER: Sara, no seas alcahueta.[2] **Las apariencias engañan.** A pesar de su aspecto de niña **dulce** y **educada,** es muy arrogante. Ha venido aquí un par de veces y apenas habla con nadie.

SARA: Bueno, ¿no será simplemente **tímida?** Es posible que **sea buena**

Javier y Sara en Ruta Maya

Vocabulario del tema

*Para describir cualidades positivas o neutras**

agradable	pleasant
atrevido/a	daring
callado/a	quiet
chistoso/a	funny
culto/a	well-educated
dulce	sweet
educado/a[†]	polite
encantador(a)	charming
hablador(a)	talkative
llamativo/a	showy, flashy
reservado/a	reserved
sensible[†]	sensitive
serio/a	serious
tímido/a	shy

*Para describir cualidades negativas**

bruto/a	stupid, brutish
cursi	tasteless, pretentious, corny
despistado/a	absent-minded
grosero/a	rude
pesado/a	tedious, annoying
presumido/a	conceited
raro/a[†]	strange
tacaño/a	stingy
testarudo/a	stubborn
tiquismiquis	picky
vago/a	lazy

Para hablar del cuerpo

el arete / el pendiente	earring
la arruga	wrinkle
la barba	beard
el bigote	moustache
la ceja	eyebrow
la cicatriz	scar
las gafas / los lentes	eyeglasses
el lunar	beauty mark, mole
el ombligo	navel
la oreja	ear
la patilla	sideburn
la peca	freckle
el pelo	hair
canoso	gray
liso	straight
rizado	curly
teñido	dyed
el piercing	piercing
el rasgo	trait, characteristic
el rostro	face
el tatuaje	tattoo
calvo/a	bald
pelirrojo/a	red-headed

—Piensa que soy su mamá.

¿Cómo son estas personas? Descríbalas hasta el más mínimo detalle.

*These adjectives are usually used with **ser** to describe inherent characteristics. In **Capítulo 3,** you will learn another list of adjectives that are most often used with **estar** to express emotional states or physical conditions.

[†]Be careful when using these words. They are false cognates.

Vocabulario del tema 17

A variety of communicative activities follows, allowing students ample opportunity to work with and acquire the new vocabulary. **Para conversar mejor** boxes provide useful idiomatic expressions for use in small-group conversations. **Nota cultural** boxes highlight one or more cultural aspects of the Spanish-speaking cultures. Each **Nota cultural** is followed by conversation questions that students can answer in pairs or small groups. The conversation questions and the communicative activity require students to use the new vocabulary from the chapter. We have chosen cultural themes for each **Nota cultural** based on the vocabulary themes in the chapter.

Puntos clave

This section of the chapter, which highlights at least one of the seven communicative functions, offers a short review of the grammatical structures that support each function. A brief exercise called **Prueba diagnóstica** allows students to check their command of the pertinent grammatical structures before moving on to the communicative activities.

Rincón cultural

This unique cultural section contains three parts. **Lugares fascinantes** presents points of interest in the chapter's country or region of focus. **¡Viaje conmigo!** is a new feature that invites students to watch the new video footage of the places featured in the **Lugares fascinantes** readings before doing the follow-up activities to those readings.

¡Viaje conmigo a España!

Gabriela y Santiago son dos videógrafos que están pasando un año viajando por el mundo hispano. Son amigos de Javier y Sara y por eso les mandan sus videoblogs. Vea el vídeo para saber lo que Gabriela les mandó sobre su viaje a España.

Video footage provided by BBC Motion Gallery

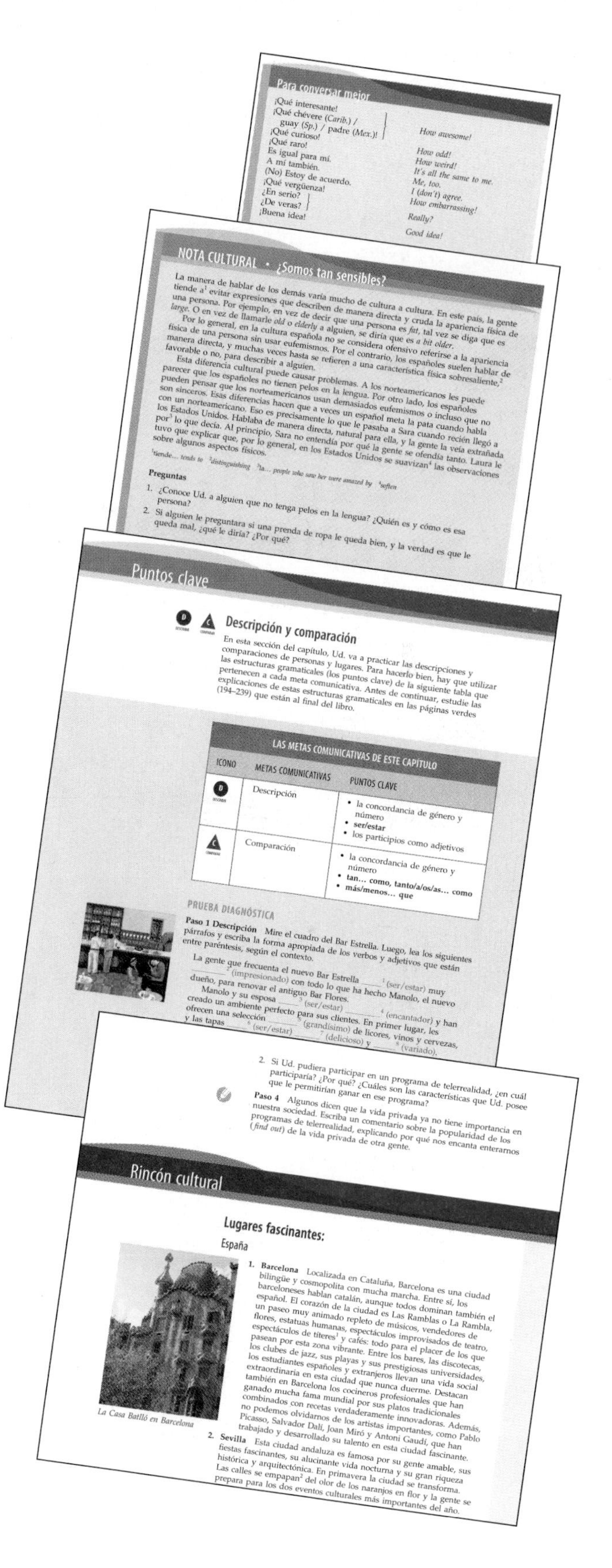

Para conversar mejor

¡Qué interesante!
¡Qué chévere (*Carib.*) / guay (*Sp.*) / padre (*Mex.*)! — *How awesome!*
¡Qué curioso! — *How odd!*
¡Qué raro! — *How weird!*
Es igual para mí. — *It's all the same to me.*
A mí también. — *Me, too.*
(No) Estoy de acuerdo. — *I (don't) agree.*
¡Qué vergüenza! — *How embarrassing!*
¿En serio? / ¿De veras? — *Really?*
¡Buena idea! — *Good idea!*

NOTA CULTURAL • ¿Somos tan sensibles?

La manera de hablar de los demás varía mucho de cultura a cultura. En este país, la gente
tiende a[1] evitar expresiones que describen de manera directa y cruda la apariencia física de
una persona. Por ejemplo, en vez de decir que una persona es *fat*, tal vez se diga que es
large. O en vez de llamarle *old* o *elderly* a alguien, se diría que es *a bit older*.
Por lo general, en la cultura española no se considera ofensivo referirse a la apariencia
física de una persona sin usar eufemismos. Por el contrario, los españoles suelen hablar de
manera directa, y muchas veces hasta se refieren a una característica física sobresaliente,[2]
favorable o no, para describir a alguien.
Esta diferencia cultural puede causar problemas. A los norteamericanos les puede
parecer que los españoles no tienen pelos en la lengua. Por otro lado, los españoles
pueden pensar que los norteamericanos usan demasiados eufemismos o incluso que no
son sinceros. Esas diferencias hacen que a veces un español meta la pata cuando habla
con un norteamericano. Eso es precisamente lo que le pasaba a Sara cuando recién llegó a
los Estados Unidos. Hablaba de manera directa, natural para ella, y la gente la veía extrañada
por[3] lo que decía. Al principio, Sara no entendía por qué la gente se ofendía tanto. Laura le
tuvo que explicar que, por lo general, en los Estados Unidos se suavizan[4] las observaciones
sobre algunos aspectos físicos.

[1]tiende... *tends to* [2]*distinguishing* [3]la... *people who saw her were amazed by* [4]*soften*

Preguntas

1. ¿Conoce Ud. a alguien que no tenga pelos en la lengua? ¿Quién es y cómo es esa persona?
2. Si alguien le preguntara si una prenda de ropa le queda bien, y la verdad es que le queda mal, ¿qué le diría? ¿Por qué?

Puntos clave

Descripción y comparación

En esta sección del capítulo, Ud. va a practicar las descripciones y comparaciones de personas y lugares. Para hacerlo bien, hay que utilizar las estructuras gramaticales (los puntos clave) de la siguiente tabla que pertenecen a cada meta comunicativa. Antes de continuar, estudie las explicaciones de estas estructuras gramaticales en las páginas verdes (194–239) que están al final del libro.

LAS METAS COMUNICATIVAS DE ESTE CAPÍTULO

ICONO	METAS COMUNICATIVAS	PUNTOS CLAVE
D (DESCRIBIR)	Descripción	• la concordancia de género y número • **ser/estar** • los participios como adjetivos
C (COMPARAR)	Comparación	• la concordancia de género y número • **tan... como, tanto/a/os/as... como** • **más/menos... que**

PRUEBA DIAGNÓSTICA

Paso 1 Descripción Mire el cuadro del Bar Estrella. Luego, lea los siguientes párrafos y escriba la forma apropiada de los verbos y adjetivos que están entre paréntesis, según el contexto.

La gente que frecuenta el nuevo Bar Estrella ____[1] (ser/estar) muy ____[2] (impresionado) con todo lo que ha hecho Manolo, el nuevo dueño, para renovar el antiguo Bar Flores.

Manolo y su esposa ____[3] (ser/estar) ____[4] (encantador) y han creado un ambiente perfecto para sus clientes. En primer lugar, les ofrecen una selección ____[5] (grandísimo) de licores, vinos y cervezas, y las tapas ____[6] (ser/estar) ____[7] (delicioso) y ____[8] (variado).

2. Si Ud. pudiera participar en un programa de telerrealidad, ¿en cuál participaría? ¿Por qué? ¿Cuáles son las características que Ud. posee que le permitirían ganar en ese programa?

Paso 4 Algunos dicen que la vida privada ya no tiene importancia en nuestra sociedad. Escriba un comentario sobre la popularidad de los programas de telerrealidad, explicando por qué nos encanta enterarnos (*find out*) de la vida privada de otra gente.

Rincón cultural

Lugares fascinantes:
España

La Casa Batlló en Barcelona

1. **Barcelona** Localizada en Cataluña, Barcelona es una ciudad bilingüe y cosmopolita con mucha marcha. Entre sí, los barceloneses hablan catalán, aunque todos dominan también el español. El corazón de la ciudad es Las Ramblas o La Rambla, un paseo muy animado repleto de músicos, vendedores de flores, estatuas humanas, espectáculos improvisados de teatro, espectáculos de títeres[1] y cafés: todo para el placer de los que pasean por esta zona vibrante. Entre los bares, las discotecas, los clubes de jazz, sus playas y sus prestigiosas universidades, los estudiantes españoles y extranjeros llevan una vida social extraordinaria en esta ciudad que nunca duerme. Destacan también en Barcelona los cocineros profesionales que han ganado mucha fama mundial por sus platos tradicionales combinados con recetas verdaderamente innovadoras. Además, no podemos olvidarnos de los artistas importantes, como Pablo Picasso, Salvador Dalí, Joan Miró y Antoni Gaudí, que han trabajado y desarrollado su talento en esta ciudad fascinante.
2. **Sevilla** Esta ciudad andaluza es famosa por su gente amable, sus fiestas fascinantes, su alucinante vida nocturna y su gran riqueza histórica y arquitectónica. En primavera la ciudad se transforma. Las calles se empapan[2] del olor de los naranjos en flor y la gente se prepara para los dos eventos culturales más importantes del año.

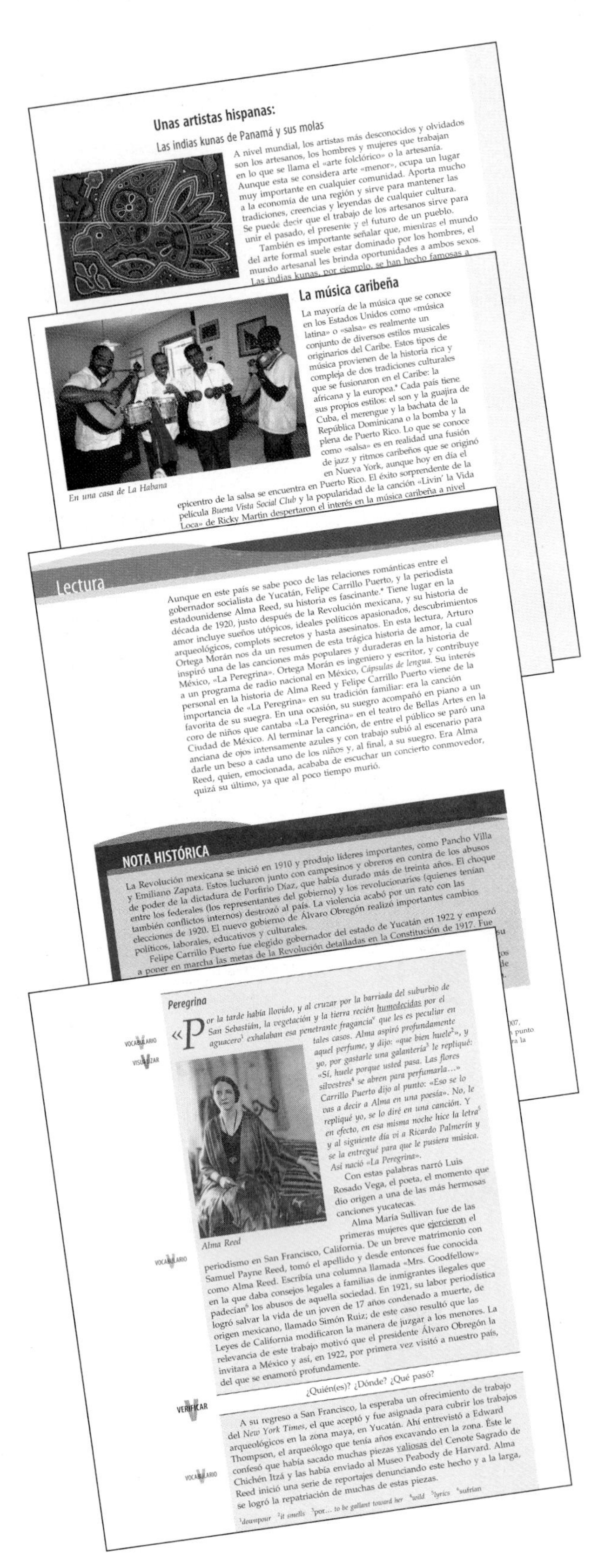

Unas artistas hispanas:
Las indias kunas de Panamá y sus molas

A nivel mundial, los artistas más desconocidos y olvidados son los artesanos, los hombres y mujeres que trabajan en lo que se llama el «arte folclórico» o la artesanía. Aunque esta se considera arte «menor», ocupa un lugar muy importante en cualquier comunidad. Aporta mucho a la economía de una región y sirve para mantener las tradiciones, creencias y leyendas de cualquier cultura. Se puede decir que el trabajo de los artesanos sirve para unir el pasado, el presente y el futuro de un pueblo.

También es importante señalar que, mientras el mundo del arte formal suele estar dominado por los hombres, el mundo artesanal les brinda oportunidades a ambos sexos. Las indias kunas, por ejemplo, se han hecho famosas a

La música caribeña

La mayoría de la música que se conoce en los Estados Unidos como «música latina» o «salsa» es realmente un conjunto de diversos estilos musicales originarios del Caribe. Estos tipos de música provienen de la historia rica y compleja de dos tradiciones culturales que se fusionaron en el Caribe: la africana y la europea.* Cada país tiene sus propios estilos: el son y la guajira de Cuba, el merengue y la bachata de la República Dominicana o la bomba y la plena de Puerto Rico. Lo que se conoce como «salsa» es en realidad una fusión de jazz y ritmos caribeños que se originó en Nueva York, aunque hoy en día el epicentro de la salsa se encuentra en Puerto Rico. El éxito sorprendente de la película *Buena Vista Social Club* y la popularidad de la canción «Livin' la Vida Loca» de Ricky Martin despertaron el interés en la música caribeña a nivel

En una casa de La Habana

Lectura

Aunque en este país se sabe poco de las relaciones románticas entre el gobernador socialista de Yucatán, Felipe Carrillo Puerto, y la periodista estadounidense Alma Reed, su historia es fascinante.* Tiene lugar en la década de 1920, justo después de la Revolución mexicana, y su historia de amor incluye sueños utópicos, ideales políticos apasionados, descubrimientos arqueológicos, complots secretos y hasta asesinatos. En esta lectura, Arturo Ortega Morán nos da un resumen de esta trágica historia de amor, la cual inspiró una de las canciones más populares y duraderas en la historia de México, «La Peregrina». Ortega Morán es ingeniero y escritor, y contribuye a un programa de radio nacional en México, *Cápsulas de lengua*. Su interés personal en la historia de Alma Reed y Felipe Carrillo Puerto viene de la importancia de «La Peregrina» en su tradición familiar: era la canción favorita de su suegra. En una ocasión, su suegro acompañó en piano a un coro de niños que cantaba «La Peregrina» en el teatro de Bellas Artes en la Ciudad de México. Al terminar la canción, de entre el público se paró una anciana de ojos intensamente azules y con trabajo subió al escenario para darle un beso a cada uno de los niños y, al final, a su suegro. Era Alma Reed, quien, emocionada, acababa de escuchar un concierto conmovedor, quizá su último, ya que al poco tiempo murió.

NOTA HISTÓRICA

La Revolución mexicana se inició en 1910 y produjo líderes importantes, como Pancho Villa y Emiliano Zapata. Estos lucharon junto con campesinos y obreros en contra de los abusos de poder de la dictadura de Porfirio Díaz, que había durado más de treinta años. El choque entre los federales (los representantes del gobierno) y los revolucionarios (quienes tenían también conflictos internos) destrozó al país. La violencia acabó por un rato con las elecciones de 1920. El nuevo gobierno de Álvaro Obregón realizó importantes cambios políticos, laborales, educativos y culturales.

Felipe Carrillo Puerto fue elegido gobernador del estado de Yucatán en 1922 y empezó a poner en marcha las metas de la Revolución detalladas en la Constitución de 1917. Fue

Peregrina

VOCABULARIO VISUALIZAR

«*Por la tarde había llovido, y al cruzar por la barriada del suburbio de San Sebastián, la vegetación y la tierra recién humedecidas por el aguacero[1] exhalaban esa penetrante fragancia que les es peculiar en tales casos. Alma aspiró profundamente aquel perfume, y dijo: «¡que bien huele[2]!», y yo, por gastarle una galantería[3] le repliqué: «Sí, huele porque usted pasa. Las flores silvestres[4] se abren para perfumarla...» Carrillo Puerto dijo al punto: «Eso se lo vas a decir a Alma en una poesía». No, le repliqué yo, se lo diré en una canción. Y en efecto, en esa misma noche hice la letra[5] y al siguiente día vi a Ricardo Palmerín y se la entregué para que le pusiera música. Así nació «La Peregrina».*

Con estas palabras narró Luis Rosado Vega, el poeta, el momento que dio origen a una de las más hermosas canciones yucatecas.

Alma Reed

VOCABULARIO

Alma María Sullivan fue de las primeras mujeres que ejercieron el periodismo en San Francisco, California. De un breve matrimonio con Samuel Payne Reed, tomó el apellido y desde entonces fue conocida como Alma Reed. Escribía una columna llamada «Mrs. Goodfellow» en la que daba consejos legales a familias de inmigrantes ilegales que padecían[6] los abusos de aquella sociedad. En 1921, su labor periodística logró salvar la vida de un joven de 17 años condenado a muerte, de origen mexicano, llamado Simón Ruiz; de este caso resultó que las Leyes de California modificaron la manera de juzgar a los menores. La relevancia de este trabajo motivó que el presidente Álvaro Obregón la invitara a México y así, en 1922, por primera vez visitó a nuestro país, del que se enamoró profundamente.

VERIFICAR

¿Quién(es)? ¿Dónde? ¿Qué pasó?

VOCABULARIO

A su regreso a San Francisco, la esperaba un ofrecimiento de trabajo del *New York Times*, el que aceptó y fue asignada para cubrir los trabajos arqueológicos en la zona maya, en Yucatán. Ahí entrevistó a Edward Thompson, el arqueólogo que tenía años excavando en la zona. Éste le confesó que había sacado muchas piezas valiosas del Cenote Sagrado de Chichén Itzá y las había enviado al Museo Peabody de Harvard. Alma Reed inició una serie de reportajes denunciando este hecho y a la larga, se logró la repatriación de muchas de estas piezas.

[1]downpour [2]it smells [3]por... to be gallant toward her [4]wild [5]lyrics [6]suffrian

Un artista hispano profiles a Hispanic artist from the country or region of focus and includes comprehension and discussion questions. Finally, **La música...** presents a short introduction to the featured musical genre and provides pre- and post-listening activities to accompany the songs that are available on the *Estampillas musicales* music CD. The follow-up activity invites students to go to YouTube™ to search out and listen to a variety of classic and contemporary musicians and singers from the featured region and then share their favorite with the class, thus opening the world of Latin music to the class.

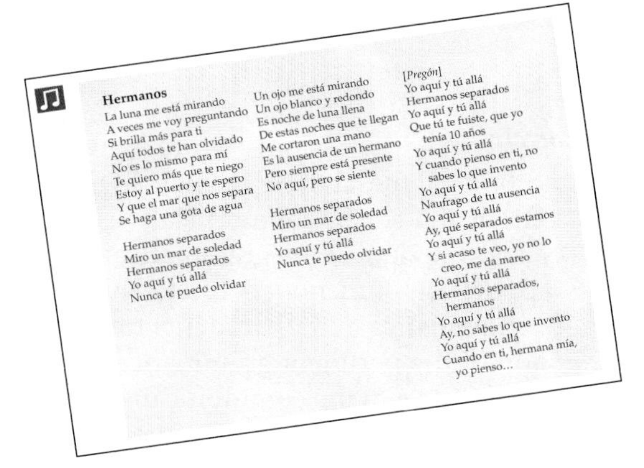

Hermanos

La luna me está mirando
A veces me voy preguntando
Si brilla más para ti
Aquí todos te han olvidado
No es lo mismo para mí
Te quiero más que te niego
Estoy al puerto y te espero
Y que el mar que nos separa
Se haga una gota de agua

Hermanos separados
Miro un mar de soledad
Hermanos separados
Yo aquí y tú allá
Nunca te puedo olvidar

Un ojo me está mirando
Un ojo blanco y redondo
Es noche de luna llena
De estas noches que te llegan
Me cortaron una mano
Es la ausencia de un hermano
Pero siempre está presente
No aquí, pero se siente

Hermanos separados
Miro un mar de soledad
Hermanos separados
Yo aquí y tú allá
Nunca te puedo olvidar

[Pregón]
Yo aquí y tú allá
Hermanos separados
Yo aquí y tú allá
Que tú te fuiste, que yo
tenía 10 años
Yo aquí y tú allá
Y cuando pienso en ti, no
sabes lo que invento
Yo aquí y tú allá
Naufrago de tu ausencia
Yo aquí y tú allá
Ay, qué separados estamos
Yo aquí y tú allá
Y si acaso te veo, yo no lo
creo, me da mareo
Yo aquí y tú allá
Hermanos separados,
hermanos
Yo aquí y tú allá
Ay, no sabes lo que invento
Yo aquí y tú allá
Cuando en ti, hermana mía,
yo pienso...

Lectura

Each chapter contains a reading that addresses the chapter theme. Pre- and post-reading activities emphasize reading strategies, comprehension, and expansion of the ideas presented in each reading for individual homework and small-group classroom discussion.

Consciousness-raising icons next to each reading highlight specific strategies. A **Vocabulario** icon VOCABULARIO in the margin alerts students to make wise strategy decisions about a new vocabulary item, such as deciphering the word based on the context, relating it to similar words they *do* know, looking it up in a dictionary, or ignoring it altogether. **Visualizar** icons VISUALIZAR remind students to visualize images of the people, places, things, and situations described at that point. A **Verificar** icon VERIFICAR and a set of short questions, positioned at logical break points within longer readings and at the end of many readings, encourage students to monitor their comprehension up to that point.

¡A escribir!

The main composition of each chapter is divided into three sections: a brainstorming activity, a guided composition based on the information gathered from the brainstorming activity, and a dialogue in which students comment on each others' composition. Additional writing activities are found throughout the text and are easily identifiable by the writing icon.

Hablando del tema

In this final section of each chapter, students converse, debate, and offer reactions to questions and situations based on chapter themes, requiring them to use higher-level speaking skills to support an opinion, discuss advantages and disadvantages, hypothesize, and so on.

Explicación gramatical

Explanations of the grammar structures associated with each communicative function can be found in the green pages near the end of the main text. An improved tabbing system provides easy reference. **¡A practicar!** exercises offer additional practice of the grammar points; the answers to all those exercises are provided in **Apéndice 1.** Explanations of additional grammatical structures can be found in the **Referencia de gramática** section at the end of the green pages.

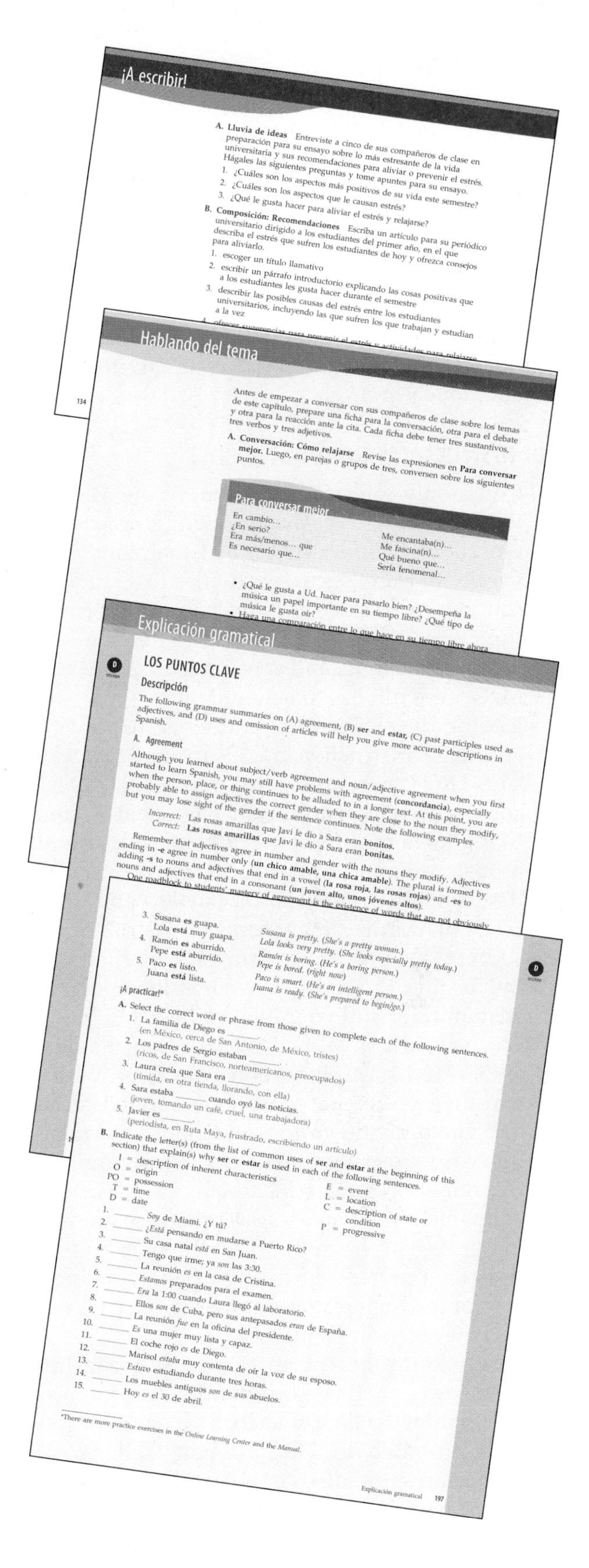

¡A escribir!

A. **Lluvia de ideas** Entreviste a cinco de sus compañeros de clase en preparación para su ensayo sobre lo más estresante de la vida universitaria y sus recomendaciones para aliviar o prevenir el estrés. Hágales las siguientes preguntas y tome apuntes para su ensayo.
1. ¿Cuáles son los aspectos más positivos de su vida este semestre?
2. ¿Cuáles son los aspectos que le causan estrés?
3. ¿Qué le gusta hacer para aliviar el estrés y relajarse?

B. **Composición: Recomendaciones** Escriba un artículo para su periódico universitario dirigido a los estudiantes del primer año, en el que describa el estrés que sufren los estudiantes de hoy y ofrezca consejos para aliviarlo.
1. escoger un título llamativo
2. escribir un párrafo introductorio explicando las cosas positivas que a los estudiantes les gusta hacer durante el semestre
3. describir las posibles causas del estrés entre los estudiantes universitarios, incluyendo las que sufren los que trabajan y estudian a la vez

134

Hablando del tema

Antes de empezar a conversar con sus compañeros de clase sobre los temas de este capítulo, prepare una ficha para la conversación, otra para el debate y otra para la reacción ante la cita. Cada ficha debe tener tres sustantivos, tres verbos y tres adjetivos.

A. **Conversación: Cómo relajarse** Revise las expresiones en **Para conversar mejor.** Luego, en parejas o grupos de tres, conversen sobre los siguientes puntos.

Para conversar mejor

En cambio...
¿En serio?
Era más/menos... que
Es necesario que...
Me encantaba(n)...
Me fascina(n)...
Qué bueno que...
Sería fenomenal...

- ¿Qué le gusta a Ud. hacer para pasarlo bien? ¿Desempeña la música un papel importante en su tiempo libre? ¿Qué tipo de música le gusta oír?

Explicación gramatical

LOS PUNTOS CLAVE

Descripción

The following grammar summaries on (A) agreement, (B) **ser** and **estar,** (C) past participles used as adjectives, and (D) uses and omission of articles will help you give more accurate descriptions in Spanish.

A. Agreement

Although you learned about subject/verb agreement and noun/adjective agreement when you first started to learn Spanish, you may still have problems with agreement (**concordancia**), especially when the person, place, or thing continues to be alluded to in a longer text. At this point, you are probably able to assign adjectives the correct gender when they are close to the noun they modify, but you may lose sight of the gender if the sentence continues. Note the following examples.

Incorrect: Las rosas amarillas que Javi le dio a Sara eran bonitos.
Correct: **Las rosas amarillas** que Javi le dio a Sara eran **bonitas.**

Remember that adjectives agree in number and gender with the nouns they modify. Adjectives ending in **-e** agree in number only (**un chico amable, una chica amable**). The plural is formed by adding **-s** to nouns and adjectives that end in a vowel (**la rosa roja, las rosas rojas**) and **-es** to nouns and adjectives that end in a consonant (**un joven alto, unos jóvenes altos**).

3. Susana **es** guapa. — *Susana is pretty. (She's a pretty woman.)*
Lola **está** muy guapa. — *Lola looks very pretty. (She looks especially pretty today.)*
4. Ramón **es** aburrido. — *Ramón is boring. (He's a boring person.)*
Pepe **está** aburrido. — *Pepe is bored. (right now)*
5. Paco **es** listo. — *Paco is smart. (He's an intelligent person.)*
Juana **está** lista. — *Juana is ready. (She's prepared to begin/go.)*

¡A practicar!*

A. Select the correct word or phrase from those given to complete each of the following sentences.
1. La familia de Diego es _______.
(en México, cerca de San Antonio, de México, tristes)
2. Los padres de Sergio estaban _______.
(ricos, de San Francisco, norteamericanos, preocupados)
3. Laura creía que Sara era _______.
(tímida, en otra tienda, llorando, con ella)
4. Sara estaba _______ cuando oyó las noticias.
(joven, tomando un café, cruel, una trabajadora)
5. Javier es _______.
(periodista, en Ruta Maya, frustrado, escribiendo un artículo)

B. Indicate the letter(s) (from the list of common uses of **ser** and **estar** at the beginning of this section) that explain(s) why **ser** or **estar** is used in each of the following sentences.

I = description of inherent characteristics
O = origin
PO = possession
T = time
D = date
E = event
L = location
C = description of state or condition
P = progressive

1. _______ *Soy* de Miami. ¿Y tú?
2. _______ ¿*Está* pensando en mudarse a Puerto Rico?
3. _______ Su casa natal *está* en San Juan.
4. _______ Tengo que irme; ya *son* las 3:30.
5. _______ La reunión *es* en la casa de Cristina.
6. _______ *Estamos* preparados para el examen.
7. _______ *Era* la 1:00 cuando Laura llegó al laboratorio.
8. _______ Ellos *son* de Cuba, pero sus antepasados *eran* de España.
9. _______ La reunión *fue* en la oficina del presidente.
10. _______ *Es* una mujer muy lista y capaz.
11. _______ El coche rojo *es* de Diego.
12. _______ Marisol *estaba* muy contenta de oír la voz de su esposo.
13. _______ *Estuvo* estudiando durante tres horas.
14. _______ Los muebles antiguos *son* de sus abuelos.
15. _______ Hoy *es* el 30 de abril.

*There are more practice exercises in the *Online Learning Center* and the *Manual.*

Explicación gramatical 197

Supplements

As a full-service publisher of quality educational products, McGraw-Hill does much more than just sell textbooks to students. We create and publish an extensive array of print and digital supplements to support instruction on your campus. Orders of new (versus used) textbooks help us defray the cost of developing such supplements, which is substantial. Please consult your local McGraw-Hill representative to learn about the availability of the following supplements that accompany this edition of *Punto y aparte.*

For Instructors and for Students

- Commonly referred to as simply the *Manual,* the *Manual que acompaña Punto y aparte* is a workbook/laboratory manual that contains a variety of exercises and activities that students can use to practice the seven communicative functions with all of the four skills: reading, writing, listening, and speaking.
- McGraw-Hill has partnered with Quia, the leading developer of online tools for foreign-language instruction and learning, to create CENTRO (**www.mhcentro.com**). CENTRO is a comprehensive learning-management system that allows you to manage your course with robust communications tools, record-keeping that can be imported to Blackboard and other CMS platforms, integration of instructor resources such as the Instructor's Manual and the Testing Program, as well as the ability to customize or add your own content.
- The new edition of *Punto y aparte* is available in CENTRO as a fully interactive eBook with a real-time voice chat feature, integrated audio and video, an integrated gradebook, and many other resources that make this a truly innovative online system for the teaching and learning of Spanish. The *Punto y aparte* eBook seamlessly integrates all the cultural multimedia content described previously, including the video footage of the **Lugares fascinantes** video program and the songs in **La música...** .
- Also new to the Fourth Edition is a dazzling video program that corresponds to the **Lugares fascinantes** section of each chapter. With footage provided by BBC Motion Gallery, the videos are presented as video blogs made by two traveling videographers who are sharing their travel experiences with friends and family. The video is available both online in CENTRO and instructors may request a complimentary DVD.
- CENTRO is also home to the online *Manual.* This digital version of the printed *Manual* is easy for students to use and ideal for instructors who want to manage students' coursework online. Identical in practice to the print version, the online *Manual* contains the full Audio Program. It also provides students with automatic feedback and scoring of their work.
- The *Estampillas musicales* CD, written and recorded for use with this program, corresponds to the **La música...** section of each chapter. The CD contains six songs, one from each of the six Spanish-speaking regions featured in *Punto y aparte.* It is available to students for purchase, and instructors may request a complimentary copy.
- The Student Edition of the Online Learning Center (**www.mhhe.com/puntoyaparte4**) provides students with a wealth of activities created especially for use with *Punto y aparte.* It includes additional vocabulary and grammar practice quizzes, cultural activities, the complete Audio Program to accompany the *Manual,* the Textbook Audio recordings (**La historia** dialogues and active vocabulary lists), the five friends animations from the Third Edition, and the Spanish Grammar Tutorials.

For Instructors Only

Punto y aparte comes with extensive and high-quality instructor resources.

- The annotated Instructor's Edition of *Punto y aparte* provides notes that offer extensive pre-text activities, teaching hints, and suggestions for using and expanding materials, as well as references to the supplementary activities in the Instructor's Manual and the Testing Program.
- Instructors have password-protected access on the Instructor Edition of the Online Learning Center and on CENTRO to instructor resources such as the Instructor's Manual, the Testing Program, the Audioscript, and the **Lugares fascinantes** Videoscript. For password information, please contact your local McGraw-Hill sales representative.

  - The Instructor's Manual is an invaluable resource, containing various syllabi in addition to detailed teaching suggestions and tips for each section of each chapter. Each chapter also provides seven to ten ready-made supplementary activities.
  - The tests and quizzes that were previously located in the Instructor's Manual have been consolidated and expanded in a separate Testing Program.
  - The Audioscript and Videoscript are transcripts of all recorded materials in the Audio Program and the new **Lugares fascinantes** video program.
- Instructors may request a complimentary copy of the **Lugares fascinantes** video program on DVD and of the *Estampillas musicales* CD.

Other Available Materials

- *Lecturas literarias: Moving Toward Linguistic and Cultural Fluency Through Literature* is a reader designed to accompany *Punto y aparte*. For those who want to offer an even stronger reading component at the intermediate level, it provides additional readings for each chapter on the chapter themes, along with pre- and post-reading and writing activities in each chapter.
- CourseSmart is a new way to find and buy eTextbooks. At CourseSmart you can save up to 50% off the cost of a print textbook, reduce your impact on the environment, and gain access to powerful web tools for learning. CourseSmart has the largest selection of eTextbooks available anywhere, offering thousands of the most commonly adopted textbooks from a wide variety of higher education publishers. CourseSmart eTextbooks are available in one standard online reader with full text search, notes and highlighting, and email tools for sharing notes between classmates. For further details, contact your sales representative or go to **www.coursesmart.com.**

Acknowledgments

We are extremely grateful to be publishing the Fourth Edition of *Punto y aparte* and would like to thank several friends, colleagues, and instructors who have aided us in myriad ways since the first days of the program. We would like to thank our colleagues Malia Lemond and Gloria Grande from the University of Texas at Austin; Moisés Castillo, Laura Flores, Anne Gebelein, Thomas Harrington, María Silvina Persino, and Gustavo Remedi, from Trinity College; and the graduate students and supervisors Inés Berkquist, Elena Castro, María Mayberry, and Lucía Osa Melero from the Department of Spanish and Portuguese at the University of Texas at Austin, who were so generous with their time and support. We thank the many instructors and friends who have participated in reviews or completed surveys of the Third Edition of *Punto y aparte*, and although we hope that they are pleased with this Fourth Edition, the appearance of their names does not necessarily constitute an endorsement of the program or its methodology.

Austin College
Patrick Duffey

Austin Community College
Tim Altanero

Birmingham-Southern College
Barbara Domcekova

> *Punto y aparte* has been by far the best-conceived text I have worked with. Excellent vocabulary section and organization, great idea to focus on the lives of the **cinco amigos,** practical suggestions in the Instructor's Manual, both teaching strategies as well as assessment.
>
> –Barbara Domcekova
> *Birmingham-Southern College*

Boston College
Christopher LaFond
Catherine Wood Lange

Bowling Green State University
Lynn Pearson

California State University, Monterey Bay
Judy Cortes

Catholic University
Martha Davis

Central Michigan University
James C. Courtad

I find this to be one of the best-conceived books I have taught with.

–James C. Courtad
Central Michigan University

George Mason University
Michelle F. Ramos-Pellicia

Gettysburg College
Dorothy Moore

Grand Valley State University
Hector Fabio Espitia

Hawai'i Pacific University
Tess Lane

Northwest Vista College
Maria Pilar Damron

San Diego State University
Esther Aguilar

Simmons College
Tulio Campos

Smith College
Molly Falsetti-Yu

Texas Christian University
Dr. Bonnie Blackwell

University of Nevada, Reno
Casilde A. Isabelli

This is a winning approach! It is the only textbook out there that addresses the problem of the gap between the second-year and third-year courses [...] By the end of the semester, the student is able to manage seven grammar categories with reading, writing, and conversing.

–Casilde A. Isabelli
University of Nevada, Reno

University of North Texas
Dr. Pierina E. Beckman
Kellye Church

University of Oklahoma, Norman
José Juan Colín

Xavier University
Irene Hodgson
David Knutson

The authors would also like to express our immense gratitude for the following individuals and institutions for their time and professionalism in helping us to "freshen up" the look of the five friends: Joel Blake (Javier), Fidel J. Jr. (Diego), Lindsay Long (Laura), Adam Pérez (Sergio), Natalia Peschiera (Sara); Elena Jurado of Café Qué Tal (San Francisco) and Mía González of Encantada Gallery (San Francisco). Special thanks are due to Jill Braaten for taking the excellent photos of these actors and locations.

It is always a pleasure to work with an organization that values teamwork above all; thus, many thanks are owed to the people at McGraw-Hill who worked behind the scenes on this Fourth Edition of *Punto y aparte*. Katherine Crouch, our sponsoring editor, was instrumental in shaping the revision plan for this edition. Max Ehrsam carefully reviewed the manuscript for matters of style, clarity, and linguistic and cultural authenticity. It was a pleasure to work with Connie Anderson as our development editor. Her conscientious, careful, and respectful approach to guiding us through the revision process was much appreciated. In addition, we are very appreciative of Misha Maclaird for her excellent work on the **Lugares fascinantes** videos. We would also like to thank the rest of the editorial team at McGraw-Hill, especially Scott Tinetti and Erin Blaze for helping guide this edition along the path from manuscript to publication. Many thanks are due to the production team at McGraw-Hill, especially Brett Coker, Natalia Peschiera, and Louis Swaim, as well as our designer, Andrei Pasternak, for the wonderful new cover and updates to the interior design for this edition. We would like to thank Stacy Best Ruel (Executive Marketing Manager), Jorge Arbujas (Marketing Manager), and the entire McGraw-Hill sales staff for their continuing efforts in promoting and making the *Punto y aparte* program such a success.

Finally, a very special thanks goes to Frank for being a source of unending support and encouragement on every level, to Guillermo for believing in us and for putting in many hours of overtime, and to our parents, who taught us the value of hard work.

To the Student

Welcome to the Fourth Edition of *Punto y aparte: Spanish in Review, Moving Toward Fluency,* a unique and exciting intermediate Spanish program! As second-year students of college Spanish, you have already studied verb tenses, the subjunctive mood, pronouns, a lot of basic vocabulary, common idioms, and so on. The goal of this course is to help you acquire the ability to use what you have learned by focusing on seven major communicative functions (**metas comunicativas**) in Spanish: describing, comparing, narrating in the past, reacting and recommending, talking about likes and dislikes, hypothesizing, and talking about the future. All your written and oral practice will involve topics that require you to demonstrate an ability to communicate those functions.

Another goal is for you to become a paragraph maker in Spanish. (In fact, the Spanish expression **punto y aparte** is used to indicate the beginning of a new paragraph!) You will also achieve greater cohesion in your speaking and writing abilities by including transition words and sentence connectors as you move toward fluency in Spanish. (Please see the list of common connectors and transition words in **Apéndice 2.**)

A third goal is for you to increase your vocabulary by adding new words to your active vocabulary and by acquiring strategies that will help you understand the meaning of unfamiliar terms. You will also notice that all the vocabulary is presented in groups of words that are thematically related. We suggest that you study the vocabulary in these thematic groups rather than as single, isolated words. You will find a consistent recycling of vocabulary throughout the text so that you will not forget vocabulary studied in **Capítulo 1** by the time you reach **Capítulo 6.**

What is unique about *Punto y aparte* and its approach is the idea of narrowing the focus of instruction to seven major communicative functions, all of which appear in every chapter from the beginning of the course. This focus on the communicative functions is supported by constant recycling of the grammatical structures needed to accurately and successfully perform those functions. In other words, the content or themes will change with each new chapter, but the seven functions will be repeated throughout the program. To facilitate your growing abilities to communicate effectively in Spanish, icons are used to remind you with which function you are working. For example, when you see the D icon D DESCRIBIR next to an activity, you know that you are working with *description* and that, in order to describe well, you must keep in mind the rules for gender/number agreement, the appropriate uses of **ser** and **estar,** and perhaps the use of past participles as adjectives. (Please see the inside back cover for a full display of the icons, the communicative functions, and the grammatical structures [**los puntos clave**] that accompany the functions.)

To accomplish each of these communicative functions, certain grammatical structures must be mastered. Therefore, *Punto y aparte* offers a wide variety of interactive tasks that allow you to practice the functions throughout the text. By doing so, you will increase your grammatical accuracy and strengthen your ability to express yourself effectively in Spanish.

Besides concentrating on the seven functions and increasing your vocabulary, we want to help you enjoy reading in Spanish. Although many reading strategies can help guide you as you approach texts written in Spanish, *Punto y aparte* concentrates on three. We like to refer to these reading strategies as "the three V's": learning *vocabulary* in context, *visualization,* and *verification.* To aid you in acquiring these strategies we have placed consciousness-raising icons next to each reading in the **Lectura** sections.

A **Vocabulario** icon V VOCABULARIO in the margin alerts you to make wise strategy decisions about a new vocabulary item, such as deciphering the word based on the context, relating it to similar words you *do* know, looking it up in a dictionary, or ignoring it altogether.

Visualizar icons VISUALIZAR remind you to visualize images of the people, places, things, and situations described at that point.

Finally, a **Verificar** icon VERIFICAR and a short set of questions, positioned at logical break points within longer readings and at the end of most readings, encourage you to monitor your comprehension up to that point. The goal of these strategies is to help you get the overall gist of the passage.

It is also very important to understand from the outset how this course differs from previous courses you may have taken. As you move toward fluency in Spanish, you should progress from being a list maker to a paragraph maker, from memorizing isolated words to learning and using groups of thematically related words, and from studying grammar structures in a vacuum to studying grammar as a support for expressing the seven communicative functions that serve as the core of the *Punto y aparte* methodology. Finally, you should also attain a deeper understanding and appreciation of Hispanic cultures through the rich and diverse **Rincón cultural** sections and through the lives of the five characters (**los cinco amigos**) who appear throughout *Punto y aparte* in their daily lives and interactions at the Ruta Maya café in Austin, Texas. The five friends are Sara Carrillo Jiménez, a Spanish graduate student; Javier Mercado Quevedo, a Puerto Rican journalist who also works at Ruta Maya; Laura Taylor, an American graduate student of Pharmacy and Health Administration and Sara's roommate; Diego Ponce Flores, a Mexican shop owner; and Sergio Wilson Flores, a Mexican-American concert promoter and Diego's cousin.

Above all, we hope that you enjoy this course and that you find yourself moving toward fluency in Spanish!

Los cinco amigos

Para empezar:

Los cinco amigos

Puntos clave
- introducción a las metas comunicativas

Tema central
- los cinco amigos

Zona de enfoque
- el café Ruta Maya en Austin, Texas

Los cinco amigos: Javier, Diego, Sara, Laura y Sergio

¡Bienvenido/a a *Punto y aparte*! A lo largo de este libro de texto y en el *Manual que acompaña Punto y aparte,* Ud. va a trabajar con siete metas comunicativas en conversaciones con sus compañeros de clase, en composiciones y en ejercicios gramaticales. También, poco a poco irá conociendo, sobre todo en la sección **La historia,** a los cinco amigos que aparecen en la foto. Todos viven en Austin, Texas.

MULTIMEDIA

Cara a cara

Lea la pequeña biografía y el perfil (*profile*) personal de cada uno de los cinco amigos. Luego, conteste las preguntas que aparecen a continuación.

SARA CARRILLO JIMÉNEZ

Sara nació en un pueblo cerca de Salamanca, España. Estudió periodismo[1] en la Universidad Pontificia de Salamanca y trabajó en una emisora[2] de radio local, en la cual sólo ofrecían programas musicales. Como quería aprender otras cosas relacionadas con el mundo de las comunicaciones, cuando a Sara le hablaron de la posibilidad de estudiar en los Estados Unidos, decidió «cruzar el charco».[3] Actualmente está acabando su maestría en Radio, Televisión y Cine y trabaja en la emisora universitaria, donde hace un programa dirigido a los hispanohablantes.

Habla Sara:
Rasgos[4] principales de mi carácter: *Soy extrovertida, franca e impaciente.*
Mi estado de ánimo en estos días: *Estoy preocupada por la tesis y por eso estoy un poco ansiosa.*
Cambios: *Hoy soy más abierta que antes, pero soy tan impaciente como siempre.*
La sugerencia que más me dan: *Que piense antes de hablar.*
Un secreto de mi pasado: *Cuando tenía 14 años, empecé a fumar.*
Lo que más me fascina: *Me fascina el ambiente relajado de Austin.*
Lo que más me molesta: *Me molesta la ropa formal.*
Si pudiera invitar a dos personas a cenar: *Invitaría a Paul McCartney y a Letizia Ortiz.*
Cuando tenga suficiente dinero, iré a: *las Islas Canarias, donde descansaré y tomaré una clase de dibujo.*

[1] *journalism* [2] *station* [3] «cruzar… *"to cross the pond"* (fig: *the Atlantic Ocean*) [4] *Traits*

Preguntas:

1. ¿Por qué decidió Sara estudiar en los Estados Unidos?
2. ¿Es tímida Sara? ¿Cómo lo sabe Ud.?
3. ¿Le gustarían a Sara las fiestas elegantes? ¿Por qué sí o por qué no?

JAVIER MERCADO QUEVEDO

Javier nació en Mayagüez, Puerto Rico. Tiene un hermano gemelo.[1] Trabaja como mesero en el café Ruta Maya, uno de los cafés de moda del centro de la ciudad. Hace dos años que Javier sacó su licenciatura en periodismo. Ahora, hace trabajos sueltos[2] para varios periódicos hispanos de los Estados Unidos, pero su sueño es conseguir un puesto de corresponsal en Latinoamérica y pasarse la vida viajando. Mientras tanto, sin embargo, está muy contento en Austin. Es soltero y no piensa casarse muy pronto, aunque es muy romántico.

[1] *twin* [2] hace… *he freelances*

Habla Javier:
Rasgos principales de mi carácter: *Soy honesto, hablador y aventurero.*
Mi estado de ánimo en estos días: *Estoy muy satisfecho porque mi vida en Austin va súper bien.*
Cambios: *Hoy tengo menos interés en Hollywood que antes, pero me interesa saber sobre la producción de películas tanto como antes.*
La sugerencia que más me dan: *Que tenga más paciencia con mi madre.*
Un secreto de mi pasado: *Pasé seis semanas viajando por Venezuela con una novia, pero le dije a mi madre que estaba allá para tomar un curso universitario.*
Lo que más me fascina: *Me fascina la clientela diversa que visita Ruta Maya.*
Lo que más me molesta: *Me molestan las personas manipuladoras y la hipocresía.*
Si pudiera invitar a dos personas a cenar: *Invitaría a Shakira y a Junot Díaz.*
Cuando tenga suficiente dinero, iré a: *México, donde trataré de entrevistar a Guillermo del Toro.*

Preguntas:

1. ¿Por qué cree Ud. que Javier trabaja en el café Ruta Maya?
2. ¿Qué característica tiene Javier que le servirá en su carrera de periodismo?
3. ¿Le gusta a Javier pasar mucho tiempo en casa? ¿Cómo lo sabe?

LAURA TAYLOR

Laura nació en Sacramento, California. Al estudiar español en la universidad se interesó mucho por la cultura hispana, así que, cuando se graduó, decidió ingresar en el Cuerpo de Paz.[1] Terminó[2] en Otavalo, cerca de Quito, Ecuador, donde trabajó en proyectos de salud rural. Después de dos años, regresó a los Estados Unidos para seguir un curso de posgrado en estudios latinoamericanos con énfasis en la salud rural. Después de graduarse, le gustaría trabajar en Latinoamérica.

Habla Laura:
Rasgos principales de mi carácter: *Soy perfeccionista, abierta y exigente.*
Mi estado de ánimo en estos días: *Estoy muy contenta porque mis clases van bien y tengo una vida social bastante activa.*
Cambios: *Hoy paso más tiempo bailando en salsatecas, pero sigo tan estudiosa como siempre.*
La sugerencia que más me dan: *Que no trate de cambiar el mundo tan rápidamente.*
Un secreto de mi pasado: *Cuando tenía 12 años, leía el diario de mi hermana mayor, Laura.*
Lo que más me fascina: *Me fascinan las culturas indígenas de los Andes.*
Lo que más me molesta: *Me molesta la intolerancia.*
Si pudiera invitar a dos personas a cenar: *Invitaría a Michelle Obama, a Evo Morales y a Rigoberta Menchú.*
Cuando tenga suficiente dinero, iré a: *las Islas Galápagos en el Ecuador, donde pasaré un rato tranquilo con mi novio Manuel.*

[1]Cuerpo... *Peace Corps* [2]*She ended up*

Preguntas:

1. ¿Cree Ud. que Laura sacó buenas notas en sus cursos universitarios? ¿Cómo lo sabe?
2. ¿Por qué se fue al Ecuador cuando terminó sus estudios?
3. ¿Piensa quedarse en los Estados Unidos cuando termine sus estudios de posgrado?

DIEGO PONCE FLORES

Diego nació en San Julián, un pueblo de México, pero fue a Monterrey a vivir con su hermano mientras estudiaba en la Universidad Tecnológica. Se mudó a los Estados Unidos hace tres años y, poco después, con la ayuda de su primo Sergio, abrió una tienda de artesanía[1] latinoamericana que se llama Tesoros.[2] Aunque se especializó en administración de empresas,[3] siempre se ha interesado por las bellas artes. Así que su tienda resulta ser una perfecta combinación de sus dos pasiones.

Habla Diego:

Rasgos principales de mi carácter: *Soy ambicioso, muy cortés y un poco inflexible.*
Mi estado de ánimo en estos días: *Estoy nervioso porque quiero abrir más tiendas, pero no sé si es el momento oportuno o no.*
Cambios: *Hoy soy menos fiestero que cuando era joven, pero aprecio mis ratos libres*[4] *tanto como antes.*
La sugerencia que más me dan: *Que deje de trabajar tantas horas y que sea menos serio.*
Un secreto de mi pasado: *Cuando tenía 17 años, fui modelo de Levi's Jeans.*
Lo que más me fascina: *Me fascina la comida exótica.*
Lo que más me molesta: *Me molesta la falta de cortesía.*
Si pudiera invitar a dos personas a cenar: *Invitaría a Bono y a Carlos Slim Helú.*
Cuando tenga suficiente dinero, iré al: *Perú, donde buscaré artesanías andinas para vender en Tesoros.*

[1]*arts and crafts* [2]*Treasures* [3]administración... *business administration* [4]ratos... *free time*

Preguntas:

1. ¿Cree Ud. que Diego nació en una ciudad industrial? ¿Por qué sí o por qué no?
2. Parece que ser dueño de Tesoros es un puesto ideal para Diego. ¿Por qué?
3. A veces Diego les parece un poco formal a sus amigos. ¿Por qué será eso?

SERGIO WILSON FLORES

Sergio nació en El Paso, Texas, pero pasó su infancia en Chihuahua, México, el estado de origen de su madre. Después, se mudó a Boston, Massachusetts, la ciudad natal de su padre. Actualmente vive en Austin con su primo, Diego, y trabaja como promotor de conjuntos musicales. De los cuatro grupos que están bajo su dirección, dos son conjuntos *tex-mex* y dos son grupos de rock. Se graduó de la universidad hace dos años, en donde se especializó en administración de empresas.

Habla Sergio:
Rasgos principales de mi carácter: *Soy alegre, bromista y optimista.*
Mi estado de ánimo en estos días: *Estoy cansado porque no duermo mucho. Escucho muchos grupos que tocan hasta muy tarde.*
Cambios: *Hoy me interesa la política más que antes, pero no tengo tanto tiempo para leer las revistas que me interesan.*
La sugerencia que más me dan: *Que trate de conseguir entradas a los conciertos de grupos famosos.*
Un secreto de mi pasado: *Tomé clases de tango para impresionar a una chica.*
Lo que más me fascina: *Me fascinan los conjuntos musicales latinos, como Los Lonely Boys y El Grupo Fantasma.*
Lo que más me molesta: *Me molesta la falta de conciencia social.*
Si pudiera invitar a dos personas a cenar: *Invitaría a Robert Rodríguez y a Julieta Venegas.*
Cuando tenga suficiente dinero, iré a: *Chile, donde asistiré al gran festival de música en Viña del Mar.*

Preguntas:

1. Se puede describir a Sergio como una persona bicultural. ¿Por qué?
2. ¿Cree Ud. que Sergio es políticamente activo en su comunidad? ¿Cómo lo sabe?
3. ¿Es Sergio una persona solitaria?

ACTIVIDADES

A. Características e intereses de los cinco amigos

Paso 1 En grupos de cuatro, completen la siguiente tabla con la información que obtuvieron de los perfiles de los cinco amigos.

	SARA	JAVIER	LAURA	DIEGO	SERGIO
Características					
Intereses					

Paso 2 Ahora, conteste las siguientes preguntas.

1. ¿Con cuál de los cinco amigos tiene Ud. más en común en cuanto a las características de su personalidad?
2. ¿Con quién hablaría si quisiera saber algo sobre la región andina?
3. Un amigo suyo quiere abrir un negocio. ¿Con cuál de los amigos debe hablar?
4. De todos los amigos, ¿cuál es el más serio / la más seria?
5. ¿A quién no le gustaría asistir a una gala en un hotel de lujo?
6. Si tuviera que estar en una isla desierta con uno de los cinco amigos, ¿con cuál preferiría estar? ¿Por qué?
7. Si estuviera en el programa *Survivor* con estos cinco amigos, ¿quién sería el primero / la primera que Ud. sacaría de la isla? ¿Por qué?
8. ¿Cuáles son tres adjetivos que lo/la describen a Ud.?
9. ¿Cuáles son tres adjetivos que describen a su mejor amigo/a?
10. ¿Cuáles son algunos de los intereses que Ud. y su mejor amigo/a tienen en común?

B. Preguntas personales Si Ud. pudiera hacerle algunas preguntas a cada uno de los cinco amigos, ¿qué preguntas les haría? A continuación hay una lista de palabras interrogativas que puede usar.

¿a quién?, ¿adónde?, ¿cómo?, ¿cuál(es)?, ¿cuándo?, ¿cuánto/a/os/as?, ¿de dónde?, ¿dónde?, ¿por qué?, ¿qué?, ¿quién?

1. A Sara: ______
2. A Javier: ______
3. A Laura: ______
4. A Diego: ______
5. A Sergio: ______

C. Perfiles de sus compañeros Entreviste a un compañero / una compañera de clase para hacerle un perfil personal, como el de los cinco amigos. Luego, escoja los dos o tres datos más interesantes sobre su compañero/a y compártalos con la clase.

Rasgos principales de su carácter:

Su estado de ánimo en estos días:

Cambios:

La sugerencia que más le dan:

Un secreto de su pasado:

Lo que más le fascina:

Lo que más le molesta:

Si pudiera invitar a dos personas a cenar:

Cuando tenga suficiente dinero, irá a:

D. ¿Quiénes son? ¿Conoce Ud. a todas las personas famosas e importantes mencionadas en los perfiles de los amigos? En el mundo hispano hay muchas personas importantes que no necesariamente se conocen en este país.

Paso 1 Busque en el Internet los nombres de tres de las siguientes personas. Tome apuntes para luego compartir con sus compañeros de clase la información que encuentre.

1. Letizia Ortiz
2. Junot Díaz
3. Evo Morales
4. Robert Rodríguez
5. Carlos Slim Helú
6. Guillermo del Toro
7. Julieta Venegas

Paso 2 En grupos de cuatro, compartan sus apuntes y escojan a dos personas de la lista a quienes les gustaría invitar a una cena especial. Después, escojan tres temas de conversación para esa noche genial. Finalmente, compartan sus ideas con el resto de la clase.

Paso 3 Imagínese que ya se celebró la cena y que fue una noche memorable, ya sea por lo bien que salió o por lo mal que salió. Escriba un correo electrónico a su mejor amigo/a explicándole lo que pasó durante la cena.

Puntos clave*

INTRODUCCIÓN

The purpose of this section of **Para empezar** is to reintroduce you to the seven **metas comunicativas** and the **puntos clave** (the grammar points needed to express those seven communicative goals). Remember that this is a *preview* of what will be covered throughout the book. You are *not* expected to have mastered these grammar points, but you should be acquainted with most of them from your previous study of Spanish.

*Nouns used as adjectives in Spanish (like **clave** in the phrase **puntos clave**) do not alter their gender and number to agree with the noun they are modifying. Other examples are: **fechas límite, hombres rana, mujeres político, perros guía.**

LAS SIETE METAS COMUNICATIVAS Y LOS PUNTOS CLAVE

ICONO	META COMUNICATIVA	PUNTOS CLAVE
D DESCRIBIR	Descripción	• la concordancia de género y número • **ser/estar** • los participios como adjetivos
C COMPARAR	Comparación	• la concordancia de género y número • **tan... como, tanto/a/os/as... como** • **más/menos... que**
P PASADO	Narración en el pasado	• el pretérito • el imperfecto • los tiempos perfectos • **hace... que**
REACCIONAR R RECOMENDAR	Reacciones y recomendaciones	• el subjuntivo en cláusulas nominales • los mandatos
G GUSTOS	Hablar de los gustos	• los verbos como **gustar** • los pronombres de complemento indirecto • el subjuntivo después de **me gusta que**
H HIPÓTESIS	Hacer hipótesis	• el pasado de subjuntivo • el condicional
F FUTURO	Hablar del futuro	• el futuro • el subjuntivo en cláusulas adverbiales

DESCRIPCIÓN: EL CAFÉ RUTA MAYA

Paso 1 Lea la siguiente descripción del café Ruta Maya.

El café Ruta Maya **es** una bodega[1] **renovada** que **está** en el distrito **teatral** de Austin. **Es** el lugar **preferido** de los cinco amigos y de hecho casi todas sus reuniones **son** allí. Las paredes **están decoradas** con carteles de **varios** países **hispanos.** Cada mes se exponen obras de **diferentes** artistas **chicanos.** Allí se celebran las culturas **hispanas,** con café estilo **cubano,** empanadas[2] y flanes[3] **sabrosos** y una **gran** muralla estilo **azteca.** Su clientela **es** muy

[1]*warehouse* [2]*turnovers* [3]*custard desserts*

Ojo

Antes de hacer esta sección, vea las páginas verdes (194–200) al final del libro para repasar cómo hacer descripciones en español.

Javier, trabajando en el café Ruta Maya

ecléctica y los fines de semana por la noche el café siempre **está lleno.**[4] Allí la gente se reúne después de ir al teatro o después de cenar para comer uno de sus **deliciosos** postres y para disfrutar de la música en vivo.[5] ¡**Es** un lugar **maravilloso**!

[4]*full* [5]en... *live*

Paso 2 Ahora, complete las oraciones con los adjetivos que están entre paréntesis. **¡OJO!** Preste atención a la concordancia entre adjetivo y sustantivo.

1. La librería favorita de Sara y Laura siempre está _____ (lleno) de estudiantes de Latinoamérica porque hay muchos libros _____ (hispano) y sirven café y postres _____ (delicioso).
2. La discoteca donde se reúnen los cinco amigos para bailar los viernes por la noche es _____ (caro), pero muy _____ (divertido).
3. El restaurante donde trabaja la prima de Laura es _____ (fabuloso). A su prima le gustan los clientes porque son muy _____ (generoso) con las propinas.

Paso 3 En parejas, describan su lugar favorito para estar con sus amigos. ¿Dónde está ese lugar? ¿Cómo es? ¿Qué tipo de personas suele (*usually*) reunirse allí? ¿Por qué les gusta tanto ese lugar?

COMPARAR

COMPARACIÓN: DOS COMPAÑERAS DE CUARTO

Paso 1 Lea la siguiente comparación entre las dos compañeras de cuarto, Laura y Sara.

Ojo

Antes de hacer esta sección, vea las páginas verdes (201–202) al final del libro para repasar cómo hacer comparaciones en español.

Laura y Sara: dos amigas bastante distintas

Aunque Laura y Sara son íntimas amigas, son muy diferentes. Laura es **más reservada que** Sara, aunque si algo le apasiona, puede ser **tan habladora como** su amiga. A las dos les encanta saber los últimos chismes[1] en España

[1]*gossip*

y Latinoamérica, por eso Sara lee **tantos blogs* como** Laura. Pero también las dos tienen intereses serios. Laura va a **más conferencias académicas que** Sara, pero está claro que Sara es **tan lista como** su amiga. Quizás se puede decir que Laura es **más intelectual que** Sara. Pero todos dicen que Sara es **la más creativa de** los cinco amigos: pinta, escribe poesía y siempre tiene **más de** cinco proyectos artísticos sin terminar. Lo bueno es que a Laura le gusta conversar **tanto como** a Sara, y con tantos intereses no les faltan temas fascinantes.

Paso 2 Ahora, haga comparaciones entre Laura y Sara, utilizando las palabras sugeridas y las indicaciones que están entre paréntesis.

MODELO: Laura / Sara: alto (+) →
Sara es más alta que Laura.

1. Laura / Sara: leer blogs* (=)
2. Sara / Laura: intelectual (−)
3. Sara / Laura: creativo (+)
4. Laura / Sara: escribir poesía (−)
5. Sara / Laura: inteligente (=)
6. Laura / Sara: asistir a conferencias (+)

Paso 3 En parejas, hagan por lo menos cuatro comparaciones entre cada uno/a de Uds. y su mejor amigo/a.

yo / mi mejor amigo/a: atlético/a, cursos este semestre, dinero, hablar por teléfono, organizado/a, pasar tiempo en Facebook, salir, serio/a,...

PASADO

NARRACIÓN EN EL PASADO: SARA Y EL DÍA INOLVIDABLE

Paso 1 Lea la siguiente narración sobre un día que Sara recordará para siempre.

Ojo

Antes de hacer esta sección, vea las páginas verdes (202–212) al final del libro para repasar cómo narrar en el pasado en español.

Cuando Sara **era** niña, siempre **visitaba** la emisora de radio donde **trabajaba** su tío. Le **fascinaba** ver cómo su tío **entrevistaba** a personas famosas. Cuando Sara **tenía** 15 años, **había** un cantante que **era** muy popular entre los jóvenes. Sus canciones **eran** muy divertidas y **tenían** mucho ritmo, así que todo el mundo **bailaba** en las discotecas al compás de[1] su música. Un día Sara **fue** a la emisora y **se encontró** con él en el estudio de grabación.[2] ¡**Estaba** tan sorprendida que **se quedó** sin habla[3]! Cuando por fin **recuperó** la voz, **se acercó** a[4] él y le **dijo** con mucha timidez: «Tú eres Miguel Bosé, ¿verdad?» El chico la **miró** y **respondió:** «Sí, y tú, ¿quién eres?» Entonces Sara **se presentó** y él le **dio** dos besos. Ese **fue** uno de los días más inolvidables de su vida.

[1]al... *to the beat of* [2]de... *recording* [3]sin... *speechless* [4]se... *she approached*

---

*En algunas partes se usa el término más formal, **la bitácora** en vez de **el blog.** Otras palabras relacionadas con **el blog** son: **el blogging, bloguear** y **el bloguero / la bloguera.**

Sara ha trabajado en varias emisoras de radio.

Paso 2 Conteste las siguientes preguntas sobre la experiencia de Sara.

1. ¿Por qué le gustaba a Sara visitar la emisora de radio?
2. ¿Por qué era muy popular Miguel Bosé?
3. ¿Qué pasó aquel día en el estudio de grabación?

Paso 3 Ahora, complete las siguientes oraciones para hablar de su propio pasado.

1. Cuando era niño/a, una vez yo…
2. El año pasado, mi mejor amigo/a y yo…
3. Al final del semestre pasado, mis profesores…
4. Cuando tenía 16 años, siempre…

REACCIONAR **R** RECOMENDAR

REACCIONES Y RECOMENDACIONES: ¡QUÉ TALENTO TIENE DIEGO!

Paso 1 Lea el siguiente párrafo sobre Diego y su familia.

Tesoros, la tienda de Diego, ha tenido mucho éxito.[1] Ahora piensa abrir otra en Arizona o Miami, pero sus padres **quieren que abra** su nueva tienda en México. Para ellos **es triste que** su querido hijo no **viva** cerca de ellos y **tienen miedo de que se quede**[2] en los Estados Unidos para siempre. Pero es obvio que Diego es un excelente hombre de negocios[3] y sus padres **esperan que tenga** mucha suerte[4] en su trabajo. Por lo menos **están contentos de que** Diego **viaje** a México para comprar artesanías tres veces al año.

[1] *success* [2] se… *will stay* [3] hombre… *businessman* [4] *luck*

Ojo

Antes de hacer esta sección, vea las páginas verdes (212–220) al final del libro para repasar cómo hacer reacciones y recomendaciones en español.

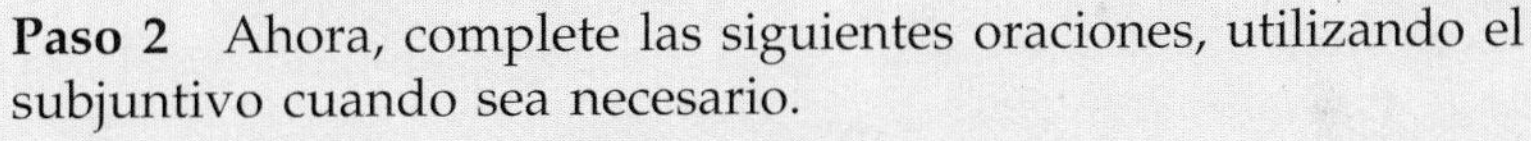

Paso 2 Ahora, complete las siguientes oraciones, utilizando el subjuntivo cuando sea necesario.

1. Es bueno que Tesoros ______ (ser) una tienda popular.
2. Los padres de Diego no quieren que él ______ (vivir) en los Estados Unidos para siempre.
3. Es evidente que Diego ______ (ser) un buen hombre de negocios.
4. Sugiero que Diego ______ (ir) a México a comprar artesanías más de tres veces al año.

Diego: un hombre con suerte en los negocios

Paso 3 Nuestros padres (hijos, abuelos, amigos…) comparten algunas de nuestras opiniones, pero no están de acuerdo con todas nuestras ideas, ¿verdad? Complete las siguientes oraciones.

1. Mis padres (hijos, abuelos, amigos) siempre recomiendan que yo…
2. Sugiero que mis padres…
3. Es bueno que mis amigos (padres, hijos)…
4. Mis amigos (padres, hijos, abuelos) piensan que es horrible que yo…

GUSTOS

HABLAR DE LOS GUSTOS: ¡QUÉ EXTROVERTIDO ES JAVIER!

Paso 1 Lea el siguiente párrafo sobre Javier y lo que más le interesa.

Si a Ud. **le interesa** saber quién es quién y quién hace qué, debe hablar con Javier. Es que a Javier **le fascina** la clientela tan variada que visita Ruta Maya. Su formación[1] de periodista puede ser el resultado de su gran interés en conocer a la gente. Desde niño, **le interesaban** los chismes,[2] mientras que a su hermano no **le importaban** para nada. La verdad es que **le encanta** enterarse de[3] lo que pasa en la vida privada de las personas. Lo único que **le fastidia**[4] es que los clientes interrumpan las conversaciones que tiene con sus amigos. Pero, de todas maneras, uno tiene que ganarse la vida,[5] ¿no?

[1]*training, education* [2]*gossip* [3]enterarse... *to find out about* [4]le... *bugs him* [5]ganarse... *earn a living*

Ojo

Antes de hacer esta sección, vea las páginas verdes (220–226) al final del libro para repasar cómo hablar de los gustos en español.

Paso 2 En parejas, escojan de cada cuadro la información que les parezca apropiada para formar siete oraciones sobre los gustos y las preferencias de los cinco amigos. Sigan el modelo.

MODELO: A Laura le encanta el Ecuador.

Sara	encantar	la comida picante	Austin
Laura	fascinar	tomar café	las revistas políticas
Sergio	fastidiar	los clientes de Ruta Maya	los blogs
los cinco amigos	gustar	las conferencias	la música tejana
Javier	interesar	bailar salsa	la comida exótica
	molestar	los conciertos	los lunes

Paso 3 Ahora, indiquen los gustos, las preferencias, las molestias, etcétera, de las siguientes personas. Pueden usar la lista de temas sugeridos en el **Paso 2** u otras ideas.

1. yo
2. mi mejor amigo/a
3. mis profesores
4. nosotros, los estudiantes de la clase

A Javier le encanta trabajar en Ruta Maya.

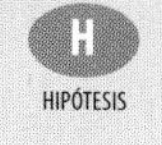
HIPÓTESIS

HACER HIPÓTESIS: LOS SUEÑOS DE SERGIO

Paso 1 Lea el siguiente párrafo sobre Sergio y lo que le gustaría hacer.

Aunque Sergio se siente feliz por lo general, a veces se pone a soñar con[1] las cosas que **haría** si **pudiera.** Por ejemplo, **le gustaría** mudarse a Los Ángeles, California. Allí **podría** conocer una comunidad y cultura mexicanoamericanas muy importantes. Además, quizás **tendría** más oportunidades profesionales, puesto que[2] Los Ángeles es ahora la capital del mundo de los espectáculos.[3] Si Sergio **llegara** a tener mucho éxito en su trabajo, **compraría** una casa al lado del mar. El único inconveniente de vivir en Los Ángeles **sería** que su familia le **quedaría** muy lejos. ¡Pero no **importaría!** Si **tuviera** tanto éxito, **dispondría** de[4] su propio avión para viajar entre Los Ángeles, Boston y México sin problema alguno.

[1]se... *he starts to dream about* [2]puesto... *since* [3]mundo... *entertainment industry* [4]dispondría... *he would have at his disposal*

Ojo

Antes de hacer esta sección, vea las páginas verdes (226–228) al final del libro para repasar cómo hacer hipótesis en español.

Sergio llevaría a sus amigos a Los Ángeles si pudiera.

Paso 2 Complete el siguiente párrafo con la forma apropiada de los verbos que están entre paréntesis.

Si yo fuera Sergio, _____ (mudarse) a Los Ángeles para conocer a más estrellas de cine. Para las vacaciones, _____ (ir) a todos los festivales musicales de Latinoamérica. Con suerte, _____ (conocer) a gente famosa como Juanes y Shakira. Si _____ (poder) hacerlo, los convencería de que fueran mis clientes. Si _____ (tener) influencia en el mundo de la música, ganaría mucho dinero. _____ (Ser) una vida genial.

Paso 3 Ahora, pensando en sus propios sueños, complete las siguientes oraciones con la forma apropiada de los verbos y su propia opinión. Luego, comparta sus respuestas con un compañero / una compañera.

1. Si yo pudiera trabajar en cualquier profesión, _____ (ser) _____ porque _____.
2. Si quisiera tener éxito en esa profesión, _____ (tener) que _____ porque _____.
3. Si ganara mucho dinero en esa profesión, yo _____ (viajar) a _____, donde _____ porque _____.

F FUTURO

HABLAR DEL FUTURO: LAS AVENTURAS DE LAURA

Paso 1 Lea la siguiente narración sobre las posibles aventuras de Laura en el futuro.

Cuando Laura **termine** sus estudios de posgrado, **irá** de nuevo al Ecuador a vivir allí. **Vivirá** en Quito, donde tal vez **trabaje** con una organización internacional. Cuando **llegue** a Quito, seguramente su novio Manuel la **recogerá** y la **llevará** a cenar. **Tendrán** mucho que decirse, ya que **habrán** pasado casi dos años sin verse. Laura no sabe cómo **irán** sus relaciones con Manuel. Como son de dos culturas distintas, los dos **tendrán** que adaptarse mucho a las actitudes, creencias y acciones del otro.

Ojo

Antes de hacer esta sección, vea las páginas verdes (228–232) al final del libro para repasar cómo hablar del futuro en español.

Paso 2 Complete las siguientes oraciones sobre Laura y Manuel con el futuro del verbo que está entre paréntesis.

1. El padre de Laura _____ (tratar) de convencerla de que se quede en los Estados Unidos.
2. Laura y Manuel _____ (estar) un poco nerviosos, pero muy contentos a la vez.
3. Manuel _____ (empezar) a ahorrar dinero.
4. Manuel _____ (tener) que adaptarse a la manera de ser de Laura, o sus relaciones no _____ (durar).

Manuel y Laura comunican por Skype.

Paso 3 Ahora, complete estas oraciones diciendo lo que Ud. hará en las siguientes circunstancias.

1. Cuando termine mis estudios,...
2. Cuando tenga 40 (50, 60,...) años,...
3. Cuando hable mejor el español,...
4. Cuando lleguen las vacaciones,...
5. Tan pronto como pueda, yo...

CAPÍTULO 1

Perspectivas:

Percepciones e impresiones

Puntos clave

DESCRIBIR COMPARAR

Temas centrales

- percepciones
- estereotipos

Zona de enfoque

- España

El Bar Estrella en el barrio de Santa Cruz (Sevilla, España)

En este capítulo, Ud. va a explorar los temas de las percepciones y los estereotipos.

Preguntas para considerar

- ¿Cuáles son los factores que influyen en las primeras impresiones que Ud. forma de una persona?
- ¿Es lógico pensar que existe un norteamericano típico o un hispano típico?
- ¿De dónde viene la información que se utiliza para crear la imagen de una persona de otra región de su país o de otra cultura?
- ¿Cuáles son los programas de televisión más populares entre sus amigos?
- ¿Hay algo que le parezca estereotipado de España y de los españoles en el cuadro que se ve en esta página?

MULTIMEDIA

 Estampillas musicales

 Lugares fascinantes

 Online *Manual* www.mhcentro.com

 Online Learning Center www.mhhe.com/puntoyaparte4

Las primeras impresiones

Situación: Javier y Sara hablan sobre los eventos relacionados con España que ocurren esta semana en Austin y de la diversa clientela que atrae el café Ruta Maya. Lea el diálogo y preste especial atención al uso del vocabulario nuevo que está **en negrita.***

Javier y Sara en Ruta Maya

SARA: Hay mucha marcha[1] en Ruta Maya para ser miércoles. ¿Qué pasa?

JAVIER: Hoy abre una exhibición fotográfica sobre la arquitectura de Antoni Gaudí y esta noche aquí al lado hay un espectáculo de flamenco.

SARA: Es **alucinante** que haya tanto interés en la cultura española. **Parece** que la mitad de la ciudad está aquí. Hay mucha gente que no conozco. ¿Quién es ese tipo sentado al lado de Diana? **Tiene mala pinta.**

JAVIER: ¿No lo reconoces? Es su hermano, David. Lo conociste hace dos años cuando visitaba a Diana.

SARA: ¡No puede ser! Era un chico tan **agradable** y **chistoso.** Recuerdo que nos hablaba de que quería ponerse su primer **tatuaje.**

JAVIER: Pues, es él. Llegó ayer de Barcelona.

SARA: Pues **se ve** ridículo con el **bigote** y las **patillas** y esa ropa tan **cursi.**

JAVIER: Cuidado, Sara, no debes **meter la pata** con Diana. A ella le gusta mucho el estilo de su hermano y cree que su ropa **está de moda.**

SARA: Oye, mira a esa muchacha con el pelo **rizado,** sentada sola en la esquina. ¡Qué guapa! ¿No te interesa?

JAVIER: Sara, no seas alcahueta.[2] **Las apariencias engañan.** A pesar de su aspecto de niña **dulce** y **educada,** es muy arrogante. Ha venido aquí un par de veces y apenas habla con nadie.

SARA: Bueno, ¿no será simplemente **tímida?** Es posible que **sea buena gente.** ¿No recuerdas que cuando conociste a Laura ella no **te cayó muy bien?**

JAVIER: Sí, me **parecía** un poco **presumida** y era demasiado **callada** y —tú me conoces— yo **hablo por los codos.**

SARA: ¡Por eso **nos llevamos** tan **bien** tú y yo!

[1]mucha… *lively social scene* [2]*matchmaker*

*Words and phrases that are boldfaced in the dialogue appear as entries in the **Vocabulario del tema** following this section.

ACTIVIDADES

A. Detective Busque en el diálogo ejemplos de las siguientes metas comunicativas: Descripción (D), Hablar de los gustos (G) y Narración en el pasado (P). Subraye cada palabra o frase que represente una (o una combinación) de estas metas comunicativas. Luego, escriba al margen la(s) letra(s) que corresponde(n) a cada ejemplo subrayado (D, G o P).

MODELOS: Lo conociste hace dos años cuando visitaba a Diana. (P)
Era un chico tan agradable y chistoso. (P) (D)

B. Comprensión Conteste las siguientes preguntas, según el diálogo.

1. ¿Qué eventos relacionados con la cultura española hay en Austin esta semana?
2. ¿Qué opina Sara del aspecto físico de David?
3. ¿Por qué no le cae bien a Javier la mujer de pelo rizado?
4. ¿Está de acuerdo Sara con la impresión que Javier tiene sobre esa chica? Explique.
5. ¿Qué opinión tenía Javier de Laura cuando se conocieron por primera vez?
6. ¿Por qué se llevan bien Sara y Javier?

C. Reacciones Complete las siguientes oraciones, basándose en la conversación de Javier y Sara. Debe utilizar uno de los conectores de la lista a la izquierda con cada oración.

MODELO: A Javier le gusta que su clientela sea diversa porque le encanta conocer a gente diferente.

1. A Sara le sorprende que...
2. Según Sara, es ridículo que el hermano de Diana...
3. A Javier no le gusta que la chica con pelo rizado...
4. Es obvio que Sara y Javier...

Conectores

en cambio	*on the other hand*
por eso	*therefore*
porque	*because*
puesto que	*since*
sin embargo	*nevertheless*
ya que	*since*

D. Diálogo En parejas, preparen un diálogo entre Sara y Diana en el que hablen de la apariencia de David, el hermano de Diana. Luego preséntenlo a la clase.

Vocabulario del tema

*Para describir cualidades positivas o neutras**

agradable	pleasant
atrevido/a	daring
callado/a	quiet
chistoso/a	funny
culto/a	well-educated
dulce	sweet
educado/a[†]	polite
encantador(a)	charming
hablador(a)	talkative
llamativo/a	showy, flashy
reservado/a	reserved
sensible[†]	sensitive
serio/a	serious
tímido/a	shy

*Para describir cualidades negativas**

bruto/a	stupid, brutish
cursi	tasteless, pretentious, corny
despistado/a	absent-minded
grosero/a	rude
pesado/a	tedious, annoying
presumido/a	conceited
raro/a[†]	strange
tacaño/a	stingy
testarudo/a	stubborn
tiquismiquis	picky
vago/a	lazy

Para hablar del cuerpo

el arete / el pendiente	earring
la arruga	wrinkle
la barba	beard
el bigote	moustache
la ceja	eyebrow
la cicatriz	scar
las gafas / los lentes	eyeglasses
el lunar	beauty mark, mole
el ombligo	navel
la oreja	ear
la patilla	sideburn
la peca	freckle
el pelo	hair
canoso	gray
liso	straight
rizado	curly
teñido	dyed
el piercing	piercing
el rasgo	trait, characteristic
el rostro	face
el tatuaje	tattoo
calvo/a	bald
pelirrojo/a	red-headed

—Piensa que soy su mamá.

¿Cómo son estas personas? Descríbalas hasta el más mínimo detalle.

*These adjectives are usually used with **ser** to describe inherent characteristics. In **Capítulo 3,** you will learn another list of adjectives that are most often used with **estar** to express emotional states or physical conditions.

†Be careful when using these words. They are false cognates.

Para hablar de las percepciones

caerle (*irreg.*) **bien/ mal (a alguien)***	to like/dislike (someone)
darse (*irreg.*) **cuenta de**	to realize
estar (*irreg.*) **de moda**[†]	to be in style
estar pasado/a de moda	to be out of style
ir (*irreg.*) **a la moda**[†]	to dress fashionably
llevarse bien/ mal con	to get along well/poorly with
parecer (parezco)	to seem, appear
parecerse a	to look like
verse (*irreg.*)[‡]	to look + *adj./adv.*

Para describir las impresiones

alucinante	incredible, impressive
degradante	degrading
deprimente	depressing
emocionante	exciting
preocupante	worrisome
repugnante	disgusting

Otras expresiones útiles

a primera vista	at first sight
las apariencias engañan	looks are deceiving
hablar por los codos[§]	to talk a lot
meter la pata	to put one's foot in one's mouth
no tener (*irreg.*) **pelos en la lengua**[§]	to speak one's mind
ser (*irreg.*) **buena/mala gente**	to be a good/bad person
tener buena/ mala pinta	to have a good/bad appearance
tener (mucha) cara	to have (a lot of) nerve

ACTIVIDADES

A. Vocabulario en contexto En parejas, indiquen si las siguientes oraciones son ciertas o falsas. Modifiquen las oraciones falsas para que sean ciertas.

	CIERTO	FALSO
1. Una persona bien educada debe tener una educación universitaria.	☐	☐
2. A la gente tacaña no le gusta gastar mucho dinero.	☐	☐
3. Ir en canoa por el Río Amazonas es algo característico de una persona atrevida.	☐	☐
4. A los estudiantes les gustan los profesores despistados porque son muy organizados.	☐	☐
5. Es probable que una persona que no tiene pelos en la lengua meta la pata con frecuencia.	☐	☐
6. A la gente mayor le encanta ver los tatuajes que lleva la gente joven hoy en día.	☐	☐
7. Las películas de Will Ferrell son deprimentes.	☐	☐

*In this construction, **caer** functions like **gustar:** Mi nueva compañera de cuarto **me cae bien,** pero sus amigas **me caen mal.**

[†]**Estar de moda** is used with things, whereas **ir a la moda** is for people: Mi **compañera de cuarto** siempre **va a la moda.** Ayer se hizo cuatro **tatuajes** simplemente porque **están de moda** ahora.

[‡]**¿Cómo me veo?** *How do I look?* **Te ves bien/guapa/cansada.** *You look fine/pretty/tired.*

[§]Literally: *to talk through your elbows; not to have hair on one's tongue*

	CIERTO	FALSO
8. Una persona que usa la ropa de su compañero/a de cuarto sin pedirle permiso tiene mucha cara.	☐	☐
9. Una persona dulce y sensible sería un policía / una mujer policía excelente.	☐	☐
10. Para mucha gente mayor, la moda de hoy es algo preocupante.	☐	☐
11. Es fácil viajar con una persona tiquismiquis porque le gusta probar cosas diferentes.	☐	☐
12. Es cursi combinar la ropa de etiqueta (*designer label*) con ropa pasada de moda como la que se vende en las tiendas de ropa de segunda mano.	☐	☐

Mónica y Penélope Cruz

B. Penélope y Mónica Cruz*

Paso 1 Lea este breve comentario sobre Penélope Cruz y su hermana, Mónica, y llene los espacios en blanco con la forma apropiada de uno de los verbos de percepción.

Mónica ________[1] (verse / parecerse) bellísma en un desfile[a] de moda en Madrid. Físicamente ________[2] (parecer / parecerse a) Penélope muchísimo. De hecho, hay gente que cuando las ve juntas no puede ________[3] (verse / darse cuenta) de quién es quién. Las hermanas son muy diferentes de personalidad, pero ________[4] (caerle / llevarse) súper bien. Siempre ________[5] (estar de moda / ir a la moda) y en 2007 empezaron a trabajar como diseñadoras[b] para la tienda de moda Mango. ________[6] (Parecer / Parecerse) que todas quieren llevar el *look* de las hermanas Cruz, lo que es una buena señal[c] para la compañía Mango.

[a]*fashion show* [b]*designers* [c]*sign*

Paso 2 Hablen en grupos de tres sobre sus compañeros de clase, su profesor(a) o unas personas famosas. Hagan una oración original con las siguientes expresiones verbales.

1. parecerse a
2. verse
3. caerle bien / mal
4. llevarse bien / mal con

C. Preguntas personales En parejas, háganse y contesten las siguientes preguntas, utilizando palabras o frases del **Vocabulario del tema.** Mientras Ud. escucha a su compañero/a, indique sus reacciones. Puede usar las expresiones de **Para conversar mejor** que aparecen a continuación. Luego, compartan con la clase lo que cada uno/a de Uds. averiguó sobre su compañero/a.

---

*Mónica Cruz is a professional ballet and flamenco dancer who has recently started a film career as well.

Ojo

Puesto que a lo largo del libro Ud. tendrá que usar todas las metas comunicativas, verá en las actividades y los ejercicios del libro algunos iconos que lo/la ayudarán a acordarse de los puntos gramaticales que debe usar en cierta situación. Estos iconos corresponden con los que están en la lista de las metas comunicativas y los puntos clave que aparece al final del libro. Si tiene alguna duda, puede consultar rápidamente esa lista o las páginas verdes que aparecen al final del libro.

Para conversar mejor

¡Qué interesante! ¡Qué chévere (*Carib.*) / guay (*Sp.*) / padre (*Mex.*)!	*How awesome!*
¡Qué curioso!	*How odd!*
¡Qué raro!	*How weird!*
Es igual para mí.	*It's all the same to me.*
A mí también.	*Me, too.*
(No) Estoy de acuerdo.	*I (don't) agree.*
¡Qué vergüenza!	*How embarrassing!*
¿En serio? ¿De veras?	*Really?*
¡Buena idea!	*Good idea!*

1. ¿Cómo es Ud.? Describa su aspecto físico y su personalidad. Describa a alguien famoso que tenga una apariencia rara. Según las revistas de chismes, ¿cómo es esa persona?

2. Haga una comparación entre Ud. y uno/a de sus mejores amigos / amigas. ¿En qué se parecen y en qué se diferencian? ¿Cómo es Ud. en comparación con sus padres? ¿Son Uds. muy parecidos o muy diferentes?

3. ¿Qué le gusta a Ud. de la moda de hoy y qué le molesta? ¿Por qué? ¿Le importa llevar ropa pasada de moda? ¿Por qué sí o por qué no? ¿Qué le recomienda a una persona que siempre quiere ir a la moda?

4. Relate una situación en la que Ud. o un amigo / una amiga haya metido la pata. ¿Dónde y con quién estaba? ¿Qué hizo o dijo? ¿Cómo reaccionaron las personas a su alrededor?

PASADO

DESAFÍO

5. Si Ud. quisiera cambiar su apariencia física para sorprender a sus padres, ¿qué haría? ¿Por qué les sorprendería?

6. ¿Qué hará la gente joven de la próxima generación con su apariencia que molestará a sus padres?

D. Fiestas fascinantes

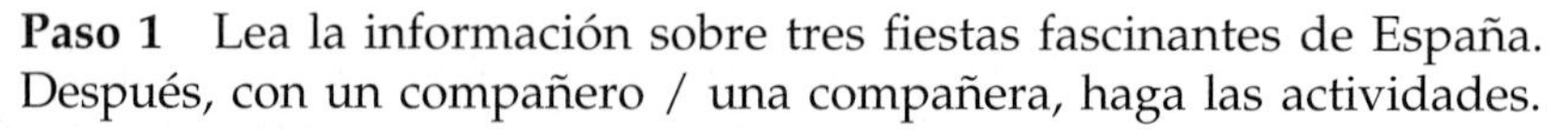

Paso 1 Lea la información sobre tres fiestas fascinantes de España. Después, con un compañero / una compañera, haga las actividades.

Los Sanfermines Los Sanfermines de Pamplona, quizás la fiesta española más conocida a nivel internacional, tienen lugar durante la semana del 7 de julio. Cada día, a las 8:00 de la mañana, cientos de personas se reúnen en las calles para correr delante de los toros que van a torear en la corrida de la tarde. Después de esta actividad tan peligrosa, la gente pasa el resto del día bebiendo y bailando por las calles.

Santiago de Compostela En esta ciudad de Galicia se celebran las fiestas del apóstol Santiago, el santo patrón de España, el 25 de julio. Cada año miles de personas de todas partes del mundo van a Santiago de Compostela para visitar la tumba del apóstol. Para llegar, muchos peregrinos[1] llegan por el «Camino de Santiago», que pasa por el norte de España desde la frontera francesa hasta la ciudad gallega.[2] Los peregrinos recorren cientos y hasta miles de millas a pie, en bicicleta o en coche.

La Tomatina En Buñol, una ciudad pequeña de Valencia, la gente puede disfrutar de un evento tan divertido como sorprendente. El último miércoles de agosto, entre el mediodía y la 1:00 de la tarde, miles de personas se dedican a tirarse,[3] unas a otras, 130 toneladas de tomates. Es una fiesta relativamente nueva, ya que empezó a mediados del siglo XX, y se está haciendo cada vez más popular.

[1]*pilgrims* [2]*Galician* [3]*to throw*

Paso 2 En parejas, contesten las siguientes preguntas.

1. ¿A cuál de las fiestas irían las siguientes personas: una persona seria, una atrevida, otra culta y otra rara? ¿A qué fiesta no deben ir las siguientes personas: una persona despistada, una tiquismiquis, otra grosera y otra reservada?
2. ¿Cuál de las fiestas le interesa más a Ud.? ¿Por qué? ¿Cuál le interesaría más a su madre, a su padre, a su profesor(a) y a su mejor amigo/a? ¿Por qué?
3. Describa una fiesta típica de su ciudad, región o país. Compárela con estas fiestas españolas.

Paso 3 Imagínese que Ud. acaba de asistir a una de estas fiestas. Describa en su blog sus experiencias durante la fiesta. Dele también recomendaciones sobre cómo pasarlo bien cuando él/ella vaya a este lugar el año que viene.

E. **Problemas repentinos** Entre todos, revisen los siguientes problemas y hagan una lista de palabras nuevas de este capítulo que los ayuden a conversar con facilidad sobre cada problema repentino. Después, en parejas, preparen un diálogo espontáneo sobre cada problema.

1. Un(a) estudiante tiene un nuevo compañero / una nueva compañera de cuarto que le cae muy mal. Habla con la directora de residencias estudiantiles para quejarse de él/ella. Describe las cosas que no le gustan. La directora piensa que el/la que se queja es demasiado tiquismiquis.
2. Francisco es muy listo pero tiene una apariencia muy rara y quiere conseguir trabajo en una compañía conservadora. Un amigo dice lo que debe hacer para cambiar su apariencia física antes de la entrevista, pero Francisco es muy testarudo.

NOTA CULTURAL • ¿Somos tan sensibles?

La manera de hablar de los demás varía mucho de cultura a cultura. En este país, la gente tiende a[1] evitar expresiones que describen de manera directa y cruda la apariencia física de una persona. Por ejemplo, en vez de decir que una persona es *fat*, tal vez se diga que es *large*. O en vez de llamarle *old* o *elderly* a alguien, se diría que es *a bit older*.

Por lo general, en la cultura española no se considera ofensivo referirse a la apariencia física de una persona sin usar eufemismos. Por el contrario, los españoles suelen hablar de manera directa, y muchas veces hasta se refieren a una característica física sobresaliente,[2] favorable o no, para describir a alguien.

Esta diferencia cultural puede causar problemas. A los norteamericanos les puede parecer que los españoles no tienen pelos en la lengua. Por otro lado, los españoles pueden pensar que los norteamericanos usan demasiados eufemismos o incluso que no son sinceros. Esas diferencias hacen que a veces un español meta la pata cuando habla con un norteamericano. Eso es precisamente lo que le pasaba a Sara cuando recién llegó a los Estados Unidos. Hablaba de manera directa, natural para ella, y la gente la veía extrañada por[3] lo que decía. Al principio, Sara no entendía por qué la gente se ofendía tanto. Laura le tuvo que explicar que, por lo general, en los Estados Unidos se suavizan[4] las observaciones sobre algunos aspectos físicos.

[1]tiende... *tends to* [2]*distinguishing* [3]la... *people who saw her were amazed by* [4]*soften*

Preguntas

1. ¿Conoce Ud. a alguien que no tenga pelos en la lengua? ¿Quién es y cómo es esa persona?
2. Si alguien le preguntara si una prenda de ropa le queda bien, y la verdad es que le queda mal, ¿qué le diría? ¿Por qué?

Actividad

H HIPÓTESIS Olivia, una amiga estadounidense de Sara, acaba de regresar de un programa de estudios en la Argentina. Ahora habla el español con mucha fluidez, tiene un novio argentino y pesa quince libras de más. Lea los tres comentarios que le hizo Sara a Olivia. Luego, en parejas, digan cómo responderían si fueran Olivia. Empiecen sus comentarios con: «Si yo fuera Olivia, yo diría... »

1. Olivia, estás más gordita. La comida argentina debe ser buenísima.
2. ¿Este muchacho de la foto es tu novio? Pues, por lo que me habías dicho, pensé que era más joven.
3. Tu español ha mejorado mucho, pero no has perdido tu acento estadounidense.

DESCRIBIR

COMPARAR

Descripción y comparación

En esta sección del capítulo, Ud. va a practicar las descripciones y comparaciones de personas y lugares. Para hacerlo bien, hay que utilizar las estructuras gramaticales (los puntos clave) de la siguiente tabla que pertenecen a cada meta comunicativa. Antes de continuar, estudie las explicaciones de estas estructuras gramaticales en las páginas verdes (194–239) que están al final del libro.

LAS METAS COMUNICATIVAS DE ESTE CAPÍTULO		
ICONO	METAS COMUNICATIVAS	PUNTOS CLAVE
D DESCRIBIR	Descripción	• la concordancia de género y número • **ser/estar** • los participios como adjetivos
C COMPARAR	Comparación	• la concordancia de género y número • **tan... como, tanto/a/os/as... como** • **más/menos... que**

PRUEBA DIAGNÓSTICA

Paso 1 Descripción Mire el cuadro del Bar Estrella. Luego, lea los siguientes párrafos y escriba la forma apropiada de los verbos y adjetivos que están entre paréntesis, según el contexto.

La gente que frecuenta el nuevo Bar Estrella ______[1] (ser/estar) muy ______[2] (impresionado) con todo lo que ha hecho Manolo, el nuevo dueño, para renovar el antiguo Bar Flores.

Manolo y su esposa ______[3] (ser/estar) ______[4] (encantador) y han creado un ambiente perfecto para sus clientes. En primer lugar, les ofrecen una selección ______[5] (grandísimo) de licores, vinos y cervezas, y las tapas ______[6] (ser/estar) ______[7] (delicioso) y ______[8] (variado). Antes, las tapas que servían en el Bar Flores no ______[9] (ser/estar) muy buenas. Doña Pepita, la dueña anterior, ya no tenía mucho interés en mantener el bar después de la muerte ______[10] (inesperado) de su marido. Venderles el bar a Manolo y a su esposa ______[11] (ser/estar) la solución ______[12] (perfecto).

(*continúa*)

Hoy _____[13] (ser/estar) viernes. _____[14] (Ser/Estar) las 4:30 de la tarde y todo _____[15] (ser/estar) preparado para una noche _____[16] (extraordinario). Las tapas _____[17] (ser/estar) listas y Mariluz ya ha llegado para practicar un poco antes de su acto. Ella _____[18] (ser/estar) de Cádiz, y su estilo de baile es _____[19] (típico) de su región. _____[20] (Ser/Estar) practicando un baile nuevo con un guitarrista _____[21] (alemán).

Mariluz va a bailar en el Bar Estrella por una hora y luego irá con Hans al Festival de Flamenco que _____[22] (ser/estar) en el Teatro Lope de Vega. Va a _____[23] (ser/estar) una noche _____[24] (estupendo).

Paso 2 Comparación Ahora, complete las siguientes comparaciones según la información de los párrafos anteriores.

1. Las tapas del Bar Estrella son _____ (mejor/peor) _____ (como/que) las tapas del Bar Flores.
2. Manolo debe tener _____ (más/menos) _____ (de/que) quince tipos de licores en su bar.
3. Doña Pepita no tenía _____ (tan/tanto) ganas de seguir con el negocio _____ (como/que) Manolo.
4. Doña Pepita está _____ (tan/tanta) contenta _____ (como/que) Manolo con la venta de su bar.
5. Al nuevo bar irán _____ (más/menos) clientes _____ (de/que) antes.
6. Seguramente, el Bar Estrella es el _____ (mejor/peor) bar _____ (de/que) la zona.

ACTIVIDADES

A. Lugares especiales

Paso 1 Lea la siguiente carta escrita por el famoso pintor español Joaquín Sorolla a su esposa acerca de un lugar que él había descubierto en la costa valenciana de España.

Valencia (noviembre de 1907)

Querida Clotilde: Estoy ya en esta playa desde las 4:00 de la tarde y he gozado mucho con el espléndido espectáculo de tanta luz y color. El día tibio[1] y agradable contribuyó, lo he desperdiciado[2] un momento viendo cosas bonitas: El agua era de un azul tan fino y la vibración de luz era una locura. He presenciado el regreso de la pesca,[3] las hermosas velas,[4] los grupos pescadores, las luces de mil colores reflejándose en el mar, la picante conversación de muchos de mis viejos modelos, me proporcionaron[5] un rato muy difícil de olvidar.

Ahora son las seis menos cuarto y he cogido el lápiz para transmitirte este rato de placer pasado en mi primera tarde en el puerto; ahora noche absoluta, es tan agradable como antes, pues como yo nunca he vivido en el puerto, el espectáculo me seduce, las sirenas, el ruido de la carga y descarga[6] sigue y las luces siguen reflejándose en el mar… […]

[1]*mild* [2]lo… *I've wasted it* (*for*) [3]*fishing* (*season*) [4]*sails* [5]regalaron [6]carga… *loading and unloading*

Paseo a orillas del mar, de Joaquín Sorolla (1863–1923)

Son las 10:30 y me voy a dormir solo... y triste, por eso, pero antes quiero decirte que la noche es colosal, hermosa, hay una luna espléndida, y el mar está más bello que durante el día, he dado un largo paseo viendo los reflejos de las luces. Hasta mañana.

Paso 2 Busque los adjetivos que Sorolla utilizó para describir las siguientes cosas.

la conversación	la luna	las velas
el día	la noche	

Paso 3 Ahora, busque las dos comparaciones que hizo Sorolla en su carta.

Paso 4 Piense en un lugar especial que Ud. conozca. Escriba cinco adjetivos que utilizaría para describir ese lugar. Luego, mencione cuatro actividades que Ud. ha hecho allí y tres emociones que ese lugar evoca en Ud.

Paso 5 Descríbale su lugar especial a un compañero / una compañera. Su compañero/a debe tratar de visualizar ese lugar especial mientras Ud. lo describe.

Paso 6 Ahora, escriba dos frases comparando el lugar especial de su compañero/a con el de Ud.

La tragedia, *de Pablo Picasso* (1881–1973)

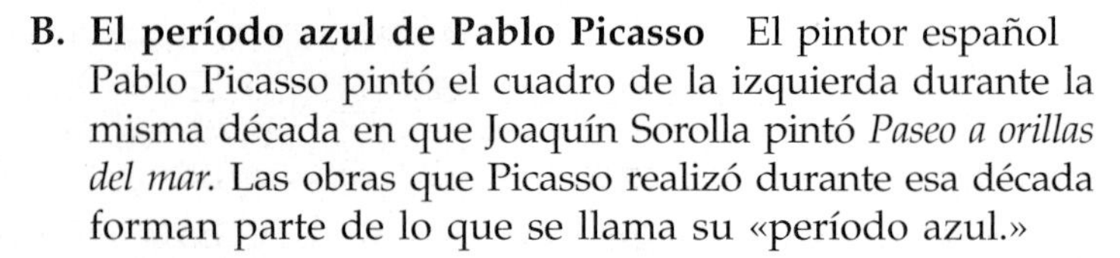

B. El período azul de Pablo Picasso El pintor español Pablo Picasso pintó el cuadro de la izquierda durante la misma década en que Joaquín Sorolla pintó *Paseo a orillas del mar.* Las obras que Picasso realizó durante esa década forman parte de lo que se llama su «período azul.»

Paso 1 En grupos de tres, describan el cuadro de Picasso. Incluyan una descripción física de la familia, algunas comparaciones entre la mujer, el hombre y el niño y una descripción de las impresiones que evoca el cuadro en Uds.

Paso 2 Hagan algunas comparaciones entre el cuadro de Picasso y la pintura de Sorolla de la Actividad A.

Paso 3 Ahora, preparen un diálogo entre las señoritas del cuadro de Sorolla y las tres personas del cuadro de Picasso. Luego, preséntenlo a la clase.

C. Las apariencias engañan ¿Cuáles son los factores que influyen en las diferentes reacciones que experimenta la gente ante las mismas personas, situaciones o cosas?

Paso 1 En parejas, observen las siguientes fotos. A primera vista, ¿qué impresión tienen Uds. de estas tres personas? Por su apariencia física, ¿qué tipo de persona será cada una de ellas? ¿Cuál será su profesión? Recuerden utilizar el vocabulario nuevo en sus descripciones. **¡OJO!** Acuérdense de que las apariencias engañan.

1.

2.

3.

Paso 2 Ahora, en grupos de cuatro, comparen algunas de las impresiones que Uds. tienen de estas personas. Incluyan en sus comentarios una explicación de los criterios que usaron para llegar a cada conclusión.

Paso 3 Su profesor(a) les va a decir quiénes son estas personas. ¿Concuerda la verdadera identidad de cada persona con la primera impresión que tuvieron Uds. de él o ella? ¿Cuáles son los factores que influyen en las primeras impresiones de alguien? Hagan una lista de esos factores y luego presenten sus ideas a la clase.

D. Los estereotipos

Paso 1 En parejas, comenten las siguientes preguntas.

¿Qué es un estereotipo? ¿De dónde viene la información que se utiliza para crear la imagen de una persona de otra región de su país o de otra cultura?

Paso 2 Lea lo que dicen los españoles de la gente de varias regiones o comunidades autónomas de España. Luego, en parejas, escojan dos a tres adjetivos que describan a los habitantes de las siguientes regiones de los Estados Unidos, según los estereotipos que Uds. conozcan. Finalmente, usen los adjetivos para escribir tres comparaciones entre los grupos.

a. «Los gallegos son supersticiosos e introvertidos.»
b. «Los andaluces son graciosos, vagos, alegres y juerguistas (*partyers*).»
c. «Los aragoneses son brutos y testarudos.»
d. «Los catalanes son arrogantes y tacaños.»

1. los tejanos
2. los de la ciudad de Nueva York
3. los jóvenes de Orange County, California
4. los de Carolina del Sur

Paso 3 Ahora, con otra pareja, comparen los estereotipos que apuntaron y las comparaciones que hicieron en el **Paso 2.** Luego, contesten las siguientes preguntas.

1. ¿Pueden nombrar a gente de cada región (políticos, actores, deportistas, activistas, amigos, etcétera)? ¿Corresponden esas personas a los estereotipos?
2. ¿Qué adjetivos piensan Uds. que los extranjeros utilizan para describir a los norteamericanos en general? ¿Qué adjetivos utiliza la gente para describir a los hispanos en general?
3. ¿Cuál es el papel de las películas y la televisión en reforzar los estereotipos de un país o una cultura? Piensen en tres programas o películas populares. ¿Cuál es la imagen que presentan de los norteamericanos? ¿de los hispanos? ¿de otras etnias o culturas?

E. La naturaleza humana Los programas de telerrealidad son muy populares en todo el mundo. Programas como *Big Brother, Survivor, American Idol, America's Next Top Model* y otros tienen sus contrapartidas en otros países: *El gran hermano, Supervivientes: Expedición Robinson, El aprendiz, Operación triunfo* y *Supermodelo.* Lea los comentarios de una española, Montserrat Ayala, y un norteamericano, Daniel Cifuentes, sobre este fenómeno.

MONTSERRAT

«Los programas de telerrealidad son escapistas. Nos permiten imaginarnos otra realidad cuando la nuestra no es tan fascinante ni complicada. En este sentido, podría decirse que son inocuos.[1] Sin embargo, tienen su lado negativo. Casi sin excepción estos programas humillan a sus participantes. Sí, es verdad que pueden salir con una nueva cara, una casa remodelada, su pareja ideal o un millón de dólares. Pero para lograr eso tienen que revelarlo todo, desnudarse[2] emocionalmente —a veces casi literalmente— ante el país entero. Se deja la dignidad ante la cámara y es, francamente, degradante.»

DANIEL

«Para mí, considero *Survivor* un programa para toda la familia. Lo empecé a ver con mis hijos desde su comienzo. Los engaños,[3] las traiciones,[4] las mentiras, la manipulación son cosas que enseñas en Naturaleza Humana 101. Mis hijos han visto a gente de color desmentir[5] y reforzar los estereotipos, a mujeres mayores ser fuertes y hombres jóvenes ser débiles, a conductores de camiones superinteligentes y a abogados tontos. Preguntas como '¿es aceptable mentir bajo ciertas circunstancias?' y '¿es la lealtad[6] tan importante?' le han ofrecido a mi familia una oportunidad para comentar temas muy importantes sobre la vida real.»

[1]*harmless* [2]*lay themselves bare* [3]*deceptions* [4]*betrayals* [5]*contradict* [6]*loyalty*

Paso 1 Haga una lista de los adjetivos que se usan en cada descripción. Diga a qué sustantivo se refiere cada uno.

Paso 2 ¿Cuál es su opinión sobre estos programas y sus participantes? Para los seis tipos de programas de telerrealidad, complete la frase modelo con su opinión sobre cada uno y su descripción de las personas que participan en estos programas. Luego compare sus respuestas con las de un compañero / una compañera. ¿Están de acuerdo? Expliquen.

Este tipo de programa es _____________ (alucinante, degradante, deprimente, emocionante, preocupante, repugnante…). En mi opinión, los participantes son _____________.

1. programas para encontrar el hombre o la mujer de sus sueños
2. programas que ponen a los participantes en gran peligro en un lugar exótico
3. programas que cambian el aspecto físico de una persona
4. programas que les dan a los participantes la oportunidad de ser cantantes famosos
5. programas que dan la oportunidad de ser una modelo famosa
6. programas que dan la oportunidad de ser un cocinero (*chef*) famoso / una cocinera famosa

Paso 3 Conteste las siguientes preguntas con un compañero / una compañera.

1. ¿Está Ud. de acuerdo con Montserrat o con Daniel? ¿Tiene una opinión completamente diferente? Explique.

2. Si Ud. pudiera participar en un programa de telerrealidad, ¿en cuál participaría? ¿Por qué? ¿Cuáles son las características que Ud. posee que le permitirían ganar en ese programa?

Paso 4 Algunos dicen que la vida privada ya no tiene importancia en nuestra sociedad. Escriba un comentario sobre la popularidad de los programas de telerrealidad, explicando por qué nos encanta enterarnos (*find out*) de la vida privada de otra gente.

Rincón cultural

Lugares fascinantes:

España

La Casa Batlló en Barcelona

1. **Barcelona** Localizada en Cataluña, Barcelona es una ciudad bilingüe y cosmopolita con mucha marcha. Entre sí, los barceloneses hablan catalán, aunque todos dominan también el español. El corazón de la ciudad es Las Ramblas o La Rambla, un paseo muy animado repleto de músicos, vendedores de flores, estatuas humanas, espectáculos improvisados de teatro, espectáculos de títeres[1] y cafés: todo para el placer de los que pasean por esta zona vibrante. Entre los bares, las discotecas, los clubes de jazz, sus playas y sus prestigiosas universidades, los estudiantes españoles y extranjeros llevan una vida social extraordinaria en esta ciudad que nunca duerme. Destacan también en Barcelona los cocineros profesionales que han ganado mucha fama mundial por sus platos tradicionales combinados con recetas verdaderamente innovadoras. Además, no podemos olvidarnos de los artistas importantes, como Pablo Picasso, Salvador Dalí, Joan Miró y Antoni Gaudí, que han trabajado y desarrollado su talento en esta ciudad fascinante.
2. **Sevilla** Esta ciudad andaluza es famosa por su gente amable, sus fiestas fascinantes, su alucinante vida nocturna y su gran riqueza histórica y arquitectónica. En primavera la ciudad se transforma. Las calles se empapan[2] del olor de los naranjos en flor y la gente se prepara para los dos eventos culturales más importantes del año. El primero, la Semana Santa, es una celebración religiosa a la que asisten miles de personas. Durante la semana antes del Domingo de la Resurrección,[3] la gente se reúne en las calles para ver pasar las procesiones realizadas por diversas cofradías.[4] Poco después de la Pascua, da inicio la Feria de Abril, que empezó en 1847 como una feria de ganado[5] con diecinueve casetas[6] y ahora cuenta con más de mil.

[1]espectáculos... *puppet shows* [2]se... *are permeated* [3]Domingo... *Easter Sunday* [4]*religious brotherhoods* [5]*cattle* [6]*booths*

La Feria de Abril, Sevilla

La Feria paraliza la ciudad durante una semana entera y la convierte en un lugar sin igual, con el desfile de caballos y enganches,[7] las casetas coloridas, la música de las sevillanas y las tradicionales corridas de toros. Sin duda, este momento del año es glorioso para la ciudad. Pero Sevilla es mucho más. Vale la pena pasear por el Barrio de Santa Cruz, antigua judería,[8] o por la calle Betis, paralela al Guadalquivir, río de suma importancia en la época del descubrimiento de América. No hay que olvidar el Parque María Luisa, sede de la Exposición de 1929, con su magnífica Plaza de España adornada con azulejos[9] hechos en el Monasterio de la Cartuja. Pasear por las calles de Sevilla es meterse en su historia, folclor y tradición.

El Alcázar (castillo) de Toledo

3. **Toledo** Durante la época medieval, Toledo era uno de los centros intelectuales y culturales más importantes de Europa. Desde 711 hasta 1492, España estuvo bajo el control de los moros,[10] quienes establecieron en Toledo un centro donde convivían las tres grandes culturas de la región: la árabe, la cristiana y la judía.[11] La influencia de los tres grupos se nota hoy sobre todo en la arquitectura, que se mantiene muy bien preservada. Caminar por las calles de Toledo es como regresar a la Edad Media. Uno puede visitar edificios que antes eran sinagogas y mezquitas[12] y que en el siglo XVI se convirtieron en iglesias católicas sin perder por completo su carácter original. También durante la época medieval funcionaba la importantísma Escuela de Traductores, que traducía documentos en árabe, castellano y latín. Sin esta escuela, es posible que nunca hubiéramos conocido la obra de filósofos tan importantes como Aristóteles, o la de matemáticos, médicos y astrónomos fundamentales de la Grecia antigua. Hoy en día, Toledo aún ofrece al visitante la oportunidad de apreciar su historia multicultural. El Museo Sefardí, creado en 1964, tiene más de 1.200 piezas representativas de los orígenes del pueblo judío, su trayectoria histórica y su dispersión geográfica. También se puede admirar la pintura religiosa de El Greco en varios edificios e iglesias de la ciudad o visitar los baños musulmanes de Tenerías, construidos en el siglo X. No es difícil entender por qué Toledo fue la capital de España hasta 1561, cuando Felipe II la trasladó a Madrid.

El Museo Guggenheim en Bilbao

4. **Bilbao** Esta ciudad es la más importante del País Vasco,[13] la región quizás más enigmática de España. Igual que Cataluña, el País Vasco es un lugar bilingüe y bicultural. La gente habla vasco, una lengua no románica cuyos orígenes no se saben a ciencia cierta. Desde hace mucho tiempo, algunos vascos quieren que su región se separe de España y tenga autonomía. La ETA es un grupo separatista militante cuyas actividades terroristas han resultado en tragedias nacionales. Sin embargo, hay muchos vascos que están indignados por

[7]*wagons* [8]*Jewish quarter* [9]*tiles* [10]*Moors* [11]*Jewish* [12]*mosques* [13]País… *Basque Country*

las actividades de la ETA y se sienten orgullosos de ser españoles y vascos a la vez. Bilbao ha sido un centro comercial desde el siglo XIV, y durante el siglo XIX tuvo un papel importante en la industrialización del país. Si bien durante la Revolución Industrial Bilbao se conocía por sus fábricas de acero,[14] su construcción de buques,[15] sus plantas químicas y su contaminación, ahora en la época posindustrial, Bilbao ha recreado su imagen. En 1997 se abrió el Museo Guggenheim, una belleza arquitectónica y un centro artístico para toda Europa. Artistas e investigadores de todas partes del mundo van para estudiar en el Guggenheim y en el Museo de Bellas Artes. También la ciudad hace mucho para promover lo mejor de la cultura vasca: su lengua, literatura, arte, historia y, por supuesto, su famosa cocina,[16] «la nueva cocina vasca.»

[14]fábricas... *steel mills* [15]*ships* [16]*cuisine*

¡Viaje conmigo a España!

Gabriela y Santiago son dos videógrafos que están pasando un año viajando por el mundo hispano. Son amigos de Javier y Sara y por eso les mandan sus videoblogs. Vea el vídeo para saber lo que Gabriela les mandó sobre su viaje a España.

Video footage provided by

BBC Motion Gallery

ACTIVIDADES

A. En parejas, contesten las siguientes preguntas sobre los cuatro lugares fascinantes.

1. ¿Por qué se puede decir que Barcelona es una ciudad bicultural? ¿Qué aspectos de la ciudad le parecen cosmopolitas?
2. ¿Cuáles son algunos de los artistas importantes que han trabajado en Barcelona? ¿Ha visto Ud. algunas obras de estos artistas? ¿Dónde?
3. ¿Por qué es interesante visitar Sevilla durante la primavera? Si Ud. sólo pudiera asistir a una de las fiestas sevillanas descritas aquí, ¿a cuál iría? ¿Por qué?
4. ¿Cuáles son algunos de los lugares históricos que se deben visitar en Sevilla?
5. ¿Por qué sería Toledo interesante para una persona a quien le fascina la historia? ¿Qué contribuciones intelectuales se hicieron allí durante la Edad Media?
6. ¿Qué tiene el País Vasco en común con Cataluña? ¿Por qué algunos españoles consideran que el País Vasco es una región peligrosa?
7. ¿Cuáles son algunos de los aspectos culturales más interesantes de Bilbao?

B. Localice en el mapa de España los cuatro lugares descritos en la sección anterior. Luego, indique el interés que tienen para Ud. esos lugares. Indique su preferencia del 1 (el lugar más interesante) al 4 (el menos interesante). Luego, turnándose con un compañero / una compañera, explique por qué a Ud. le interesa más el número 1 y por qué le interesa menos el número 4. Haga por lo menos tres comparaciones entre los dos lugares cuando presente su explicación.

C. Ahora que Ud. ha leído sobre los lugares y ha visto el vídeoblog de Gabriela, escriba un blog sobre un viaje imaginario que Ud. haya hecho a uno de los lugares fascinantes de España. Siga el siguiente bosquejo.

P PASADO
REACCIONAR R RECOMENDAR

Acabo de volver de España. El viaje fue _____________.
Iba a ir a _____________ porque…
Pero al final decidí ir a _____________ porque…
Primero…. Luego…. Otro día….
Pero lo mejor fue que un día conocí a _____________ (una persona famosa) en…
Como pueden ver, fue un viaje _____________.
Si mis amigos piensan visitar España, recomiendo que…

Un artista hispano:

Antoni Gaudí

Antoni Gaudí (1852–1926) fue uno de los arquitectos más originales y una de las figuras más emblemáticas de Barcelona. Formó parte del modernismo catalán, un movimiento artístico asociado con el *Art Nouveau* internacional.

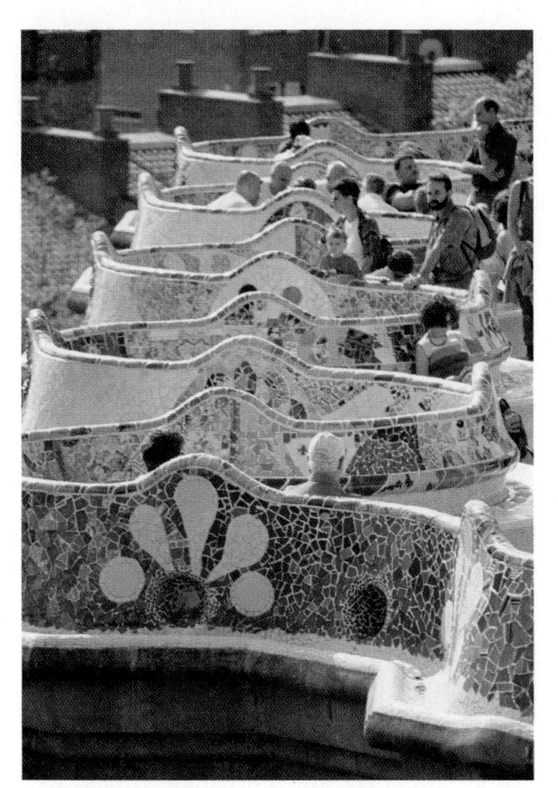

El Parque Güell

Para Gaudí, la estructura de un edificio era sólo una parte de la arquitectura. Construir un edificio también implicaba cubrir las fachadas[1] y llenar los interiores de esculturas,[2] pinturas y muebles[3] que reflejaban una unidad íntegra.[4] Por eso, en distintos momentos de su carrera estudió pintura, escultura, diseño interior y cómo hacer muebles.

Casa Batlló y Casa Milá son dos de sus obras más famosas. Gaudí utilizó materiales tradicionales, como piedras, ladrillos[5] y azulejos de una manera totalmente original y trató de evitar completamente las líneas rectas.[6] Es conocido por su uso de mosaicos de colores vibrantes, sus extraordinarios hierros forjados[7] y sus diseños inspirados en la naturaleza y las formas animalescas. El Parque Güell es quizás la obra más creativa de Gaudí. En este parque se puede apreciar el ingenio juguetón[8] del arquitecto. Hay bancos coloridos en forma de serpientes de mar, una fuente con una escultura de dragón cubierta de mosaicos y una gran plaza abierta rodeada de paredes ondulados.[9]

En 1883, Gaudí, un católico devoto, se hizo cargo de la catedral la Sagrada Familia. Con la muerte inesperada del arquitecto en 1926, esta creación artística única se quedó sin terminar, pero hoy en día es uno de los iconos más importantes de esa gran ciudad catalana. Definitivamente, Barcelona debe gran parte de su carácter al genio de Antoni Gaudí.

[1]*façades* [2]*sculptures* [3]*furniture* [4]unidad... *integrated whole* [5]*bricks* [6]líneas... *straight lines* [7]hierros... *wrought-iron works* [8]*playful* [9]*undulating, rolling*

PREGUNTAS

1. Gaudí es considerado uno de los arquitectos más brillantes del mundo. ¿Cuáles son los elementos que hacen sus estructuras tan originales? ¿Qué impresión tiene Ud. sobre su estilo?
2. ¿Cómo es el estilo de arquitectura en su recinto (*campus*) universitario? ¿Puede imaginar un edificio del estilo gaudiano allí? ¿Dónde localizaría ese edificio? ¿Cómo sería? ¿Permitiría el presidente / la presidenta de su universidad la construcción de algo tan original? Expliquen.

ACTIVIDAD

Busque imágenes en Internet de una de las siguientes obras de Gaudí: El Capricho de Gaudí en Comillas, el viaducto, los bancos o la entrada al Parque Güell, el interior de la Pedrera (Casa Milá), la catedral de la Sagrada Familia, la Casa Vincens. Presente la imagen más alucinante a la clase con una breve descripción. Pida reacciones de sus compañeros de clase. Utilice expresiones como **Es fascinante, impresionante, alucinante, sorprendente que...**

La música española

El flamenco «clásico» viene de la cultura gitana en el sur de España. En reuniones familiares y fiestas particulares, se reunían los gitanos andaluces para tocar guitarra, bailar y cantar canciones de temas melancólicos o dolorosos. Hoy en día sigue siendo una música muy social tocada en fiestas que empiezan a las 10:00 de la noche y terminan al día siguiente. Varios guitarristas se turnan cantando y tocando mientras que el público acompaña a los músicos y bailadores, haciendo ritmo con las palmas.[1] Hay que notar también la manera de cantar, el *cante jondo,* un canto profundo, de lamento o tristeza. Así que la voz, la guitarra, el cajón[2] y las palmas son los «instrumentos» que se asocian con el flamenco clásico.

El flamenco es una forma artística apasionada

A mediados de los años 70, con la llegada de Camarón de la Isla y del guitarrista Paco de Lucía, empezó lo que se conocía como el «flamenco contemporáneo». A través de los años, el contacto con géneros diferentes ha provocado una fusión que hoy en día vemos en flamenco-blues, flamenco-chill, flamenco-pop, flamenco-rock, flamenco-jazz, flamenco-salsa, flamenco-punk y flamenco-rap. Son estilos que han captado el interés de las nuevas generaciones. La canción «Matemáticas» es un ejemplo de flamenco-pop, un género musical que combina elementos tradicionales de música flamenca con ciertos atributos de la música contemporánea que incluyen el uso de la guitarra eléctrica y temas menos dolorosos.

[1]*palms of the hand* [2]*box*

ACTIVIDADES

A. Antes de cantar En «Matemáticas» Ud. escuchará una historia de amor y sufrimiento que es parte del flamenco tradicional, pero también apreciará la poesía y el juego de palabras que evocan una sensibilidad más contemporánea. Al principio escuchará el sonido clásico. También, durante la mayor parte de la canción podrá apreciar las palmas, que son una parte integral de la música flamenca.

1. ¿Ha escuchado Ud. la música de los Gipsy Kings o de otro grupo de flamenco? ¿Le gusta?
2. ¿Cuáles son los instrumentos musicales que anticiparía escuchar en una canción flamenca?
3. ¿Cuál de los géneros de flamenco fusión le interesaría escuchar?
4. En una canción titulada «Matemáticas», ¿qué tipo de vocabulario habrá?

B. ¡A cantar! Escuche la canción «Matemáticas» que se puede encontrar en el CD *Estampillas musicales.*

Matemáticas

Veinte para despertar
Veinte para recordar
Veinte, te quiero decir
Veinte, vamos a subir
Otros veinte y tenemos cien
Cien maneras de vivir
Otros cien para morir
Que me porte bien o mal
Yo te quiero hasta mil
Yo te quiero hasta mil

Ah, yo te quiero hasta mil
Ah, yo te quiero hasta mil

Mil maneras de volar
Mil fronteras que cruzar
Más de mil cosas que
aprender
Para sólo un poder
Y una vida nada más
Y las matemáticas
Nunca me dejaron en paz
Nunca me dejaron en paz

Ah, yo te quiero hasta mil
Ah, yo te quiero hasta mil

Mira cómo me tienes adentro
Tu paraíso es un infierno
Me vuelve loco y me calma
Y se me destroza el alma
Me vuelves loco
Me vuelves loco
Yo te quiero hasta mil
Me vuelves loco
Yo te quiero hasta mil
Me vuelves loco
Me vuelves loco
Yo te quiero hasta mil

Ah, yo te quiero hasta mil

C. **Después de cantar** En parejas, contesten las siguientes preguntas.

1. ¿Pueden Uds. identificar los instrumentos musicales que se escuchan en esta canción?
2. ¿Cuáles son las palabras que expresan el sufrimiento que el amor le causa al cantante?
3. ¿Cómo es esta canción similar a una canción de los Gipsy Kings? ¿Cuáles son los elementos del flamenco-pop?

D. **¡A escuchar!** Para apreciar más el flamenco contemporáneo, vaya a YouTube™ y escuche la música de Paco de Lucía o Camarón de la Isla. Para conocer el flamenco fusión, escuche a Bebe (flamenco-punk), Rosario Flores (flamenco-pop), Pata Negra (flamenco-blues), Chambao (flamenco-chill), Concha Buica (flamenco-africano), La Shica (flamenco-rap) o Pitingo (flamenco-gospel). Luego, con sus compañeros de clase, comparta sus impresiones sobre los artistas y las canciones que escucharon, utilizando frases como **Me gusta(n)... porque..., Me encanta que..., Es impresionante/fantástico que..., Me sorprende que...** y **Es evidente que....**

Lectura

Esta lectura viene de una serie biográfica de la revista popular *Vanidades,* titulada «Salvador Dalí: La novela de su vida». En esta sección, la autora, Eunice Castro, narra el tiempo que Dalí pasó en la Escuela de Bellas Artes de San Fernando, en Madrid.

NOTA HISTÓRICA

Salvador Dalí fue uno de los pintores más importantes del arte moderno. Captó la atención del mundo no sólo por su genio artístico manifestado en sus cuadros, esculturas, ilustraciones de libros, escenarios y vestuario de ballet, publicidad y diseño de joyas, sino también por su personalidad provocadora, su apariencia física llamativa y su excentricidad. Dalí escribió numerosos libros en los que explica sus ideas sobre el arte. En una entrevista declaró lo siguiente:

> «El surrealismo soy yo. Soy el único surrealista perfecto y trabajo dentro de la gran tradición española... Tuve la certeza de que yo era el salvador del arte moderno, el único capaz de sublimar, integrar y racionalizar todas las experiencias revolucionarias de los tiempos modernos, dentro de la gran tradición clásica del realismo y el misticismo, que es la misión suprema y gloriosa de España... »

Salvador Dalí

Antes de leer

A. Para comentar Trabaje con un compañero / una compañera. Miren la foto de Dalí y comenten los siguientes temas.

1. Describan la apariencia física de Dalí en la foto. ¿Cómo influye la apariencia física del artista en cómo percibimos su personalidad? Basándose en este retrato de Dalí, describan su personalidad con muchos detalles.
2. Si vieran a una persona así caminando por la calle, ¿qué pensarían y qué harían?
3. Piensen en otras personas famosas cuya apariencia física es especialmente llamativa. ¿Qué impresión tienen Uds. de su personalidad?
4. ¿Creen Uds. que la sociedad tolera el hecho de que los artistas, actores y cantantes tengan una apariencia física rara y personalidad extravagante? ¿Por qué?

B. Acercándose al tema Lea el título de la ficha en la página siguiente y las nueve palabras y frases asociadas con el tema de la vida estudiantil de Salvador Dalí. Con un compañero / una compañera, decidan si los espacios en blanco requieren un sustantivo, un verbo o un adjetivo. Luego, completen las oraciones con la forma apropiada de las palabras de la ficha.

1. Desde joven, ___________ de Dalí era algo rara con su pelo largo y sus patillas ___________.
2. El día de su examen final, Dalí llevaba una chaqueta de cuadros y una gardenia enorme y olorosa. A los que lo vieron les parecía ___________.

Un estudiante excéntrico		
la apariencia física	la falta de respeto	el payaso[1]
examinar	expulsar	meter la pata
borracho/a	llamativo/a	presumido/a

[1]*clown*

3. Antes del examen, Dalí había tomado un vaso de un licor para estar «inspirado». Así que llegó al examen ___________.
4. Antes de escoger sus tres preguntas, Dalí exclamó que los profesores eran incompetentes para juzgarlo, y salió del salón. ¡Qué ___________ era!
5. El director lo ___________ de la Escuela para siempre por ___________ ante los profesores.

Ojo

VISUALIZAR = Al ver este icono Ud. debe imaginarse lo que se describe o lo que pasa en esa parte del relato.

VOCABULARIO = Si no sabe el significado de una palabra, piense en las palabras relacionadas, búsquela en un diccionario u olvídela por completo.

Salvador Dalí: La novela de su vida

Ese mismo año de la muerte de doña Felipa, Dalí decidió ingresar en la Escuela de Bellas Artes de San Fernando, en Madrid. En el mes de octubre, vestidos de luto[1] por la reciente muerte de doña Felipa, su padre y su hermana lo acompañaron a Madrid, donde debía tomar el examen de ingreso en San Fernando y resolver el problema de vivienda.

Don Salvador traía una recomendación de un amigo para la Residencia de Estudiantes, adjunta a la Institución Libre de Enseñanza, una escuela elitista progresista y auténtica. Una verdadera excepción en los años 20.

En la Residencia, Dalí conocería a García Lorca, a Luis Buñuel y a otras figuras de la incipiente vanguardia artística y literaria de la época.

En esa época, el pintor era un joven apuesto,[2] de grandes ojos oscuros, alto, pero de constitución más bien frágil. Pero su estilo de arreglarse era insólito.[3] Él llevaba pelo largo y frondosas patillas hasta la comisura[4] de los labios (cosa que no estaba de moda) y le comenzaba a crecer un bigotillo de curiosos perfiles.[v]* [...]

—Dalí fue el hazmerreír* de todos —diría un condiscípulo. —Lo llamábamos el «señor patillas». [...]

A pesar de su aspecto, Dalí fue bien acogido[5] en la Residencia de Estudiantes en cuanto descubrieron su talento pictórico. Allí la alegría, las fiestas y las bromas de los jóvenes corrían a la par que las serias tertulias[6] donde discutían sobre arte, literatura, teatro, poesía, cine y religión. [...]

[1]de... *in mourning* [2]*handsome* [3]*unusual* [4]comisura... *corners of his mouth* [5]*welcome* [6]*gatherings*

VERIFICAR

¿Quién(es)? ¿Dónde? ¿Qué pasó?

*__Visualizar__ icons refer to words and phrases that are followed by a superscripted *v*. **Vocabulario** icons in the margin refer to words and phrases that are underlined within the text.

No tardó Dalí en tener problemas en San Fernando, al asumir una actitud protagónica en una protesta estudiantil, que se rebelaba[7] a admitir como catedrático[8] de la Escuela al pintor Torres García.

—Alumno Salvador Dalí, está expulsado de la Escuela por un año —lo castigó la Junta Directiva.

VOCABULARIO

Sus familiares se solidarizaron con él, pero cuando regresó a casa se llevaron una inesperada sorpresa.

—Estás transformado —exclamó su padre al recibirlo.

Dalí parecía otra persona. Él vestía un elegante traje de corte inglés como sus compañeros de la Residencia y llevaba el cabello cortado a la moda y bien engominado.[9] Sus espectaculares patillas habían desaparecido.

VISUALIZAR

Pero eso no era todo. Don Salvador pudo apreciar que su hijo también había evolucionado pictórica e intelectualmente.[v] [...]

Llegó el día de los exámenes teóricos finales del curso, programados para el 14 de junio de 1926. Dalí hizo lo inconcebible. Se presentó ante el Tribunal Académico, que ya estaba reunido en sesión pública dispuesta a examinarlo, con una llamativa chaqueta a cuadros y una enorme y olorosa gardenia en el ojal.[10v]

VISUALIZAR

—Parecía un payaso —lo criticaron todos los que lo vieron.

Dalí, que nunca bebía, antes se había tomado un vaso de licor para estar «inspirado», según él.

VOCABULARIO

Eran las 12:30 minutos del día, cuando el Dr. Manuel Menéndez lo invitó a extraer tres bolas numeradas del bombo que contenían las lecciones que él debía explicar. De pronto, sorpresiva e irrespetuosamente, Dalí proclamó:

—¡No! Como todos los profesores de la Escuela de San Fernando son incompetentes para juzgarme, me retiro.

—¡Fuera! —rugió el director.

Así, Dalí obtuvo la expulsión definitiva de la Escuela de San Fernando.

—Estoy convencido de que mi hijo será para siempre un hombre sin oficio ni beneficio —dijo su padre, disgustado.[11]

[7]se... *refused* [8]*head of department* [9]*slicked-down* [10]*lapel* [11]*very upset*

VERIFICAR

¿Quién(es)? ¿Dónde? ¿Qué pasó?

Después de leer

A. Comprensión Conteste las siguientes preguntas, según la lectura.

1. ¿Qué acababa de pasar en su vida personal cuando Dalí entró a la Escuela de Bellas Artes?
2. ¿A quiénes conoció Dalí en la Residencia de Estudiantes? ¿Quiénes son estas personas?
3. ¿Qué pensaron los otros estudiantes de Dalí? ¿Por qué?

4. ¿Cómo era el ambiente social e intelectual de la Residencia de Estudiantes?
5. ¿Por qué fue expulsado de San Fernando la primera vez?
6. ¿Cómo había cambiado Dalí cuando regresó a casa después de esta primera expulsión?
7. ¿Cómo se presentó Dalí a sus exámenes finales?
8. ¿Qué hizo Dalí que provocó su expulsión definitiva de la Escuela de Bellas Artes?

DESCRIBIR

B. El Museo de Dalí Complete el siguiente párrafo con la forma correcta de **ser** o **estar,** según el contexto. Trate de visualizar este alucinante museo mientras lee.

El Museo de Dalí se encuentra en Figueras, un pueblo que _____[1] a tan sólo una hora y media de Barcelona. Vale la pena ir porque _____[2] uno de los museos más fascinantes de España. El visitante debe _____[3] preparado para vivir una experiencia única. Al llegar a Figueras, lo primero que sorprende al visitante _____[4] que el techo del edificio _____[5] decorado con más de veinte huevos blancos gigantescos. Cada cuarto del museo _____[6] lleno de una extravagante combinación de pinturas, muebles, esculturas, joyas y decoraciones surrealistas. En el interior del complejo se encuentra la tumba donde _____[7] enterrado el artista. Visitar la casa y el museo de Dalí _____[8] como entrar en otro mundo: un mundo surrealista.

C. Dalí News En 1945, Dalí creó su propio diario, el *Dalí News.* Junto a la información sobre las actividades del pintor, este diario contenía anuncios de productos inventados por él, como el «Dalinal».

Dalinal

¿Sufre usted tristeza intelectual periódica? ¿Depresión maníaca, *mediocridad congénita, imbecilidad gelatinosa,* piedras de diamante en los riñones, impotencia o frigidez? Tome **Dalinal,** la chispa artificial que logrará estimular su ánimo de nuevo.

Paso 1 Imagínese que Ud. es periodista y tiene que entrevistar a Dalí sobre su nuevo diario. Un(a) estudiante hace el papel del periodista y otro/a el del excéntrico Dalí. Juntos preparen una lista de preguntas para hacer la entrevista, y luego presenten su diálogo delante de la clase.

Paso 2 En grupos pequeños, preparen algunos testimonios sobre la efectividad de «Dalinal». Escriban un párrafo para presentar a la clase, describiendo cómo cambió su vida. Pueden empezar así: **«Dalinal» es alucinante. Antes tenía..., era..., sufría de.... Ahora...**

D. Para discutir En grupos pequeños, comenten las siguientes preguntas.

1. Castro dice que en la Residencia de Estudiantes, «la alegría, las fiestas y las bromas de los jóvenes corrían a la par que las serias tertulias donde discutían sobre arte, literatura, teatro, poesía, cine y religión». ¿Cómo es la vida en las residencias estudiantiles de su universidad? ¿Cómo se compara con la de la residencia de Dalí, Lorca y Buñuel?
2. Cuando Dalí regresó a casa la primera vez, su padre notó varios cambios en la apariencia física y el intelecto de su hijo. Cuando Ud. regrese a casa la próxima vez, ¿qué cambios notará su familia?
3. ¿Cuál es su reacción ante la actitud de Dalí con respecto a los profesores de la Escuela de San Fernando? ¿Ha sentido Ud. a veces algún impulso similar?

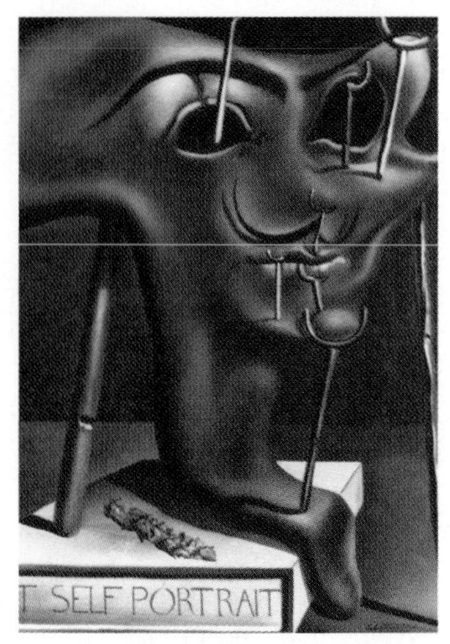

Autorretrato blando con beicon frito

E. **Autorretrato blando con beicon frito** El mismo Dalí definió este autorretrato como «el guante de mí mismo», ya que quiere ser un autorretrato antipsicológico en el que en vez de pintar el alma —es decir, lo interior—, decidió pintar únicamente lo exterior, o sea, la piel. «Como soy el más generoso de todos los pintores, me ofrezco siempre como alimento para de esta manera alimentar nuestra época de forma suculenta», declaró Dalí en 1962.

1. ¿Cuál es la impresión inmediata que tienen Uds. al ver el autorretrato de Dalí?
2. ¿Cuáles son los adjetivos que Uds. utilizarían para describir *Autorretrato blando con beicon frito?*
3. ¿Qué piensa Ud. de la explicación que nos dio Dalí sobre su autorretrato?

¡A escribir!

A. **Lluvia de ideas**

Paso 1 Lea la siguiente opinión sobre los programas de telerrealidad, expresada por un ex concursante.

Ser concursante es muy emocionante: hay fotos de paparrazi, entrevistas para las revistas de chismes, dinero, fiestas con celebridades. La posibilidad de ser rico y famoso te afecta mucho. Salir en la tele y saborear la fama es alucinante. Pero nada está garantizado. Tienes que tener cuidado y no dejar que se te suba a la cabeza.

Paso 2 La clase entera debe hablar sobre cómo la fama puede afectar la vida de la gente desconocida que de repente se vuelve famosa. Su profesor(a) puede anotar en la pizarra algunas de las ideas sobresalientes.

B. **Composición: Descripción** Imagínese que su profesor(a) o uno de los cinco amigos ha ganado uno de los siguientes programas de telerrealidad: *Survivor, The Apprentice* o *American Idol.* Su vida ha cambiado completamente. Escriba un artículo para una revista de chismes sobre la nueva vida de su profesor(a) o uno de los cinco amigos. Exagere la información para hacer el artículo más interesante. Siga el siguiente bosquejo.

1. escoger un título llamativo (por ejemplo: **Sara Carrillo y Paul McCartney en una villa privada de Ibiza o Nuevas tiendas de Diego Ponce conectadas con la Mafia)**
2. escribir una oración introductoria, usando por lo menos tres adjetivos para describir a la persona y el programa en el que participó
3. escribir un párrafo que describa la vida de esta persona antes de participar en la competencia de ___________ (nombre del programa). **(Era..., Tenía..., Iba a..., Salía con..., Estaba...)**
4. describir su vida actual y cómo ha cambiado después de la competencia. Hable sobre sus gustos y preferencias en cuanto a la moda, sus vacaciones, la gente famosa con quien pasa tiempo ahora, etcétera.
5. revelar algo escandaloso o fascinante que haya hecho esta persona recientemente
6. hablar de sus planes para el futuro
7. escribir una conclusión

C. **Diálogo** Lea el artículo de un compañero / una compañera y luego presente un diálogo espontáneo entre Ud. y la persona descrita en su artículo. Ud. es muy atrevido/a y franco/a en sus preguntas y la persona responde de una manera muy presumide y arrogante.

Hablando del tema

Antes de empezar a conversar con sus compañeros de clase sobre los siguientes temas, prepare una ficha para la conversación, otra para el debate y otra para la reacción ante la cita. Vea la explicación de las fichas en el **Apéndice 1.**

SÍNTESIS

A. **Conversación: Los programas de telerrealidad** Revise las expresiones de **Para conversar mejor.** Luego, en parejas o grupos de tres, conversen sobre los siguientes puntos.

Para conversar mejor

Al público le encanta ver...
Es fascinante...
Fue alucinante cuando en un episodio...
Me fascina(n)...
Me molesta(n)...
No lo podía creer.
Para mí, es evidente que...
Y tú, ¿qué opinas?

- Describa dos de los programas de telerrealidad que Ud. haya visto o de los cuales haya oído hablar. Describa cómo es cada programa, incluyendo su meta principal, una descripción de los participantes, sus acciones y la clase de dilema moral que surge en este tipo de programa.
- Compare dos de estos programas, dando la mayor cantidad de detalles que pueda. Incluya ejemplos de escenas específicas que Ud. haya visto.
- Explique por qué estos programas han sido tan populares.

B. Debate: El derecho de vestirse tal como uno quiera Revise las expresiones de **Para debatir mejor** y lea las dos opiniones sobre este tema que se presentan a continuación. Después, prepare tres argumentos a favor y tres en contra del derecho de vestirse como uno quiera sin que ninguna autoridad intervenga. Luego, presente sus argumentos en un debate. No sabrá cuál de los siguientes puntos de vista tendrá que defender.

Para debatir mejor

A FAVOR	EN CONTRA
Así es.	De ninguna manera.
Exacto.	Lo siento, pero…
Podría ser.	No sabes lo que dices.
Tienes razón.	Temo que estés equivocado/a.

- «Los reglamentos de cualquier institución (educativa o empresarial) deben reservarse el derecho de dictar cómo los estudiantes o empleados se deben vestir y llevar el pelo, y si es permitido llevar pendientes o tatuajes visibles en la escuela o en el lugar de trabajo.»
- «Ni los tatuajes, ni los pendientes ni el pelo largo o teñido afectan de manera alguna la habilidad de una persona de trabajar bien o de tener éxito en los estudios o en el trabajo. En una democracia, todos tienen el derecho de vestirse y llevar el pelo como quieran.»

C. Reacción: Percepciones Revise las expresiones de **Para reaccionar mejor.** Luego, reaccione ante la siguiente cita. Añada razones que apoyen sus opiniones.

«Los estadounidenses no hablan de manera directa, lo cual le da la impresión a la gente de otras culturas que los estadounidenses no son honestos ni sinceros.»

Para reaccionar mejor

Creo/Opino/Supongo que…	Es posible que…
Es bueno/malo que…	Es verdad que…
Es ridículo que…	No está mal que…

CAPÍTULO 2

Conexiones:

Nuestras raíces

Punto clave

PASADO

Temas centrales
- conexiones
- relaciones entre las generaciones
- la familia y la inmigración

Zona de enfoque
- el Caribe

Un barrio de La Habana (Cuba)

En este capítulo, Ud. va a explorar el tema de los lazos (*ties*) que tiene con la familia y con el lugar donde nació o se crió (*you were raised*).

Preguntas para considerar

- ¿Cómo es Ud. en comparación con sus padres?
- ¿Es natural que haya conflictos familiares entre las generaciones?
- ¿Cómo se sentiría si tuviera que dejar su país de origen y nunca pudiera regresar?
- ¿Cómo cambian las relaciones entre personas de diferentes generaciones cuando también hay diferencias culturales?
- ¿Cómo podemos mantener las conexiones con la familia y nuestras raíces en este mundo moderno?
- ¿Cuántas generaciones se representan en el cuadro que se ve en esta página?
- ¿Es raro ver a personas de diferentes generaciones interactuando en el barrio donde Ud. vive, o es algo común?

MULTIMEDIA

¡La quiero mucho, pero me vuelve loco!

Situación: Hace cinco días la madre de Javier llegó de Puerto Rico para visitarlo en Austin. Javier habla con Laura sobre la visita y las **expectativas** que su madre tiene de él. Lea el diálogo y preste especial atención al uso del vocabulario nuevo que está **en negrita.**

¿Se queja Ud. de sus padres cuando está con sus amigos?

LAURA: ¿Por qué estás tan callado, Javi? Todo va bien con la visita de tu madre, ¿no?

JAVIER: Bueno, tú sabes cómo es cuando viene. **Me vuelve loco.**

LAURA: La verdad es que me parece menos **exigente** esta vez. No te **regañó** ni una vez en todo el fin de semana. Y es tan **cariñosa** como siempre.

JAVIER: Pues tienes razón. **Se portó** bien, aunque en privado me dijo varias veces que me ve más americanizado que nunca. Y no deja de **quejarse** de que mi hermano Jacobo **se haya mudado** a Seattle. Para ella es **insoportable** que sus hijos estén lejos y que pierdan sus **valores** culturales.

LAURA: Pero, ¿ha leído tus artículos sobre las familias inmigrantes y los reportajes que hiciste sobre la pintura de Nick Quijano? Casi todo lo que haces profesionalmente tiene que ver con la cultura hispana. ¿No es cierto?

JAVIER: Sí, sí. Está muy **orgullosa** de mí y siempre **alaba** mis logros, pero al mismo tiempo le gusta **quejarse** de sus hijos **rebeldes** y **egoístas.**

LAURA: Las relaciones **íntimas** son difíciles a larga distancia. Quiere que su «tribu» esté cerca de ella. Eso lo entiendo.

JAVIER: Es difícil. A mí me encanta Puerto Rico. De hecho, si no vuelvo cada seis meses lo **extraño** mucho, pero como tú sabes, mi vida aquí ha sido fenomenal. ¡Tengo tantas oportunidades!

LAURA: Estoy segura que, en el fondo[1], tu madre lo entiende. Habla con ella y pídele su **apoyo.**

JAVIER: Tienes razón. Debo hablar de modo más **abierto** con ella.

[1]en... *deep down*

ACTIVIDADES

A. Detective Busque en el diálogo ejemplos de las siguientes metas comunicativas: Comparación (C), Reacciones y recomendaciones (R), Narración en el pasado (P) y Hablar de los gustos (G). Subraye cada palabra o frase que represente una (o una combinación) de estas metas comunicativas. Luego, escriba al margen la(s) letra(s) que corresponde(n) a cada ejemplo subrayado (C, R, P o G).

MODELOS: No te regañó ni una vez en todo el fin de semana. (P)
Para ella es insoportable que sus hijos estén lejos. (R)

B. Comprensión Conteste las siguientes preguntas, según el diálogo.

1. ¿Cómo se ha portado la madre de Javier durante esta visita?
2. ¿Javier tiene paciencia con su madre? Explique su respuesta.
3. ¿Cómo expresa Javier su aprecio por su cultura?
4. Aunque a Javier le encanta Puerto Rico, ¿por qué no vive allí?
5. ¿Qué le aconseja Laura a Javier?

REACCIONAR
R
RECOMENDAR

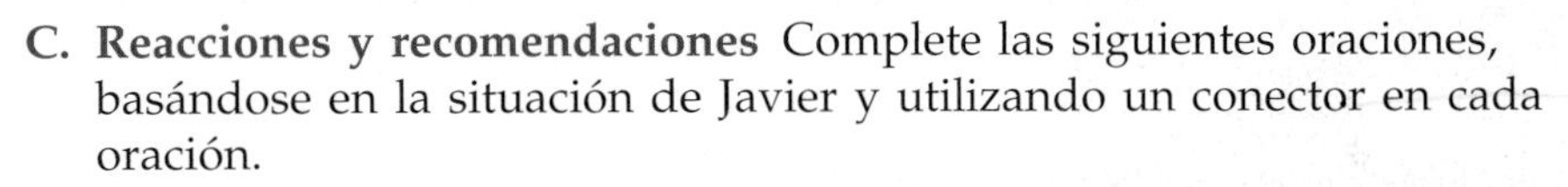

C. Reacciones y recomendaciones Complete las siguientes oraciones, basándose en la situación de Javier y utilizando un conector en cada oración.

MODELO: A la Sra. de Mercado no le gusta que sus hijos estén tan lejos, puesto que los quiere mucho.

1. A Javier no le gusta que su madre...
2. Yo recomiendo que Javier...
3. Es una lástima que el hermano de Javier...
4. Es obvio que la madre de Javier...

D. Diálogo En parejas, preparen una conversación telefónica en la que Javier argumente que Jacobo es el que debe regresar a la isla, porque él —Jacobo— está casado y tiene hijos que deben criarse cerca de sus abuelos.

Conectores

además	*besides*
para que + *subjuntivo*	*so that*
por eso	*therefore*
por otro lado	*on the other hand*
puesto que	*since*
sin embargo	*nevertheless*

Vocabulario del tema

*Para describir a los parientes**

abierto/a	open
cariñoso/a	loving
comprensivo/a	understanding
conservador(a)	conservative
decepcionado/a	disappointed
entrometido/a	meddlesome
estricto/a	strict
exigente	demanding
indulgente	lenient
involucrado/a	involved
mandón/mandona	bossy
orgulloso/a	proud
protector(a)	protective
quejón/quejona	complaining

Para describir a los niños problemáticos†

egoísta	selfish
ensimismado/a	self-centered
envidioso/a	envious
inquieto/a	restless
insoportable	unbearable
malcriado/a	ill-mannered
mimado/a	spoiled
rebelde	rebellious
sumiso/a	submissive
travieso/a	mischievous

Para hablar de las relaciones familiares

acostumbrarse (a)	to adjust (to)
alabar	to praise
apoyar	to support (emotionally)
castigar	to punish
compartir	to share
contar (ue) con	to count on
criar(se) (me crío)	to bring up; to be raised
cuidar (de)	to take care of
extrañar‡	to miss (someone/something)
heredar	to inherit
lamentar	to regret
mantener	to maintain
mudarse	to move (*residence*)
obedecer (obedezco)	to obey
pelearse	to fight
portarse	to behave
quejarse (de)	to complain (about)
regañar	to scold
volverle loco/a	to drive (someone) crazy

—Esta es la señora que ocupaba la cama contigua a la mía en maternidad.

COSPER

¿Por qué es chistosa esta tira cómica?

Para describir las relaciones familiares

disfuncional	dysfunctional
estable	stable
estrecho/a	close (*relationship between people or things*)
íntimo/a	close (*relationship between people*)

*Remember to use **ser** with adjectives when describing inherent characteristics and **estar** when referring to emotional or physical states.

†These terms can also be used to describe adults. See the **Vocabulario del tema** from **Capítulo 1** (pages 17–18) for adjectives used to describe people in more positive terms.

‡This verb expresses the emotion that people feel when they are far from someone or something they love. To express the same emotion in Spain, the phrase **echar de menos** is used.

pésimo/a	awful, terrible
unido/a	close-knit

COGNADOS: **la armonía, la estabilidad, la protección, la unidad**

Para hablar de los miembros de la familia

los antepasados	ancestors
el benjamín / la benjamina	baby of the family
el/la gemelo/a	twin
el/la hermanastro/a	stepbrother, stepsister
el/la hijo/a adoptivo/a	adopted child
el/la hijo/a único/a	only child
la madrastra	stepmother
el/la medio/a hermano/a	half brother, half sister
el padrastro	stepfather

Para hablar de las relaciones intergeneracionales

la brecha generacional	generation gap
el comportamiento	behavior
la comprensión	understanding
la desilusión	disappointment
la esperanza	hope
la expectativa	expectation
el malentendido	misunderstanding
los (buenos/ malos) modales	(good/bad) manners
las raíces	roots
los valores	values

ACTIVIDADES

A. Vocabulario en contexto En parejas, completen las siguientes oraciones con la palabra más apropiada, según el contexto. Hagan los cambios necesarios para que haya concordancia. Luego, ofrezcan su opinión o un consejo para cada situación.

1. Es posible que un hijo único se sienta ______ (inquieto, envidioso) cuando llega un nuevo hermanito. Por eso, pienso que los padres...
2. Es probable que la benjamina de una familia sea ______ (entrometido, mimado). Para que la benjamina no se porte mal, toda la familia debe...
3. Es normal que los adolescentes sean un poco ______ (rebelde, sumiso). Para mantener unas relaciones íntimas con sus hijos adolescentes, los padres deben...
4. A los niños no les gusta que sus padres los ______ (regañen, extrañen) en público. Pero a veces...
5. Una persona que se cría en un ambiente ______ (sano, estricto) durante su niñez (*childhood*) puede ser rebelde durante la adolescencia. Por eso, creo que...
6. Los padres tacaños no quieren que sus propios hijos ______ (hereden, apoyen) su dinero. Si los hijos quieren el dinero, deben...
7. Los psicólogos sugieren que los padres ______ (castiguen, apoyen) a sus hijos cuando tengan problemas morales. Si no lo hacen...
8. Muchas veces los malentendidos ocurren por falta de (*lack of*) ______ (comprensión, comportamiento) entre las generaciones. Es importante...

B. Las relaciones intergeneracionales En el dibujo se ven tres generaciones de mujeres cubanas en el porche de la casa de la abuela. En parejas, lean las descripciones de cada mujer y luego contesten las preguntas. Traten de usar los verbos nuevos de este capítulo. Compartan sus respuestas con el resto de la clase.

1. La madre es mandona. ¿Qué hace ella que le vuelve loca a su hija?
2. La abuela es indulgente. ¿Qué hace para mimar (*spoil*) a su nieta?
3. La hija está un poco ensimismada estos días. ¿Qué hace que le molesta a su madre?
4. La madre es quejona. ¿De qué se queja durante estos días en la playa?
5. La abuela es muy protectora. ¿Cuáles son las cosas que no permite que haga su nieta?

C. Preguntas personales En parejas, hagan y contesten las siguientes preguntas. Reaccione ante las respuestas de su compañero/a con las frases de **Para conversar mejor.** Después, compartan sus respuestas con el resto de la clase.

Para conversar mejor

¡Qué bien/difícil!
¡Qué suerte!
¡Qué horror!
No me digas. / No lo puedo creer.
¿De veras? / ¿En serio?
¡Qué malo/a eras!
(No) Estoy de acuerdo.
(No) Tienes razón.
Claro. / Por supuesto.
Suena bien, pero…

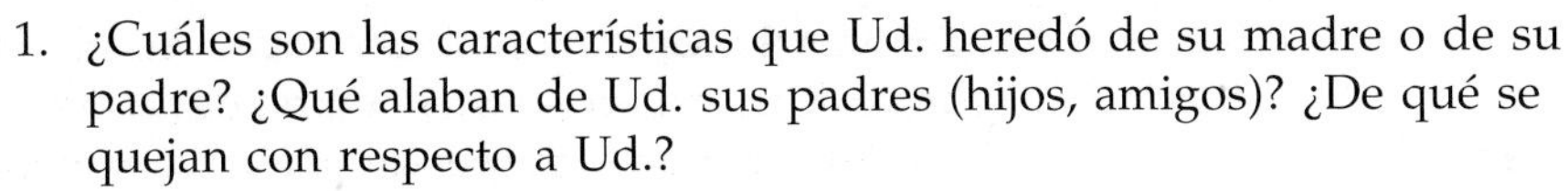

1. ¿Cuáles son las características que Ud. heredó de su madre o de su padre? ¿Qué alaban de Ud. sus padres (hijos, amigos)? ¿De qué se quejan con respecto a Ud.?

2. ¿Cómo era Ud. cuando tenía 5 años? ¿Y cuando tenía 15 años? ¿Qué travesuras hacía en su niñez?
3. ¿Cómo eran sus padres cuando Ud. era niño/a o adolescente? ¿Estrictos, conservadores, protectores? ¿Abiertos, indulgentes? ¿...? ¿Son diferentes ahora que Ud. es adulto/a? Explique.

4. ¿Qué recomienda Ud. que hagan los padres divorciados para mantener sus relaciones con sus hijos? ¿Qué problemas puede haber entre hermanastros?

5. Cuando era joven, ¿vivía en el mismo lugar o se mudaba varias veces su familia? ¿Vivía cerca de sus abuelos u otros parientes? ¿Tenía mucho contacto con sus primos? ¿Tenía un(a) pariente favorito/a?

6. ¿Qué recomienda que hagan las familias modernas para mantener relaciones familiares estrechas? ¿Piensa que es importante escoger una universidad o un trabajo profesional que le permita estar cerca de sus parientes?

D. Pasado, presente, futuro: «De tal palo, tal astilla»*

Paso 1 ¿Cómo es Ud. en comparación con sus padres (como son ahora o como eran antes)? Vea las siguientes características personales y diga cómo es Ud. en comparación con su madre y su padre.

¿MÁS, MENOS O IGUAL QUE SU PADRE?		¿MÁS, MENOS O IGUAL QUE SU MADRE?	
1. ambicioso/a	6. abierto/a	1. ambicioso/a	6. abierto/a
2. sensible	7. rebelde	2. sensible	7. rebelde
3. involucrado/a en la política	8. religioso/a	3. involucrado/a en la política	8. religioso/a
	9. exigente		9. exigente
4. tiquismiquis	10. conservador(a)	4. tiquismiquis	10. conservador(a)
5. quejón, quejona		5. quejón, quejona	

Paso 2 En grupos de cuatro, comparen sus respuestas y comenten lo siguiente: ¿Son Uds. muy parecidos a sus padres o muy diferentes? ¿Creen Uds. que las diferencias tienen que ver más con la personalidad de cada uno, con el sexo o con el hecho de que son de generaciones distintas?

DESAFÍO

Paso 3 Hoy en día los avances en el campo de la genética son alucinantes. Es posible que en el futuro diseñemos a nuestros hijos. ¿Diseñaría Ud. a su hijo/a si pudiera? Explique por qué sí o por qué no. Si lo hiciera, ¿qué características tendría? ¿En qué aspectos se parecería a Ud.? ¿En qué aspectos sería diferente?

***De tal palo, tal astilla** is a saying whose English equivalent is *Like father, like son.*

E. **Problemas repentinos** Entre todos, revisen los siguientes problemas y hagan una lista de las palabras nuevas de este capítulo y del **Capítulo 1** que los ayuden a conversar con facilidad sobre cada problema repentino. Después, en parejas, preparen un diálogo espontáneo sobre cada problema.

1. Ud. es maestro/a de primer grado. Está exasperado/a por el comportamiento de un estudiante, Nacho. Llame al padre / a la madre del niño para decirle que su hijo está portándose muy mal en la escuela. El padre / La madre insiste en que su hijo es un angelito inocente.
2. Un hijo mimado / Una hija mimada pelea con su padre/madre porque cree que su padre/madre debe darle un coche nuevo y más dinero para comprar ropa. El padre / La madre quiere que su hijo/a sea popular, pero en el fondo sabe que debe ser más estricto/a con él/ella.

NOTA CULTURAL • Nombres raros: El caso de Venezuela

Los nombres raros son comunes en algunos países latinoamericanos como, por ejemplo, en Venezuela. Al ponerle un nombre a su hijo/a, algunos padres buscan inspiración en figuras históricas internacionales; otros, en estrellas del cine o famosos deportistas; los más intrigantes, en la pura creatividad. En el registro electoral venezolano encontrará nombres como Hitler Adonys Rodríguez Crespo, Hochiminh Jesús Delgado Sierra, Dwight Eisenhower Rojas Barboza, Hiroshima Jennifer Bravo Quevedo. Otros nombres únicos son Alkaselser, Air Jordan, Batman, Yesaidú (*Yes I do*) y Yahoo. A otros venezolanos les gusta mezclar algunas letras de los nombres de sus parientes para crear uno nuevo. Por ejemplo, Raftina viene de Rafael y Robertina y Yolimar viene de Yolanda y Mario. En 2007 La Asamblea Nacional propuso una ley que prohibiría nombres raros porque un nombre ridículo o extravagante es muy dañino para la autoestima de un niño, una niña o un(a) adolescente. Pero a muchos venezolanos no les gustó que el gobierno tratara de controlar los nombres de sus hijos. Al final, el gobierno retiró la propuesta, dándoles a sus ciudadanos la libertad de ser creativos en el momento de ponerle un nombre a sus hijos.

Preguntas

1. ¿Qué le parece la creatividad de algunos venezolanos al escoger nombres para sus hijos?
2. ¿Qué le parece la idea de ser nombrado/a en honor de un lugar? ¿Le gustan los nombres como París, Dakota, Cleveland, Austin, Madison?
3. ¿Cuáles son los nombres más raros que Ud. ha escuchado? Piense, tal vez, en los nombres que las celebridades les ponen a sus hijos. ¿Por qué cree Ud. que los padres escogieron esos nombres para sus hijos?
4. ¿Por qué escogieron sus padres su nombre? ¿Sabe Ud. qué significa su nombre? ¿Le gusta su nombre?

Actividad

C COMPARAR Imagínese que Ud. está casado/a con una persona venezolona y que van a tener un bebé. Su dilema es que la familia venezolana tiene expectativas sobre el nombre que le pondrá a su hijo/a. Todos los hermanos de su esposo/a venezolano/a les han puesto a sus hijos nombres que combinan los nombres de parientes queridos. Vea la lista que debe usar para inventar un nombre original. María, Concha, Lucía, Gabriela, Marta, Isabel, Héctor, Roberto, José, Paco, Ignacio, Fernando. Cree un nombre para una niña y uno para un niño. Luego, comparta los nombres con la clase y decidan cuál es el más bonito, el más feo y el más original.

Puntos clave

Narración en el pasado

En esta sección del capítulo, Ud. va a practicar la narración en el pasado. Para hacerlo bien, hay que utilizar las estructuras gramaticales (los puntos clave) de la siguiente tabla que pertenecen a la meta comunicativa. Antes de continuar, estudie las explicaciones de estas estructuras gramaticales en las páginas verdes que están al final del libro.

LA META COMUNICATIVA DE ESTE CAPÍTULO		
ICONO	META COMUNICATIVA	PUNTOS CLAVE
P PASADO	Narración en el pasado	• el pretérito • el imperfecto • los tiempos perfectos • **hace... que**

PRUEBA DIAGNÓSTICA

En el cuadro verá a un niño que se llama Miguel. Lea lo que él, ya adulto, cuenta sobre una persona importante en su vida. En la página siguiente, llene los espacios en blanco con la forma apropiada del pretérito o del imperfecto (según el contexto) de los verbos que están entre paréntesis.

Yo ________[1] (criarse) en un vecindario típico de La Habana, Cuba, donde todo el mundo ________[2] (conocerse). ________[3] (Tener) amigos de todas las edades. En particular, ________[4] (haber) un hombre, don Enrique Pozo, el zapatero, que ________[5] (ser) el vecino favorito de todos los niños. Él siempre nos ________[6] (contar) cuentos chistosos. Cuando ________[7] (empezar) a asistir a la escuela primaria, don Enrique siempre ________[8] (sentarse) en las escaleras frente a su tienda para saludarme después de las clases.

Un día, mientras don Enrique me ________[9] (hablar) de mis clases, me ________[10] (decir) que ________[11] (irse) a los Estados Unidos. Yo ________[12] (sentirse) fatal al oír de su plan. Los primeros meses lo ________[13] (extrañar) muchísimo. Poco a poco ________[14] (acostumbrarse) a vivir sin él. Pero cinco años más tarde, mi familia ________[15] (mudarse) a Miami. ¡Adivinen con quién ________[16] (encontrarse) mis padres y yo en un restaurante cerca de nuestra nueva casa! ¡A don Enrique! ¡________[17] (Ser) increíble! ¡Qué coincidencia más alucinante!

Expresiones útiles

Las siguientes expresiones le pueden servir para narrar en el pasado.

Para contar una historia

además, también
al mismo tiempo
después
de vez en cuando
en cambio
finalmente, al final
luego, entonces
mientras
por eso, por lo tanto
por último, por fin...
primero, segundo

Para añadir emoción a su historia

Te voy a contar algo increíble (estupendo, ridículo) que le pasó a...	*I'm going to tell you something incredible (wonderful, ridiculous) that happened to . . .*
Escucha lo que le sucedió a...	*Listen to what happened to . . .*
Pero eso no fue nada.	*But that was nothing.*
Ahora viene lo peor.	*Now comes the worst part.*
Se dio cuenta de* que...	*He/She realized that . . .*
De repente / De golpe	*Suddenly*
¡Cataplún!	*Crash!*
¡Paf!	*Bang!*

*__Realizó__ is never appropriate here, as **realizar** means *to fulfill, accomplish.*

Para reaccionar ante una historia

¡Bárbaro! / ¡Fenomenal!	
¡De ninguna manera!	*No way!*
¡Imagínate!	*Imagine that!*
¡Pobrecito/a!	*Poor thing!*
¡Qué chévere/guay/padre!	*Awesome!*
¡Qué lío!	*What a mess!*
¡Qué mala onda/pata!	*What a bummer!*

ACTIVIDADES

Las siguientes actividades le darán la oportunidad de narrar en el pasado. Recuerde que se suele usar el imperfecto para hacer descripciones en el pasado y para hablar de lo que hacía una persona habitualmente. En cambio, se usa el pretérito para adelantar (*advance*) el argumento de una historia.

A. Cuando era más joven Termine las siguientes oraciones. Luego, compártalas con un compañero / una compañera, quien va a hacerle preguntas sobre cada situación. Utilice las expresiones útiles para contar lo que pasó y para reaccionar ante los cuentos de su compañero/a.

1. Cuando tenía _________ años, siempre...
2. Una vez, mientras estaba en la escuela secundaria,...
3. De pequeño/a, antes de dormir me gustaba...
4. Un día, cuando tenía _________ años,...
5. Cuando era niño/a, una persona muy importante en mi vida era...

B. Verdades y mentiras

Paso 1 Lea las siguientes preguntas y marque **sí** o **no** al lado de cada pregunta. **¡OJO!** Cuando responda, debe **mentir** en sus respuestas por lo menos **dos** veces. Después, su compañero/a tratará de adivinar (*guess*) cuándo ha mentido.

¿Alguna vez ha (conjugue el verbo que está entre paréntesis para hacerle las preguntas a su pareja)...

	SÍ	NO
1. (utilizar) un documento de identidad falso?	☐	☐
2. (estar) obsesionado/a con una persona famosa?	☐	☐
3. (decir) una mentira gorda a sus padres?	☐	☐
4. (salir) con alguien que haya conocido a través de un servicio del Internet?	☐	☐
5. (heredar) dinero que no esperaba?	☐	☐
6. (compartir) un secreto que había prometido guardar?	☐	☐
7. (viajar) a un país de habla española?	☐	☐
8. (portarse) de una manera insoportable enfrente de sus amigos?	☐	☐

Paso 2 Mire las respuestas de su compañero/a. Pídale detalles sobre las respuestas que Ud. cree que son mentiras. Algunas preguntas posibles para pedir detalles son: **¿Qué pasó? ¿Cuántos años tenías? ¿Se enojó? ¿Cómo te sentiste?**

Paso 3 Después de interrogar a su compañero/a, presente a la clase la afirmación de su compañero/a que le parezca la más interesante o atrevida. La clase decidirá si es verdad o mentira.

C. **Un regalo especial** Lea sobre un regalo especial que la abuela les dio a Javier y a su hermano gemelo, Jacobo, cuando cumplieron 4 años. Esta serie de acciones forma la columna (*backbone*) de la historia. Note que cada acción adelanta la narración. Trabajando con un compañero / una compañera, hagan el relato más interesante y completo añadiendo descripciones, emociones e información de trasfondo (*background*). También deben utilizar algunas de las **Expresiones útiles** (en las páginas 52–53) para conectar los eventos.

- La abuela entró al salón con un regalo muy grande para los dos.
- Javier y Jacobo corrieron hacia su abuela.
- Ella les dio el paquete.
- Quitaron (*Took off*) el papel para abrirlo.
- Descubrieron una caja de bloques de madera.
- Empezaron a jugar con los bloques inmediatamente.

D. Los hermanos se pelean En parejas, miren los siguientes dibujos. Juntos, escriban el cuento de lo que les pasó a Javier y a su hermano gemelo, Jacobo, cuando jugaban con sus bloques. Las siguientes palabras los ayudarán para añadir detalles a su cuento: gritar (*to yell*), pedir perdón, torre (*tower*), tumbar (*to knock down*).

E. Las hermanas Mirabal

Paso 1 En parejas, lean en la página siguiente la historia de las hermanas Mirabal, heroínas de la República Dominicana. Llenen los espacios en blanco con la forma del pretérito o del imperfecto, según el contexto. Prepárense para explicar la razón por la cual escogieron cada conjugación. Vean la tabla de usos del pretérito y del imperfecto en las páginas verdes 202–212.

Patria, Minerva y María Teresa Mirabal

Las hermanas Mirabal, Patria, Minerva, María Teresa y Dedé _________[1] (tener) una vida relativamente acomodada durante el comienzo de la dictadura de Rafael Leónidas Trujillo en la República Dominicana (1928–1961). La dictadura trujillista _________[2] (ser) totalitaria, opresiva y sangrienta.[a] Cuando _________[3] (asistir) a la escuela secundaria, Patria, Minerva y María Teresa, conocidas como «las Mariposas», _________[4] (empezar) a trabajar con la resistencia clandestina. _________[5] (Ser) un trabajo sumamente peligroso, ya que Trujillo _________[6] (castigar) a sus opositores con la tortura y hasta con la muerte. De hecho, por sus actividades rebeldes, la policía de Trujillo _________[7] (encarcelar)[b] a las tres por un tiempo en el famoso centro de tortura, «La 40».

En 1960, Trujillo _________[8] (decidir) parar las actividades de las hermanas para siempre. El 25 de noviembre, mientras las hermanas _________[9] (viajar) para ver a sus esposos, quienes _________[10] (estar) en la Prisión «La Victoria», unos hombres _________[11] (parar) su coche. _________[12] (Sacar) a las hermanas y a su chofer del coche, los _________[13] a un cañaveral[c] y los _________[14] (asesinar). Así, las Mariposas _________[15] (dejar) a la cuarta hermana, Dedé, quien ha dedicado su vida cuidando el legado[d] de sus valientes hermanas. Sus vidas _________[16] (ser) breves, pero _________[17] (tener) un impacto enorme en la historia de su país.

[a]*bloody* [b]*jailed* [c]*sugar cane field* [d]*legacy*

Paso 2 Conteste las siguientes preguntas.

1. ¿Quién era Trujillo? ¿Cómo era su régimen?
2. ¿Quiénes eran las Mariposas? ¿Por qué trabajaban con la resistencia clandestina?
3. ¿Qué le pasó a Dedé?

REACCIONAR
R
RECOMENDAR

Paso 3 En parejas, haciendo el papel de las personas indicadas, llenen el espacio en blanco con la forma apropiada de los verbos que están entre paréntesis. Después, completen las oraciones que siguen para expresar las reacciones de los que hablan.

1. Durante la escuela secundaria, las maestras de las hermanas Mirabal les decía:

   «Es importante que Uds. _________ (ser) sumisas y obedientes.

   Tenemos miedo de que...»
2. Sus amigos de la resistencia les decían:

   «Es necesario que Uds. nos _________ (ayudar) a esconder las armas para la revolución contra Trujillo. No nos gusta que Trujillo...»
3. Su hermana Dedé les decía:

   «Tengan cuidado. Temo que Trujillo las _________ (encarcelar) otra vez. Es posible que...»

F. La inmigración y las nuevas generaciones

Paso 1 Lea esta entrevista que tiene opiniones de tres inmigrantes caribeños, sobre cómo el vivir en los Estados Unidos ha afectado su vida familiar.

El entrevistador: ¿Cómo te sientes, más latinoamericano o más estadounidense? ¿Eso afecta tus relaciones con tu familia?

Yolanda Rodríguez, dominicano americana (21 años). «Llegué aquí a los 15 años, así que vamos a decir que todavía me siento como dominicana, pero con claras influencias norteamericanas. Mis padres quieren que estudie, que tenga una carrera buena, pero como mujer también se espera que yo esté muy apegada[1] a la familia; que ayude a cuidar a mis abuelitos, por ejemplo. Veo que mis amigos estadounidenses no tienen muchas obligaciones familiares y que a ellos les importa más su vida social que su vida familiar.»

Julio Martínez, puertorriqueño (48 años). «Yo soy 100% boricua,[2] pero mi familia… no tanto. Mis hijos llevan una vida muy ocupada aquí en Nueva York y me parece que sus amigos son más importantes que su propia familia. Mis nietos no hablan ni una palabra de español y no saben nada de la historia de Puerto Rico. Me gustaría poder cantarles y leerles en mi idioma. Creo que nuestras relaciones se afectan por la distancia cultural. Ellos no me entienden.»

Ana Rosario Pozo, cubanoamericana (14 años). «Nací y me crié aquí. Aunque valoro mi herencia cubana, tengo que admitir que me siento más estadounidense que cubana. Muchas veces mis padres no me entienden para nada. Quiero poder salir con mis amigas, quizás tener un novio, pero my madre es muy estricta. Necesito más libertad que la que ella tenía en Cuba. Ella llevaba una vida muy protegida y nunca discutía[3] con sus padres. Yo la respeto pero quiero que entienda que estoy en los Estados Unidos ahora.»

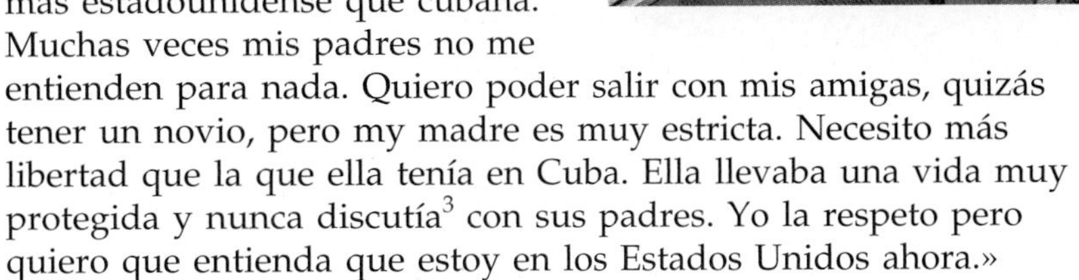

[1]*attached* [2]*Puerto Rican* [3]*argued*

Paso 2 En parejas, imagínense lo que hizo cada entrevistado/a en cada situación.

a. Yolanda le dijo a su madre que iba a la biblioteca para estudiar, pero en realidad…
b. Julio les llamó a sus nietos a su casa diciéndoles que estaba muy enfermo, pero en realidad…
c. Ana le dijo a su madre que salía con sus amigas, Brooke y Maya, pero en realidad…

Paso 3 En grupos de tres, ofrezcan un consejo a Yolanda, a Julio y a Ana utilizando las formas verbales indicadas abajo. Roten los papeles para que cada uno/a tenga la oportunidad de practicar las diferentes formas verbales. Escriban sus consejos en un papel.

ESTUDIANTE A: Utilice «Debe…»
ESTUDIANTE B: Utilice «Tiene que…»
ESTUDIANTE C: Utilice «Recomiendo que…»

Rincón cultural

Lugares fascinantes:

El Caribe

El Malecón, La Habana

1. **La Habana, Cuba** Antes de la Revolución Cubana, La Habana era la ciudad más cosmopolita del Caribe. Hoy, aunque muchos de los edificios necesitan reparaciones, hay museos y monumentos de gran interés y belleza. El capitolio,[1] por ejemplo, es casi igual en estilo y tamaño al que hay en Washington, D.C. El Museo Árabe, de estilo mudéjar,[2] tiene una réplica exacta de un mercado del Oriente Medio.[3] Otros lugares fascinantes incluyen el Museo de la Revolución, el Museo de Carros Antiguos, el majestuoso Gran Teatro de La Habana —sede del famoso Ballet Nacional de Cuba y la Ópera Nacional—, el Castillo de los Tres Reyes del Morro y otras fortalezas del siglo XVI. Dado que la música es omnipresente en la isla, el Museo Nacional de Música es un lugar que uno no debe perderse. Tiene una colección impresionante de tambores[4] africanos que muestra la historia y el desarrollo de la música cubana. Cuba tiene fama por su riqueza artística: hay festivales de hip-hop cubano; de música contemporánea, ballet y jazz; de nuevo cine latinoamericano y mucho más. También, por su clima tan agradable, la gente disfruta

[1]*capitol building* [2]estilo de arte que combina lo cristiano con lo árabe [3]Oriente… *Middle East* [4]*drums*

de estar en las calles. El Malecón, una avenida marítima de siete kilómetros, es conocido como «el sofá habanero» por ser un lugar donde la gente se sienta para charlar, cantar y ver la puesta del sol. Es curioso ver por todas partes coches estadounidenses de los años 50 en muy buenas condiciones. También uno se puede mover en coco-taxis, que son motocicletas de tres ruedas en forma de coco y pintadas de amarillo. Sin lugar a dudas, La Habana tiene mucho que ofrecer.

Práctica de béisbol, San Pedro de Macorís

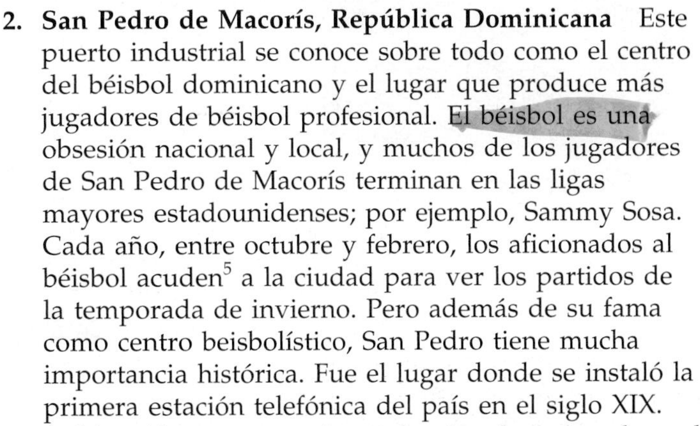

2. **San Pedro de Macorís, República Dominicana** Este puerto industrial se conoce sobre todo como el centro del béisbol dominicano y el lugar que produce más jugadores de béisbol profesional. El béisbol es una obsesión nacional y local, y muchos de los jugadores de San Pedro de Macorís terminan en las ligas mayores estadounidenses; por ejemplo, Sammy Sosa. Cada año, entre octubre y febrero, los aficionados al béisbol acuden[5] a la ciudad para ver los partidos de la temporada de invierno. Pero además de su fama como centro beisbolístico, San Pedro tiene mucha importancia histórica. Fue el lugar donde se instaló la primera estación telefónica del país en el siglo XIX. Además, la ciudad ha sido un centro de producción de azúcar, lo cual la convirtió en un centro de riqueza a principios del siglo XX. La producción azucarera atrajo a la zona a trabajadores de ascendencia africana, quienes han contribuido de manera profunda a la cultura, la música, la danza y las prácticas religiosas de la ciudad. Hoy en día, San Pedro está experimentando un renacimiento, con la atención que recibe por sus contribuciones al béisbol y por su industria.

El Viejo San Juan

3. **El Viejo San Juan, Puerto Rico** La ciudad más antigua del territorio estadounidense y la segunda más antigua de las Américas, el Viejo San Juan (el centro colonial que ahora forma parte de la zona metropolitana de San Juan) ofrece una fascinante mezcla de lo viejo y lo nuevo. Aquí se puede visitar fortalezas[6] españolas como El Morro y San Cristóbal; la Catedral de San Juan, donde yacen[7] los restos del conquistador Juan Ponce de León; las murallas[8] originales que protegían la ciudad y casas coloniales que datan de los siglos XVI y XVII. También se puede simplemente pasear por las calles empedradas[9] y visitar sus hermosas plazas, como el Parque de las Palomas, donde cada día se reúnen familias puertorriqueñas para dar de comer a los centenares de palomas que habitan la plaza. En cuanto a lo moderno, por la noche, el centro colonial se convierte en una zona de entretenimiento, con sus bares, clubes de salsa y teatros, frecuentados por puertorriqueños jóvenes y mayores. Además, el Viejo San Juan tiene uno de los puertos más importantes de las Américas y, junto con la zona metropolitana, es un centro burocrático, financiero y farmacéutico. Si uno se cansa de la vida urbana, puede escaparse al Yunque, un bosque lluvioso que queda a sólo 22 millas.

[5]van [6]*fortresses* [7]*lie buried* [8]*city walls* [9]*cobblestoned*

El teleférico de Mérida

4. **Mérida, Venezuela** Fundada en el siglo XVI como capital del estado de Mérida y localizada entre los picos[10] más altos de los Andes venezolanos, esta ciudad tiene mucho que ofrecer para complacer[11] una variedad de gustos. La respetada Universidad de los Andes atrae a muchos estudiantes, incluso a los extranjeros. Se puede estudiar por un semestre, un año o un verano en esta bella ciudad, cuyo ambiente natural y vida cultural son tan atractivos. Mérida es un centro cultural que hospeda,[12] entre otras cosas, un festival internacional de violín cada año en el mes de enero. Para los que prefieren estar al aire libre, el estado de Mérida goza de cuatro parques nacionales, más de 400 lagunas y muchísimas cascadas. Es famoso por sus deportes de aventura, como el andinismo,[13] el esquí, el parapente,[14] la bicicleta de montaña y el *rafting* en aguas blancas. Para llegar a los puntos de partida para muchas de estas actividades, se puede experimentar otra aventura: ¡montarse en el teleférico[15] más alto y largo del mundo! Los golosos[16] no deben perder la oportunidad de visitar la heladería más famosa del mundo, la Heladería Coromoto. Desde 1991 esta heladería aparece en el *Libro Guinness de los Récords* porque ofrece 832 sabores de helado.

[10]*mountain peaks* [11]*satisfy* [12]*hosts* [13]*mountain climbing* [14]*paragliding* [15]*cable car* [16] Los… *Those who have a sweet tooth*

¡Viaje conmigo al Caribe!

Vea el vídeo para saber lo que Santiago les mandó a Javier y Sara sobre su viaje al Caribe.

Video footage provided by

BBC Motion Gallery

ACTIVIDADES

A. Conteste las siguientes preguntas sobre los cuatro lugares fascinantes.

1. ¿Cuáles son los atractivos culturales de La Habana, Cuba? ¿A cuál de estos lugares le gustaría visitar y por qué?
2. ¿Cuáles son algunos de los indicios que muestran la importancia de la música en Cuba?
3. ¿Por qué le interesaría San Pedro de Macorís, República Dominicana, a un fanático de los deportes?
4. Nombre dos hechos históricos interesantes asociados con San Pedro de Macorís.

5. ¿De qué manera es el Viejo San Juan, Puerto Rico, una mezcla de lo antiguo y lo moderno? ¿Qué puede hacer si quiere pasar un rato disfrutando de la naturaleza?
6. ¿Por qué podría ser interesante estudiar un semestre en Mérida, Venezuela? ¿A quién le interesaría más, a un estudiante tiquismiquis o a un estudiante atrevido? ¿Por qué?
7. Unos de los sabores de helado que vende la Heladería Coromoto son cerveza, pasta con queso parmesano, rosas, whisky y ajo (*garlic*). ¿Le interesaría probar uno de estos sabores? ¿Normalmente cuál es su sabor de helado favorito?

B. Localice los cuatro lugares en el mapa del Caribe y póngale a cada uno un número del 1 (el más interesante) al 4 (el menos interesante) para indicar el grado de interés que Ud. tiene en visitar estos lugares. Turnándose con un compañero / una compañera, explique por qué a Ud. le interesa más el número 1 y por qué le interesa menos el número 4. Haga por lo menos tres comparaciones entre los dos lugares cuando presente su explicación.

C. Ahora que Ud. ha leído sobre los lugares y ha visto el videoblog de Santiago, imagínese que Ud. es agente de viajes. Escriba un correo electrónico al padre de la familia López Montero ofreciéndole recomendaciones para su reunión familiar en el Caribe. Hay seis personas que viajan: la abuela, el padre, la madrastra, unos gemelos de 17 años y la benjamina de 8 años. Siga el siguiente bosquejo que está en la página siguiente.

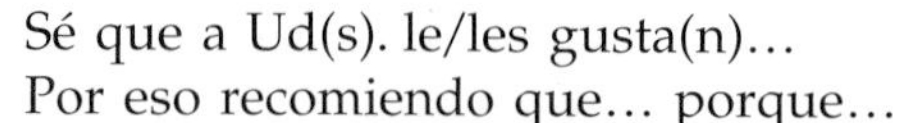

Sé que a Ud(s). le/les gusta(n)...
Por eso recomiendo que... porque...
Entiendo que Uds. necesitan...
El año pasado otro cliente fue con su familia a esta misma ciudad y les gustó mucho. Le adjunto unos comentarios que me mandó el cliente cuando regresó: «Fue un viaje maravilloso. El primer día..., Todos los días..., Una tarde... y la última noche...»
Estoy seguro/a de que...

La siesta, *de Nick Quijano (n. 1953)*

Un artista hispano:

Nick Quijano

Nick Quijano nació en Nueva York en 1953 de padres puertorriqueños. Cuando tenía 14 años, su familia regresó a Puerto Rico permanentemente. Por eso, Quijano debe su formación cultural a Puerto Rico y su arte refleja una celebración del espíritu de la gente de la Isla. A causa de la situación especial de Puerto Rico, que ha sido territorio de los Estados Unidos desde 1898, la lucha entre los esfuerzos para asimilar y a la vez resistir las influencias y los valores estadounidenses ha sido parte central del arte puertorriqueño a lo largo del siglo XX. Muchos de los artistas contemporáneos están motivados por la búsqueda[1] de una identidad puertorriqueña única.

En su arte, Nick Quijano celebra con gran afecto la vida familiar y la omnipresencia de la espiritualidad en la vida cotidiana[2] de su gente. También muestra el gran componente africano que se encuentra en la Isla.

En *La siesta,* Quijano representa a su abuela materna durmiendo en un sofá. Los colores vivos y la riqueza de los detalles reflejan el sentimiento nostálgico y cariñoso que el artista tiene hacia su familia. Cada objeto tan cuidadosamente colocado[3] en la sala simboliza parte de la cultura puertorriqueña que el artista no quiere perder.

[1]*search* [2]*daily* [3]*placed*

PREGUNTAS

1. ¿Cuál es la situación política que hace que la identidad puertorriqueña sea única?
2. Describa la pintura.
3. Si Nick Quijano pintara una escena familiar para Ud., ¿qué objetos le pediría que pusiera en el cuadro?

ACTIVIDAD

Los objetos que se encuentran en *La siesta* representan la conexión íntima con los miembros de la familia y también muestran la importancia de la religión en la vida cotidiana. Indique el simbolismo de los siguientes objetos y explíquele a un compañero / una compañera el porqué de su selección.

	OBJETO	SÍMBOLO
1.	_____ la estatua de la Virgen Milagrosa (*Miraculous*)	a. la educación
		b. la generosidad
2.	_____ la taza de café	c. la espiritualidad
3.	_____ el retrato del padre	d. la hospitalidad
4.	_____ los lentes, el recado (*note*), la carta	e. el respeto
5.	_____ el perro	

En una casa de La Habana

La música caribeña

La mayoría de la música que se conoce en los Estados Unidos como «música latina» o «salsa» es realmente un conjunto de diversos estilos musicales originarios del Caribe. Estos tipos de música provienen de la historia rica y compleja de dos tradiciones culturales que se fusionaron en el Caribe: la africana y la europea.* Cada país tiene sus propios estilos: el son y la guajira de Cuba, el merengue y la bachata de la República Dominicana o la bomba y la plena de Puerto Rico. Lo que se conoce como «salsa» es en realidad una fusión de jazz y ritmos caribeños que se originó en Nueva York, aunque hoy en día el epicentro de la salsa se encuentra en Puerto Rico. El éxito sorprendente de la película *Buena Vista Social Club* y la popularidad de la canción «Livin' la Vida Loca» de Ricky Martin despertaron el interés en la música caribeña a nivel mundial. Los instrumentos esenciales para crear los ritmos latinos incluyen las claves, las maracas, los bongos, los timbales, las congas, la guitarra y el bajo, entre otros. La canción «Hermanos» es una guajira. Tal vez Ud. conoce la famosa canción cubana «Guantanamera», otro ejemplo de guajira.

ACTIVIDADES

A. Antes de cantar Ud. va a escuchar «Hermanos», una canción cuyo tema tiene que ver con una hermana y un hermano cubanos, separados por el exilio de ella. Notará en la letra de la canción un refrán corto,

---

*Aunque los habitantes originales del Caribe fueron, por supuesto, indígenas, por enfermedades y maltrato de los europeos, los habitantes originales casi desaparecieron. Sus formas musicales prácticamente no tuvieron ningún impacto en la música caribeña.

repetido y el «pregón» que es una improvisión fuera de la estructura normal de la canción.

1. ¿Ha visto Ud. las películas *Buena Vista Social Club, Lost City, Mad Hot Ballroom* o *Los Mambo Kings?* ¿Le gustaron? Explique.
2. ¿Ha visto *Dancing with the Stars* o *So You Think You Can Dance* en la tele? Si los ha visto, ¿cuáles son los bailes latinos que bailan los competidores?
3. ¿Cuáles son los instrumentos que se espera escuchar en una canción caribeña?
4. En una canción cuyo título es «Hermanos», ¿qué tipo de vocabulario habrá?

B. ¡A cantar! Escuche la canción «Hermanos» que se puede encontrar en el CD *Estampillas musicales.*

Hermanos

La luna me está mirando
A veces me voy preguntando
Si brilla más para ti
Aquí todos te han olvidado
No es lo mismo para mí
Te quiero más que te niego
Estoy al puerto y te espero
Y que el mar que nos separa
Se haga una gota de agua

Hermanos separados
Miro un mar de soledad
Hermanos separados
Yo aquí y tú allá
Nunca te puedo olvidar

Un ojo me está mirando
Un ojo blanco y redondo
Es noche de luna llena
De estas noches que te llegan
Me cortaron una mano
Es la ausencia de un hermano
Pero siempre está presente
No aquí, pero se siente

Hermanos separados
Miro un mar de soledad
Hermanos separados
Yo aquí y tú allá
Nunca te puedo olvidar

[*Pregón*]
Yo aquí y tú allá
Hermanos separados
Yo aquí y tú allá
Que tú te fuiste, que yo tenía 10 años
Yo aquí y tú allá
Y cuando pienso en ti, no sabes lo que invento
Yo aquí y tú allá
Naufrago de tu ausencia
Yo aquí y tú allá
Ay, qué separados estamos
Yo aquí y tú allá
Y si acaso te veo, yo no lo creo, me da mareo
Yo aquí y tú allá
Hermanos separados, hermanos
Yo aquí y tú allá
Ay, no sabes lo que invento
Yo aquí y tú allá
Cuando en ti, hermana mía, yo pienso…

C. Después de cantar En parejas, contesten las siguientes preguntas sobre la canción «Hermanos».

1. ¿Pueden Uds. identificar los instrumentos que se escuchan en esta canción?
2. ¿Cuáles son las palabras de la canción que más claramente expresan la dolorosa separación de los dos hermanos?
3. ¿Qué sabemos del hermano que se fue? ¿Es mayor que el que canta? ¿Es hombre o mujer?
4. ¿Qué emociones evoca la canción? Reaccionen ante los sentimientos expresados por la canción.
5. ¿Cuáles son las palabras más pegadizas (*catchy*) de la canción?

D. ¡A escuchar! Para apreciar la gran variedad de música caribeña que hay, vaya a YouTube™ y escuche unos de los siguientes cantantes o grupos, según sus gustos: música tradicional (Celia Cruz, Tito Puente), nueva trova cubana (Pablo Milanés, Silvio Rodríguez), reggaetón (Don Chezina, Daddy Yankee, Don Omar), rap cubano (Orishas), merengue dominicano y bachata (Juan Luis Guerra, Frank Reyes). Luego, comparta sus impresiones de los artistas y sus canciones con sus compañeros de clase utilizando frases como **Me gusta(n)... porque..., Me encanta que..., Es impresionante/fantástico que..., Me sorprende que...** y **Es evidente que...**

Lectura

Esta lectura viene de una entrevista que le hizo Mauricio Vicent a Benito Zambrano, un cineasta español, antes de que empezara a rodar su película *Habana Blues*. Su respeto y profundo amor por Cuba empezaron cuando estudiaba cine en ese país, de 1992 a 1994. Concebida como un homenaje a

NOTA HISTÓRICA

En 1959, Fidel Castro y sus tropas revolucionarias tomaron control de La Habana, poniendo fin a la dictadura sanguinaria[1] de Fulgencio Batista. Al asumir el poder, Castro y su gobierno optaron por el modelo económico comunista y se aliaron con el bloque soviético. La Revolución trajo muchos cambios a la isla: reforma educativa, eliminación de las clases sociales, reforma agraria, ayuda a los pobres, disminución del prejuicio racial y sexista. Por esta razón recibió mucho apoyo, especialmente de las clases populares. Al mismo tiempo, alienó a mucha gente, en particular a los que no estaban de acuerdo con los ideales marxistas y a las clases media-alta y alta, quienes perdieron muchos de los beneficios que habían gozado bajo el régimen de Batista. Por eso, muchos dejaron la isla y se mudaron a los Estados Unidos y a España. Aunque la Revolución trajo cambios positivos, sigue siendo un régimen totalitario que no tolera opiniones disidentes y que comete abusos de los derechos humanos.

La entrevista que va a leer hace referencia al «período especial en tiempos de paz», durante la primera mitad de los 1990. Con el colapse de la Unión Soviética, Cuba perdió su principal aliado político y comercial y entró en una gran depresión económica. El país perdió el 80% de sus exportaciones e importaciones incluyendo la comida, la medicina y el petróleo. La gente sufrió de hambre y malnutrición y faltaron muchas necesidades básicas. Miles de cubanos arriesgaron la vida saliendo de la isla en balsas (*rafts*) inestables y peligrosas para emigrar a los Estados Unidos.

Por las relaciones diplomáticas tensas entre los Estados Unidos y Cuba, es difícil viajar entre los dos países. Muchos cubanos y cubano-americanos pasan años sin ver a sus familiares, aunque recientemente hemos visto una relajación de las restricciones de visitas familiares impuestas por los Estados Unidos.

[1]*bloody*

Cuba, *Habana Blues* presenta la historia de dos jóvenes, Ruy y Tito, que llevan años persiguiendo el sueño de convertirse en estrellas de la música. Tito vive con su abuela, una gran dama de la música, y Ruy vive con Caridad, la madre de sus dos hijos. La relación de la pareja está en crisis, por lo que Caridad piensa marcharse ilegalmente a Miami con los dos niños. La situación de los tres se exacerba cuando unos productores españoles llegan a la isla y descubren el talento extraordinario de Ruy, Tito y su banda. Les ofrecen un contrato y la posibilidad de salir de Cuba, pero las condiciones del contrato son pésimas y a los dos les provocan conflictos artísticos y ético-morales. Mientras lea, piense en el mensaje que Zambrano quiere comunicar y si le interesa ver la película después de leer la entrevista.

Antes de leer

A. Para comentar Trabaje con un compañero / una compañera. Comenten los siguientes temas.

1. ¿Qué tipo de película le gusta: acción, horror, romántica, biográfica, musical, ciencia ficción, animación, comedia? ¿Cuál fue la última película que vio?
2. Según el cartel y el título, ¿qué tipo de película cree Ud. que es *Habana Blues?*
3. ¿Qué libertades necesitan los músicos para crear y compartir su música? En su opinión, ¿cuáles son los desafíos (*challenges*) que enfrentan los artistas jóvenes bajo un régimen totalitario?
4. ¿Cómo decide si va a ver una película? ¿Lee Ud. reseñas o críticas antes de ir a verlas o cuenta con las sugerencias de sus amigos?

B. Acercándose al tema Lea el título de la ficha y las nueve palabras asociadas con la película. Con un compañero / una compañera, decida si los espacios en blanco requieren un sustantivo, un verbo o un adjetivo. Luego, escoja la palabra apropiada de la ficha para completar las oraciones.

1. Zambrano escribió el ________ de *Habana Blues* para celebrar el espíritu del país donde estudió.
2. No le interesó enfatizar (*emphasizing*) las ________ de Cuba, haciendo una caricatura de la isla y su gente, sino pintarla con mucho respeto.

Entrevista con Zambrano		
el conflicto	el guión	la miseria
enfrentar	equivocarse	triunfar
complicado/a	creativo/a	simplón / simplona

3. Por eso, no quiso presentar una visión ________ del país, sino mostrar la complejidad de la vida allí.
4. Zambrano dice que los que piensan que la Revolución cubana es intocable ________. Cree que la gente joven debe ayudar a transformar el país.
5. Los personajes de su película ________ una realidad difícil: la separación de la familia cubana, la emigración a los Estados Unidos y las concesiones que hay que hacer para poder ________ en el extranjero.
6. Cuando uno es parte de una sociedad como esta, tan ________, donde todo el mundo vive prácticamente al día, con un nivel de ________ y de tensiones muy fuertes, se puede llegar a perder los límites de la dignidad.
7. La película habla de eso: la historia del protagonista es un poco la del reencuentro con su propia dignidad y su sentido ________ que no le deja vender su alma.

Entrevista: Benito Zambrano, Director de Habana Blues

Después del éxito de *Solas,* con el que consiguió cinco premios Goya en 1999, el director andaluz Benito Zambrano se prepara para rodar su segundo largometraje[1] en Cuba, *Habana Blues,* una historia sobre dos jóvenes músicos cubanos que luchan por sacar adelante su proyecto artístico en medio de las dificultades de la sociedad cubana de hoy.

VOCABULARIO

Benito Zambrano, de 38 años, se graduó en 1994 en la Escuela Internacional de Cine y Televisión de San Antonio de los Baños (La Habana), y cuenta que desde entonces se debía y le debía a Cuba este «homenaje». «A mí siempre me pareció muy importante el esfuerzo[2] y la voluntad de los creadores cubanos por intentar hacer su obra, por tratar de hacer arte, cultura, pese a[3] las circunstancias», afirma el cineasta, que acaba de pasar por la isla en busca de grupos musicales para su película.

EL PAÍS:* ¿Qué es *Habana Blues*?

BENITO ZAMBRANO: Yo siempre quise agradecerle a Cuba todo lo que he aprendido aquí y lo que ha supuesto[4] para mí. Cuba ha sido la etapa más importante de mi vida, la mayoría y las mejores cosas que he escrito las he hecho aquí, incluido el guión de Solas, que en principio era un

[1]*feature film* [2]*efforts* [3]pese... *despite* [4]lo... *what it has meant*

**El País* es un periódico español.

proyecto para ser filmado en América Latina. *Habana Blues*, que también ha nacido en Cuba, cuenta las peripecias[5] de dos jóvenes de La Habana que hacen música medio alternativa, medio marginal, y tratan de sacar adelante su proyecto. A través de su historia se hace un recorrido[6] por la realidad cubana actual, con sus conflictos y dificultades.

VOCABULARIO

Benito Zambrano

EL PAÍS: ¿Un retrato crítico?

BENITO ZAMBRANO: Creo que hacer el retrato crítico de la realidad de Cuba es responsabilidad y misión de los cineastas cubanos. En mi caso, me conformo con hacer una historia que no sea simplona, sino medianamente seria, que sea respetuosa y no se mofe ni escarbe[7] en las miserias de Cuba, pero que diga algo al pueblo cubano.

VOCABULARIO

EL PAÍS: Pero sí aparecerá la picaresca del cubano para sobrevivir, los problemas que perturban a la gente…

BENITO ZAMBRANO: Salen conflictos que van a influir en los personajes y que existen en la realidad: la separación de la familia cubana, la emigración a Estados Unidos, las concesiones que hay que hacer para poder triunfar en el extranjero, el enfrentamiento[8] de ideas…

VOCABULARIO

EL PAÍS: ¿Y el equilibrio entre supervivencia y dignidad?

BENITO ZAMBRANO: Cuando uno es parte de una sociedad como esta, tan complicada, donde todo el mundo vive prácticamente al día, con un nivel de conflicto y de tensiones muy fuertes, se puede llegar a perder los límites de la dignidad. La película también habla de eso: la historia del protagonista es un poco la del reencuentro con su propia dignidad y con su sentido como creador.

EL PAÍS: ¿Qué tiene *Habana Blues* de musical?

BENITO ZAMBRANO: Como género, no sería un musical clásico, pero es una película en la que la música va a jugar un papel protagonista. Pensamos hacer también un disco, aunque aún no tenemos decididos los grupos. Aquí estos días hemos visto a Interactivo, a X Alfonso; en Madrid, a la gente de Habana Abierta y contamos con la ayuda de Pavel. Queremos algo que tenga que ver con la fusión del rock, el jazz, el hip-hop con la música afrocubana, la música más alternativa que atrapa a los jóvenes cubanos de hoy.

[5]*adventures* [6]viaje [7]no… *neither mocks nor digs* [8]*confrontation*

EL PAÍS: Han pasado casi diez años desde que se graduó en la Escuela de Cine de San Antonio de Baños. ¿Cómo es la Cuba que ha encontrado hoy?

BENITO ZAMBRANO: Materialmente, encuentro que el país está mejor. A mí me tocó[9] vivir años duros, de 1992 a 1994, los años convulsos y difíciles del llamado período especial,[†] cuando ocurrió la crisis de los balseros[10] y toda esa historia. Hoy hay más transporte público, menos cortes de luz, sin duda la población vive menos estresada. Sin embargo, veo una degradación de otro tipo, hay problemas internos y también espirituales, quizás más ocultos, pero que siguen ahí porque los problemas no se han resuelto.[V]

VISUALIZAR

EL PAÍS: ¿La Revolución cubana se ha quedado estancada?

VOCABULARIO

VISUALIZAR

BENITO ZAMBRANO: Todo ha de ser movible, todo tiene que adaptarse a su tiempo. El agua que sale de un manantial[11] es cristalina y comienza como torrente, pero en cuanto se estanca[12] se pudre.[13] [V] Quien piense que la Revolución cubana llegó a lo mejor y que debe ser intocable, está equivocado. La gente joven que está viviendo en este país necesita de cambios y de transformaciones. Cuba tiene que sacar lo mejor de sí mismo para dar un salto hacia adelante, y lo mejor de sí mismo son sus gentes, es su pueblo; y tiene que confiar en la gente que vive en este país.

VOCABULARIO

[...]

[9]A... *It was just my luck* [10]*boat people seeking refuge in the United States* [11]*spring* [12]se... *it stands still* [13]se... *it becomes rotten*

[†]Se refiere al «período especial en tiempos de paz.» Ver la **Nota histórica,** página 65.

Después de leer

A. Comprensión Conteste las siguientes preguntas, según la lectura.

1. ¿Qué admira Zambrano del artista cubano? ¿A qué circunstancias se refiere?
2. ¿Por qué le interesó a Zambrano hacer una película sobre Cuba?
3. ¿Cuál es la trama básica de *Habana Blues*, según Zambrano? Resúmala con sus propias palabras.
4. ¿Por qué dice Zambrano que su película no es crítica de Cuba? ¿Está Ud. de acuerdo con su punto de vista?
5. ¿Cuáles son los problemas de la vida cubana que sí salen en la película?
6. ¿Por qué cree Ud. que Zambrano dice que la vida en Cuba es complicada?
7. ¿Qué tipos de música salen en la película?
8. ¿Cómo es diferente la Cuba de ahora que en los años 90 cuando Zambrano estudió allí?
9. ¿Qué necesitan los jóvenes cubanos, según Zambrano?

10. Según Zambrano, ¿cuál es el estado de la Revolución cubana hoy en día? ¿Cuál será su salvación?
11. Antes de que salga una nueva película, es normal que el director / la directora haga entrevistas para promocionarla. ¿Cree Ud. que lo que dice Zambrano en esta entrevista captaría el interés del público? ¿A Ud. le interesa ver *Habana Blues*?

B. Los personajes intrigantes de *Habana Blues*

DESCRIBIR

Paso 1 Ud. acaba de conocer a Ruy, Tito y Caridad, los protagonistas de *Habana Blues*, en una fiesta. Trabajando en parejas, miren sus fotos en esta página y en la página siguiente y túrnese con un compañero / una compañera para describir a cada uno/a —cómo son físcamente y cómo son sus personalidades. Usen el vocabulario nuevo de los Capítulos 1 y 2 cuando puedan.

1. Ruy: a. aspecto físico b. personalidad
2. Tito: a. aspecto físico b. personalidad
3. Caridad: a. aspecto físico b. personalidad

REACCIONAR

RECOMENDAR

Paso 2 En parejas, lean las siguientes afirmaciones sobre los tres personajes para obtener más información clave sobre ellos. Después, reaccionen ante cada afirmación y expresen su opinión sobre cada situación. ¿Qué tiempos verbales deben usar en cada caso?

Para reaccionar: **Es deprimente/mejor/ sorprendente/terrible/triste que...**
Para opinar: **Creo/Opino/Pienso/Supongo que...**

1. Ruy es un cantante talentoso que toca en una banda con su mejor amigo. Quiere a su familia, pero su pasión por la música le hace tomar muchas malas decisiones.
2. Cuando dos productores españoles llegan a Cuba, descubren el talento extraordinario de Ruy, Tito y su banda y quieren llevarlos a España. El contrato que les ofrecen es una miseria—ganarán poquísimo dinero y tienen que criticar su país y su cultura.
3. Ruy se niega a vender el alma a los productores españoles a pesar de haber luchado por tanto tiempo para alcanzar sus sueños. Opta por quedarse en Cuba.
4. Tito sabe claramente que no puede quedarse en Cuba. En sus 28 años nunca ha salido de la isla; por eso acepta las condiciones miserables del contrato de los españoles. Sin embargo, no puede imaginar su vida personal o profesional sin su amigo Ruy.

Ruy, un músico talentoso

Tito y Ruy, íntimos amigos

Ruy, Caridad y sus hijos: ¿Cómo sobrevivirá la familia?

5. Los dos amigos se pelean y sus sueños se encuentran amenazados (*threatened*).
6. Caridad, la esposa de Ruy, es una mujer independiente y fuerte. Está harta de (*She's fed up with*) las aventuras de Ruy con otras mujeres y de su incapacidad de contribuir dinero a la familia.
7. Por eso, Caridad toma la decisión casi desesperada de salir de Cuba para Miami. Es un gran riesgo montarse en una lancha por la noche con los niños y arriesgar así sus vidas.
8. Ruy se desespera al pensar que no volverá a ver a sus hijos.

Paso 3 Piensen en los siguientes personajes o personas y, utilizando la información que saben de ellos, imaginen dos gustos o disgustos de cada uno/a. Usen los verbos que están a continuación u otros que se conjugan como gustar.

dar igual fascinar gustar interesar molestar preocupar

1. Ruy y Tito
2. Caridad
3. los hijos de Ruy y Caridad
4. Benito Zambrano

C. La música en Cuba

Paso 1 Llene el siguiente párrafo con la forma correcta de los verbos que están entre paréntesis para aprender más sobre la música en la vida cotidiana de Cuba.

La música es una parte esencial de la vida cubana. A pesar de las dificultades que sufre la gente, está claro que la música _______[1] (ser) sumamente importante en sus vidas. Es impresionante que el simple acto de pasear por las calles de La Habana te _______[2] (dar) la sensación de estar en un concierto espontáneo. No es raro que un grupo de músicos _______[3] (llegar) a una plaza con sus instrumentos y poco después todo el barrio _______[4] (estar) fuera bailando. Según el director de *Habana Blues*, la gente hasta camina por las calles con un ritmo musical. ¿Es posible que _______[5] (ser) genético? Zambrano quería captar este amor por la música en su película. Para él es importante que la gente que vea *Habana Blues* _______[6] (entender) lo esencial que es la música en la vida cotidiana de los cubanos.

Paso 2 Con un compañero / una compañera, conteste las siguientes preguntas.

1. ¿Cree Ud. que la música es una parte esencial de la vida cotidiana de la gente joven de su país? ¿En qué sentido? Explique.
2. ¿Piensa que hay un aprecio por la música de diferentes generaciones en este país? ¿Le gustan algunos músicos de la generación de sus padres? ¿Cuáles? ¿Aprecian sus padres la música de su generación?
3. Cuando ve una película, ¿presta atención a la banda sonora que acompaña la película? ¿Ha comprado la banda sonora de alguna película? ¿Cuál? Explique por qué le gustó.

D. Para discutir En grupos de cuatro, comenten las siguientes preguntas.

1. ¿Cuál es su sueño más importante, el que más marque su identidad (i.e., ser médico/a o político / mujer política, ser rico/a, ayudar a niños abandonados)? ¿Estaría Ud. dispuesto/a (*willing*) a hacer cualquier cosa para alcanzar ese sueño? ¿Qué estaría dispuesto/a a hacer?
2. ¿Ha tenido Ud. un mejor amigo / una mejor amiga con quien haya tenido un serio desacuerdo? ¿un amigo íntimo / una amiga íntima que se haya mudado lejos? ¿Cómo afectó ese desacuerdo o esa mudanza las relaciones entre Uds.?
3. ¿Ha tenido Ud. que tomar la decisión de dejar lo familiar —su casa, su estado— y mudarse por los estudios, el trabajo o el amor?
4. ¿Cómo se sentiría Ud. si tuviera que irse de su lugar de origen y jamás pudiera regresar? ¿Qué haría para mantener sus conexiones con ese lugar y con la gente que se quedó allí?
5. ¿Qué pasará cuando las familias cubanas puedan viajar con más libertad entre los Estados Unidos y Cuba?

E. Una decisión difícil Dadas las relaciones diplomáticas tan difíciles entre los Estados Unidos y Cuba en el momento de su partida, Caridad sabía que si se iba de la isla era posible que nunca pudiera regresar y que sus hijos nunca volvieran a ver a su padre. A pesar de todo eso, tomó la decisión de marcharse con sus hijos.

Escriba una carta de Caridad a Ruy, escrita un año después de su mudanza a Miami. Describa su vida en Miami. Incluya información sobre los dos hijos.

¡A escribir!

A. Lluvia de ideas

Paso 1 Lea las siguientes opiniones de Adela, una joven dominicana, y de un abuelo estadounidense.

ADELA: Veo a mis padres y mis abuelos casi todos los días. Me encanta el apoyo y la seguridad que me dan, pero a veces me siento atrapada sin la posibilidad de explorar y ver el mundo.

ABUELO: Sólo veo a mis hijos y mis nietos dos o tres veces al año porque viven lejos de nosotros. Todos tienen una carrera excelente que les gusta y tienen muchos amigos. Pero tengo poca influencia en la vida de ellos, y me siento muy frustrado y triste al no poder compartir la cultura que es mi herencia y un poco de mi sabiduría (*wisdom*) con mis nietos.

Paso 2 Ahora, entre todos en la clase preparen una lista de las ventajas de vivir cerca de su familia y otra lista de las desventajas.

Conectores

al contrario
en cambio
por otro lado

B. Composición: Ventajas y desventajas Imagínese que Ud. es periodista y escriba un artículo sobre la vida familiar. Siga el bosquejo.

1. escoger un título provocativo
2. escribir una oración introductoria usando como mínimo dos adjetivos
3. describir las ventajas de convivir con la familia utilizando ejemplos específicos
4. describir las desventajas de vivir cerca de los parientes utilizando ejemplos específicos
5. ofrecerles consejos a los que vivan cerca de su familia para independizarse, y consejos a los que vivan lejos para mantener las relaciones familiares a larga distancia
6. escribir la conclusión

C. Diálogo Lea el ensayo de un compañero / una compañera y luego invente un diálogo entre el abuelo y Adela en el que hablen de sus frustraciones y se ofrezcan consejos.

Hablando del tema

Antes de empezar a conversar con sus compañeros de clase sobre los temas de este capítulo, prepare una ficha para la conversación, otra para el debate y otra para la reacción ante la cita. Vea la explicación de las fichas en el **Apéndice 1.**

A. Conversación: Las familias de hoy Revise las expresiones de **Para conversar mejor.** Luego, en parejas o grupos de tres, conversen sobre los siguientes puntos.

Para conversar mejor

En mi caso...
Fue deprimente/preocupante cuando...
Ha sido igual para mí.
Lo mejor es que...
Me encanta (que)...
Mi situación ha sido diferente.
Para mí, es evidente que...
Pensaba que...

- Hable sobre las ventajas y desventajas de tener padres muy involucrados en su vida. ¿Cuánta influencia deben tener los padres en las vidas de sus hijos mayores?
- ¿Cuánta influencia deben tener los hijos en las decisiones de sus padres? Por ejemplo, si un padre divorciado / una madre divorciada quiere casarse otra vez, ¿deben los hijos tener voto en la elección de pareja?
- Si los padres divorciados se casan otra vez, juntando así a dos familias, puede ser difícil para una persona acostumbrarse a la nueva situación. Haga recomendaciones para que los hermanastros y los padrastros se llevan bien.

B. Debate: Los asilos para ancianos Revise las expresiones de **Para debatir mejor** y lea las dos opiniones sobre este tema que se presentan a continuación. Después, prepare tres argumentos a favor y tres en contra de la necesidad de que los abuelos vivan en casa con sus hijos.

Para debatir mejor

A FAVOR	EN CONTRA
Eso es.	No es siempre así.
Estoy de acuerdo.	¿Hablas en serio?
Muy bien dicho.	Lo siento, pero…
No cabe duda.	Todo lo contrario.

«Los abuelos son una parte integral de la familia extendida. Por eso es importante que cuando sean muy mayores y enfermos vivan en casa con sus hijos y no en un asilo para ancianos.»

«En un asilo de ancianos, los mayores lo pasan mejor, con amigos de su edad, y están mejor cuidados, rodeados de médicos y enfermeros. Los asilos de ancianos modernos son excelentes lugares para pasar los últimos años.»

C. Reacción: La adolescencia Revise las expresiones de **Para reaccionar mejor.** Luego, reaccione ante la siguiente cita. Añada razones que apoyen sus opiniones.

Para reaccionar mejor

Creo/Opino/Supongo que…	Es posible que…
Es bueno/malo que…	Es verdad que…
Es difícil que…	No tiene sentido que…

«Es natural y aun necesario que un(a) adolescente pase por un período rebelde para llegar a ser una persona independiente y realizada.»

CAPÍTULO 3

Pasiones y sentimientos:

Las relaciones humanas

Punto clave

REACCIONAR
R
RECOMENDAR

Temas centrales

- el amor
- los sentimientos
- las pasiones

Zona de enfoque

- México

El Callejón del Beso (*Guanajuato, México*)

En este capítulo Ud. va a explorar los temas de las pasiones y las relaciones sentimentales.

Preguntas para considerar

- ¿Qué nos atrae de otra persona?
- ¿Qué hace que las relaciones sentimentales sean duraderas o pasajeras (*fleeting*)?
- ¿Qué emociones surgen en las relaciones humanas?
- En el cuadro que se ve en esta página, se representa el amor prohibido. Hoy en día, ¿tienen los padres una influencia fuerte en la selección de la pareja de sus hijos?

MULTIMEDIA

Buscando el equilibrio

Sergio le da consejos a su primo Diego.

Situación: Diego le habla a Sergio sobre una reunión emocionante que tuvo hace dos días. También le confiesa que sus **relaciones sentimentales** con su novia Cristina han sufrido recientemente por su obsesión con el trabajo. Lea el diálogo y preste especial atención al uso del vocabulario nuevo, que está **en negrita.**

SERGIO: Hombre, qué gusto verte aquí en Ruta Maya. ¿Qué me cuentas?

DIEGO: Pues estoy muy **emocionado** y tenía que compartir unas noticias con alguien. Anteayer me reuní con Lupe Flores, la nueva directora del Museo Mexic-Arte, para hablar del proyecto que propuse hace tres meses.

SERGIO: ¿Te refieres a la exhibición de pinturas y fotos de parejas mexicanas famosas?

DIEGO: Sí. Lupe está tan entusiasmada como yo con la posibilidad de montar la exhibición en febrero. Pensamos incluir a Diego Rivera y a Frida Kahlo, a La Malinche y a Hernán Cortés, y a Felipe Carrillo Puerto y a Alma Reed, entre otros. Hace años que **sueño con** este proyecto.

SERGIO: ¡Qué padre! Así que conseguiste **un compromiso** oficial de Lupe para hacerlo.

DIEGO: Pues oficial, oficial, no. Lupe quiere reunirse conmigo de nuevo.

SERGIO: Uy, primo, ¿estás seguro que es necesario reunirse tanto?

DIEGO: ¿Qué estás insinuando?

SERGIO: Nada, nada. No quiero **meterme en líos** con Cristina.

DIEGO: Espera, ¿qué pasa?

SERGIO: Es que hablé con Cristina ayer y me dijo que la **dejaste plantada** y ahora, escuchándote, creo que fue la noche en que estuviste con Lupe.

DIEGO: Sí, ya lo sé. Cristina está muy **enojada** conmigo. **Se puso rabiosa** y hasta me dijo que quería **romper conmigo.**

SERGIO: La entiendo, mano. Cristina **te quiere** mucho y **merece** mejor **trato.** Uds. son **almas gemelas** y no quiero que algún día lamentes tus decisiones por culpa de Lupita y tu trabajo.

DIEGO: Tienes toda la razón. Conversar con alguien tan **apasionada** por el arte como Lupe fue **genial.** Se me fue el tiempo por completo.

SERGIO: Cuidado con Lupita.

DIEGO: No, no es lo que que tú estás pensando. **Coqueteamos** un poco, pero no hay absolutamente nada entre nosotros.

SERGIO: ¿Dirías lo mismo si fuera Cristina reuniéndose con otro hombre y **dejándote plantado** a ti?

ACTIVIDADES

A. Detective Busque en el diálogo ejemplos de las siguientes metas comunicativas: Descripción (D), Narración en el pasado (P), Comparación (C) e Hipótesis (H). Subraye cada palabra o frase que represente una (o una combinación) de estas metas comunicativas. Luego, escriba al margen la(s) letra(s) que corresponde(n) a cada ejemplo subrayado (D, P, C o H).

MODELOS: Se puso rabiosa y hasta me dijo que quería romper conmigo. (P)
Pues estoy muy emocionado. (D)

B. Comprensión

1. ¿Por qué está emocionado Diego?
2. ¿Cuál es la exhibición que piensa montar?
3. ¿Por qué puede causarle problemas con Cristina este trabajo?
4. ¿Por qué piensa Sergio que lo que está haciendo Diego es peligroso?
5. ¿Está Ud. de acuerdo con Diego o con Sergio?

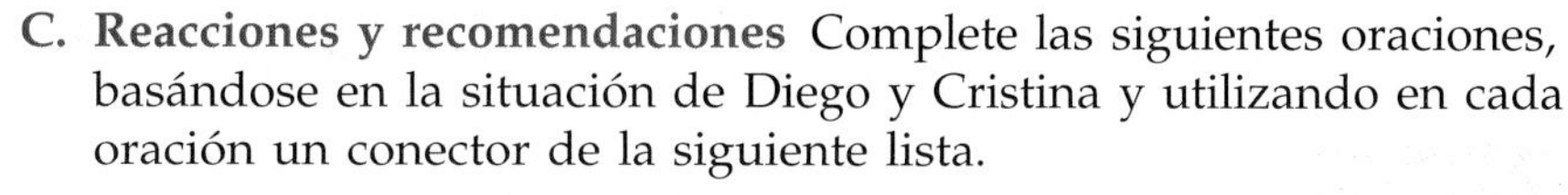

C. Reacciones y recomendaciones Complete las siguientes oraciones, basándose en la situación de Diego y Cristina y utilizando en cada oración un conector de la siguiente lista.

Conectores
en cambio
para que + *subjuntivo*
por eso
porque
sin embargo
ya que

MODELO: Es una lástima que Diego trabaje tanto porque ahora no tiene tiempo para sus amigos.

1. Qué bueno que Diego…
2. Creo que Cristina…
3. Es interesante que Sergio…
4. Dudo que Diego y Cristina…

D. Diálogo En parejas, preparen una conversación entre Diego y Cristina en la que hablen de lo que pasó esa noche cuando Diego la dejó plantada.

Vocabulario del tema

Para hablar de las relaciones sentimentales

abrazar	to hug
atraer (*irreg.*)	to attract
besar	to kiss
casarse (con)	to marry, get married (to)
confiar (confío) en	to trust in
coquetear	to flirt
dejar a alguien	to leave someone
dejar plantado/a	to stand (someone) up
discutir	to argue
divorciarse (de)	to get a divorce (from)
enamorarse (de)	to fall in love (with)
merecer (merezco)	to deserve
meterse en líos	to get into trouble
odiar	to hate
piropear	to compliment (romantically)*
ponerse (*irreg.*)	to become, get†
querer (*irreg.*)	to love
romper con	to break up with
salir (*irreg.*) **con**	to date
ser fiel	to be faithful
soñar (ue) con	to dream about

Verbos para influir

aconsejar	to advise
recomendar (ie)	to recommend
rogar (ue)	to beg
sugerir (ie, i)	to suggest

Para describir las relaciones sentimentales‡

dañino/a	harmful
duradero/a	lasting
exitoso/a	successful
genial	wonderful
inolvidable	unforgettable
pasajero/a	fleeting
tempestuoso/a	stormy

—Mi amor . . . prométeme que nunca más volverás a ordenar en francés . . .

Describa la «noche inolvidable» de esta pareja.

Para describir las emociones‡

alucinado/a	amazed
apasionado/a	passionate
apenado/a	pained, sad
asqueado/a	repulsed
asustado/a	frightened
avergonzado/a	embarrassed
cauteloso/a§	cautious
celoso/a	jealous
confundido/a	confused
deprimido/a	depressed
emocionado/a	excited
enfadado/a, **enojado/a**	angry
halagado/a	flattered

*__Piropear__ and __piropo__ carry a special significance in Hispanic culture. See the __Nota cultural__ on pages 83–84.

†Remember that **ponerse** is used with adjectives to communicate the English concept of *to become/get + adjective* when describing emotional or physical states.

Me puse nerviosa.	I became/got nervous.
Él se puso rojo.	He blushed. (*Literally:* He became/got red.)

‡Remember to use **ser** with adjectives when describing inherent characteristics and **estar** when referring to emotional or physical states.

§**Cauteloso/a** is only used with **ser.**

harto/a (de)	fed up (with), sick (of)
nostálgico/a	nostalgic; homesick
rabioso/a	furious
satisfecho/a	satisfied

Más sobre las relaciones sentimentales

el alma gemela	soul mate
la amistad	friendship
el compromiso	commitment
el equilibrio	balance
el fracaso	failure
la media naranja*	other half
el noviazgo	courtship
el piropo	(romantic) compliment
el resentimiento	resentment
el riesgo	risk
el soltero / la soltera	single person
el trato	treatment

ACTIVIDADES

A. ¿Está Ud. de acuerdo? Lea las siguientes opiniones con un compañero / una compañera. Comenten por qué están de acuerdo o no con esas afirmaciones. Deben reaccionar ante las opiniones de su compañero/a.

Para conversar mejor

Desde mi punto de vista...
En mi opinión... / Yo creo que...
Estoy completamente de acuerdo.
Me sorprende que creas eso.
No estoy de acuerdo en absoluto.
Pero, ¿qué dices?
¡Qué barbaridad!
Tienes toda la razón.

1. No es prudente salir con alguien que siempre coquetea con otros.
2. Es natural sentirse enojado/a si alguien lo/la deja plantado/a.
3. Es esencial hacer todo lo posible para no divorciarse nunca.
4. Una amistad entre personas sin intereses similares es imposible.
5. No es una buena idea casarse con una persona súper guapa.
6. Enamorarse de una persona de otro país es meterse en líos.
7. Las personas apasionadas con su trabajo u otro interés particular no hacen buenos amigos.
8. Sería genial conocer a la futura pareja a través del Internet.

B. Un viaje a México

Paso 1 Mire los adjetivos en la página siguiente y fíjese en la diferencia entre las terminaciones **-ado/a** (del participio pasado) y **-ante** o **-ente** y en los verbos que se usan en cada caso.

*Literally: *the half of an orange.*

ESTAR		SER	
alucinado/a	*amazed*	alucinante	*amazing*
deprimido/a	*depressed*	deprimente	*depressing*
emocionado/a	*excited*	emocionante	*exciting*
fascinado/a	*fascinated*	fascinante	*fascinating*
impresionado/a	*impressed*	impresionante	*impressive*
preocupado/a	*worried*	preocupante	*worrisome*
relajado/a	*relaxed*	relajante	*relaxing*
soprendido/a	*surprised*	sorprendente	*surprising*

Paso 2 Marisol y Sean, los dueños de Ruta Maya, están pensando hacer un viaje a México para relajarse y escaparse de las presiones del negocio. Lea la información sobre los tres lugares que consideran visitar y después complete el diálogo con el mejor adjetivo. Haga los cambios necesarios para la concordancia. **¡OJO!** A veces hay más de una respuesta posible.

¡México lindo, México fascinante, México sorprendente!

Zitácuaro, Michoacán *Más de 20 millones de mariposas monarca[1] emigran a Zitácuaro cada año para pasar el invierno. Debido a la cantidad enorme de mariposas, la tierra se convierte en una alfombra[2] multicolor mientras que las ramas[3] de los árboles se inclinan bajo su peso.*

La Barranca del Cobre *Este cañón, localizado en el estado de Chihuahua, es más profundo que el Gran Cañón en los Estados Unidos. Hay un tren que pasa por el cañón, desde el cual los turistas pueden apreciar unas vistas espléndidas. Durante los últimos 100 kilómetros de este viaje, el tren pasa por 39 puentes[4] y 86 túneles.*

La Laguna Catemaco *Esta es una laguna formada por el cráter de un volcán en el estado de Veracruz. En una de las islas, en el centro de la laguna, se encuentra un grupo de monos pescadores.[5] El área también es conocida por su festival de brujos, celebrado en el mes de marzo, conocido como «marzo mágico».*

¡Visítenos hoy!

[1]mariposas... *monarch butterflies* [2]*carpet* [3]*branches* [4]*bridges* [5]monos... *fishing monkeys*

MARISOL: Últimamente me he sentido un poco _________.[1] Necesito unas vacaciones para levantarme el ánimo.

SEAN: ¡Qué buena idea! ¿Por qué no vamos a México? Queda cerca y los precios son buenos en esta época del año.

MARISOL: ¡Sí! Mira este folleto sobre las vacaciones en México. Zitácuaro me parece un lugar _________.[2] No puedo creer que haya tantas mariposas.

SEAN: Sí, me quedé _________[3] cuando leí que podían hacer que las ramas de un árbol se inclinaran bajo su peso, pero estoy más _________[4] con la idea de ir en tren por la Barranca del Cobre.

MARISOL: Es verdad que suena ___________,[5] pero estoy _________[6] porque este tipo de viaje no me parece _________[7] y necesitamos descansar.

SEAN: En ese caso otro lugar muy tranquilo es la Laguna Catemaco. Los monos pescadores en Catemaco son _________[8] y el volcán debe ser _________.[9]

MARISOL: Bueno, estoy muy _________[10] con la posibilidad de ir a México, pero busquemos más información en el Internet antes de tomar una decisión.

SEAN: Está bien. Tienes razón.

Paso 3 Complete las siguientes frases de manera original, usando la información sobre los tres lugares.

1. Me parece fascinante que…
2. Es alucinante que…
3. Es sorprendente que…

Paso 4 Imagínese que Marisol y Sean ya están en México pasándolo bien en uno de los tres lugares. Escríbales una tarjeta postal a los empleados de Ruta Maya como si Ud. fuera Marisol o Sean.

C. **Preguntas personales** En parejas, contesten las preguntas que están en las páginas siguientes, utilizando palabras del **Vocabulario del tema.** Mientras escucha a su compañero/a, reaccione con algunas expresiones de **Para conversar mejor.** Luego, deben compartir con la clase lo que cada uno/a averiguó sobre su compañero/a.

Para conversar mejor

¡Qué barbaridad!
¡Qué bueno!
¡Qué chévere/guay/padre!
¡Qué horror!
¡Qué lío!
¡Qué suerte!
¡Qué vergüenza!
¡Bárbaro!
¡Fenomenal!
¿De veras? ¿En serio?
Sí, tienes razón.
¿Tú crees?
(No) Estoy de acuerdo.

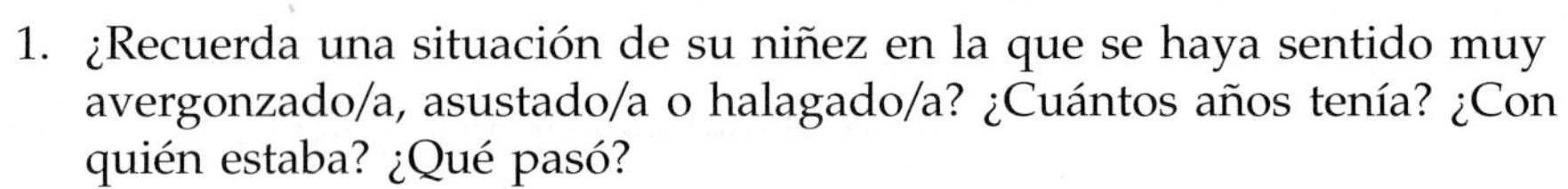

1. ¿Recuerda una situación de su niñez en la que se haya sentido muy avergonzado/a, asustado/a o halagado/a? ¿Cuántos años tenía? ¿Con quién estaba? ¿Qué pasó?

2. ¿Qué actividades le apasionan a Ud.? ¿Cree que pasa demasiado o poco tiempo haciendo las actividades que le apasionan? Explique su opinión. ¿Ha formado amistades a través de esas actividades? Describa cómo son esas amistades.

3. ¿Qué consejos le daría a un hombre cuya novia rompió con él a través del correo electrónico?

4. Haga una comparación entre el comportamiento de una pareja que tiene relaciones exitosas y una pareja que tiene relaciones dañinas. ¿Qué les recomienda a las dos parejas? ¿Qué haría Ud. para no meterse en líos en sus relaciones sentimentales?

D. **¿Qué nos atrae?** Piense en su grupo de amigos íntimos. ¿Tienen todos una personalidad semejante? ¿Tienen Uds. los mismos intereses?

Paso 1 Llene la siguiente tabla indicando con una X cuáles de los adjetivos se pueden aplicar a su propia personalidad y a la personalidad de su mejor amigo/a. Luego, indique cuáles de las actividades les interesan a Ud. y a su mejor amigo/a. Finalmente, añada algunas características y algunos intereses de Ud. y su mejor amigo/a que no aparezcan en la tabla.

CARACTERÍSTICAS			INTERESES		
ADJETIVOS	YO	MI MEJOR AMIGO/A	ACTIVIDADES	YO	MI MEJOR AMIGO/A
atrevido/a			chismear		
cómico/a			cocinar		
estudioso/a			hacer ejercicio		
fiestero/a			ir a los bares		
hablador(a)			ir de compras		
independiente			jugar videojuegos		
práctico/a			leer		
religioso/a			mirar deportes		
testarudo/a			mirar telenovelas		
tranquilo/a			tomar el sol		
¿ ?			viajar		
¿ ?			¿ ?		
¿ ?			¿ ?		

Paso 2 Ahora, calcule los resultados.

1. ¿Cuántas características tienen en común?
2. ¿Cuántos intereses comparten?
3. Comparta esta información con un compañero / una compañera de clase, explicándole por qué ha sido exitosa su amistad con su mejor amigo/a.

Paso 3 En grupos de tres, compartan los resultados y comenten las siguientes preguntas.

1. ¿Cree Ud. en la idea de que los polos opuestos se atraen?
2. ¿Pueden ser exitosas las relaciones entre personas muy diferentes?
3. En una amistad duradera, ¿qué es más importante: poseer características personales similares o compartir muchos intereses?
4. ¿De qué manera puede una pasión interferir en las relaciones interpersonales?
5. ¿Conoce Ud. a alguien que tenga una pasión que lo/la haya alejado (*has distanced him/her*) de sus amigos o familiares?

NOTA CULTURAL • Los piropos

Imagínese la siguiente situación: Varios chicos están reunidos en un lugar público, charlando.[1] De repente, ven pasar un coche descapotable,[2] último modelo, de una buena empresa[3] automovilística. Uno de los chicos exclama: «¡Vaya máquina!». Ahora tenemos una situación similar, pero esta vez los chicos ven pasar a una chica muy guapa y no pueden evitar un comentario: «¡Vaya monumento!». Estos chicos acaban de piropear a una joven atractiva.

El piropo es una forma de expresión muy hispana que los chicos usan normalmente para halagar a las chicas. Cuando los piropos son alabanzas discretas, cuando tienen gracia[4] y son inofensivos, pueden ser bien recibidos por las chicas. Por desgracia, las cosas que se dicen no siempre son un modo inocente de coqueteo. Es posible que reflejen el mal gusto y la grosería de quien las dice y, por lo tanto, pierden su validez como piropos y pasan a ser algo diferente y desagradable. Cuando esto ocurre, la reacción de la chica será de disgusto y rechazo.

A algunas mujeres hispanas les puede agradar que las piropeen por la calle, siempre que se trate de un verdadero piropo y no de una barbaridad obscena. Es indudable que hasta los piropos más simpáticos implican una coquetería «sensual», pero cuando un chico traspasa los límites permitidos ya no se trata de un sencillo piropo, sino de una agresión que nunca será bien recibida.

[1]hablando [2]*convertible* [3]compañía [4]tienen... *they're charming*

Preguntas

1. En grupos de tres, comenten la costumbre de piropear a las mujeres. ¿Son sexistas los piropos?
2. ¿Piensan que a los hombres les gustaría escuchar piropos sobre su aspecto físico mientras caminan por la calle? Expliquen.

(*continúa*)

Actividad

En grupos de tres, lean los siguientes piropos e indiquen cuál es el más cursi, el más romántico, el más poético y el más tonto.

1. Si yo fuera pintor, te haría un retrato y lo llamaría *Perfección*.
2. Quisiera ser lluvia para caerte encima.
3. ¡Tantas curvas y yo sin frenos!
4. Si mi corazón volara, tu alma sería mi aeropuerto.
5. Estoy buscando diosas para una nueva religión y acabo de elegirte a ti.
6. Beyoncé es una bruja junto a ti.
7. Eres mi príncipe y siempre lo serás, y yo tu princesa hasta la eternidad.
8. Quisiera ser gato para vivir siete vidas a tu lado.

E. **Problemas repentinos** Entre todos, revisen los siguientes problemas y hagan una lista de las palabras nuevas de este capítulo y de los capítulos anteriores que los ayuden a conversar con facilidad sobre cada uno. Después, en parejas, preparen un diálogo espontáneo sobre cada problema repentino.

1. Un novio / Una novia acaba de mandarle una tarjeta virtual (o flores virtuales) para el Día de San Valentín a través del Internet en vez de una tarjeta convencional o flores de verdad. Su pareja está furiosa y él/ella no comprende su reacción.
2. Una persona acaba de conocer a un hombre/una mujer a través del Internet. Su mejor amigo/a es muy cauteloso/a y cree sin la menor duda que no es prudente salir con esa persona, pero la primera persona está seguro/a de que esa persona es su media naranja.

Puntos clave

Reacciones y recomendaciones

En esta sección del capítulo, Ud. va a practicar las reacciones y recomendaciones. Para hacerlo bien, hay que utilizar las estructuras gramaticales (los puntos clave) de la siguiente tabla que pertenecen a la meta comunicativa. Antes de continuar, estudie las explicaciones de estas estructuras gramaticales en las páginas verdes que están al final del libro.

LA META COMUNICATIVA DE ESTE CAPÍTULO		
ICONO	META COMUNICATIVA	PUNTOS CLAVE
REACCIONAR R RECOMENDAR	Reacciones y recomendaciones	• el subjuntivo en cláusulas nominales • los mandatos

PRUEBA DIAGNÓSTICA

Una estudiantina en Hacienda de los Santos Álamos, México

A. El subjuntivo Las estudiantinas son grupos de jóvenes universitarios que pasean por la ciudad de noche, vestidos de trovadores medievales, cantando canciones tradicionales y serenatas románticas. La costumbre empezó en España en el siglo XIII e inmigró a las Américas. Además de ser una gran diversión, es una buena manera de ganarse un poco de dinero para los gastos de la universidad. Lea la siguiente historia sobre unos futuros tunos y llene los espacios en blanco con la forma apropiada de los verbos que están entre paréntesis.

Beto y su amigo, Esteban, quieren ser músicos en una estudiantina de su universidad. Esperan que ______[1] (ser) una buena manera de ganar dinero y de conocer a muchachas. Pero la madre de Beto no quiere que él ______[2] (ser) parte de la estudiantina hasta el año que viene porque teme que ______[3] (interesarse) demasiado por la música y que no ______[4] (hacer) su tarea. Sus hermanos mayores fueron tunos y desean que Beto ______[5] (seguir) la tradición familiar. Pero su madre sabe que es muy posible que el benjamín de la familia ______[6] (meterse) en líos. Los hermanos creen firmemente que Beto ______[7] (poder) aprender a encontrar un buen equilibrio entre sus estudios y la música. Además, ellos saben que su amigo, Esteban, es un estudiante muy serio y esperan que ______[8] (ayudar) a su hermano menor a organizar su tiempo. ¡Ojalá que su madre ______[9] (escuchar) a sus hijos mayores!

B. Los mandatos Beto y Esteban ya son tunos. Complete las siguientes oraciones con los mandatos que les da el director de la estudiantina. Como el director es también estudiante, utilice la forma informal del imperativo.

1. «Beto, ______ (hacer) la tarea antes de practicar con la estudiantina. No ______ (posponer) el trabajo.»
2. «Esteban y Beto, ______ (divertirse) durante sus presentaciones pero no ______ (coquetear) tanto con las muchachas del público.»
3. «Beto, ______ (venir) a la plaza para tocar a las 10:00 de la noche. No ______ (llegar) tarde.»
4. «Muchachos, ______ (practicar) sus instrumentos todos los días. No ______ (olvidarse) de su compromiso con la estudiantina.»

Expresiones útiles

Las siguientes expresiones le pueden servir para expresar sus sentimientos y sus opiniones. ¿Cuáles de ellas requieren el subjuntivo?

Para alabar

Es impresionante que…	*It's impressive/awesome that . . .*
Estoy orgulloso/a de que…	*I'm proud that . . .*
Estoy súper contento/a de que…	*I'm super-happy that . . .*
Me alegro de que…	*I'm glad that . . .*
Qué bueno que…	*How great that . . .*

Para quejarse

¡Esto es el colmo!	*This is the last straw!*
Estoy decepcionado/a de/porque…	*I'm disappointed by/because . . .*
No me gusta que…	*I don't like it that . . .*
Ya estoy harto/a (de que…)	*I'm fed up already (that) . . .*
Ya no puedo soportarlo/la más.	*I can't stand it/him/her anymore.*

Para pedir perdón

Lo siento mucho.	*I'm very sorry.*
Mil disculpas/perdones.	*A thousand pardons.*
Perdón, me equivoqué.	*Sorry, I made a mistake.*
Se me olvidó por completo.	*I totally forgot.*
Siento que…	*I'm sorry that . . .*

Para enfatizar una respuesta negativa

Me importa tres narices/un pepino.	*I couldn't care less.*
¡Ni hablar!	*No way!*
Ni se te ocurra. / Ni lo pienses.	*Don't even think about it.*
¡Ni soñarlo!	*In your dreams!*

Para reaccionar ante una situación

No es para tanto.	*It's not such a big deal.*
¡Qué chévere/guay/padre!	*How cool!*
¡Qué cara tiene!	*What nerve he/she has!*
¡Qué horror!	*How awful!*
¡Qué vergüenza!	*How embarrassing!*

ACTIVIDADES

Las siguientes actividades le darán la oportunidad de practicar la expresión de reacciones y recomendaciones. Recuerde que debe usar el subjuntivo en la mayoría de los casos y a veces los mandatos.

A. Algunas situaciones delicadas Trabaje con un compañero / una compañera. Hagan un diálogo para las siguientes situaciones. Luego, añadan su opinión sobre cada situación.

1. Dos novios discuten en una fiesta porque la novia piensa que el novio está coqueteando con otra mujer.

   El novio avergonzado: Perdóname, mi amor. Siento que…

   La novia celosa: ¡Esto es el colmo! Estoy harta de que…

   ¿Creen Uds. que la novia debe perdonar a su novio? Expliquen.

2. Una madre se queja porque su hija y su nuevo novio se besan en público constantemente.

   La madre estricta: Es preocupante que Uds.… Y estoy decepcionada porque…

   La hija egoísta: No es para tanto, mamá. Me importa un pepino que…

   ¿Creen Uds. que la madre tiene una preocupación razonable? Expliquen.

3. Dos amigas discuten porque una deja plantada a la otra constantemente. Lo acaba de hacer por tercera vez este mes.

   La amiga harta: ¡Ya no puedo soportarlo más! Me molesta que… Tienes que…

   La amiga despistada: Se me olvidó por completo. Siento que… Pero espero que…

   ¿Creen Uds. que esta amistad vaya a durar mucho más? Expliquen.

4. Un padre y su hijo hablan de su nueva hermanastra (una niña muy habladora) y de cómo los dos se llevan bien y lo bueno que es que el hijo trate de acostumbrarse a su nueva familia.

   El padre cariñoso: Estoy muy orgulloso de que… y espero que…

   El hijo dulce: A veces me vuelve loco porque habla por los codos, pero me alegro de que… y sé que es importante que…

   ¿Creen Uds. que las expectativas de esta familia son realistas? Expliquen.

B. El Callejón del Beso

Paso 1 Hay muchas versiones de la leyenda del «Callejón del Beso», lugar de una historia romántica en la ciudad de Guanajuato, México. Trabajando en parejas, lean la versión que está en la página siguiente y llenen los espacios en blanco con la forma apropiada del pretérito o del imperfecto (según el contexto) de los verbos que están entre paréntesis.

El Callejón del Beso, Guanajuato, México

Hace muchos años, en un pequeño callejón de la ciudad de Guanajuato, ________[1] (vivir) un matrimonio de dinero con su única hija, Carmen. Un día Luis, un minero pobre, ________[2] (ver) a Carmen en la iglesia y los dos ________[3] (enamorarse). Los padres de Carmen ________[4] (querer) que su hija se casara con un español rico y por eso ________[5] (oponerse) definitivamente a las relaciones entre los jóvenes. Pero Luis y Carmen ________[6] (quererse) desesperadamente y a pesar de las amenazas[a] de su padre, Carmen ________[7] (salir) al balcón de su cuarto que daba al balcón del cuarto de Luis al otro lado del callejón y así los jóvenes enamorados ________[8] (pasar) horas hablándose.

Una noche el padre de Carmen los ________[9] (ver) besándose desde un balcón al otro y ________[10] (ponerse) tan rabioso que ________[11] (jurar) matar a Carmen si volvía a verla con Luis. Pero Carmen ________[12] (estar) tan enamorada de Luis que no ________[13] (poder) soportar la separación y ________[14] (volver) al balcón y a las charlas románticas. Unas semanas después, el padre de Carmen ________[15] (entrar) al cuarto de su hija mientras ella ________[16] (hablar) con Luis desde su balcón y en una furia ________[17] (matar) a su única hija con una daga.[b] Luis no ________[18] (poder) vivir sin el amor de Carmen y, desesperado, ________[19] (suicidarse) tirándose desde la boca de la mina donde trabajaba.

Hoy en día, según la leyenda, si dos enamorados se besan con amor en el tercer escalón[c] del mismo callejón, tendrán quince años de buena fortuna. Pero si pasan sin darse un beso, tendrán siete años de mala suerte.

[a]*threats* [b]*dagger* [c]*step*

Paso 2 En parejas, hagan mini-conversaciones como si fueran los protagonistas y las personas a su alrededor. Completen las oraciones para expresar sus deseos y opiniones. Usen su imaginación y el vocabulario nuevo de este capítulo cuando sea posible.

1. EL PADRE: No quiero que Luis...
   CARMEN: Pienso que...
2. LUIS: Es necesario que nosotros...
   CARMEN: Dudo que...
3. LA MADRE DE CARMEN: Temo que tu padre...
   CARMEN: Te pido que...
4. UN VECINO RICO: Estoy seguro de que...
   SU HIJA, UNA AMIGA DE CARMEN: Ojalá que...

C. Una noche desilusionante

Paso 1 En parejas, miren los siguientes dibujos y comenten lo que les pasó a Diego y Cristina la semana pasada.

Paso 2 ¿Qué le dijo Cristina a Diego al día siguiente? Preparen un diálogo entre los dos.

Paso 3 Ahora, ofrezcan a la pareja cuatro consejos utilizando los siguientes verbos: **aconsejar, recomendar, rogar, sugerir.**

D. ¿Es posible salvar este matrimonio?

Paso 1 Mire el dibujo de una pareja que lleva muchos años de casados. Son diferentes y tienen expectativas distintas de la vida romántica. Use las claves que están a continuación para describir a la pareja. Incluya muchos detalles en su descripción. Luego, compare sus respuestas con las de un compañero / una compañera.

1. Don Nacho es... Siempre está... Por eso...
2. Doña Fermina es... En este momento está... Es obvio que...
3. A doña Fermina le gusta(n)... Le encanta(n)... Le fastidia que...
4. A doña Fermina le molesta que su esposo... Ella prefiere que... Sin embargo...
5. Para escaparse de su realidad, doña Fermina... Es triste que... Es mejor que...

Paso 2 Trabajando en parejas, díganle a don Nacho lo que tiene que hacer para salvar su matrimonio. Utilicen mandatos formales.

E. Una pareja famosa Las tempestuosas pero apasionadas relaciones sentimentales entre Diego Rivera y Frida Kahlo son ya famosísimas. Se casaron, se separaron y se casaron de nuevo, pero las aventuras amorosas de los dos imposibilitaron su felicidad absoluta. Diego mismo admitió que cuanto más amaba a Frida más quería hacerle daño. Este conflicto se refleja a menudo en los cuadros de Frida.

Diego Rivera y Frida Kahlo

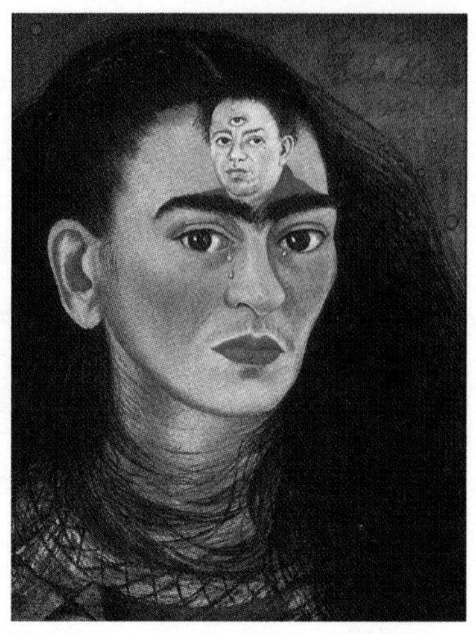

Diego y yo, *de Frida Kahlo (1907–1954)*

Paso 1 Aquí hay un artículo sobre cómo se enamoraron Diego y Frida. Lea el artículo. Haga un círculo alrededor de los verbos que están en el pretérito y subraye los que están en el imperfecto. Luego, con un compañero / una compañera, comente las razones posibles por las que se usaron esos tiempos verbales en cada caso.

¿QUÉ VIERON EL UNO EN EL OTRO? LA HISTORIA DE LA CHISPA[1] QUE INCENDIÓ[2] ESTOS CORAZONES

La pintora mexicana Frida Kahlo se enamoró locamente del pintor Diego Rivera cuando apenas tenía 15 años. «Mi ambición es tener algún día un hijo de Diego Rivera», les dijo Frida a sus amigas. «Algún día se lo voy a hacer saber.»

Como Rivera estaba casado y tenía veinte años más que ella, Frida no llegó a conseguir su objetivo hasta siete años más tarde, cuando la voluntariosa[3] estudiante volvió a «la carga[4]»: fue a ver a Diego a la Escuela de Arte, lo hizo bajar de una enorme escalera desde la que trabajaba en un mural, le pidió opinión sobre sus pinturas... y el pintor se sintió muy intrigado por la atrevida chica que había sufrido un espantoso accidente y tenía una pierna destrozada, pero que tenía una cara exótica y bella y mostraba un espíritu indomable. Así fue como, ya divorciado y lleno de curiosidad por aquella mujer con quien «podía hablar de todos los temas de la Tierra», la empezó a cortejar,[5] hasta que Guillermo Kahlo, el padre de Frida, decidió hablarle a Diego. «Mire, Rivera, quiero hacerle una advertencia. Mi hija Frida es una chica inteligente, pero... tiene un demonio oculto.[6]» A lo que el pintor contestó: «Yo lo sé, Sr. Kahlo, yo lo sé.» Kahlo respiró tranquilo: «Ah, qué bien Rivera, he cumplido con mi deber y ya me siento en paz habiéndole advertido.» Y con esa semibendición del padre de Frida, la pareja contrajo matrimonio el 21 de agosto de 1929, sin que nunca Diego le hiciera la pregunta clave.

[1]*spark* [2]*ignited* [3]*willful* [4]la... *the task at hand* [5]*court* [6]*hidden*

Paso 2 Complete lo siguiente.

1. Después de haber visto la fotografía de Diego y Frida y el cuadro de Frida, y después de haber leído el artículo sobre los dos, describa la personalidad de Frida. Luego, haga una comparación de los atributos físicos de la pareja.
2. ¿Qué hizo Frida para que Diego se fijara en ella?
3. ¿Por qué cree Ud. que a Diego le interesó la joven artista?
4. En su opinión, ¿es posible que unas relaciones duren si un hombre tiene veinte años más que su esposa? ¿Por qué sí o por qué no?

HIPÓTESIS

DESAFÍO

5. Si su padre le dijera a su novio/a que Ud. es una persona encantadora pero que tiene problemas psicológicos, ¿cómo se sentiría? ¿Qué le diría a su padre?

Rincón cultural

Lugares fascinantes:

México

Una estudiantina guanajuatense

1. **Guanajuato** Esta ciudad al norte de la capital es un lugar muy romántico donde hay algo para todos los gustos. Al entrar en la ciudad uno cree que ha regresado en el tiempo, por la bella arquitectura colonial. Uno de los atractivos de la ciudad son las tradicionales estudiantinas: grupos de jóvenes estudiantes que se pasean por la ciudad de noche, vestidos de trovadores medievales, cantando serenatas para ganar dinero. Llevan grupos de turistas por las calles empedradas contándoles leyendas de la ciudad, como la del Callejón del Beso.[1] Otros atractivos de Guanajuato son el Museo de Diego Rivera, que está en la casa donde nació el artista, y el Teatro Juárez, considerado uno de los mejores de México. Cada año el Festival Internacional Cervantino atrae a artistas, músicos, bailarines, actores, cantantes y más de 150.000 visitantes de todas partes del mundo. Para las personas con gustos más macabros, hay que ver el Museo de las Momias. En Guanajuato, los cadáveres se momifican de forma natural a causa de los minerales que existen en la tierra y el agua que bebe la gente. Cuando las familias de los muertos no pueden pagar el cementerio, los cuerpos momificados se instalan en el Museo de las Momias.

[1]Callejón... Véase la página 88.

El Zócalo en México D.F.

2. **México, D.F.**[2] Esta megaciudad, con más de 20 millones de habitantes, es la capital del país y una de las ciudades más grandes del mundo. Fue construida simbólicamente encima de Tenochtitlán, la antigua capital de los aztecas, cuyas ruinas no se encontraron sino hasta el siglo XX, durante las excavaciones para la construcción del metro. El D.F., como la conocen los mexicanos, siempre ha sido el centro político y cultural del país. Es una ciudad con muchos lugares públicos para pasearse, como el Parque Alameda, el Zócalo y el Parque de Chapultepec, donde muchas familias pasan sus días libres. También están los famosos canales de Xochimilco. Hace siglos, sus canales interminables formaban una parte importante del comercio de la ciudad. Hoy en día, los canales, con sus trajineras[3] adornadas de flores, le ofrecen a todo el mundo una manera agradable de disfrutar de la naturaleza y uno de los sitios más pintorescos del Distrito Federal. Igual que muchas ciudades latinoamericanas, el D.F. es un lugar donde coexiste lo viejo con lo moderno. Hay elegantes casas coloniales, iglesias barrocas y rascacielos que sirven de testigos de la larga historia de la ciudad. Una de las joyas del D.F. es el Museo Nacional de Antropología, cuyos edificios hospedan tesoros de las culturas indígenas del país.

«El castillo», la gran pirámide de Chichén Itzá

3. **Yucatán** Muchos conocen este lugar sobre todo por sus bellas playas, como las de Cozumel y Cancún. Por las aguas cristalinas del Caribe, son lugares ideales para hacer snorkling o bucear. Sin embargo, la Península de Yucatán contiene otros tesoros importantes. Cuna[4] de la civilización maya, allí se encuentran algunas de las ruinas precolombinas más importantes del continente americano, como las de Chichén Itzá. Chichén Itzá fue un centro religioso de los mayas. El templo mayor da evidencia de los avances de los mayas en la arquitectura, las matemáticas y la astronomía. En el equinoccio de primavera (el 21 de marzo) el juego de luz solar en las crestas de la escalera norte crea la ilusión de que una serpiente desciende hacia el pie de la pirámide. Este efecto les indicaba a los mayas que era hora de sembrar el maíz. En contraste, en el equinoccio de otoño (el 21 de septiembre), el ascenso de la serpiente indicaba el inicio de la cosecha. Actualmente, todos los años hay grandes festivales en estas fechas para celebrar el inicio de la primavera o la llegada del otoño. Gente de todas partes del mundo llega para conectarse con la espiritualidad del lugar.

[2]D.F. = Distrito Federal = *Mexico City* [3]*decorative boats for hire* [4]*Cradle*

4. Oaxaca La ciudad de Oaxaca es una de las más diversas y bellas de la República mexicana. Su impresionante Jardín Etnobiológico muestra la diversidad biológica y étnica de este estado al sur de la capital. Cerca de Oaxaca se encuentra la zona arqueológica de Monte Albán, donde los zapotecas construyeron su ciudad sagrada —aún muy bien preservada— alrededor del año 500 A.C.[5] En la ciudad de Oaxaca, la herencia de las culturas prehispánicas se nota todos los días en su cocina, su música y la alegría y colorido de sus fiestas, calles y mercados. El Zócalo es el centro de la vida oaxaqueña, con sus mercados al aire libre, sus iglesias coloniales, sus puestos llenos de tejidos y artesanías, y sus cafés y restaurantes. Entre las comidas y bebidas típicas están los chapulines[6] fritos, varios moles,[7] el mezcal y el café de olla, hervido con canela y caña de azúcar. Cada julio, durante dos semanas, esta ciudad de 200.000 habitantes se inunda con más de 50.000 personas que vienen a participar en la Guelaguetza. En esta gran fiesta relacionada con el ciclo agrícola, los indígenas de las siete regiones del estado hacen demostraciones de la música y baile de su región y hacen ofrendas de productos típicos de su tierra.

[5]«Antes de Cristo» [6]*grasshoppers* [7]*flavorful sauces*

¡Viaje conmigo a México!

Vea el vídeo para saber lo que Gabriela les mandó a Javier y Sara sobre su viaje a México.

Video footage provided by

BBC Motion Gallery

ACTIVIDADES

A. En parejas, contesten las siguientes preguntas sobre los cuatro lugares fascinantes.

1. ¿Por qué es Guanajuato un buen lugar para una luna de miel?
2. ¿Cuáles son algunas de las atracciones turísticas en Guanajuato?
3. ¿Por qué se considera la Ciudad de México una megaciudad?
4. ¿Qué fue Tenochtitlán y cuál fue su importancia? ¿Se puede visitar hoy en día?

(*continúa*)

5. ¿Por qué se considera el Museo Nacional de Antropología una de las joyas más interesantes del D.F.?
6. ¿Por qué le interesaría a un arqueólogo visitar Yucatán?
7. ¿Cuáles son dos de los lugares en Oaxaca que le interesaría visitar y dos comidas o bebidas que le gustaría probar?
8. ¿Qué es la Guelaguetza?

B. Localice los cuatro lugares fascinantes de México en el siguiente mapa y póngale a cada uno un número del 1 (el más interesante) al 4 (el menos interesante) para indicar el grado de interés que Ud. tiene en visitar estos lugares. Luego, turnándose con un compañero / una compañera, explique por qué a Ud. le interesa más el número 1 y por qué le interesa menos el número 4. Haga por lo menos tres comparaciones entre los dos lugares cuando presente su explicación.

C. Ahora que Ud. ha leído sobre los lugares y ha visto el videoblog de Gabriela, escriba un relato sobre un viaje imaginario que Ud. haya hecho con su novio/a a uno de los lugares fascinantes de México. Describa lo que hicieron y explique por qué siguen siendo pareja o por qué han roto. Siga el siguiente bosquejo.

Nuestro viaje a _______ fue _______
Primero..., Luego..., Más tarde..., Finalmente...
(narración en el pasado con cuatro verbos en el pretérito y cuatro en el imperfecto)
Nos encantó / Nos encantaron...
Durante el viaje me di cuenta de que él/ella...
Al final de diez días juntos, decidimos que nuestra relación...
Si una pareja piensa ir a México para su luna de miel, (no) recomiendo que... porque...

Baile de las calaveras, *de José Guadalupe Posada*

Clavera Catrina *de José Guadalupe Posada*

Un artista hispano:

José Guadalupe Posada

El artista mexicano José Guadalupe Posada nació en Aguascalientes en 1852. Desde muy pequeño le gustaba dibujar. A los 19 años hizo sus primeras caricaturas políticas para una revista local. En 1888 se marchó[1] a la capital, donde empezó a producir miles de grabados[2] que reflejaban los intereses, los miedos y la conciencia del pueblo mexicano.

Posada fue prolífico. Hizo más de 20.000 dibujos a lo largo de su vida. Gran parte de su obra artística se centra en «las calaveras[3]». En estas caricaturas, Posada capta un tema muy presente en la conciencia mexicana: la muerte. Sin embargo, sus calaveras no representan la muerte triste y solemne, sino la humanidad, la vanidad y la alegría de la vida. Creó miles de imágenes de gente humilde, políticos, revolucionarios, ricos y criminales haciendo todo tipo de actividades humanas. Posada documentó en sus grabados una gran variedad de escándalos, chismes, crímenes horribles y catástrofes naturales. A través de sus dibujos trazó una crítica social con sentido del humor. Entre sus calaveras más populares está la de *Don Chepito Marihuano*, un soltero de la clase alta, rico y ridículo. Los grabados de *Don Chepito* relatan una serie de aventuras de amor, peligro y violencia. Su comportamiento tiene que ver con su costumbre de fumar marihuana.

La calavera más famosa de Posada es la *Calavera Catrina*. Esta imagen de una mujer joven de la clase alta, con un sombrero elegante, se ha convertido en icono mexicano. Los grabados de Posada aparecieron en muchísimos periódicos: foro público donde la gente mexicana podía apreciar su arte. Por esta razón, para los muralistas Diego Rivera y José Clemente Orozco, Posada fue un precursor del movimiento nacionalista en el arte público. Diego Rivera dijo: «Analizando la obra de José Guadalupe Posada puede realizarse el análisis más completo de la vida social del pueblo de México».

En el primer grabado, *Baile de las calaveras*, se pueden ver todos los esqueletos coqueteando, bailando, bebiendo y cantando, replicando las mismas actividades que hacían en vida. El segundo es la famosísima *Calavera Catrina*.

[1]se... se fue [2]*engravings* [3]*skulls*

PREGUNTAS

1. ¿Qué tipo de arte hizo Posada? ¿Cuáles eran los temas más importantes para él?
2. ¿Qué tipo de figura usa para representar la muerte? ¿Cómo retrata esas figuras?
3. ¿Dónde publicaba su arte? ¿Por qué era bueno publicar su arte así?
4. ¿Por qué opinaba Diego Rivera que el arte de Posada es clave para realizar un análisis social del pueblo mexicano?

DESCRIBIR

ACTIVIDAD

La *Calavera Catrina* es un icono presente en muchos géneros del arte mexicano. Busque en el Internet los diferentes tipos de imágenes de calaveras que se ven durante la celebración del Día de los Muertos en México. Presente la imagen más interesante a la clase y comente las diversas expresiones artísticas que celebran en esta fiesta de los muertos.

La música mexicana

Los Tigres del Norte, tocando en Vina del Mar, Chile

¿Qué es la música mexicana? Muchas personas, al hablar de la música mexicana, piensan en los grupos de mariachis con sus trajes de charro, sombreros enormes y guitarras, trompetas y violines. Esta es ciertamente una de las formas de la música mexicana que ha penetrado en la imaginación popular estadounidense. Sin embargo, «mariachi» no se refiere a un estilo de música, sino a un grupo de músicos que toca varios estilos de música de diferentes regiones de México. Cada estilo tiene su propio ritmo e instrumentos, además de su propio baile y traje típicos. También, la variedad de guitarras que se usan en la interpretación de la música mexicana es sorprendente, así como los diversos géneros musicales (la chilena, el gusto, la polka, el ranchero, el son, el huapango, el norteño) que, como joyas preciosas, forman una parte integral de la cultura mexicana. Esta cultura se ha transmitido de generación a generación porque los niños típicamente aprenden las canciones y los bailes de su región en las escuelas primarias, además de géneros musicales de otras regiones. Saber bailar o cantar piezas de la propia región es saber expresar con orgullo el amor por la tierra natal. «La Mariquita» es un tipo de canción llamado «gusto». Es música folclórica, de la gente del campo.

ACTIVIDADES

A. Antes de cantar Al principio escuchará el violín, acompañado por la guitarra y el bajo acústico. El rasgueo de la guitarra produce el ritmo que es típico de este estilo de canción. Note que el ritmo del violín es muy fluido y que, comparado con el de la guitarra, es menos rígido. Conteste las siguientes preguntas.

1. ¿Ha oído Ud. la música de algún cantante mexicano? ¿Le gustó?
2. ¿Qué tipo de vocabulario se usará en una canción romántica cuyo título es «La Mariquita» (nombre cariñoso que se le da a una mujer)?
3. ¿Conoce algunas canciones con el tema del amor no correspondido? ¿Cuáles son?

B. ¡A cantar! Escuche la canción «La Mariquita» que se puede encontrar en el CD *Estampillas musicales*.

La Mariquita

Ay cielos, ay qué dolor
Vide[1] una garza[2] morena
Hay muertos que no hacen
ruido
Y son mayores sus penas
[*Se repite.*]

Ay, que le da
Que le da y vamos a ver
A ver cómo corre el agua
Vamos a verla correr
Ay, que le da
Que le da y vamos a ver
El agua que se derrama[3]
No se vuelve a recoger

Mariquita quita quita
Quítame del padecer[4]
El rato que no te veo
Loco me quiero volver
[*Se repite.*]

Ay, soledad
soledad y vamos a ver
A ver cómo corre el agua
Vamos a verla correr
Ay, soledad
Soledad y vamos a ver
El agua que se derrama
No se vuelve a recoger

Lucero de la mañana[5]
De la mañana lucero
Si supieras, vida mía
Lo bastante que te quiero
[*Se repite.*]

Ay, que le da
Que le da y vamos a ver
A ver cómo corre el agua
Vamos a verla correr
Ay, que le da
Que le da y vamos a ver
El agua que se derrama
No se vuelve a recoger

[1]Vi [2]*heron* [3]se... *is spilled* [4]*suffering* [5]Lucero... *Morning Star* (*Venus*)

C. Después de cantar En parejas, contesten las siguientes preguntas sobre la canción «La Mariquita».

1. ¿Es la canción optimista o pesimista? ¿Qué palabras de la letra apoyan su opinión?
2. ¿Qué partes de la canción son las más pegadizas (*catchy*)?
3. ¿Escuchó unas canciones folclóricas mexicanas como «Allá en el rancho grande», o «Cielito lindo» cuando aprendía el español? ¿Hay otras que recuerda?

D. ¡A escuchar! Para apreciar más la gran variedad de música mexicana regional, vaya a YouTube™ y escuche la música de Luis Miguel (los boleros), Los Tigres del Norte, Los Panchos, Linda Ronstadt o Lucero. Luego, para conocer la música contemporánea de México, escuche a Julieta Venegas, Paulina Rubio, Víctor García, Maná o Thalía. Luego, comparta con sus compañeros de clase sus impresiones sobre los artistas y las canciones que escuchó utilizando frases como **Me gusta(n)... porque... , Me encanta que... , Es impresionante/fantástico que... , Me sorprende que...** y **Es evidente que... .**

Lectura

Aunque en este país se sabe poco de las relaciones románticas entre el gobernador socialista de Yucatán, Felipe Carrillo Puerto, y la periodista estadounidense Alma Reed, su historia es fascinante.* Tiene lugar en la década de 1920, justo después de la Revolución mexicana, y su historia de amor incluye sueños utópicos, ideales políticos apasionados, descubrimientos arqueológicos, complots secretos y hasta asesinatos. En esta lectura, Arturo Ortega Morán nos da un resumen de esta trágica historia de amor, la cual inspiró una de las canciones más populares y duraderas en la historia de México, «La Peregrina». Ortega Morán es ingeniero y escritor, y contribuye a un programa de radio nacional en México, *Cápsulas de lengua.* Su interés personal en la historia de Alma Reed y Felipe Carrillo Puerto viene de la importancia de «La Peregrina» en su tradición familiar: era la canción favorita de su suegra. En una ocasión, su suegro acompañó en piano a un coro de niños que cantaba «La Peregrina» en el teatro de Bellas Artes en la Ciudad de México. Al terminar la canción, de entre el público se paró una anciana de ojos intensamente azules y con trabajo subió al escenario para darle un beso a cada uno de los niños y, al final, a su suegro. Era Alma Reed, quien, emocionada, acababa de escuchar un concierto conmovedor, quizá su último, ya que al poco tiempo murió.

NOTA HISTÓRICA

La Revolución mexicana se inició en 1910 y produjo líderes importantes, como Pancho Villa y Emiliano Zapata. Estos lucharon junto con campesinos y obreros en contra de los abusos de poder de la dictadura de Porfirio Díaz, que había durado más de treinta años. El choque entre los federales (los representantes del gobierno) y los revolucionarios (quienes tenían también conflictos internos) destrozó al país. La violencia acabó por un rato con las elecciones de 1920. El nuevo gobierno de Álvaro Obregón realizó importantes cambios políticos, laborales, educativos y culturales.

Felipe Carrillo Puerto fue elegido gobernador del estado de Yucatán en 1922 y empezó a poner en marcha las metas de la Revolución detalladas en la Constitución de 1917. Fue conocido como «El Dragón de los Ojos Verdes» y «El Apóstol de la Raza de Bronce» por su apoyo feroz de la gente indígena. Sólo gobernó veinte meses, pero su gobierno socialista abrió 417 escuelas, fundó la Universidad Nacional del Sureste, dio a la gente indígena cargos públicos, otorgó derechos políticos a la mujer —incluyendo el voto—, comenzó el reparto de tierras y apoyó la exploración de las ruinas mayas en las zonas arqueológicas de la región.

---

*La autobiografía de Alma Reed, *Peregrina: mi idilio socialista con Felipe Carrillo Puerto* (2007, editada por Michael K. Schuessler con prólogo de Elena Poniatowska) da al público un punto de vista más íntimo del período de la Revolución mexicana, época muy importante para la historia de méxico.

Antes de leer

A. Para comentar En grupos de tres, contesten las siguientes preguntas.

1. ¿Qué políticos de este u otro país han sido defensores de los pobres? ¿Cuál era/es su visión para la gente menos afortunada o explotada?
2. ¿Se ha enamorado Ud. alguna vez de algún lugar que haya visitado, ya sea en su propio país o en el extranjero? ¿Por qué se enamoró de ese lugar?
3. ¿Conoce Ud. alguna canción cuyas letras hayan sido inspiradas por una persona real?

B. Acercándose al tema Lea el título de esta ficha y las nueve palabras asociadas con el tema del amor trágico. Con un compañero / una compañera, decida si los espacios en blanco requieren un sustantivo, un verbo o un adjetivo. Luego, complete las oraciones con la forma apropiada de las palabras de la ficha.

Una historia de amor		
el dolor	la crisis	el preparativo
dejar	divorciarse	enamorarse
apasionado/a	apenado/a	utópico/a

1. Al llegar a Yucatán, Alma conoció a Felipe y ____________ de inmediato de ese hombre ____________ y visionario.
2. Creció entre ellos un amor intenso. Compartían ideales similares, enmarcados por sus sueños ____________ de crear un mundo más justo.
3. Pero Felipe estaba casado con hijos y su relación con Alma les causó mucho ____________. Sin embargo, su amor por Alma era tan fuerte que ____________ de su mujer e hizo planes para casarse con Alma.
4. Alma volvió a San Francisco para empezar los ____________ para la boda, pero Felipe, mientras tanto, se encontró con una ____________ política de fuertes dimensiones en Yucatán.
5. Doce días antes de la boda, Felipe fue asesinado por los enemigos del estado. Así ____________ a su alma gemela destrozada y profundamente ____________.

Peregrina

VOCABULARIO

VISUALIZAR

«Por la tarde había llovido, y al cruzar por la barriada del suburbio de San Sebastián, la vegetación y la tierra recién humedecidas por el aguacero[1] *exhalaban esa penetrante fragancia*[V] *que les es peculiar en tales casos. Alma aspiró profundamente aquel perfume, y dijo: «que bien huele*[2]*», y yo, por gastarle una galantería*[3] *le repliqué: «Sí, huele porque usted pasa. Las flores silvestres*[4] *se abren para perfumarla...» Carrillo Puerto dijo al punto: «Eso se lo vas a decir a Alma en una poesía». No, le repliqué yo, se lo diré en una canción. Y en efecto, en esa misma noche hice la letra*[5] *y al siguiente día vi a Ricardo Palmerín y se la entregué para que le pusiera música. Así nació «La Peregrina».*

Alma Reed

Con estas palabras narró Luis Rosado Vega, el poeta, el momento que dio origen a una de las más hermosas canciones yucatecas.

VOCABULARIO

Alma María Sullivan fue de las primeras mujeres que ejercieron el periodismo en San Francisco, California. De un breve matrimonio con Samuel Payne Reed, tomó el apellido y desde entonces fue conocida como Alma Reed. Escribía una columna llamada «Mrs. Goodfellow» en la que daba consejos legales a familias de inmigrantes ilegales que padecían[6] los abusos de aquella sociedad. En 1921, su labor periodística logró salvar la vida de un joven de 17 años condenado a muerte, de origen mexicano, llamado Simón Ruiz; de este caso resultó que las Leyes de California modificaron la manera de juzgar a los menores. La relevancia de este trabajo motivó que el presidente Álvaro Obregón la invitara a México y así, en 1922, por primera vez visitó a nuestro país, del que se enamoró profundamente.

VERIFICAR

¿Quién(es)? ¿Dónde? ¿Qué pasó?

A su regreso a San Francisco, la esperaba un ofrecimiento de trabajo del *New York Times*, el que aceptó y fue asignada para cubrir los trabajos arqueológicos en la zona maya, en Yucatán. Ahí entrevistó a Edward Thompson, el arqueólogo que tenía años excavando en la zona. Éste le confesó que había sacado muchas piezas valiosas del Cenote Sagrado de Chichén Itzá y las había enviado al Museo Peabody de Harvard. Alma Reed inició una serie de reportajes denunciando este hecho y a la larga, se logró la repatriación de muchas de estas piezas.

VOCABULARIO

[1]*downpour* [2]*it smells* [3]por... *to be gallant toward her* [4]*wild* [5]*lyrics* [6]sufrían

VOCABULARIO

Felipe Carrillo Puerto

En febrero de 1923, su camino se cruzó con el de Felipe Carrillo Puerto, gobernador de Yucatán. Personaje de fuerte personalidad e ideas socialistas, que tenía años luchando por los indígenas mayas y que se encontraba en la cúspide de su carrera. Dicen, quienes fueron testigos,[7] que fue un amor a primera vista. Durante ese año, vivieron un intenso romance que desembocó[8] en el divorcio de Carrillo Puerto y una promesa de boda que nunca se consumó. Este tiempo, vio coincidir[9] a una pareja de soñadores enamorados, a un poeta (Luis Rosado Vega) y a un músico (Ricardo Palmerín); que en una canción dejaron una eterna huella[10] de aquella historia.*

VERIFICAR ¿Quién(es)? ¿Dónde? ¿Qué pasó?

VISUALIZAR VOCABULARIO VOCABULARIO

El 3 de enero de 1924, mientras Alma Reed hacía los preparativos para la boda en San Francisco, Carrillo Puerto moría fusilado[11] en la ciudad de Mérida por tropas de Adolfo de la Huerta que se habían rebelado contra el presidente Álvaro Obregón. Se cuenta que, cuando era conducido al paredón,[12] sacó de uno de sus bolsos un anillo[13] y le pidió a uno de sus ejecutores que lo entregara a Pixan Halel, en maya: Alma y Caña (Reed).[V] La herida en el corazón de Alma Reed nunca cerró. No obstante, siguió trabajando intensamente en lo que le gustaba… el periodismo. En 1928, conoció a José Clemente Orozco y se convirtió en su admiradora y promotora, exponiendo sus trabajos en New York. Cuentan las malas lenguas que hubo entre ellos una relación sentimental, que no llegó a mayores porque Orozco era casado y Alma nunca olvidó a Felipe. Su labor de promotora de artistas mexicanos se extendió también a David Alfaro Siqueiros. En 1961, el presidente Adolfo López Mateos reconoció el amor que Alma Reed tenía por México y le otorgó el Águila Azteca.[14]

[7]*witnesses* [8]*culminated* [9]vio… *saw the coming together of* [10]*print, mark* [11]*shot* [12]lugar de fusilamiento [13]*ring* [14]Águila… *The Order of the Aztec Eagle, the highest honor awarded by the Mexican government to a foreign national, for services given to Mexico or humankind in general*

VERIFICAR ¿Quién(es)? ¿Dónde? ¿Qué pasó?

*Se refiere aquí a la canción «La Peregrina».

En un día del año 1965, una anciana de mirada azul dormido, se acercó al entonces senador por Yucatán,[V] Carlos Loret de Mola y le dijo: «Usted ocupará algún día la silla de Felipe, yo no lo veré como gobernador porque moriré pronto; pero quiero pedirle que cuando yo muera, me sepulten[15] en Mérida, cerca de Felipe». Unos meses después, el 20 de noviembre de 1966, Alma Reed murió a los 77 años en la Ciudad de México, a causa de un cáncer en el estómago. Tuvo que esperar casi un año para que uno de sus viejos amigos recuperara sus cenizas[16] que habían quedado retenidas por falta de pago en las funerarias Gayosso. Fue entonces que Loret de Mola, aún sin ser gobernador, cumplió el último deseo de Alma Reed y hoy sus restos yacen[17] en la Ciudad Blanca, muy cerca de los de Felipe Carrillo Puerto. Así respondió «La Peregrina» a esa plegaria[18] que nació cuando coincidieron: un par de soñadores enamorados, un músico y un poeta.

[15]*bury* [16]*ashes* [17]*lie* [18]*prayer*

Después de leer

A. Comprensión Conteste las siguientes preguntas sobre la nota histórica y la lectura.

1. ¿Qué hacía Alma Reed antes de ir a México? ¿Qué evento hizo que viajara a México?
2. ¿Qúe hizo Alma después de entrevistar al arqueólogo Edward Thompson?
3. ¿Por qué fue Felipe Carrillo Puerto tan importante para la gente indígena yucateca?
4. ¿Cuál era la situación matrimonial de Carrillo cuando conoció a Reed?
5. ¿Qué pasó días antes de la boda de Alma y Felipe?
6. ¿Qué hizo Felipe minutos antes de ser fusilado?
7. ¿Cómo mantuvo Alma contacto con su querido México después de perder a su alma gemela?
8. ¿Qué favor quería Alma del senador Carlos Loret de Mola?

B. La famosa canción «La Peregrina»

Paso 1 Complete el siguiente párrafo con la forma correcta del pretérito, del imperfecto o del pluscuamperfecto (según el contexto).

La Peregrina

Cuando dejes mis palmeras
y mi tierra,
Peregrina del semblante
encantador:
No te olvides, no te olvides
de mi tierra,
no te olvides, no te olvides
de mi amor.

Alma Reed llegó a México por primera vez en 1921. Al bajar del tren un grupo de mariachis __________[1] (estar) allí para cantar una serenata a la esposa de un diplomático mexicano que __________[2] (haber / viajar) en el mismo tren con Alma. La primera canción que __________[3] (cantar) fue «Alma de mi alma». Alma __________[4] (pensar) que la canción __________[5] (ser) para ella y __________[6] (estar) tan afectada que __________[7] (empezar) a llorar. Luego __________[8] (abrazar) al representante del presidente Obregón, que __________[9] (haber / venir) a recogerla. Dos años más tarde, al escuchar la historia de la reacción emotiva de Alma ante la canción «Alma de mi alma», Felipe __________[10] (querer) regalarle una canción que contara la historia de una joven de California que __________[11] (haber / venir) a México para entrevistar al gobernador y cómo ellos ______________[12] (haber / enamorarse). Con la ayuda del poeta Luis Rosado Vega y el compositor Ricardo Palmerín __________[13] (nacer) la famosísima canción «La Peregrina».

Paso 2 En parejas, contesten las siguientes preguntas sobre la canción.

1. ¿Cómo piensa que Alma se sintió cuando se dio cuenta de que la canción no era para ella?
2. ¿Cómo se sentiría si alguien escribiera una canción dedicada a Ud. y luego esta canción se convirtiera en una canción popular a nivel nacional?

C. Para discutir

1. El padre de Alma le contaba cuentos sobre sus viajes a México. Estos cuentos despertaron en la niña un profundo interés en México y su gente. ¿Recuerda Ud. algunas historias de su infancia que todavía tengan un impacto en su vida? ¿Le contaron sus padres o abuelos cuentos de otros lugares o personas que hayan hecho que Ud. quisiera aprender más sobre otras culturas o viajar a otros países?
2. Algunas personas se sienten atraídas por personas de otras culturas. Otros creen que las diferencias culturales tienen un impacto negativo en las relaciones. ¿Cuál es su opinión? ¿Se casaría Ud. o saldría con una persona de otra cultura? En su opinión, ¿se aceptan las relaciones interétnicas o interculturales en su comunidad?
3. Los editores de Alma Reed le pidieron que fuera a México para entrevistar al gobernador socialista de Yucatán, al que le decían «la copia tropical de Abraham Lincoln». ¿Qué dos o tres preguntas habrá preparado Reed para hacerle a Felipe Carrillo antes de conocerlo?
4. Hoy en día, en este país la palabra «socialista» evoca pánico para mucha gente. ¿Por qué cree Ud. que esta palabra está tan cargada de connotaciones negativas?

D. **Reacciones** En parejas, imagínense que son mexicanos/as que viven durante la época de Alma Reed y Felipe Carrillo Puerto. Lean las siguientes oraciones y reaccionen ante cada una con una expresión como **Es triste que…, Es increíble que…, Es bueno que…** Explique su reacción a cada una.

1. Alma defiende a jóvenes mexicanos en los Estados Unidos y, en particular, a uno que es acusado falsamente de asesinato.
2. Como el nuevo gobernador de Yucatán, Felipe Carrillo Puerto da su primer discurso al público en la lengua maya.
3. Aunque Felipe está casado con otra mujer, Alma y Felipe son almas gemelas. Están verdaderamente enamorados y comparten los mismos ideales y sueños utópicos.
4. Un momento antes de ser fusilado, el gobernante yucateco llama a uno de sus ejecutores, pone en sus manos un anillo y le dice: «Entrégaselo a *Pixán Halal*».[a]

[a]*Pixán* significa **alma** en lenguaje maya-quiché y *Halal* significa **junco** (*reed*).

E. **El telegrama** Alma estaba ensayando para su boda en el Hotel Fairmont de San Francisco, con su vestido de novia y azahares (*orange blossoms*) tras las orejas, cuando de repente le pasaron un telegrama que acababa de llegar al hotel donde vivía. El telegrama decía: «Felipe Carrillo Puerto Asesinado».

Paso 1 En parejas, escriban cuatro o cinco oraciones describiendo lo que pasó cuando Alma leyó el telegrama.

Paso 2 Escríbanle a Alma una breve nota de pésame (*condolence*). Palabras útiles: **afectado/a, el dolor, el sentimiento, la tristeza**

¡A escribir!

A. **Lluvia de ideas** En grupos pequeños, generen ideas para crear una historia de amor que cada uno de Uds. va a escribir como composición.

1. **¿Dónde?** Hagan una lista de cinco lugares posibles donde pueda empezar la acción de su cuento.
2. **¿Quién(es)?** Luego, hagan una lista de cinco personas que puedan formar parte del conflicto entre los amantes de su historia.
3. **¿Qué pasó?** Finalmente, hagan una lista de cinco situaciones que puedan utilizar en la trama de su historia.

B. Composición: Narración en el pasado Escoja un lugar, una persona y una trama para su historia de amor. Siga el siguiente bosquejo.

1. escoger un título intrigante
2. escribir un párrafo introductorio explicando dónde se conocieron los amantes de su historia de amor
3. describir a los amantes con muchos detalles, su apariencia física y sus sentimientos
4. explicar cómo la entrada de una tercera persona complica la vida de los amantes
5. escribir una conclusión describiendo cómo terminó la historia

C. Diálogo Lea la historia de amor de un compañero / una compañera y luego preparen Uds. un diálogo entre una de las personas de cada historia en el que cuenten lo que pasó un año después.

Hablando del tema

Antes de empezar a conversar con sus compañeros de clase sobre los siguientes temas, prepare una ficha para la conversación, otra para el debate y otra para la reacción ante la cita.

A. Conversación: Las amistades íntimas Revise las expresiones en **Para conversar mejor.** Luego, en parejas o grupos de tres, conversen sobre los siguientes puntos.

Para conversar mejor

Al principio pensaba que...
Creo que...
En nuestro caso...
Fue alucinante/chistoso cuando...
No hay ninguna duda que...
Nos conocimos en....
Es evidente que...
Teníamos... en común.

- Describa una de sus amistades más íntimas. ¿Qué intereses comparte con su amigo/a?
- ¿Cómo se conocieron Uds.?
- Haga una comparación entre sus propias características personales y las de este amigo íntimo / esta amiga íntima.
- ¿Qué recomienda Ud. que hagan los demás para establecer y fomentar relaciones íntimas y duraderas?

B. Debate: Cómo conocer a su media naranja Revise las expresiones en **Para debatir mejor.** Después, prepare tres argumentos a favor y tres en contra sobre el uso del Internet para conocer a su media naranja. Luego, presente sus argumentos en un debate. No sabrá qué lado tendrá que defender.

Para debatir mejor

A FAVOR	EN CONTRA
Así es.	De ninguna manera.
Exacto.	Lo siento, pero…
Podría ser.	No sabes lo que dices.
Tienes razón.	Temo que estés equivocado/a.

«Hoy en día, si Ud. no quiere buscar pareja en un bar o someterse a citas a ciegas, conocer a una persona genial a través del Internet es una buena opción. Puede saber de antemano (*beforehand*) cómo es su aspecto físico, cuáles son sus intereses y cómo es su personalidad.»

«Para muchos solteros, con el ritmo de vida tan acelerado que llevan, conocer a su pareja a través de un servicio del Internet es una pérdida de tiempo. Las citas rápidas (*speed dating*) les dejan conocerse cara a cara y saber inmediatamente si hay química o no.»

C. Reacción: Ciertas diferencias no son posibles Revise las expresiones en **Para reaccionar mejor.** Luego, reaccione ante la siguiente cita. Añada razones que apoyen sus opiniones.

Para reaccionar mejor

Creo/Opino/Supongo que…
Es bueno/malo que…
Es difícil que…
Es poco probable que…
Es posible que…
Es verdad que…

«Me sería imposible casarme o tener una amistad íntima con una persona de otro partido político.»

CAPÍTULO 4

La vida moderna:

Las obligaciones y el tiempo libre

Punto clave

GUSTOS

Temas centrales

- el estrés
- el ocio
- el humor

Zona de enfoque

- El Cono Sur

La Plaza Dorrego en Buenos Aires

MULTIMEDIA

Estampillas musicales

Lugares fascinantes

Online *Manual*
www.mhcentro.com

Online Learning Center
www.mhhe.com/puntoyaparte4

En este capítulo Ud. va a explorar el tema de sus obligaciones, en cuanto a sus estudios y el trabajo, y lo que hace para pasarlo bien y relajarse.

Preguntas para considerar

- ¿Se siente Ud. estresado/a por sus obligaciones académicas y su trabajo?
- ¿Qué hace para aliviar el estrés?
- ¿Cuáles son las actividades que lo/la ayudan a relajarse?
- ¿Tiene Ud. un lugar especial para escaparse de vez en cuando?
- ¿Qué importancia tiene el humor en su vida diaria?
- La escena que se ve en esta página muestra uno de los escapes de la vida diaria en la Argentina. ¿Qué papel desempeñan la música y el baile en su vida?

Hay que ser más fiesteros

¡Tienes que relajarte, Diego!

Situación: Los cinco amigos pasaron un largo fin de semana en un rancho cerca de San Antonio. El dueño, Francisco Ramos, tiene una casa alucinante. Cada cuarto está decorado con artesanías de los países hispanos que Fran ha visitado. Como es de imaginar, a Diego le encantó. Lea el diálogo y preste especial atención al uso del vocabulario nuevo, que está **en negrita.**

DIEGO: Uds. tenían razón. Pasar un fin de semana fuera era exactamente lo que necesitaba para **relajarme. Lo pasé de maravilla.** Me siento totalmente **renovado.**

SARA: Pues tú **trabajas como una mula.** Verte **tenso** y **agotado** nos tenía a todos preocupados.

DIEGO: Aprecio su preocupación por mi **bienestar** y les prometo que ahora con la ayuda de Francisco en Tesoros voy a tomar más tiempo para **cargar las pilas.** Pero…

SARA: Pero ¿qué? No empieces.

DIEGO: Mira, Sara, tienes que entender algo: me fascina mi trabajo, me anima, me emociona poder compartir…

SARA: Ya lo sé. Es que extrañamos al viejo Diego que bailaba, cocinaba y nos hacía **reírnos a carcajadas** hasta las 4:00 de **la madrugada.**

DIEGO: Como te dije, voy a **tratar de** tener más equilibrio en mi vida. Pero para **tener éxito** en mi trabajo y **realizar** mis sueños, tengo que estar **dispuesto a** trabajar duro.

SARA: La verdad es que los cinco somos muy trabajadores y entendemos tu dedicación, pero quiero que sepas que nos encantó verte tan **animado, bromeando** con todos y **disfrutando de** la vida.

DIEGO: Fue realmente un fin de semana perfecto. Francisco es buenísima gente y estoy súper contento de que pueda trabajar conmigo en Tesoros. Va a cambiar mi vida.

SARA: ¡Ojalá! Cristina estará muy **satisfecha** si de verdad funciona.

DIEGO: Sí, estaba **hasta las narices** conmigo y con mi trabajo. Pero me da mucho gusto decirte que ya invité a Cristina a **un espectáculo** en Nueva York para su cumpleaños y dejaré a Francisco encargado de la tienda.

SARA: ¡Adiós, **aguafiestas.** Hola, querido Diego!

ACTIVIDADES

A. **Detective** Busque en el diálogo ejemplos de las siguientes metas comunicativas: Reacciones y recomendaciones (R), Narración en el pasado (P), Hablar de los gustos (G) y Hablar del futuro (F). Subraye cada palabra o frase que represente una (o una combinación) de estas metas comunicativas. Luego, escriba al margen la(s) letra(s) que corresponde(n) a cada ejemplo subrayado (R, P, G o F).

MODELOS: Sí, <u>estaba</u> hasta las narices conmigo y con mi trabajo. (P)
Verte tenso y agotado <u>nos preocupaba</u> a todos. (G) (P)

B. **Comprensión** Conteste las siguientes preguntas, según el diálogo.

1. ¿Por qué está tan contento Diego?
2. ¿De qué se queja Sara?
3. ¿Cómo era Diego antes?
4. ¿Por qué puede Diego cambiar su vida ahora?
5. ¿Quién estará contenta con este cambio y por qué?

C. **Reacciones y recomendaciones** Complete las siguientes oraciones sobre la conversación de Diego y Sara, utilizando un conector en cada oración.

MODELO: Es bueno que Diego pueda tomar un poco de tiempo para cargar las pilas, ya que trabajar demasiado no es bueno para la salud.

1. Es interesante que su amigo Francisco…
2. Es una lástima que Diego…
3. Sara cree que Diego…
4. Es preocupante que en la vida moderna…

Conectores

además
en cambio
para que + *subjuntivo*
por lo tanto
porque
puesto que
sin embargo
ya que

D. **Diálogo** En parejas, preparen un diálogo entre Sergio y Cristina en el que hablen de lo que harán Diego y ella cuando vayan a Nueva York y de cómo ella puede asegurarse de que Diego no trabaje mientras estén allí. Luego, preséntenlo a la clase.

Vocabulario del tema

Para hablar de las obligaciones

aprovechar(se) (de)	to take advantage of
aumentar	to increase
desvelarse	to stay awake all night
disminuir	to decrease
madrugar	to get up early
mejorar	to improve (make better)
ponerse al día	to catch up
posponer (*like* **poner**)	to postpone
realizar	to accomplish, fulfill (a goal)
seguir + -ndo	to keep doing something
tener éxito	to be successful
trabajar como una mula*	to work like a dog
tratar de	to try to

Para describir el estado de ánimo

agobiado/a	overwhelmed
agotado/a	exhausted
angustiado/a	distressed
animado/a	in good spirits
desanimado/a	bummed
descansado/a	rested
dispuesto/a (a)	willing (to)
entusiasmado/a	enthusiastic
estresado/a	stressed (out)
harto/a	fed up
hasta las narices	fed up to here
quemado/a	burned out
relajado/a	relaxed
renovado/a	renewed
satisfecho/a	satisfied
tenso/a	tense
vago/a†	lazy

Para hablar del tiempo libre

aliviar	to relieve
cargar las pilas	to recharge one's batteries
charlar	to chat
disfrutar de	to enjoy

De vacaciones: ¿Cómo carga Ud. sus pilas?

entretener(se) (*like* **tener**)	to entertain (oneself)
estar de buen/mal humor	to be in a good/bad mood
pasarlo bien/mal	to have a good/bad time
relajarse	to relax
reunirse (me reúno) (con)	to get together (with)
tener mucha marcha	to have a lively social scene

Para hablar del humor

bromear	to joke around
levantar el ánimo	to lift the spirits
reírse (i, i) (me río) a carcajadas	to laugh out loud
sonreír(se) (*like* **reír**)	to smile
la broma	practical joke
el chiste	joke
la risa	laughter
chistoso/a	funny
comiquísimo/a	hilarious

*Literally: *to work like a mule*

†**Vago** used with **estar** indicates a temporary condition, whereas when used with **ser** it indicates an inherent characteristic.

entretenido/a	entertaining
de mal gusto	in poor taste

Para describir las diversiones

el/la aguafiestas	party pooper
el bienestar	well-being
el chisme	gossip
el espectáculo	show, performance
la madrugada	early morning
los ratos libres	free time
el recreo	recreation
la resaca	hangover

Expresiones útiles para hablar del tiempo libre

¡Que lo pase/ pases/pasen bien! ¡Que se divierta / te diviertas / se diviertan!	Have a good time!
¿Cómo lo pasó/ pasaste/pasaron?	How was it?, Did you have a good time?
Lo pasé muy bien / de maravilla / fatal.	I had a great time / a blast / a terrible time.

ACTIVIDADES

A. Vocabulario en contexto

Paso 1 Indique quién hace las siguientes cosas: Ud., su madre, padre, hermano/a, hijo/a, amigo/a, compañero/a de cuarto, nadie, etcétera.

1. Les levanta el ánimo a los que están quemados.
2. Trabaja como una mula y no es capaz de relajarse.
3. Está dispuesto/a a desvelarse para ayudar a un amigo con un proyecto.
4. Sabe los chismes de todos sus amigos y también de los ricos y famosos.
5. Piensa que es importantísimo tener éxito profesional.
6. Siempre sonríe y está animado/a.
7. Está agobiado/a porque con frecuencia pospone el trabajo que tiene que hacer.
8. Aprovecha sus ratos libres para ponerse al día con los estudios o el trabajo.
9. Sigue bromeando aunque todos están hartos de sus bromas.

Paso 2 En parejas, compartan sus respuestas del **Paso 1.** Escojan dos situaciones y amplíen sus respuestas para dar ejemplos concretos de lo que hace la persona indicada en cada situación.

B. Decisiones

Paso 1 Conteste las siguientes preguntas y explíquele sus respuestas a un compañero / una compañera.

	SÍ	NO
1. Después de haberse desvelado en una fiesta fantástica, ¿madrugaría Ud. al día siguiente para hacer ejercicio antes de asistir a su primera clase?	☐	☐
2. ¿Pospondría una entrevista para un trabajo importante si tuviera la oportunidad de asistir a un concierto de su grupo musical favorito?	☐	☐

	SÍ	NO
3. ¿Iría a clase con una resaca tremenda?	☐	☐
4. ¿Estaría dispuesto/a a suspender sus estudios por un año para trabajar en Cancún?	☐	☐
5. ¿Gastaría más de 200 dólares en una de las siguientes cosas: un partido de fútbol, una obra de teatro de *Broadway* en Nueva York, un concierto, una botella de vino, un suéter, un masaje?	☐	☐
6. ¿Iría de compras para aliviar el estrés?	☐	☐
7. Después de trabajar como una mula todo el día, ¿iría a un lugar con mucha marcha para pasarlo bien?	☐	☐

Paso 2 Según las respuestas y las explicaciones ¿es su compañero/a una persona atrevida o cautelosa? Explique por qué.

C. **Preguntas personales** En parejas, contesten las siguientes preguntas. Mientras escucha a su compañero/a, reaccione con algunas expresiones de **Para conversar mejor.** Luego, revelen a la clase lo que cada uno/a averiguó de su compañero/a.

Para conversar mejor

¡Increíble!	Estoy de acuerdo.
¡Qué chistoso!	Es igual para mí.
¿De veras?	Yo (A mí) también/tampoco.
¿En serio?	¡Fenomenal!
¡Qué horror!	¡Qué idea más buena!

1. Describa a la persona más fiestera que Ud. conozca. ¿Qué le gusta hacer a esta persona en las fiestas? ¿Les molesta a los otros invitados lo que hace esta persona? Explique su respuesta.

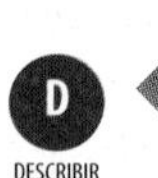

2. ¿Qué hace el aguafiestas típico? ¿Es Ud. extrovertido/a o introvertido/a en una fiesta? ¿Ha sido alguna vez un(a) aguafiestas? Explique su respuesta.

3. ¿Es la música una parte importante de su vida? ¿Qué tipo de música le gusta escuchar cuando se siente estresado/a, nostálgico/a, de buen humor, triste?

   Si pudiera conocer a cualquier cantante o músico, ¿a quién le interesaría conocer? ¿Por qué?

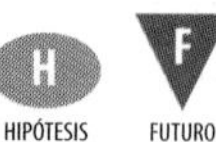

4. ¿Qué le gusta hacer para aliviar el estrés?

   Si fuera el decano / la decana (*dean*) encargado/a de (*in charge of*) los servicios estudiantiles, ¿qué recursos ofrecería para ayudar a los estudiantes a disminuir el estrés?

   ¿Qué hará durante las próximas vacaciones para relajarse?

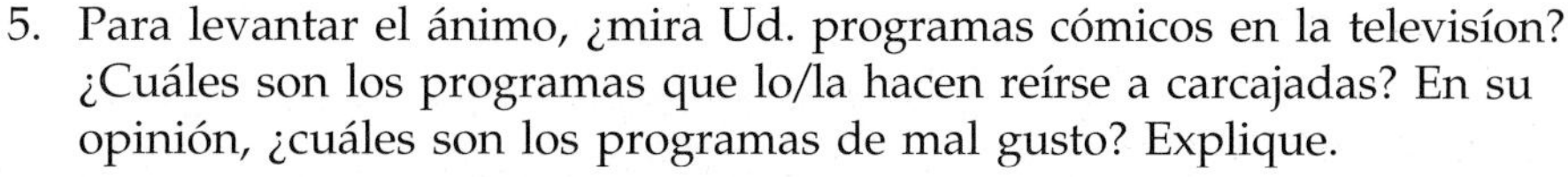

5. Para levantar el ánimo, ¿mira Ud. programas cómicos en la televisíon? ¿Cuáles son los programas que lo/la hacen reírse a carcajadas? En su opinión, ¿cuáles son los programas de mal gusto? Explique.

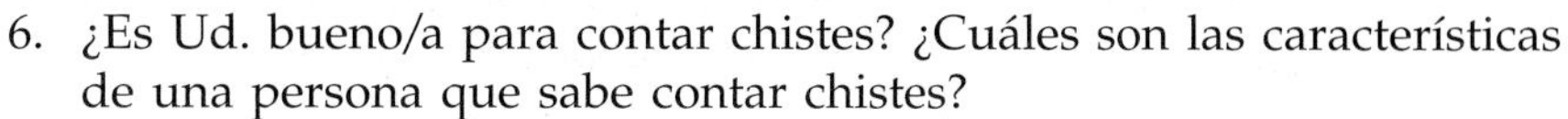

6. ¿Es Ud. bueno/a para contar chistes? ¿Cuáles son las características de una persona que sabe contar chistes?

D. Para combatir el estrés

Paso 1 Lea las descripciones de tres lugares excelentes para divertirse en el Cono Sur durante el mes de febrero, cuando las temperaturas del verano son perfectas y el ambiente es alucinante.

1. **Punta del Este, Uruguay** Es una ciudad que está en la costa del Océano Atlántico y es un lugar favorito de los ricos y famosos para veranear. Se considera como «la Riviera de Sudamérica». La playa está rodeada de bellos bosques de pinos; las olas, de más de diez pies de altura, son perfectas para hacer surfing. Hay grandes mansiones, pistas de golf y tenis y casinos lujosos.
2. **Viña del Mar, Chile** Es una ciudad balnearia[1] que fue fundada hace más de 100 años. Tiene lujosas villas de comienzos del siglo XX con torrecillas miradores[2] que dan al mar,[3] así como casas modernas de estilo elegante. Cada mes de febrero se celebra allí el gran Festival de Música de Viña del Mar, en el que tocan músicos hispanos de todo el mundo. Este festival es tal vez la reunión de estrellas hispanas más grande del mundo.

3. **Buenos Aires, Argentina** Es conocida como «el París de Sudamérica». Se puede encontrar cafés en casi todas las esquinas, desde los más elegantes y caros hasta los más sencillos. En el centro de la ciudad hay más de 70 cines. Las representaciones teatrales en Buenos Aires, por otro lado, son más numerosas que en París o Nueva York. La vida nocturna es alucinante. Se dice que en la calle Corrientes, la calle principal, nunca se duerme. ¡Las discotecas y los clubes no cierran de la madrugada!

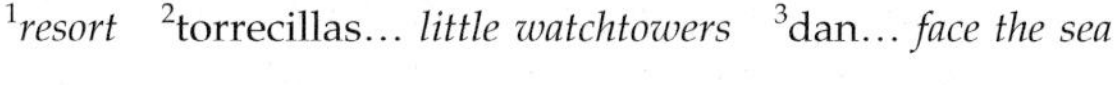

[1]*resort* [2]torrecillas... *little watchtowers* [3]dan... *face the sea*

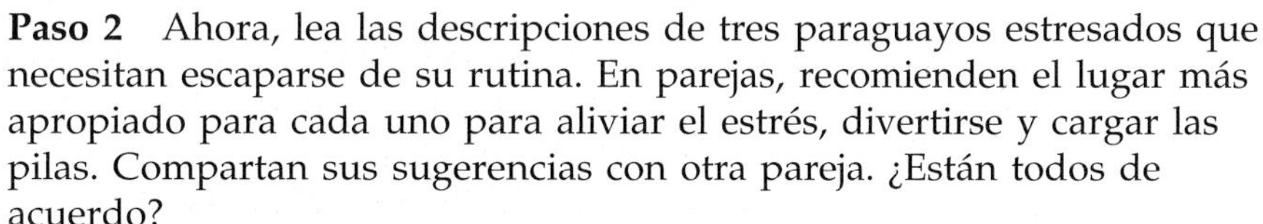

Paso 2 Ahora, lea las descripciones de tres paraguayos estresados que necesitan escaparse de su rutina. En parejas, recomienden el lugar más apropiado para cada uno para aliviar el estrés, divertirse y cargar las pilas. Compartan sus sugerencias con otra pareja. ¿Están todos de acuerdo?

1. Arturo Baca, un actor que está angustiado porque no consiguió un papel en un espectáculo, dado que no sabe bailar bien.
2. Teresa Palacios, una estudiante que está hasta las narices con sus estudios y con su ex novio, quien sigue llamándola tres veces al día.
3. Carolina Castañeda, una bibliotecaria que está desanimada porque vive en un pueblo pequeño, sin mucha marcha.

   Arturo, sabemos que Ud.... Sin embargo, le aconsejamos que...

   Teresa, es muy importante que Ud.... Por eso sugerimos que...

   Carolina, recomendamos que... porque...

E. **Problemas repentinos** Entre todos, revisen los siguientes problemas y hagan una lista de palabras nuevas de este capítulo y de los capítulos anteriores que los ayuden a conversar con facilidad sobre cada problema repentino. Después, en parejas, preparen un diálogo espontáneo sobre cada problema.

1. Un consejero/Una consejera y una persona que está «quemada» por el exceso de trabajo están en una sesión de terapia. El/La paciente se queja de su trabajo y el consejero / la consejera trata de convencerle de que tome clases de baile o música para aliviar el estrés.
2. Una persona muy bromista trata de levantarle el ánimo a un amigo / una amiga que está desanimado/a porque tiene que posponer sus vacaciones.

NOTA CULTURAL • ¿Quiénes son los más fiesteros?

La primera vez que Diego recibió una invitación para ir a una fiesta en los Estados Unidos, se sorprendió mucho. ¡La invitación indicaba la hora en que iba a terminar la fiesta! Eso nunca pasaría en el mundo hispano, en donde se indica la hora en que comienza una fiesta (algo que no siempre se respeta), pero se considera de mala educación decirles a los invitados que tienen que irse a una hora determinada. La costumbre estadounidense puede resultar un choque cultural para los hispanos. De hecho, a Javier le molesta tanto que él se niega a ir a una fiesta si la invitación indica cuándo va a terminar.

En el mundo hispano, el invitado tiene derecho a quedarse todo el tiempo que quiera en una reunión o una fiesta, y el anfitrión tiene el deber de atenderlo. En el Ecuador, Laura asistió a una boda que empezó a las 7:00 de la noche y no terminó hasta las 7:00 de la mañana del día siguiente. Era muy diferente de las bodas estadounidenses que ella conocía, pero no parecía que los novios estuvieran enojados con sus invitados. Al contrario, se rieron, cantaron y bailaron con los otros hasta que se fue la última persona. Sergio también prefiere las fiestas alegres y largas de su familia mexicana a las cenas cortas y secas que tiene con su familia de los Estados Unidos.

En fin, cada cultura es diferente y hay que respetar las costumbres especiales. Sin embargo, cuando Ud. vaya a una fiesta en un país hispano, ¡no se sorprenda si no termina nunca!

Preguntas

1. ¿Por qué sería de mal gusto ponerle horas fijas a una fiesta en Latinoamérica?
2. ¿Qué le parece a Ud. la flexibilidad que hay en el mundo hispano en cuanto al horario de las fiestas? ¿Por qué?
3. ¿A qué hora suelen empezar y terminar las bodas en su país? ¿Le gustaría ir a una boda que durara hasta la mañana siguiente?

Actividad

En parejas, escriban un diálogo en el que uno de Uds. haga el papel de un anfitrión / una anfitriona estadounidense que está cansado/a y quiere pedirles a sus invitados, de manera educada, que se vayan. La otra persona será un invitado hispano / una invitada hispana que no entiende las indirectas (*discreet hints*) de su anfitrión/anfitriona.

Puntos clave

GUSTOS

Hablar de los gustos

En esta sección del capítulo, Ud. va a practicar la meta comunicativa **Hablar de los gustos.** Para hacerlo bien, hay que utilizar las estructuras gramaticales (los puntos clave) de la siguiente tabla que pertenecen a la meta comunicativa. Antes de continuar, estudie las explicaciones de estas estructuras gramaticales en las páginas verdes que están al final del libro.

LA META COMUNICATIVA DE ESTE CAPÍTULO		
ICONO	META COMUNICATIVA	PUNTOS CLAVE
G GUSTOS	Hablar de los gustos	• los verbos como **gustar** • los pronombres de complemento indirecto • el subjuntivo después de **me gusta que...**

PRUEBA DIAGNÓSTICA

Un amigo argentino de Javier nos habla de la importancia del fútbol en su país. Llene los espacios en blanco con la forma más apropiada del verbo que está entre paréntesis, junto con el pronombre de complemento indirecto adecuado.

Desde niño, (a mí) __________[1] (encantar) ver el fútbol con mi padre y mi abuelo. (A nosotros) __________[2] (emocionar) especialmente los campeonatos[1] grandes, como la Copa Libertadores o la Copa Mundial.

No somos solamente fanáticos «de sofá». Mi padre juega en una liga de hombres de su edad y, cuando yo siento mucho estrés, __________[3] (dar ganas de) correr por el campo de fútbol y patear la pelota duro.[2] Desde luego, __________[4] (convenir) hacer ejercicios para aliviar las tensiones en vez de fumar o tomar alcohol.

En contra de lo que se suele pensar, el fútbol no es un espacio exclusivamente masculino. Es cierto que a mi madre y mi abuela __________[5] (aburrir) los partidos de fútbol, pero a muchas chicas jóvenes __________[6] (fascinar) este deporte tanto como a los chicos. Hay cada vez más ligas femeninas. A algunos de mis amigos __________[7] (fastidiar) que las chicas ocupen «sus» campos de fútbol en los parques, pero a mí no. De hecho, __________[8] (caer fenomenal) las chicas deportistas.

Un partido de la Copa Mundial entre Brasil y Honduras

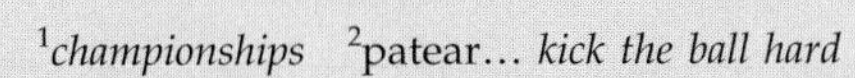
[1]*championships* [2]patear... *kick the ball hard*

Expresiones útiles*

Para hablar de lo que le gusta

me apetece(n)	*I feel like*
me cae(n) bien/fenomenal	*I really like (person or people)*
me conviene(n)	*It's good (a good idea) for me to*
me da(n) ganas de	*I feel like*
me emociona(n)	*I'm excited by*
me encanta(n)	*I love, really like*
me fascina(n)	*I'm fascinated by*
me importa(n)	*I care about*
me interesa(n)	*I'm interested in*

Para expresar lo que no le gusta

me aburre(n)	*I'm bored by*
me cae(n) mal/fatal	*I don't like (person or people)*
me da(n) asco	*I'm disgusted by*
me disgusta(n)	*I'm annoyed by*
me fastidia(n) me molesta(n)	*I'm bothered by*
me preocupa(n)	*I'm worried about*

Para expresar indiferencia

me da igual me da(n) lo mismo me es igual	*I don't care, it's all the same to me*
no me importa(n)	*I don't care (about)*
no me interesa(n)	*I'm not interested (in)*

ACTIVIDADES

Las siguientes actividades le darán la oportunidad de practicar las metas comunicativas. Habrá un énfasis particular en expresar los gustos.

A. La vida nocturna Se dice que los argentinos nunca duermen. Buenos Aires es una ciudad de mucha marcha. Muchos extranjeros que visitan esta capital porteña quedan alucinados por su intensa actividad nocturna. Pero Buenos Aires tiene competencia: Madrid y Nueva York tienen también mucha movida.

---

*Note that for all of these **gustar**-like constructions, if they are immediately followed by **que** + *verb phrase*, the verb in that following verb phrase must be in the subjunctive.

Me molesta *que* mis vecinos *hagan* ruido después de la medianoche.

but

Me molesta *el ruido*. (followed by a noun)

and

Me molesta *desvelarme* por el ruido que hacen mis vecinos. (followed by an infinitive)

Paso 1 Lea los siguientes anuncios sobre la vida nocturna en Buenos Aires, Madrid y Nueva York.

La marcha mundial

Buenos Aires
A medianoche termina la primera sesión designada para los chicos menores de 18 años y empieza la marcha de verdad. Los boliches[1] porteños antes se quedaban abiertos hasta las 5:00, pero hace cuatro años, una nueva ley require que cierren a las 3:00.

¡OJO!
Cuidado con los patovicas.[2] Son personal que ofrece servicio de seguridad para los locales de baile pero recientemente han sido muy agresivos hacia los clientes jóvenes.

Madrid
En general, los lugares para ir a bailar abren a las 20 horas, pero este horario es para la juventud, menores de 16 años. Los jóvenes tienen que salir a las 23:00 cuando abren otra vez para los mayores. Las discotecas suelen permanecer abiertas hasta las 3:00 ó 4:00 aunque los sábados y domingos se extiende hasta las 5:00.

¡OJO!
Mucha gente que vive cerca de las discotecas se queja de «la contaminación sonora» que causan las discotecas madrileñas.

Nueva York
Las discotecas de Nueva York están casi vacías hasta las 22 horas, pero a partir de la medianoche empieza la bulla[3] y sigue hasta que cierran las puertas a las 4:00. Van los mayores de 18 ó 21 años.

¡OJO!
En las discos más de moda los sacabullas[4] determinan quién entra y quién no. Así que es recomendable vestirse de moda y esperar que tenga suerte. Es una movida muy esnob.

[1]*disco bars* [2]*bouncers* [3]*commotion* [4]*bouncers*

Paso 2 En parejas, formen oraciones completas con los elementos que están entre las diagonales. Luego, reaccionen a cada oración, añadiendo el por qué de sus reacciones. Sigan el modelo.

MODELO: los vecinos madrileños / molestar / el ruido que producen las discotecas

Es necesario que… porque… →

A los vecinos madrileños les molesta el ruido que producen las discotecas.

Es necesario que los vecinos se quejen con las autoridades, porque tienen el derecho de dormir tranquilos por la noche.

1. los madrileños jóvenes / molestar / el horario restrictivo

   No es justo que… porque…

2. los sacabullas en los clubes neoyorquinos / importar / la apariencia física de los clientes

   Es frustrante que… porque…

(*continúa*)

3. los chicos argentinos menores de 18 años / encantar / bailar

   No les gusta que... porque...
4. los padres de los jóvenes / preocupar / la agresividad de los patovicas argentinos

   Es importante que... porque...
5. las mujeres / convenir / vestirse a la última moda si quieren entrar en los clubes de Nueva York

   Es ridículo que... porque...

Paso 3 En grupos pequeños, hablen de un lugar con mucha marcha en su ciudad. ¿Tienen que vestirse bien para entrar? ¿Cómo está decorado el lugar? ¿Quién frecuenta este lugar? ¿Por qué es tan popular?

Paso 4 Escriba un anuncio para la gente joven de su ciudad sobre un lugar nuevo con mucha marcha.

B. El mate: Un ritual de la amistad

Paso 1 Lea la siguiente descripción del mate y lo que significa para la gente del Cono Sur.

Un gaucho con su mate

Quizás más que cualquier otra actividad, el ritual del mate refleja la esencia del Cono Sur. Es una práctica cultural que cruza las fronteras entre profesiones, etnicidades, géneros y clases sociales. El mate se hace de yerba mate, una hierba amarga[1] similar al té, y se toma sobre todo en compañía de amigos en un ritual elaborado que tiene sus raíces en la época precolombina. Es típico utilizar un recipiente especial que también se llama «mate». Se pasa este recipiente de persona a persona y cada uno bebe el mate por la misma bombilla.[2]

No es simplemente otra bebida caliente como el café o el té; el mate tiene sus propios mitos y tradiciones. El ritual del mate enfatiza la importancia de convivir con los amigos, colegas y familiares. Provee un momento para conversar y relajarse. Simboliza la amistad, el respeto, el cariño y la generosidad. Una invitación a tomar mate es una señal de que a uno le han aceptado en el grupo, y sería falta de educación negarse a[3] tomarlo.

[1]*bitter* [2]*straw* [3]negarse... *to refuse*

Paso 2 Contesten las siguientes preguntas en grupos de cuatro.

1. ¿Por qué creen Uds. que a las personas del Cono Sur les gusta el mate?
2. ¿Qué les parece la tradición de tomar mate? ¿Les gustaría probarlo? ¿Por qué sí o por qué no? ¿Les molestaría compartir la misma bombilla con otras personas? Expliquen.
3. Si Uds. estuvieran en la Argentina por un año, ¿qué bebidas o comidas les gustaría tener disponibles (*available*) para aliviar su nostalgia para su propio país?

Paso 3 En parejas, pensando en el ritual del mate y en sus propios rituales con sus amigos, formen oraciones con la información dada. **¡OJO!** Recuerden que los verbos para expresar gustos requieren el subjuntivo después de **que.**

1. los uruguayos / encantar / que el ritual del mate / ser un evento social
2. los argentinos / fastidiar / que en el mundo moderno / no haber tiempo para relajarse
3. mis amigos y yo / encantar / que nuestro café favorito / estar cerca del campus
4. los estudiantes / gustar / que los cafés locales / dejarles quedarse por horas sin molestarlos

C. Los pasatiempos de los argentinos En parejas, lean cada afirmación y completen las tres oraciones que siguen.

Clase de tango

1. En Buenos Aires dan clases de tango al mediodía. La gente baila por una hora y vuelve a trabajar renovada.
   a. A los jefes no les preocupa que... por eso...
   b. Es bueno que... porque...
   c. Es ridículo que... porque...
2. El tango es mucho más que un baile: se baila, se escucha, se toma su *look;* también es una manera de cuidar la salud y de encontrar amor y compañía.
   a. No me interesa que... porque...
   b. Para los tangueros es importante que... por eso...
   c. Es obvio que... sin embargo...
3. Finlandia y Japón son unos de los países donde más se baila el tango.
   a. Me sorprende que... porque...
   b. Es posible que... pero...
   c. Dudo que... porque...

Unos aficionados apasionados

4. Según Mónica, una amiga argentina de Sergio, los hombres de su familia están tan obsesionados con el fútbol que, cuando hay partido los fines de semana, no prestan atención a nada más.
   a. A Mónica le molesta que... pero...
   b. Ella piensa que... porque...
   c. Espera que... porque...
5. A veces un equipo poco conocido le gana a uno de los equipos de mejor reputación. Por eso, el fútbol permite creer en milagros.
   a. A los aficionados del fútbol les encanta que... por eso...
   b. Es bueno que... porque...
   c. Es verdad que... sin embargo...

(*continúa*)

6. Las mujeres aficionadas al fútbol, unidas a sus hombres por la pasión por el deporte, disfrutan de mejores relaciones románticas.
   a. A los hombres les gusta que... por eso...
   b. Dudo que... porque...
   c. Estoy seguro/a de que... pero...

D. Viva el teatro

Paso 1 Lea el siguiente artículo sobre la popularidad del teatro en la Argentina. Luego, en parejas, contesten las preguntas.

¡Viva el teatro!

En una época en que los argentinos no pueden permitirse grandes lujos, comprar una entrada, entrar en una sala y esperar la magia que se esconde tras el telón está poniéndose de onda.[1] Una saludable onda que es el tema de conversación para el café después de la función y para el resto de la semana, y que a cambio no exige grandes gastos. Hay espectáculos con localidades desde 10 pesos... un peso menos de lo que cuesta ir al cine...

[1] de... de moda

1. ¿Por qué creen Uds. que a los argentinos les interesa tanto el teatro?
2. ¿Cuál fue la última obra de teatro que Uds. vieron y por qué fueron a verla? ¿Creen Uds. que los estadounidenses irían al teatro con más frecuencia si les costara lo mismo que una entrada al cine? Expliquen.
3. A muchos argentinos les fascina tanto el teatro que toman clases de actuación. ¿Les gustaría a Uds. tomar clases de teatro? ¿Harían de «*extra*» en una película si les ofrecieran la oportunidad? ¿Les gustaría ser actores/actrices? Expliquen sus respuestas.

Paso 2 Vea el anuncio en la página siguiente para varias obras de teatro que se presentan esta semana en Buenos Aires. Luego, en parejas, traten de llegar a un acuerdo sobre qué obra les gustaría ver. Expresen lo que les gusta y lo que les disgusta en cuanto a una obra de teatro.

Este fin de semana hay diversas opciones para todos los gustos, desde comedias hasta dramas. Solo, con amigos o en pareja se puede disfrutar del teatro porteño.[1] Algunas de las obras que están en cartelera son:

Cinco mujeres con el mismo vestido
La obra transcurre durante una elegante fiesta de casamiento. Entradas $20, $30 y $40.*

El método Gronholm
Cuatro candidatos al puesto de ejecutivo de una multinacional se enfrentan en la entrevista final. Entradas $25, $30, $35 y $40.

No seré feliz pero tengo marido
Una mirada irónica y sarcástica sobre el matrimonio; el espectáculo de mayores carcajadas desde que se inventó el matrimonio. $20, $30 y $40.

Chicago
Broadway viene a Buenos Aires. Electrizante comedia musical que cuenta una historia de avaricia, asesinato y el mundo del espectáculo. $35, $45 y $55.

Shangay, té verde y sushi en 8 escenas
Una pareja se separa en medio de un restaurante chino. Entradas desde $12, incluye té verde y maní japonés.

Póker de viernes
Teatro improvisado. Un espectáculo de improvisación que es siempre igual y siempre distinto. Carcajada garantizada. $10.

[1]de Buenos Aires

Rincón cultural

Lugares fascinantes:

El Cono Sur

La Patagonia, Argentina

1. **La Patagonia, Argentina** Esta zona inmensa al extremo sur del país sirve de frontera con Chile. (Hay una Patagonia chilena también.) Aunque compone una tercera parte del territorio argentino, sólo el 5 por ciento de la población habita la región. Es un terreno muy diverso con llanos desiertos,[1] un distrito de lagos y montañas (los Andes). Allí se han encontrado importantes restos de dinosaurios. Charles Darwin pasó por la Patagonia y fue uno de los lugares que más le intrigó, y las famosas aventuras de Butch Cassidy y el Sundance Kid los llevaron a la Patagonia para escaparse de las autoridades. Estos compraron tierra en Cholila, donde construyeron una casa y una pequeña tienda. También robaron varios bancos en

[1]llanos... *deserted plains*

*In Argentina, as in other countries that use the peso, the dollar sign is used.

Santa Cruz y en San Luis. Se quedaron allí por cinco años hasta 1907, cuando vendieron la casa y se escaparon a la cordillera.[2] A Butch Cassidy le gustaban las montañas de la Patagonia porque le recordaban el paisaje de su estado natal, Utah. La naturaleza de la Patagonia la hace un destino para los más atrevidos. Hay muchas opciones para hacer actividades al aire libre: pescar, montar a caballo, montar en bicicleta, hacer andinismo,[3] esquiar y navegar en kayac. Entre los varios parques nacionales están el Parque Nacional Nahuel-Huapi, un bosque petrificado de 15.000 hectáreas creado para preservar la flora y la fauna nativas de la zona; el Parque Nacional Los Glaciares con el famoso Glaciar Moreno, uno de los pocos glaciares del mundo que sigue avanzando; y la Cueva de las Manos, donde las paredes están marcadas de huellas de manos humanas que datan de cerca de entre 13.000 y 9.500 A.C.

El Observatorio Paranal, Chile

2. **El Observatorio Paranal, Chile** Este observatorio está localizado encima del Cerro[4] Paranal, una montaña de 2.635 metros en el Desierto de Atacama en el norte de Chile. Este lugar se considera el más seco del mundo, y es hogar de flamencos, géiseres, un valle lunar y volcanes nevados de casi 6.000 metros de altura. Es también el sitio perfecto para poner un observatorio: ofrece 350 noches despejadas[5] al año, un aire extremadamente seco y estabilidad atmosférica. Es poco probable que los seres humanos quieran vivir allá y hace falta[6] una zona aislada para que no haya contaminación[7] de luz para el observatorio. El Observatorio Paranal es un centro internacional de astronomía. Allí se encuentra el telescopio más grande y avanzado del mundo. Científicos de todas partes del mundo van allí para realizar investigaciones astronómicas.

Montevideo, Uruguay

3. **Montevideo, Uruguay** El centro de la vida política, económica y cultural del Uruguay es Montevideo. Fundada en 1726, es hoy en día una ciudad cosmopolita donde se concentra más de la mitad de la población uruguaya. Se sitúa en la orilla oriental[8] del Río de la Plata, que divide el Uruguay y la Argentina. El centro histórico es la Ciudad Vieja. Allí se encuentra el Mausoleo de Artigas (la tumba del héroe de la independencia uruguaya, José Gervasio Artigas) en la Plaza Independencia, y el Palacio Salvo, que, con veintiséis pisos, fue el edificio más alto de Sudamérica cuando se inauguró en 1927. Otra zona de interés es el Barrio Sur, donde a principios del siglo XIX unos esclavos fugitivos del Brasil se instalaron y establecieron las bases de la cultura afrouruguaya. Montevideo goza de un magnífico puerto natural, lo cual hace de esta ciudad un importante centro de comercio. El Mercado del Puerto era uno de los mejores mercados

[2]*mountain range* [3]hacer... *mountain climbing* [4]*Hill* [5]*clear* [6]hace... *there needs to be* [7]*pollution* [8]orilla... *eastern shore*

del continente cuando se inauguró en 1868. Ahora ofrece parrillas[9] típicas con las famosas carnes uruguayas y también restaurantes elegantes. Los sábados por la tarde hay un ambiente de fiesta, con artistas, artesanos y músicos. Montevideo ofrece una vida cultural muy activa y sofisticada. Los montevideanos se pueden entretener en los bares de tango, candombe (música afrouruguaya) y rock; en los cines internacionales, en los múltiples teatros y, por supuesto, viendo partidos de fútbol—la pasión nacional.

Las Cataratas del Iguazú

4. **Las Cataratas del Iguazú** Estas impresionantes cataratas, cuatro veces más grandes que las del Niágara, se encuentran en la frontera entre la Argentina, el Brasil y el Paraguay. El español Álvar Núñez Cabeza de Vaca las «descubrió» en 1541. Quedó impresionado no sólo por esas fabulosas cascadas, sino también por la naturaleza que las rodeaba. Vio un bosque lleno de orquídeas, begonias, pájaros exóticos y 500 clases diferentes de mariposa. Las cataratas entran a formar parte del Río Iguazú —cuyo nombre significa «grandes aguas» en guaraní[10]— con una fuerza tremenda, creando nubes de vapor de 30 metros de altura. Dentro de las nubes el juego de luz solar crea arcos iris[11] radiantes. Una de las cascadas que forman las cataratas se conoce como «La Garganta del Diablo». Hay un hotel de lujo[12] que está ubicado dentro del Parque Nacional Iguazú. Es el único hotel que ofrece a sus huéspedes una exclusiva vista a la Garganta del Diablo desde sus habitaciones y restaurantes. El sonido del agua de las cataratas es tan fuerte que puede escucharse a todas horas.

[9]*casual restaurants that serve grilled meats* [10]lengua indígena de la zona
[11]arcos... *rainbows* [12]de... *luxury*

¡Viaje conmigo al Cono Sur!

Vea el vídeo para saber lo que Santiago les mandó a Javier y Sara sobre su viaje al Cono Sur.

Video footage provided by

BBC Motion Gallery

ACTIVIDADES

A. En parejas, contesten las siguientes preguntas sobre los cuatro lugares fascinantes.

1. ¿Cómo es la geografía de la Patagonia? ¿Cuáles son sus atractivos turísticos?
2. ¿Qué personas famosas pasaron tiempo en la Patagonia? ¿Qué hicieron allí?
3. ¿Por qué es el Cerro Paranal un lugar idóneo para poner un telescopio?
4. ¿Por qué es Montevideo importante para el Uruguay?
5. Si fuera Ud. a Montevideo, ¿qué podría hacer en el Mercado del Puerto?
6. ¿Cómo se llamaba el primer europeo en conocer las Cataratas del Iguazú?
7. Describa los atractivos naturales de las cataratas y sus alrededores.
8. ¿Por qué puede ser difícil dormir en el hotel de lujo en el Parque Nacional Iguazú?

B. Localice los cuatro lugares fascinantes del Cono Sur en el mapa y ponga un número del 1 al 4 para indicar el grado de interés que Ud. tiene en investigar y explorar estos lugares. Turnándose con un compañero / una compañera, explique por qué a Ud. le interesa más el número 1 y por qué le interesa menos el número 4. Cuando presente su explicación, haga por lo menos tres comparaciones entre los dos lugares.

C. Ahora que Ud. ha leído sobre los lugares y ha visto el videoblog de Santiago, imagínese que Ud. es una de las siguientes personas que quiere hacer un viaje al Cono Sur. Escriba un correo electrónico a un agente de viajes explicándole lo que le fascina sobre el Cono Sur, lo que le gusta hacer cuando viaja, lo que le molesta de ciertos hoteles, lo que le preocupa sobre la comida y el clima y lo que le interesa aprender antes de su viaje.

- Un(a) guía que hace deportes extremos quiere ir a la Patagonia.
- Un astrónomo / Una astrónoma quiere ir al Desierto de Atacama.
- Un actor / Una actriz súper rico/a quiere ir a Montevideo.
- Un hombre / Una mujer de las Cataratas del Niágara quiere ir a Iguazú.

Una artista hispana:

Maitena Burundarena

Maitena Burundarena nació en Buenos Aires en 1962. Es conocidísima en Sudamérica y Europa por sus tiras cómicas llenas de sarcasmo, ironía, realismo y mucho humor. Empezó en los años 80 como ilustradora gráfica para varios diarios y revistas de la Argentina. En 1993, salieron por primera vez sus tiras cómicas en una página de humor semanal de *Para ti,* una revista femenina de la Argentina. Maitena llamó *Mujeres alteradas* a su serie de viñetas, que trata el tema del mundo femenino. Maitena es una gran observadora de la humanidad y sus tiras representan situaciones cotidianas que todos reconocen. Tanto mujeres como hombres pueden relacionarse con las situaciones que retrata. Parecen ser fragmentos pequeños de la vida, pero en sus manos se convierten en chistes que nos hacen reír y ver las cosas de una manera diferente. Las mujeres de sus viñetas son casadas, solteras, viudas, adolescentes, jóvenes y viejas. Las hay guapas, feas, trabajadoras estresadas, amas de casa agotadas y novias frustradas; es decir, hay de todo. Nadie escapa el ojo observador de Maitena. La periodista y novelista española Rosa Montero dice: «Leer a Maitena es una auténtica experiencia. Sus viñetas son como un espejo de la vida cotidiana, pero hay algo más, lo que hace de ella una artista de genio: te hace pensar, y esa es la finalidad del arte. Todo arte es un intento de entender cómo somos, y Maitena es una artista en el sentido más profundo y absoluto de la palabra». Hoy en día, Maitena es tan célebre que sus tiras cómicas y viñetas aparecen en más de 30 países y han sido traducidas a doce idiomas.

La tira cómica titulada *Esos momentos en que no podés contener tu estúpida risa* refleja las varias situaciones que ocurren en la vida diaria que nos hacen reír a carcajadas.

Esos momentos en que no podés contener tu estúpida risa

PREGUNTAS

1. ¿De qué se tratan las tiras cómicas de Maitena?
2. Según Rosa Montero, ¿cuál es el objeto principal de todo arte?
3. ¿Lee Ud. algunas tiras cómicas? ¿Cuáles son y por qué le gustan?
4. ¿Cómo respondería Ud. ante la risa inapropiada en cada una de las seis situaciones que presenta la tira cómica de la página anterior? ¿Qué le diría a la persona que está riéndose a carcajadas para mostrar su sorpresa o disgusto?

ACTIVIDAD

Busque en el Internet las tiras cómicas de Maitena y las de Quino, otro caricaturista argentino. *Mafalda* es el nombre de una tira cómica de Quino y trata de una niña precoz que se preocupa por todos los problemas de la sociedad moderna. Escoja una tira cómica que le guste de cada artista y preséntelas a la clase. En grupos de tres, hagan comparaciones entre los dos artistas en cuanto al estilo de sus dibujos, los temas que trata y lo cómico que son. Luego, decidan cuál es la más cómica y la más satírica entre todas las que se han presentado en su grupo.

Unos tambores típicos del candombe, Montevideo, Uruguay

La música uruguaya

Generalmente, cuando se trata de la música del Cono Sur, lo primero que viene a la mente es, sin duda, el tango. Sin embargo, en el Cono Sur hay muchos otros estilos musicales: la música folclórica, la música de protesta de los años 60 y 70 conocida como «La nueva canción», la música clásica, el rock en español y muchos estilos más. Lo que muchos no saben es que el tango mismo proviene del candombe, un género musical de origen afrouruguayo que llegó con los esclavos que fueron llevados a la fuerza a ese país a mediados del siglo XVIII. El candombe ha sobrevivido hasta hoy y se encuentra no sólo en muchas grabaciones de música uruguaya, sino también en la vida actual del país. Hoy en día, es muy común ver grupos de gente tocando candombe en las calles de distintos barrios.

Aunque el candombe ha experimentado algunas transformaciones, mantiene dos de sus características originales: la forma de tocar y los instrumentos básicos. Estos instrumentos son los tamboriles o tambores. Los hay de tres tamaños distintos, cada uno con una voz diferente: piano, chico y repique. Cada cual cumple una función rítmica determinada que tiene que ver con el lenguaje propio del candombe. Muchos músicos se han inspirado en el ritmo particular del candombe, y han creado diferentes composiciones a lo largo del siglo XX y hasta hoy.

«Candombe del Piedras» es el resultado de un proyecto muy especial: *Esperando salir,* un CD de canciones escritas por jóvenes encarcelados en el Uruguay y tocadas por músicos profesionales. El proyecto lo llevó a cabo Proyectos Culturales, una organización no gubernamental de Montevideo, Uruguay. Trabaja con niños y adolescentes de poblaciones marginadas o que están internados en centros carcelarios. Proyectos Culturales les ofrece a estos adolescentes programas culturales, artísticos y pedagógicos.

ACTIVIDADES

A. Antes de cantar En la canción «Candombe del Piedras», se oyen los sentimientos de un joven encarcelado. Como no tiene licencia* para salir, se ha quedado en la cárcel aburrido, pensando en su familia. «El Piedras» se refiere a la parte del complejo penitenciario donde está encarcelado el joven. Conteste las siguientes preguntas.

1. ¿Qué palabras expresan la nostalgia que uno siente cuando no puede ver a su familia por mucho tiempo?
2. ¿Qué harán los encarcelados para pasar el tiempo? Si Ud. estuviera en la cárcel, ¿cómo se sentiría y qué haría para pasar el tiempo?
3. ¿Sabe de alguna canción, poema, libro o película que trate de la experiencia de estar encarcelado? ¿Cuál es y qué temas trata?

B. ¡A cantar! Escuche la canción «Candombe del Piedras» que se puede encontrar en el CD *Estampillas musicales.*

Candombe del Piedras

Es de mañana, estamos todos.
Miro pa'[1] 'fuera y veo poco.
Poquito a poco me rompo el coco.[2]
Sin la licencia me como el bocho.[3]

Todos los días la misma historia
Con la rutina, así es la vida,
Ladrando[4] un poco
Acá en el Piedras.

Fumando solo,
Fumando un pucho,[5]
Tranquilo y nada.
Que pasa el tiempo,
Que falta poco,
Pa' la licencia,
Pa' estar en casa.

Con mi familia,
Que extraño mucho.
Tengo las ganas
De estar en casa.

Así es la historia
Acá en el Piedras.
Nos despedimos,
Tocando[6] un poco.
[*Se repite varias veces.*]

[1]para [2]me... *I think too much* [3]me... *I worry too much* [4]solicitando algo insistentemente sin obtener respuesta [5]cigarrillo [6](*double meaning*) *playing the instrument; escaping from prison*

C. Después de cantar En parejas, contesten las siguientes preguntas sobre la canción «Candombe del Piedras».

1. ¿Qué instrumentos musicales se escuchan en esta canción?
2. ¿Cómo es un día típico para el joven encarcelado?
3. ¿Qué emociones evoca la canción en Uds.?

D. ¡A escuchar! Para apreciar más la gran variedad de música del Cono Sur, vaya a YouTube™ y escuche la música de protesta de Mercedes Sosa, Violeta Parra y Victor Jara, el tango clásico de Carlos Gardel y Astor Piazzolla, el tango nuevo de Daniel Melingo y Lidia Borda, la música folclórica argentina de Atahualpa Yupanqui, la nueva canción chilena de Inti-Illimani, el rock chileno de Los Prisioneros, el electro-pop melodramático del grupo argentino Miranda, el pop chileno de Kudai o las canciones de Jorge Drexler, el compositor y cantautor uruguayo que

---

*Se refiere a un permiso para salir de la cárcel por un tiempo corto, según la gravedad del delito y la buena conducta del encarcelado mientras cumple su sentencia judicial.

ganó un Grammy en 2005 por su canción original «Al otro lado del río», de la película *Diarios de motocicleta*. Luego, comparta sus impresiones de los artistas y sus canciones con sus compañeros de clase, utilizando frases como **Me gusta(n)... , porque... , Me encanta que... , Es impresionante/ fantástico que... , Me sorprende que...** y **Es evidente que... .**

Lectura

La siguiente lectura, escrita por Rebeca Rojas Rodríguez, trata sobre las diversas maneras en que diferentes grupos de jóvenes chilenos expresan su identidad. El artículo presenta algunos de los grupos que son omnipresentes en la ciudad capital de Santiago. Este fenómeno sociológico en el que los jóvenes sienten la necesidad de diferenciarse de la generación anterior es un hecho reciente. Antes de los años 50 los jóvenes se vestían igual y hacían más o menos las mismas cosas que los mayores. En 1955 la famosa película *Rebelde sin causa* con James Dean presentó al mundo un joven aislado e incomprendido que se convirtió en un icono de rebeldía de su generación. Fue durante estos años que vimos el comienzo de la diferenciación juvenil y la tendencia entre los jóvenes de agruparse según sus gustos e intereses. Luego, en los años 60, aparecieron los hippies, los motociclistas, los rockeros y, más tarde, los *punks*, los *breakdancers* y otros grupos. Hoy en día, vemos la manifestación de la indivualidad generacional en las llamadas «tribus urbanas». Son distintos grupos que se reúnen en los mismos lugares, llevan el mismo corte de pelo, se visten parecido, hablan parecido y escuchan la misma música. Aunque el artículo que va a leer hace referencia a Santiago, Ud. verá que tiene relación con grupos de jóvenes similares alrededor del mundo.

Antes de leer

A. Para comentar En grupos de tres, contesten las siguientes preguntas.

1. ¿A qué edad empezó a notar que existían grupos muy distintos entre sus contemporáneos?
2. ¿Pasaba Ud. todo el tiempo con el mismo grupo en la escuela secundaria o tenía amigos de varios grupos diferentes?
3. Y ahora, ¿pasa tiempo con un grupo en particular? ¿Cuáles son los intereses que unen a ese grupo?
4. ¿Siente la necesidad de vestirse y comportarse de una manera muy diferente a la de sus padres? ¿Se nota una diferencia entre el estilo de vida de sus padres y el de sus abuelos? Explique.
5. Aparte del estilo de ropa que lleva, ¿de qué otra manera puede una persona expresar su identidad?

B. Acercándose al tema Lea el título de la ficha que está en la página siguiente y las nueve palabras asociadas con el tema del artículo. Con un compañero / una compañera, decida si los espacios en blanco requieren un sustantivo, un verbo o un adjetivo. Luego, escoja la palabra apropiada de la ficha para completar las oraciones.

Las tribus urbanas		
el extremo	la filosofía	la técnica
adoptar	manifestar	tildar[1]
entretenido/a	llamativo/a	satánico/a

[1]*to brand*

1. En muchos centros urbanos la gente joven _________ su deseo de distinguirse por medio de un estilo de vida extravagante y muestras de originalidad en su manera de vestir.
2. Entre las tribus urbanas de Santiago es fácil reconocer a los emos o «emocionales», porque llevan muchos piercings, expansores en la oreja y tatuajes. Hay quienes los _________ de depresivos o *freaks*.
3. Los hiphoperos llevan ropa muy _________ y joyas muy costosas. Son *breakdancers* que sólo se preocupan por mejorar su _________ y estar en buen estado físico.
4. Los góticos juegan con el ocultismo y conceptos _________ y nunca se les ve con las Peloláis, las chicas de pelo largo y muy liso cuyo pasatiempo favorito es ir de compras.
5. Es fácil reconocer a los Punkies, con sus cortes de pelo originales, todo tipo de piercings y su _________ anarquista.
6. Los Otakus son amantes de la música y la animación japonesa. Algunos están tan apasionados que _________ la personalidad de sus personajes favoritos y se visten como ellos.

Chile: Tribus urbanas, rostros que buscan una identidad

En los últimos años, han surgido variadas tribus urbanas de adolescentes que buscan diferenciarse a través de algún estilo estético e ideológico con el cual, sin embargo, sólo logran homogeneizarse aún más con aquellos que comparten los mismos gustos e ideas. Es así como la búsqueda de originalidad se vuelve identificación y lo individual se vuelve colectivo, en el ámbito de agrupaciones que definen la actitud frente al mundo de estos jóvenes que aún cursan la enseñanza media.[1]

Una tribu urbana es una subcultura que se origina y se desarrolla en una urbe o ciudad congregando generalmente jóvenes que comparten un mismo estilo de vida. Según algunos críticos y analistas, el fenómeno no es nada más que la búsqueda de aquella identidad tan añorada[2] por los

[1]enseñanza... *secondary education* [2]deseada

adolescentes, pero también se trata de un reclamo[3] social por sentirse desplazados o rechazados,[4] sin posibilidades de surgir.

Se trata de adolescentes entre los 14 y los 22 años de edad aproximadamente que organizan y difunden sus ideologías a través del Internet. Por ello, no son un fenómeno regional ni aislado sino que tienden a afectar grandes sectores del mundo globalizado, en especial las naciones más digitalizadas. En el mundo de los fotolog, encontramos algunas de estas tribus que construyen su identidad a través de una imagen y se pueden clasificar en:

Emos: El término viene de «emocionales», porque así se definen quienes pertenecen a esta tribu urbana, lo que implica enfrentar la vida desde una perspectiva netamente[5] emocional, donde hay que pensar con el corazón y no con la cabeza. Se trata de jóvenes entre 13 y 20 años que buscan... «pacificar el mundo a través de la propia paz interior y contagiar, sin contacto alguno, sus emociones a los demás». Son de pocos amigos y pasan gran parte del día escuchando música funk; es por eso que hay quienes los tildan de «depresivos», ...o *freaks*. Se juntan en el Portal Lyon o en el EuroCenter de Santiago, porque en estos lugares pueden encontrar con facilidad los discos de sus grupos favoritos (Mychemical Romance, Braid, Mineral y The get up kids), además de aquellas prendas de vestir con las que podemos fácilmente identificarlos. Es decir, jeans holgados[6] dejando ver sus boxers o sus calzones de colores con motivos infantiles en el caso de las niñas, polerones[7] canguro,... muchos piercing, expansores en la oreja y tatuajes.[V]

Pokemones: Son una «evolución» de los emos, es decir, nacen de ellos, pero con el tiempo han logrado algunas diferencias. Visten pantalones caídos, llevan peinados muy producidos y cortes de pelo que parecen tijereteados,[8] además de chasquillas chuecas[9] y mucho gel. A diferencia de los emos, no son depresivos y gustan de las fiestas y del reggaetón.

[...]

[3]*claim* [4]*rejected* [5]*distinctly* [6]*loose-fitting* [7]*sweatshirts* [8]*all hacked up*
[9]chasquillas... *crooked bangs*

Hiphoperos: Se visten con ropa muy ancha y por lo general deportiva, aunque entre ellos hay muchas diferencias. Por un lado, están los que cantan, hacen su propia música y con sus letras protestan contra las injusticias, mientras que quienes bailan se llaman *breakdancers* y sólo se preocupan de mejorar su técnica, estar en buen estado físico y cada día hacer un salto[10] más espectacular. El hiphopero además usa las pantis de su mamá en la cabeza, tiene elásticos en sus pantalones para que no le llegue a las zapatillas llenas de argollas de lata de bebida[11] y más joyas costosas y raras tenga, más hiphopero es.

VOCABULARIO

Góticos: [...] Según sus propias declaraciones, «los góticos son mucho más que sólo vestirse de negro y pintarse el rostro de blanco,[V] ser gótico es arte y cultura». Pero lejos del movimiento social que representa el término, los jóvenes que pertenecen a esta tribu mantienen en pie algunas actividades en las cuales no dimensionan[12] el real peligro que corren. Juegan con el ocultismo y variados conceptos satánicos sin por eso sentirse herejes.[13] [...]

VISUALIZAR

Otakus: Son amantes de la música y la animación japonesa; tanta es su pasión que algunos se visten y adoptan la personalidad de sus personajes favoritos. Organizan sus propias fiestas con disfraces e intercambio de ñoñerías[14] que sólo ellos entienden. Coleccionan chapitas[15] de las series, llevan para todos lados una carpeta con dibujos y cosas varias, se llaman con apelativos que sólo ellos comprenden (generalmente se trata de nombres japoneses), participan en maratones de la misma serie de animé o películas japonesas y escuchan solamente las bandas sonoras[16] de sus series o música japonesa en general.

VOCABULARIO

Peloláis: Son las chicas que gustan tener el pelo largo y muy liso, no se hacen grandes peinados y su ropa siempre está a la moda.[V] La mayoría estudia en colegios privados, hablan inglés y su pasatiempo favorito es salir a vitrinear.[17]

VISUALIZAR

[...] **Punkies:** El punk es amigo de todo lo que saque de quicio a un jefe de personal,[18] es decir, cortes de pelo inverosímiles,[19] desiguales, tal vez con cresta[20] y con sus mechas pintadas,[21] pantalones ajustados y llamativos, botas de cuero y complementos del «sado».[V] Es capaz de agujerearse cualquier parte del cuerpo con los llamados piercing, es anarquista y reacciona contra todo tipo de imposición, porque considera que el término «punk» debe ser sinónimo de individualismo total, libertad única y placer específico.

VOCABULARIO VISUALIZAR

VOCABULARIO

La lista de tribus urbanas daría para mucho más y, a la vez, se necesitarían constantes actualizaciones debido a que cada cierto tiempo surge una nueva agrupación. Por el momento, estas tribus que hemos mencionado parecen ser las más cotizadas[22] en la actualidad urbana de

[10]*jump* [11]argollas... *soft drink can tabs* [12]*understand* [13]*heretics* [14]*silly things* [15]*trading cards* [16]bandas... *soundtracks* [17]*window-shop* [18]saque... *drives a manager crazy* [19]*increíble* [20]*spikes* [21]mechas... *streaks* [22]*important*

nuestro país. Ellas nos muestran los múltiples aspectos de una juventud inquietante que preferimos ignorar u observar de lejos, porque nos atemoriza descubrir cuánto de nosotros hay en ellos.

VOCABULARIO

Después de leer

A. Comprensión Conteste las preguntas, según la lectura.

1. ¿Piensa la autora que los jóvenes de las tribus urbanas son verdaderamente originales? Explique.
2. ¿Por qué podría ser atractivo para un(a) joven de una ciudad grande unirse a una tribu?
3. ¿Cuál ha sido el rol del Internet en el fenómeno de las tribus urbanas?
4. En su opinión, de las tribus que describe la autora, ¿cuáles son las más extremistas?
5. ¿Cuáles de estos grupos se encuentran en su ciudad o universidad? ¿Cuáles son las características de cada uno?
6. ¿Por qué dice la autora que los adultos prefieren ignorar los diversos aspectos de las tribus? ¿Por qué los atemorizan estos aspectos? ¿Está Ud. de acuerdo con su explicación?

B. La búsqueda de la originalidad Cada tribu urbana busca diferenciarse a través de algún estilo estético e ideológico. ¿Han logrado distinguirse unas tribus de otras?

COMPARAR

Paso 1 En grupos de tres, preparen comparaciones entre dos de las tribus urbanas indicadas.

los emos / los pokemones	los otakus / los góticos
los punkies / los góticos	las peloláis / los hiphoperos

GUSTOS

Paso 2 Expliquen sus comparaciones al resto de la clase y luego decidan si un(a) joven del primer grupo de cada pareja comparada podría tener una amistad con alguien de la segunda tribu, a pesar de sus diferencias. Expliquen por qué creen que serían posibles o imposibles tales amistades. ¿Qué cosas o actividades les pueden gustar a los jóvenes de las dos tribus y que les podría molestar?

C. Para discutir En grupos pequeños, hablen de los siguientes temas.

1. ¿Cree Ud. que la expresión de la individualidad a través de la manera de vestirse, llevar el pelo o ponerse piercings y tatuajes es un importante paso hacia la independencia personal?
2. ¿Se podría considerar a las hermandades (*fraternities*) y las hermandades de mujeres (*sororities*) como tribus? ¿Por qué sí o por qué no?
3. No todos los grupos se distinguen por cómo se visten. ¿Puede pensar en algún grupo que se identifique por otras características? ¿Cuál es?

(*continúa*)

4. ¿Cree Ud. que es posible ser verdaderamente individual en esta sociedad? ¿Por qué sí o por qué no?
5. ¿Cuáles son las ventajas y desventajas de siempre estar con personas que piensan igual que Ud.?
6. Entre las diferentes tribus puede haber conflictos por la gran diversidad de ideas estéticas e ideológicas. Incluso unas tribus son víctimas de la intolerancia hasta el punto de sufrir ataques físicos. En los centros urbanos donde hay muchas tribus, ¿debe hacer el gobierno un esfuerzo para fomentar la tolerancia entre las tribus?

D. Una tribu nueva Escriba un anuncio para su blog sobre una nueva tribu de su creación. Describa el tipo de persona que quiere que sea parte de su tribu; cómo se vestirá, cuáles serán sus intereses y gustos, y otros detalles.

¡A escribir!

A. Lluvia de ideas Entreviste a cinco de sus compañeros de clase en preparación para su ensayo sobre lo más estresante de la vida universitaria y sus recomendaciones para aliviar o prevenir el estrés. Hágales las siguientes preguntas y tome apuntes para su ensayo.

1. ¿Cuáles son los aspectos más positivos de su vida este semestre?
2. ¿Cuáles son los aspectos que le causan estrés?
3. ¿Qué le gusta hacer para aliviar el estrés y relajarse?

B. Composición: Recomendaciones Escriba un artículo para su periódico universitario dirigido a los estudiantes del primer año, en el que describa el estrés que sufren los estudiantes de hoy y ofrezca consejos para aliviarlo.

1. escoger un título llamativo
2. escribir un párrafo introductorio explicando las cosas positivas que a los estudiantes les gusta hacer durante el semestre
3. describir las posibles causas del estrés entre los estudiantes universitarios, incluyendo las que sufren los que trabajan y estudian a la vez
4. ofrecer sugerencias para prevenir el estrés y actividades para relajarse
5. escribir una conclusión

C. Diálogo Lea el artículo de un compañero / una compañera y luego, trabajando juntos/as, creen un diálogo entre dos consejeros/as en el que hablen de cómo se están preparando para ayudar a los estudiantes estresados que llegarán a su oficina al final del semestre.

Hablando del tema

Antes de empezar a conversar con sus compañeros de clase sobre los temas de este capítulo, prepare una ficha para la conversación, otra para el debate y otra para la reacción ante la cita. Cada ficha debe tener tres sustantivos, tres verbos y tres adjetivos.

A. **Conversación: Cómo relajarse** Revise las expresiones en **Para conversar mejor.** Luego, en parejas o grupos de tres, conversen sobre los siguientes puntos.

Para conversar mejor

En cambio...	Me encantaba(n)...
¿En serio?	Me fascina(n)...
Era más/menos... que	Qué bueno que...
Es necesario que...	Sería fenomenal...

- ¿Qué le gusta a Ud. hacer para pasarlo bien? ¿Desempeña la música un papel importante en su tiempo libre? ¿Qué tipo de música le gusta oír?
- Haga una comparación entre lo que hace en su tiempo libre ahora y lo que hacía cuando estaba en la secundaria.
- Si fuera rico/a, ¿adónde iría para escaparse de sus obligaciones diarias? ¿Qué haría allí?

B. **Debate: La tecnología** Revise las expresiones en **Para debatir mejor.** Después, prepare tres argumentos a favor y tres en contra sobre la omnipresencia de la tecnología en nuestras vidas. Luego, presente sus argumentos en un debate. No sabrá qué lado tendrá que defender.

Para debatir mejor

A FAVOR	EN CONTRA
Eso es.	Eso no tiene sentido.
Estoy de acuerdo.	¿Hablas en serio?
Muy bien dicho.	Lo siento, pero...
No cabe duda.	Todo lo contrario.

«La tecnología, que se creía que iba a mejorar la vida, ha aumentado el nivel de estrés en la vida diaria.»

«La tecnología es súper importante para mis estudios, mi trabajo y mi vida social. Sin tener contacto constante con mis amigos, mi vida sería mucho más estresante.»

C. **Reacción: La mejor terapia: reírse** Revise las expresiones en **Para reaccionar mejor.** Luego, reaccione ante la siguiente cita. Añada razones que apoyen sus opiniones.

Para reaccionar mejor

Creo/Opino/Supongo que...	Es posible que...
Es absurdo/ridículo que...	Es verdad que...
Es bueno/malo que...	No tiene sentido.

«Según unos estudios recientes, la felicidad es contagiosa. Por cada amigo/a feliz que tenga una persona, su propia felicidad aumenta un 9 por ciento.»

CAPÍTULO 5

El mundo actual:

Participación cívica y acción global

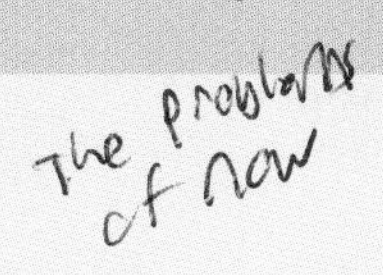

Punto clave

HIPÓTESIS

Temas centrales

- los problemas actuales
- la gente indígena
- el activismo

Zona de enfoque

- la región andina

Un pueblo boliviano

En este capítulo, Ud. va a explorar el tema del mundo actual.

Preguntas para considerar

- ¿Cuáles son los problemas sociales más importantes de hoy?
- ¿Qué puede hacer el individuo para participar activamente en su sociedad?
- ¿Cómo nos afectan personalmente los acontecimientos mundiales?
- ¿Qué importancia tiene la política en su vida diaria?
- La escena que se ve en esta página representa un pueblo boliviano durante una campaña presidencial. ¿Cómo cambia el ambiente en su universidad y su ciudad durante las campañas nacionales y locales?

MULTIMEDIA

Estampillas musicales

Lugares fascinantes

Online *Manual*
www.mhcentro.com

Online Learning Center
www.mhhe.com/puntoyaparte4

Este mundo nuestro

¡Qué buena oportunidad!

Situación: Laura y Sergio y están en Ruta Maya hablando sobre una oportunidad que tiene Laura de ir al Ecuador. Lea el diálogo y conteste las preguntas que lo siguen. **¡OJO!** Preste especial atención al uso del vocabulario nuevo **en negrita.**

LAURA: ¿Recuerdas ese correo que recibí de Luis Alberto en el que me ofreció un trabajo con Médicos Sin Fronteras en Colombia y Bolivia durante la primavera?

SERGIO: Claro. ¿Lo has aceptado?

LAURA: No. Es que cuando le dije a Luis Alberto cuánto protestaba mi padre por su miedo al **terrorismo, el narcotráfico** y **los secuestros** en esa parte de Latinoamérica, me sugirió otra oportunidad. Francamente, **vale la pena** considerarla.

SERGIO: Dime.

LAURA: Habrá un congreso en el Ecuador sobre **los desafíos** más **urgentes** para Latinoamérica y quieren **promoverlo** en los Estados Unidos. Buscan personas que preparen **reportajes** en inglés para **la prensa** norteamericana.

SERGIO: Pero, ¿por qué estaría tu padre más tranquilo con ese plan?

LAURA: Por dos razones: porque nosotros estaríamos allí sólo diez días en vez de un semestre entero y porque actualmente el Ecuador está bastante estable.

SERGIO: ¿Nosotros?

LAURA: Sí. Cuando Javi **se enteró del** congreso se entusiasmó muchísimo. Como sabes, ya ha escrito mucho sobre **los esfuerzos** y **el poder** de los jóvenes estadounidenses en la última elección que hubo aquí.

SERGIO: Sí, claro. Lo recuerdo bien.

LAURA: Pues, en el Ecuador hay **una campaña** para **promover** la participación de **los ciudadanos** jóvenes. A Javi le gustaría preparar un artículo comparando el activismo político juvenil en los Estados Unidos con el de Latinoamérica.

SERGIO: ¡Qué padre! ¿Y tú piensas **llevar a cabo** algún estudio para tu tesis?

LAURA: Sí. Asistiría a los discursos sobre **los esfuerzos** que han hecho para **combatir la desnutrición** y **el analfabetismo.** También, Luis Alberto me prometió que me presentaría a unos chamanes **activistas.** Si pudiera entrevistarlos sobre sus conocimientos médicos tradicionales, tendría más información para mi tesis.

SERGIO: Sería fenomenal.

ACTIVIDADES

A. Detective Busque en el diálogo ejemplos de las siguientes metas comunicativas: Descripción (D), Narración en el pasado (P), Hablar de los gustos (G), Hacer hipótesis (H) y Hablar del futuro (F). Subraye cada palabra o frase que represente una (o una combinación) de estas metas comunicativas. Luego, escriba al margen la(s) letra(s) que corresponde(n) a cada ejemplo subrayado (D, P, G, H o F).

MODELOS: ¿Por qué estaría tu padre más tranquilo con ese plan? (H)
Luis Alberto me prometió que me presentaría a unos chamanes activistas. (P) (D)

B. Comprensión Conteste las siguientes preguntas, según la situación.

1. ¿Por qué no quería el padre de Laura que ella trabajara con Médicos Sin Fronteras?
2. ¿Cuál es la solución que propuso Luis Alberto?
3. ¿Por qué cree Laura que su padre aceptará el nuevo plan?
4. ¿Qué haría Javier si fuera al Ecuador?
5. ¿Cómo ayudaría a Laura el viaje?
6. ¿Por qué cree Sergio que la idea de Laura es buena?

C. Reacciones y recomendaciones Complete las siguientes oraciones sobre la situación, utilizando un conector en cada oración.

MODELO: Es bueno que Laura...
Es bueno que Laura pueda regresar a Sudamérica puesto que le fascinó su último viaje allí. Sin embargo, debe tratar de tener en cuenta los sentimientos y preocupaciones de su papá.

1. El padre de Laura no cree que...
2. Qué bueno que Javier...
3. Es obvio que el congreso...
4. Laura espera que...

Conectores

además
en cambio
para que + *subjuntivo*
por lo tanto
porque
puesto que
sin embargo
ya que

D. Diálogo En parejas, preparen un diálogo en el que el padre de Laura hable con Javier para pedirle que cuide a su hija. El señor Taylor debe enumerar todas sus preocupaciones y Javier debe responder a cada una de manera que lo convenza de que los dos van a estar bien y que Laura es una mujer fuerte que sabe cuidarse a sí misma.

Vocabulario del tema

Para hablar de los problemas actuales

el analfabetismo	illiteracy
la crisis	crisis
los derechos humanos	human rights
el desafío	challenge
la desigualdad	inequality
la desnutrición	malnutrition
la explotación	exploitation
la gente indígena (*but* **los indígenas**)	indigenous people
la guerra	war
el hambre (*but* **mucha hambre**)	hunger
la huelga	strike
la injusticia	injustice

la manifestación	demonstration
el narcotráfico	drug traffic; drug trafficking
la pobreza	poverty
el prejuicio	prejudice
la salud	health
el secuestro	kidnapping; hijacking
el SIDA	AIDS
el subdesarrollo	underdevelopment
en vías de desarrollo	developing
desarrollado/a	developed
el terrorismo	terrorism

Para hablar de las soluciones

el bienestar	well-being
la campaña	campaign
el/la ciudadano/a	citizen
la cuestión	issue
la diversidad	diversity
el esfuerzo	effort
el/la líder	leader
el liderazgo	leadership
la lucha	fight; struggle
la paz	peace
el poder	power
la política	politics; policy
los recursos	resources
la tolerancia	tolerance
el tratamiento	treatment

Acciones para hablar de las soluciones

colaborar (con)	to help; work (with)
combatir	to combat
desarrollar	to develop
donar	to donate
elegir (i, i) (elijo)	to elect
enterarse (de)	to become informed (about)
financiar	to finance
hacer de voluntario/a	to volunteer
invertir (ie, i)	to invest

—Es el arma más terrible. Ojalá el hombre no la utilice jamás. Acabaría con la raza humana . . .

En su opinión, ¿cuál es el arma más terrible de la humanidad?

llevar a cabo	to carry out
postularse	to run for office
promover (ue)	to promote
resolver (ue)	to resolve
salvar	to save (*someone, something*)
valer (*irreg.*) **la pena**	to be worth it

Para hablar de las noticias

la prensa	press
el reportaje	report
los titulares	headlines

Para hablar de una situación

alarmante	alarming
alentador(a)	encouraging
chocante	shocking
desesperante	infuriating
desilusionante	disappointing
horripilante	horrifying
impresionante	impressive
inquietante	disturbing
polémico/a	controversial

COGNADOS: **activista,* alarmista, altruista, egoísta, extremista, idealista, oportunista, optimista, pesimista, urgente**

*These words that end in "**-ista**" are used to refer to both males and females: **la activista, el hombre egoísta,** etc.

ACTIVIDADES

A. Vocabulario en contexto

Paso 1 Complete las siguientes oraciones con la palabra más apropiada, según el contexto, y luego indique si está Ud. de acuerdo con ellas o no.

	SÍ	NO
1. La causa principal de la pobreza es ________ (el analfabetismo / el hambre).	☐	☐
2. Los estudiantes egoístas hacen de voluntario porque quieren ________ (desarrollar / salvar) el mundo.	☐	☐
3. ________ (La campaña / La crisis) del SIDA es uno de los problemas más alarmantes hoy en día.	☐	☐
4. El nivel de ________ (desnutrición / prejuicio) infantil en este país es inquietante: demasiados niños no comen tres comidas al día.	☐	☐
5. Si todos los ciudadanos ________ (hacer de voluntario / participar en una huelga) una vez por semana, podríamos resolver todos nuestros problemas sociales.	☐	☐
6. La prensa de este país debe hacer más reportajes sobre otros países porque la gente debe ________ (elegir / enterarse) más de lo que pasa en el resto del mundo.	☐	☐
7. Un buen líder / Una buena líder debe ________ (invertir / financiar) su campaña electoral con donaciones de los ricos y poderosos.	☐	☐
8. Si una persona se postula para presidente de un país, debe tener una opinión fuerte sobre las ________ (cuestiones / campañas) polémicas.	☐	☐

Paso 2 En parejas, expliquen por qué están de acuerdo o no con cada oración.

REACCIONAR
R
RECOMENDAR

B. En la prensa

Paso 1 Turnándose con su compañero/a, lean en voz alta cada reportaje sobre la región andina. Después de cada reportaje, reaccionen ante la información leída, utilizando expresiones como: **Es horrible que..., Es inquietante que..., Es impresionante que....**

Luego, hagan recomendaciones para asegurar que sigan adelante las soluciones que se han iniciado. Utilicen los nuevos verbos de este capítulo, como **llevar a cabo, promover** y **desarrollar.** Después, digan cómo estas iniciativas afectarán a las personas involucradas, utilizando la forma verbal **seguir** + *gerundio.*

MODELO: Es impresionante que tantos bolivianos puedan leer ahora. Recomiendo que, después de aprender a leer, los adultos bolivianos asistan a clases por la noche. Así seguirán aprendiendo nuevas destrezas.

1. **Bolivia** estará libre de analfabetismo gracias a un acuerdo de cooperación con Cuba y Venezuela. Más de 50.000 voluntarios bolivianos trabajaron en el proyecto «Yo, Sí Puedo» utilizando el

Los objetivos de las Naciones Unidas para el nuevo milenio

1 Erradicar la pobreza extrema y el hambre

2 Lograr la enseñanza primaria universal

3 Promover la igualdad entre los géneros y la autonomía de la mujer

4 Reducir la mortalidad infantil

5 Mejorar la salud materna

6 Combatir el VIH/SIDA el paludismo y otras enfermedades

7 Garantizar la sostenibilidad del medio ambiente

8 Fomentar una asociación mundial para el desarrollo

método cubano de alfabetización audiovisual. Cuba donó 30.000 televisores, 30.000 reproductores de vídeo y 30.000 cintas de grabación para implementar el proyecto de alfabetismo. Venezuela colaboró también, donando más de 8.000 paneles solares para que el programa pudiera llegar a las comunidades campesinas.

Reacción: Recomendación: Futuro:

2. En **el Perú,** 20 millones de sus ciudadanos sufren de hambre crónica. Científicos nacionales y extranjeros piensan que la harina de coca,[1] por su alto valor nutritivo y medicinal, puede ayudar a erradicar el hambre y la desnutrición de muchos peruanos. Es una cuestión de enriquecer los alimentos con la harina de coca y promover la idea con una agresiva campaña de concientización[2] alimentaria para desarrollar esta alternativa para combatir el hambre en las zonas pobres.

   Reacción: Recomendación: Futuro:

3. En Guayaquil, **Ecuador,** existen aproximadamente 1.000 pandillas,[3] unas muy violentas. El Ministerio de Bienestar Social promueve un programa para mejorar el sistema educativo y el uso del tiempo libre de los jóvenes que están en riesgo.[4] Ofrece «otras armas», como talleres sobre trabajos manuales, la creación de microempresas,[5] la formación de equipos de deportes y la promoción de concursos[6] culturales, tales como grafiti, bailes y música. Sin embargo, para llevar a cabo esta estrategia, la colaboración de otras instituciones nacionales y organizaciones no gubernamentales del extranjero será necesaria.

   Reacción: Recomendación: Futuro:

4. En 2008, las Naciones Unidas estimaron que había 3 millones de desplazados[7] en **Colombia.** La Fundación Pies Descalzos fue creada en 1995 por la cantante colombiana Shakira, con el propósito de proporcionar oportunidades para los niños desplazados, víctimas de la violencia en su país. Su objetivo principal es financiar y desarrollar programas en las áreas de educación, nutrición, apoyo psicológico y salud a la población joven de pocos recursos. En la actualidad,[8] existen cinco escuelas en regiones seriamente afectadas por la violencia, donde miles de niños reciben ayuda con sus necesidades.

   Reacción: Recomendación: Futuro:

[1]harina... *cocaine flour* [2]campaña... *campaign to raise public awareness* [3]*gangs* [4]En... *at risk* [5]*small businesses* [6]*competitions* [7]*displaced people* [8]En... *Currently*

Paso 2 En parejas, lean los ocho objetivos de la Organización de las Naciones Unidas (la ONU) para el nuevo milenio. Después, contesten las siguientes preguntas.

1. ¿Cómo ayudará cada iniciativa descrita en el **Paso 1** con la realización de los objetivos de la ONU?
2. ¿Creen que sea posible realizar estos objetivos a nivel mundial antes del 2020? ¿Por qué?

C. **Preguntas personales** En parejas, contesten las siguientes preguntas, utilizando el **Vocabulario del tema.** Luego, compartan sus ideas con la clase.

1. ¿Ha experimentado personalmente algún prejuicio o ha visto de cerca el maltrato de alguien por ser diferente? ¿Qué pasó? ¿Cómo reaccionó Ud.?

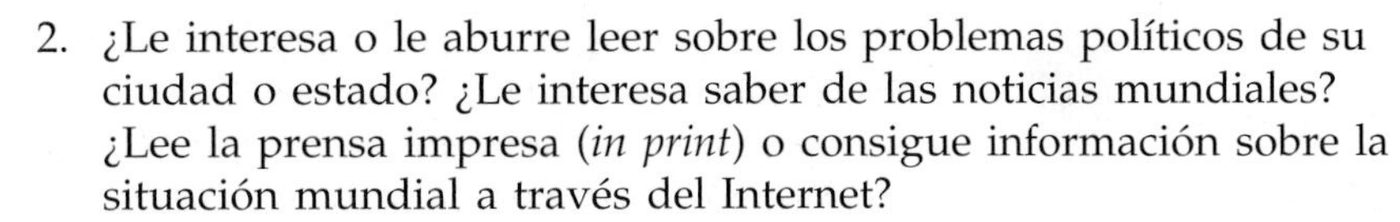

2. ¿Le interesa o le aburre leer sobre los problemas políticos de su ciudad o estado? ¿Le interesa saber de las noticias mundiales? ¿Lee la prensa impresa (*in print*) o consigue información sobre la situación mundial a través del Internet?

3. ¿Cuáles son algunas de las recomendaciones que Ud. le haría al gobernador / a la gobernadora de su estado/provincia para resolver los problemas de su estado/provincia?

4. En su opinión, ¿cuáles son dos de los problemas más inquietantes que los futuros líderes del mundo tendrán que resolver? Haga una comparación entre estos dos problemas explicando cómo son similares y cómo son diferentes.

5. En cuanto a su actitud hacia los problemas del mundo actual, ¿es Ud. activista, alarmista, extremista, idealista, optimista o pesimista? Explique su respuesta.

D. Noticias positivas

Paso 1 Lea el siguiente artículo y subraye cinco verbos que indiquen lo que hará una estación de radio colombiana para transmitir noticias positivas de su país.

Informativo colombiano de radio sólo transmite «noticias positivas»

SANTA FE DE BOGOTÁ, Colombia, 9 de diciembre (EFE).- El «circuito Todelar de Colombia», una de las principales organizaciones de radio de este país, empezó por primera vez en la historia nacional un programa especial de 120 horas continuas con «noticias positivas» de su país.

Hasta el próximo viernes serán entrevistados más de 600 ciudadanos colombianos que destacan en diferentes disciplinas, tras[1] ser localizados en una investigación que duró cuatro meses, declaró el director de noticias, César Fernández.

El programa, que se transmitirá por las 40 emisoras del circuito de emisoras para toda Colombia, tiene proyección internacional y pretende mostrar la «cara real» de esta nación latinoamericana, que ha soportado duras acciones del narcotráfico y la violencia.

Estaciones como «105.9 Aquí Colombia», de Nueva York, emitirá para Estados Unidos durante los cinco días la «positiva» jornada radial.

«Vamos a demostrar que tenemos muchos valores y que hay una buena semilla[2] humana en Colombia. Somos milliones y milliones de buenos frente a unos pocos que se destacan por sus delitos», agregó Fernández.

Con las once estrofas[3] del himno nacional, que por primera vez se interpretaron completas en una red[4] de emisoras, Todelar comenzó la «jornada de creer en Colombia y en sus habitantes».

Personalidades como el Nobel de Literatura (1982) Gabriel García Márquez, el científico Manuel Elkin Patarroyo, el pintor y escultor Fernando Botero y cientos de colombianos que viven por todo el mundo, que destacan por sus labores profesionales, desfilarán[5] por los micrófonos de Todelar.

[1]después de [2]*seed* [3]*verses* [4]*network* [5]*will parade*

Paso 2 Ahora, en parejas, escriban cuatro titulares positivos sobre este país, utilizando el vocabulario nuevo de este capítulo.

Paso 3 En grupos de tres, lean los titulares que cada uno/a acaba de escribir y luego reaccionen y hagan recomendaciones como si fueran una de las personas indicadas en la siguiente lista. Traten de usar palabras nuevas en sus reacciones y frases como **Es fantástico que..., Es posible que..., Es evidente que..., Es impresionante que..., Dudo que..., Es alentador que..., Tengo miedo de que...** y **No creo que....**

- una persona idealista
- una persona paranoica
- una persona pesimista

E. **Problemas repentinos** Entre todos, revisen los siguientes problemas y hagan una lista de palabras nuevas de este capítulo y de los capítulos anteriores que los ayuden a conversar con facilidad sobre cada problema repentino. Después, en parejas, preparen un diálogo espontáneo sobre cada problema.

1. Una persona está tratando de reclutar[1] a un(a) estudiante para hacer de voluntario en Latinoamérica. El/La estudiante le pregunta cómo podría ayudar. El reclutador / La reclutadora menciona los problemas que hay y cómo los voluntarios pueden ayudar. Está muy apasionado/a y lleno/a de entusiasmo cuando habla de los proyectos de voluntariado. Al/A la estudiante le interesa, pero no es muy atrevido/a: reacciona con muchas dudas ante la idea de hacer de voluntario y expresa su miedo por no saber suficiente español para trabajar allí.
2. Su primo/a anuncia que ha vendido todas sus posesiones para ir al Perú y trabajar con la gente indígena. Trate de convencerlo/la de que es una locura total lo que quiere hacer. Su primo/a responde a sus reacciones con sorpresa y desilusión ante sus dudas y falta de idealismo.

[1]*recruit*

NOTA CULTURAL • La vida política de los jóvenes hispanos

Para muchos jóvenes hispanos, el activismo político es una parte importante de la vida diaria. A nivel general, los jóvenes se mantienen al día en cuestiones de política de manera consistente. Creen que es importante leer el periódico, mirar el noticiero[1] en la televisión o buscar las noticias en el Internet. No sólo saben cuál es la situación de su propia nación, sino que también están muy enterados de la política internacional. En los cafés y los bares que frecuentan los jóvenes, es común oír fuertes discusiones sobre la situación mundial, además de conversaciones sobre los deportes, el cine y los últimos chismes.

Sin embargo, el interés en la política con frecuencia va más allá de la conversación. Es muy común que los estudiantes universitarios y de escuela secundaria participen en huelgas generales y manifestaciones para protestar contra ciertas injusticias, como la subida[2] del precio de los boletos de autobús, la matrícula de las clases o los impuestos, o cuando algún político comete un fraude. Además, no es raro ver protestas contra las intervenciones estadounidenses en Latinoamérica o en otras partes del mundo. Las acciones de los jóvenes, a veces pacíficas, a veces más agresivas, demuestran una fuerte creencia en el poder de la voz del pueblo.

[1]*newscast* [2]*rise*

Preguntas

1. ¿En qué actividades políticas participa Ud.?
2. ¿Ha participado alguna vez en una manifestación o huelga para protestar contra algo? ¿Por qué participó? ¿Cuáles fueron los resultados de la manifestación o huelga?
3. ¿Cuáles son las mejores maneras de protestar contra la injusticia? ¿Por qué cree así?

Actividad

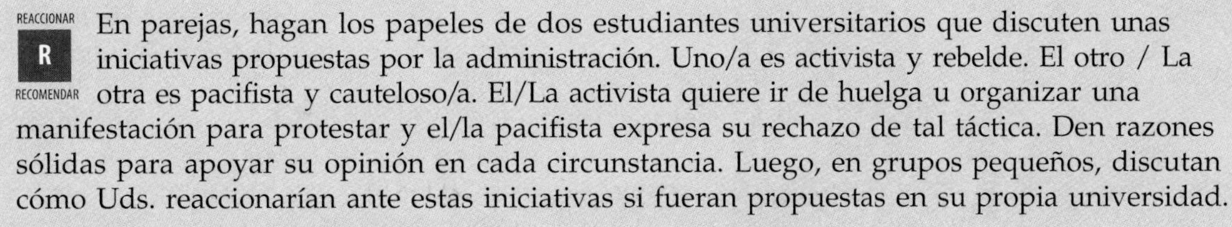

En parejas, hagan los papeles de dos estudiantes universitarios que discuten unas iniciativas propuestas por la administración. Uno/a es activista y rebelde. El otro / La otra es pacifista y cauteloso/a. El/La activista quiere ir de huelga u organizar una manifestación para protestar y el/la pacifista expresa su rechazo de tal táctica. Den razones sólidas para apoyar su opinión en cada circunstancia. Luego, en grupos pequeños, discutan cómo Uds. reaccionarían ante estas iniciativas si fueran propuestas en su propia universidad.

1. El presidente de la universidad quiere invertir un millón de dólares en reclutar a mejores atletas.
2. La administración anuncia que duplicará el costo del estacionamiento en el recinto universitario y que las multas por mal estacionamiento se triplicarán.
3. Para ahorrar dinero, se despedirá al 20 por ciento de los profesores y más clases se darán por el Internet.

Puntos clave

Hacer hipótesis

En esta sección del capítulo, Ud. va a practicar la meta comunicativa **Hacer hipótesis.** Para hacerlo bien, hay que utilizar las estructuras gramaticales (los puntos clave) de la siguiente tabla que pertenecen a la meta comunicativa. Antes de continuar, estudie las explicaciones de estas estructuras gramaticales en las páginas 226–228.

LA META COMUNICATIVA DE ESTE CAPÍTULO		
ICONO	META COMUNICATIVA	PUNTOS CLAVE
H HIPÓTESIS	Hacer hipótesis	• el pasado de subjuntivo • el condicional

Una manifestación en La Paz, Bolivia

PRUEBA DIAGNÓSTICA

Lea la siguiente entrevista a un estudiante boliviano que participó en una manifestación. Conjugue los verbos que están entre paréntesis para expresar situaciones hipotéticas.

REPORTERO: ¿Qué ________[1] (hacer) Ud. para mejorar la situación de la gente indígena de su país si ________[2] (ser) ministro del gobierno?

OSWALDO: Si ________[3] (tener) el apoyo necesario, ________[4] (poder) coordinar las luchas políticas y sociales de todas las comunidades indígenas.

REPORTERO: ¿Qué ________[5] (necesitar) para llevar a cabo tal coordinación?

OSWALDO: Si ________[6] (poder) contar con los fondos del gobierno, ________[7] (desarrollar) una campaña agresiva para comunicarnos mejor con las comunidades rurales. Sé que los jóvenes universitarios de mi país ________[8] (ayudar) con esta coordinación si ________[9] (saber) que sus esfuerzos ________[10] (promover) la justicia social.

REPORTERO: Muchas gracias. Me gusta su optimismo y espero verlo algún día de ministro o incluso presidente de nuestro país.

Expresiones útiles

Para hablar del mundo actual

actualmente	*currently*
desgraciadamente	*unfortunately*
francamente	*frankly*
seguramente	*surely*
verdaderamente	*truly*
de hecho	*in fact*
el hecho de que + *subjuntivo**	*the fact that*
en cuanto a	*as far as . . . is concerned*
hoy (en) día	*nowadays*

*Traditionally, the phrase **el hecho de que** has always been followed by the subjunctive. In *Punto y aparte* and elsewhere, however, you may notice it followed by the indicative. This shift in usage seems to be due in part to influences from the English language and in part to the fact that some native Spanish speakers report choosing between the subjunctive and the indicative according to how certain or uncertain they are of the truth or validity of the statement following the phrase.

Actividades

Las siguientes actividades le darán la oportunidad de practicar las metas comunicativas. Habrá un énfasis particular en hacer hipótesis, utilizando el condicional y el pasado de subjuntivo.

A. La cadena En parejas, formen una serie de oraciones hipotéticas, utilizando la última cláusula de la primera oración para formar la cláusula hipotética de la segunda oración, como en el modelo. A ver hasta qué punto cada pareja lleva su serie de oraciones.

MODELO: Si Laura fuera a Bolivia y Colombia, su padre estaría inquieto.
Si su padre estuviera inquieto, Laura lo calmaría.
Si Laura calmara a su padre, ella podría pasarlo bien en su viaje.
Si ella pudiera pasarlo bien en su viaje,...

1. Si yo fuera presidente/a de esta universidad,...
2. Si yo pudiera conocer a cualquier líder mundial,...
3. Si tuviera un millón de dólares para donar,...
4. Si yo trabajara para la Fundación Pies Descalzos con su fundadora, Shakira,...
5. Si mis padres decidieran hacer de voluntario en Latinoamérica,...

B. ¿Qué diría o haría? En parejas, comenten lo que Uds. dirían o harían en las siguientes situaciones. Utilicen las expresiones útiles de arriba cuando sea posible y expliquen el porqué de sus respuestas.

1. si su madre o padre se postulara para líder de este país
2. si Ud. y sus amigos tuvieran que luchar en una guerra
3. si Ud. fuera pacifista durante una guerra internacional
4. si un voluntario de la Cruz Roja tratara de reclutarlo/la para ir a Bolivia
5. si sus compañeros de clase quisieran protestar contra el precio de la matrícula de esta universidad
6. si viera a una persona con hambre en la calle
7. si su compañero/a de cuarto fuera paranoico/a

C. La medicina tradicional: ¿Debemos respetarla o rechazarla?

Paso 1 Lea el artículo en la página siguiente. Mientras lee, busque cognados que lo/la ayuden a entender mejor el tema.

LA MEDICINA TRADICIONAL:
¿Debemos respetarla o rechazarla?

Hierbas medicinales, La Paz, Bolivia

Por siglos los indígenas del Amazonas han recurrido a sus alrededores para buscar tratamientos para las enfermedades. Normalmente, cada tribu cuenta con un chamán que usa plantas tropicales y ritos elaborados para curar una variedad de enfermedades. Hasta hace poco, la medicina occidental calificaba a estos chamanes de embusteros,[1] pero últimamente varias escuelas de medicina norteamericanas han empezado a ofrecer cursos en el Amazonas para que los médicos, enfermeros y farmacéuticos aprendan de la sabiduría tradicional de los chamanes.

Sin embargo, este interés también trae problemas. Muchas compañías farmacéuticas internacionales han llegado al Amazonas para explotar los recursos naturales y buscar curas para las enfermedades que afligen a los países desarrollados. Las tribus se quejan de que las compañías hagan acuerdos con los gobiernos nacionales pero no con las tribus, que no respeten sus prácticas tradicionales, que los dejen sin recursos para atender a su propia gente y que sólo les interesen las plantas que tienen un valor monetario. Es más, alegan que el dinero generado con sus propios recursos nunca llega a manos de las tribus. Según se estima, las tribus amazónicas reciben sólo un 0,001 por ciento del dinero que se obtiene de la venta de sus plantas. Además, las tribus temen perder[2] su cultura y su modo de vida, por el contacto excesivo con culturas más modernas y poderosas. Para aquellas, la globalización no es positiva porque amenaza su mera[3] existencia.

[1]de... *as tricksters* [2]temen... *are afraid of losing* [3]*mere*

Paso 2 En parejas, terminen las siguientes oraciones haciendo el papel de la persona indicada.

UNA ESTUDIANTE DE MEDICINA

1. Me fascina que...
2. Si yo _________ (poder) estudiar con un chamán,...

UN CHAMÁN

3. Me molesta que...
4. Si nosotros _________ (tener) más poder y control,...

LA PRESIDENTA DE UNA COMPAÑÍA FARMACÉUTICA

5. Es importantísimo que...
6. Si nuestra compañía _________ (descubrir) en el Amazonas una cura para el cáncer,...

DESAFÍO

Paso 3 Los miembros del Pacto Andino (Bolivia, Colombia, el Ecuador, el Perú y Chile) están desarrollando leyes modelo para la conservación y el uso sostenible de materia biológica. Estas leyes les darán más poder a las naciones y tribus locales del Amazonas para que todas puedan controlar y beneficiarse más de los recursos naturales de la zona. En parejas, terminen las siguientes oraciones para decir qué pasará cuando se cumplan esas leyes.

1. Cuando _________ (haber) más leyes para proteger los derechos de las tribus,...
2. A menos que _________ (desarrollarse) un buen plan de uso sostenible para estos recursos, la gente del Amazonas...
3. Con tal de que las tribus _________ (tener) más control sobre la venta de sus plantas regionales,...
4. Con estas leyes, antes de que las compañías multinacionales _________ (explotar) los recursos de una zona,...
5. Tan pronto como _________ (haber) más cooperación entre las compañías y las tribus,...

Paso 4 En parejas, busquen un argumento a favor y otro en contra de cada una de las siguientes afirmaciones. Después, expresen sus propias opiniones sobre cada afirmación. Cuando terminen, compartan sus ideas con el resto de la clase.

1. Podemos aprender mucho de las culturas «subdesarrolladas», incluso en áreas tan avanzadas como la medicina.
2. Los indígenas pueden beneficiarse de la presencia de las compañías farmacéuticas extranjeras en sus tierras.
3. Los países «primermundistas» deben dejar en paz a estas tribus y buscar curas para sus enfermedades en otras partes.
4. Aunque las compañías destruyan la forma de vivir de los indígenas, es importante seguir explotando los recursos del Amazonas porque muchas más personas podrán curarse con los medicamentos que se encuentran allí.
5. La globalización es un fenómeno del que todos se pueden beneficiar.

D. Evo Morales y Barack Obama En 2005, Evo Morales, un indígena aymara, fue elegido el primer presidente indígena de cualquier país andino. En 2008, Barack Obama fue elegido el primer presidente afroamericano de los Estados Unidos. Durante sus campañas hablaron de los problemas más inquietantes de sus países respectivos.

Paso 1 En parejas, lean las siguientes descripciones de algunas de las cuestiones que los dos líderes enfrentaron cuando eran candidatos. Después, preparen la reacción que Uds. piensan que cada candidato tuvo ante la cuestión y la promesa que hizo para remediar la situación. Para la reacción, utilicen expresiones como **No es justo que…, No creo que…** y **Es alarmante que….** Para la promesa, empiecen con **Si fuera presidente/a…** y incluyan varias palabras nuevas de este capítulo, por ejemplo: **colaborar con, combatir, desarrollar, financiar** y **promover.**

Evo Morales, presidente de Bolivia

Evo Morales:

1. En las culturas andinas, la hoja de coca se usa para hacer té y se mastica (*it is chewed*) para aliviar el soroche (*altitude sickness*). Por la guerra estadounidense contra las drogas, los indígenas que antes se ganaban la vida cultivando la coca para usos tradicionales ahora no pueden sostener a sus familias.
2. Las compañías multinacionales quieren tomar control de los recursos naturales, como el gas.
3. Bolivia es uno de los países más pobres de Latinoamérica. Para colmo de males, el 10 por ciento más rico de la población gana veinticinco veces más al año que el 40 por ciento más pobre.

Barack Obama, presidente de los Estados Unidos

Barack Obama:

4. La guerra de Irak, que costaba más de 4 mil millones de dólares al mes en 2003, ha subido a más de 12 mil millones mensuales. En términos concretos, en el 2008, cada familia estadounidense pagó más de 1.000 dólares al mes para financiar la guerra.
5. Hay cerca de 41 millones de personas sin seguro médico. El sistema de salud de los Estados Unidos es el único entre las democracias industrializadas que no provee seguro médico universal para todos los ciudadanos.
6. La subcontratación de trabajos a países en vías de desarrollo ha causado la pérdida de trabajos en los Estados Unidos.

Paso 2 En grupos de tres, discutan lo difícil que es cumplir con las promesas electorales después de las elecciones. Hablen de si Uds. piensan que es posible que cada presidente lleve a cabo sus promesas a lo largo de su administración. Utilicen expresiones como **Dudo que…, Estoy seguro/a de que…, Es probable que…** y **Espero que….**

Paso 3 Vea la pintura que representa un pueblo boliviano durante una campaña política en la primera página de este capítulo. En parejas, hagan una lista de las promesas que Uds. piensan que el candidato le hace al pueblo para ganar su voto. Utilicen el vocabulario nuevo, tratando de incorporar por lo menos cinco de los nuevos verbos y otras palabras nuevas también.

Paso 4 Escriba un breve discurso político como si fuera un candidato andino / una candidata andina, en el que hable de la pobreza, el analfabetismo y los derechos humanos. En su discurso, complete las siguientes oraciones:

1. Si yo __________ (ser) presidente/a...
2. Si nosotros __________ (tener) una sociedad más justa...
3. Tan pronto como __________ (terminar) las elecciones...
4. En cuanto yo __________ (poder),...

F FUTURO

E. Un futuro más justo y pacífico

Paso 1 En parejas, conjuguen el verbo que está entre paréntesis y terminen las oraciones explicando cómo será el mundo en el futuro.

1. Cuando todos los niños del mundo __________ (tener) suficiente comida,...
2. Tan pronto como los derechos humanos __________ (respetarse) en todos los países,...
3. Después de que __________ (encontrarse) una cura para el SIDA,...
4. En cuanto todos los padres de Bolivia __________ (tener) un trabajo que les pague bien,...
5. Hasta que los países desarrollados no les __________ (dar) más dinero a los países pobres,...
6. Para que __________ (haber) menos terrorismo,...
7. Cuando más personas __________ (hacer) de voluntarias,...

Paso 2 En grupos de tres, hablen de los cambios que Uds. esperan ver en este país en los próximos diez años.

Rincón cultural

Lugares fascinantes:

La región andina

1. **Cuzco y Machu Picchu, Perú** Localizada a unos 3.000 metros sobre el nivel del mar, Cuzco fue la capital del imperio inca antes de que los españoles la conquistaran en 1533. Símbolo de la mezcla racial y cultural en el Perú, en Cuzco todavía se puede escuchar tanto el quechua como el español en sus calles y apreciar las ruinas de

Machu Picchu, Perú

edificios y paredes incas, sobre las que los españoles construyeron iglesias barrocas y casas coloniales. La Catedral y la Iglesia de la Merced contienen colecciones magníficas del arte colonial, mientras que las ruinas de Coricancha, un edificio que en la época de los incas estaba recubierto de oro, y el Museo de Arqueología dan testimonio a la grandeza del imperio inca. Si Ud. tiene la oportunidad de visitar Cuzco, es imprescindible que vaya a Machu Picchu. Estas ruinas en lo alto de los Andes fueron una vez un importante centro de la civilización inca. En 1911, un profesor de la Universidad de Yale, Hiram Bingham, descubrió este lugar arqueológico. Allí se puede admirar el Templo Mayor, una plaza sagrada, acueductos, fuentes y otras maravillas arquitectónicas. Aunque es difícil llegar allí, algunos de los que visitan Machu Picchu consideran la experiencia como algo mágico e intensamente espiritual.

Cartagena de Indias, Colombia

2. **Cartagena, Colombia** Esta ciudad caribeña, fundada en 1533 por el español Pedro de Heredia, llegó a ser uno de los puertos españoles más importantes de la época. Por su estratégica posición geográfica, con una bahía protegida de los vientos, sufría ataques frecuentes de piratas y otros conquistadores, lo cual motivó la construcción de una gran muralla,[1] dos castillos (San Felipe de Barajas y San Fernando de Bocachica) y otras defensas. Por eso se le dio a Cartagena el nombre de «la Ciudad Heroica». Hoy en día es una de las ciudades amuralladas mejor conservadas del mundo. La arquitectura militar y religiosa (La Catedral, la Iglesia Santo Domingo, el Convento de San Pedro Claver) y los museos (el Museo de Oro, el Museo Arqueológico, el Museo Colonial y el Museo de Arte Moderno) más las preciosas playas conocidas por la variedad de colores que cambian según la hora del día hacen de esta bella ciudad caribeña un lugar de gran interés turístico. También hay una rica vida cultural: el Festival Internacional del Cine, que tiene lugar en marzo; la Fiesta de los Acordeones, que se celebra en agosto; y el Festival de Jazz, bajo la luna en diciembre. Gabriel García Márquez, ganador del Premio Nobel de Literatura en 1982, vivió en Cartagena durante varias épocas de su vida y hoy en día pasa tiempo allí en su casa, donde ritualmente escribe en las primeras horas de la mañana en su despacho[2] que da al mar. Está claro por qué esta bella ciudad histórica sirve de inspiración al gran escritor.

3. **Las Islas Galápagos, Ecuador** A unas 500 millas de la costa ecuatoriana está el archipiélago de las Islas Galápagos, formadas de piedra volcánica, que, a pesar de su apariencia austera, ofrecen una enorme variedad de flora y fauna. Fue en estas islas donde el científico Charles Darwin empezó a formular su teoría de la evolución en 1835.

[1]*city wall* [2]*office*

Las Islas Galápagos, Ecuador

En 1959, se constituyó el Parque Nacional Galápagos. Allí trabajan organizaciones, como la Fundación Charles Darwin, para conservar los tesoros naturales. Es un ecosistema diverso y complejo donde cohabitan animales marinos y terrestres. Entre las especies que allí se encuentran hay delfines, pingüinos, orcas, ballenas azules y jorobadas,[3] focas,[4] iguanas marinas y una extraordinaria variedad de pájaros. Por supuesto, no nos podemos olvidar de la gigantesca tortuga galápago, que llega a pesar hasta 550 libras y vivir hasta 150 años. La más famosa de estas tortugas se llama George: tiene 95 años; es decir, es todavía un jovencito. Hoy la flora y la fauna de las islas se encuentran amenazadas por la introducción de otras especies y por la intervención humana. El gobierno ecuatoriano junto con la UNESCO y la Unión Mundial para la Conservación están tomando medidas importantes para proteger las islas.

La Paz con el Nevado Illimani al fondo

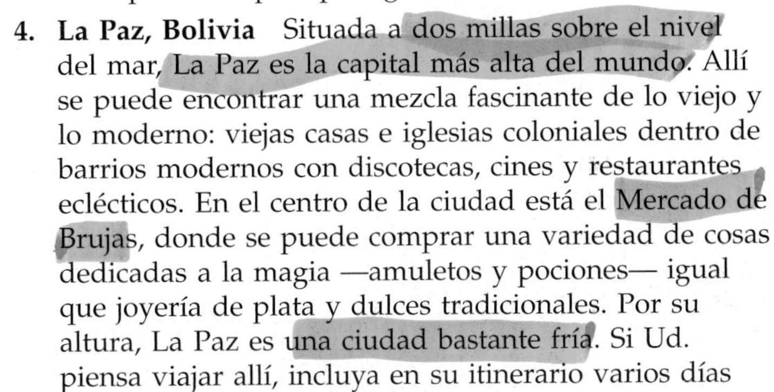

4. **La Paz, Bolivia** Situada a dos millas sobre el nivel del mar, La Paz es la capital más alta del mundo. Allí se puede encontrar una mezcla fascinante de lo viejo y lo moderno: viejas casas e iglesias coloniales dentro de barrios modernos con discotecas, cines y restaurantes eclécticos. En el centro de la ciudad está el Mercado de Brujas, donde se puede comprar una variedad de cosas dedicadas a la magia —amuletos y pociones— igual que joyería de plata y dulces tradicionales. Por su altura, La Paz es una ciudad bastante fría. Si Ud. piensa viajar allí, incluya en su itinerario varios días de descanso al principio para recuperarse de los efectos a veces graves del soroche: enfermedad provocada por el cambio de altitud y la falta de oxígeno en las alturas que puede provocar fuertes dolores de cabeza, escalofríos y vómitos. No muy lejos de la capital, a unos 13.000 pies sobre el nivel del mar, queda el lago navegable más alto del mundo, el Lago Titicaca. Dentro del lago están las islas del Sol y de la Luna, con sus palacios, jardines y templos de la civilización inca.

[3]*humpbacked* [4]*seals*

¡Viaje conmigo a la región andina!

Vea el vídeo para saber lo que Gabriela les mandó a Javier y Sara sobre su viaje a la región andina.

Video footage provided by

BBC Motion Gallery

ACTIVIDADES

A. En parejas, contesten las siguientes preguntas sobre los cuatro lugares fascinantes.

1. ¿Por qué se puede considerar Cuzco un lugar mestizo?
2. ¿Cuáles son algunas de las atracciones turísticas de Cuzco y sus alrededores?
3. ¿Por qué podría ser Cartagena un lugar interesante para visitar?
4. ¿Por qué se considera importante proteger las Islas Galápagos?
5. ¿Qué acontecimiento científico ocurrió en las Islas Galápagos?
6. ¿Por qué es famosa La Paz? ¿Cuáles son algunos de sus atractivos fascinantes?
7. ¿Por qué tiene fama el Lago Titicaca?

B. Localice los cuatro lugares fascinantes de la región andina en el mapa y ponga un número del 1 al 4 para indicar el grado de interés que Ud. tiene en visitar estos lugares. Turnándose con un compañero / una compañera, explique por qué a Ud. le interesa más el número 1 y por qué le interesa menos el número 4. Haga por lo menos tres comparaciones entre los dos lugares cuando presente su explicación.

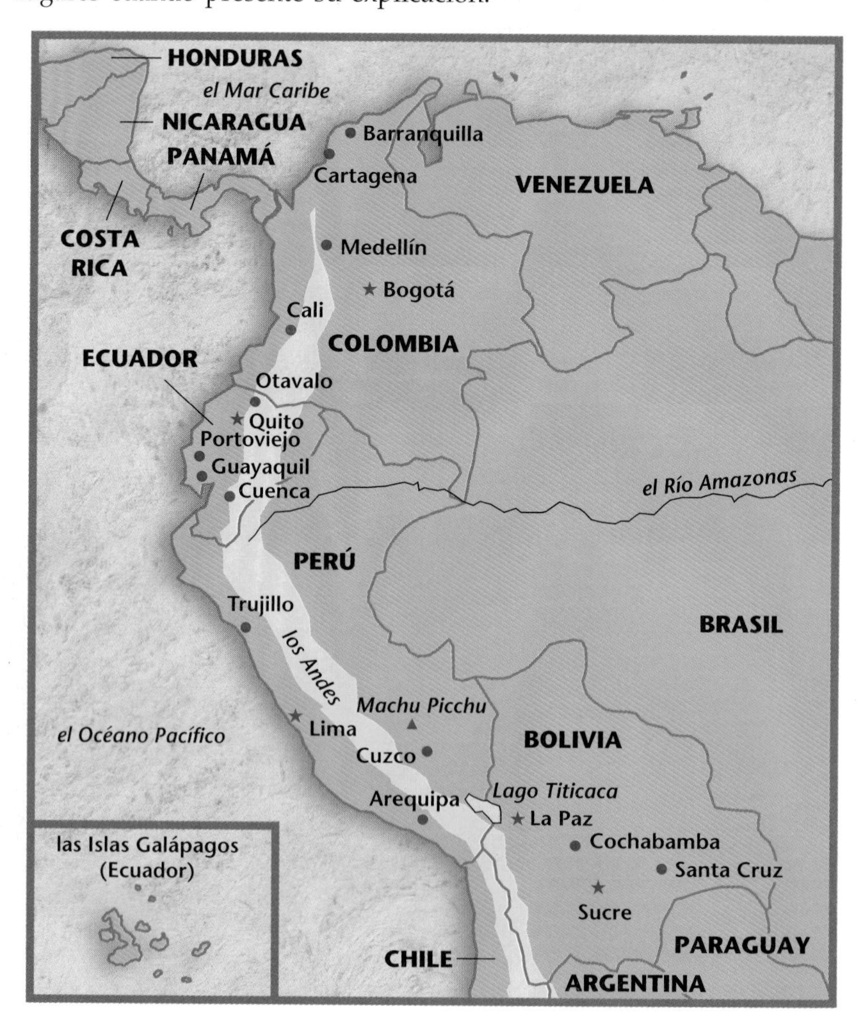

SÍNTESIS

C. Ahora que ha leído sobre los lugares y ha visto el videoblog de Gabriela, para cada uno de los cuatro lugares, prepare unos apuntes para argumentar y debatir con un compañero / una compañera sobre el mejor sitio para llevar a cabo dos eventos. Incluya en sus apuntes algunas de las siguientes metas comunicativas: descripción, comparación, recomendación, gustos, hipótesis, futuro. No sabrá qué sitio le tocará defender hasta el momento en que comience la actividad.

Ahora, su instructor(a) le dirá qué lugar debe defender. En parejas, realicen un debate para decidir el mejor sitio para uno de los siguientes eventos.

1. ¿Cuál es el mejor lugar para un congreso sobre la pobreza mundial?
2. ¿Cuál es el mejor lugar para la reunión anual de la compañía REI?

Un artista hispano:

Gonzalo Endara Crow

Gonzalo Endara Crow nació en Quito, Ecuador, en 1936. Ganador de muchos premios nacionales e internacionales, Endara Crow participa por medio de su arte en el surrealismo y en la corriente literaria del realismo mágico,* cuyo representante más famoso es el escritor colombiano Gabriel García Márquez.

Después de la noche, *de Gonzalo Endara Crow*

*El realismo mágico es un movimiento literario en el que se combinan hechos de la vida diaria con imágenes de la fantasía y del subconsciente.

El arte de Endara Crow es una maravilla de colores y fantasía, pero a la vez representa la realidad americana. Muestra un mundo donde conviven lo tradicional y lo moderno, la realidad y la imaginación, la vida material y la vida espiritual. Su pintura es verdaderamente mestiza,* mezclando lo indígena campesino tradicional con lo occidental moderno. El protagonista de sus obras de arte es un anónimo pueblo colonial andino. Es un pueblo en el que el tiempo se ha detenido, donde la modernidad pasa por encima de él.

En los cuadros de Endara Crow, cada color y cada objeto tienen un valor simbólico. El conjunto artístico forma una fábula que narra la vida de los pueblos ecuatorianoandinos. Fíjese en el cuadro *Después de la noche* (página 155) y piense en la simbología de los colores y objetos representados.

PREGUNTAS

Conteste las siguientes preguntas, según el cuadro y la lectura sobre el arte de Endara Crow.

1. ¿Por qué vuelan (*fly*) los trenes por encima del pueblo? ¿Por qué cree Ud. que no se representa ninguna estación de trenes?
2. ¿Qué cree que implica *Después de la noche,* el título del cuadro?
3. ¿Por qué son tan pequeñas las personas y por qué parecen todas iguales?
4. ¿Qué aspectos de la vida de un pueblo pequeño nunca se ven afectados por el tiempo? ¿Qué cosas nunca cambiarán?
5. ¿Opina Ud. que la modernización siempre mejora la vida humana? Dé ejemplos para apoyar su opinión.

ACTIVIDAD

Identifique y explique el simbolismo de los siguientes objetos en el cuadro *Después de la noche.*

OBJETO	SIMBOLISMO
1. _____ el tren de colores brillantes	**a.** el mestizaje
2. _____ el tren negro	**b.** la esperanza
3. _____ los habitantes del pueblo	**c.** el amanecer (*dawn*)
4. _____ los globos (*balloons*)	**d.** la felicidad
5. _____ los arcos iris	**e.** la noche

La música andina

Una gran parte de la música andina refleja la fuerte influencia de las diversas culturas indígenas de la región. Para crear esta música distintiva y reconocible por el mundo entero, se han combinado instrumentos tanto europeos como autóctonos.[1] Aunque los instrumentos de los indígenas precolombinos eran muy variados, predominaban los instrumentos de viento. Entre los que todavía se usan hoy en día están las zampoñas o sikus,[2] la quena[3] y las tarkas, una

[1]*native* [2]*pan pipes* [3]*a notched flute*

*mezcla de lo indígena con lo europeo

Un hombre tocando una quena en Cuzco, Peru

flauta rectangular. La preferencia andina por los tonos altos, para imitar los sonidos de la naturaleza, influyó en la modificación de instrumentos europeos para que se acomodaran mejor a los gustos andinos. Esto se aprecia en el uso del violín y en la creación del charango, una suerte[4] de guitarra andina.

En «Himno al Inca», Ud. escuchará la quena y el charango al principio, acompañados por la guitarra, el bombo (un tambor típico de la región) y otros instrumentos de percusión. En la primera parte, cuyo ritmo vuelve al fin de la canción, se oye el ritmo y los acordes típicos del huayno, un estilo de canción y baile andino, mezclado con la cumbia, un ritmo colombiano. Después, la canción se transforma para reflejar la fuerte influencia africana que hay en la costa del Perú. En esta parte, se oye la guitarra, el bajo eléctrico, el güiro (un instrumento de percusión caribeño) y el cajón: una caja de madera que primeramente era un cajón de pescado en el que el músico se sentaba y pegaba con las manos.

[4]*kind*

ACTIVIDADES

A. Antes de cantar Va a escuchar «Himno al Inca», una canción cuyo tema tiene que ver con el sufrimiento y la valentía de la cultura indígena desde la Conquista. Aunque alude al gran imperio inca, que dominaba la mayor parte de la región cuando llegaron los españoles, «Himno al Inca» es un homenaje a todos los grupos indígenas que han sobrevivido hasta hoy. Conteste las siguientes preguntas.

1. ¿Ha oído Ud. alguna vez alguna canción de la región andina? ¿Le gustó? ¿Dónde o en qué ocasión la oyó?
2. ¿Qué tipo de vocabulario espera encontrar en una canción cuyo título es «Himno al Inca»?
3. ¿Conoce algunas canciones contemporáneas que combinen estilos de los años 80 ó 90 con la música rap, por ejemplo?

B. ¡A cantar! Escuche la canción «Himno al Inca» que se puede encontrar en el CD *Estampillas musicales.* Luego, comparta sus impresiones de los artistas y sus canciones con sus compañeros de clase, utilizando frases como **Me gusta(n)... porque..., Me encanta que..., Es impresionante/fantástico que..., Me sorprende que...** y **Es evidente que....**

Himno al Inca

Incansable alma indígena
Incandescente obsidiana
Impenetrable su tristeza
Incomparable su belleza

Imperdonable la conquista
Incalculable la miseria
Invisible su existencia
Inevitable su cultura

Aymara y Aguaruna
Quechua, Urus y Huambisa
Mestizo, Ayacucho y Ancash
Mascho-Piro del Río Purú
[*Se repite dos veces más.*]

C. **Después de cantar** En parejas, contesten las siguientes preguntas sobre la canción «Himno al Inca».

1. ¿Cuáles son los instrumentos que reconoció en esta canción?
2. ¿Cuál es el mensaje principal de la canción?
3. ¿Notó Ud. el juego de palabras en la canción? Explique.
4. ¿Qué parte de la canción refleja la influencia africana que hay en el Perú?

D. **¡A escuchar!** Para apreciar más la música andina criolla, vaya a YouTube™ y escuche la música de Chabuca Granda o los valses criollos de Eva Ayllon. Para conocer mejor la música afroperuana, escuche a Gabriel Alegría (jazz afroperuano), Susana Baca (ganadora de un Grammy en 2005) o el extraordinario grupo de danza y música Perú Negro. Otros músicos peruanos de interés son Grupo 5 (cumbia) y Nosequien y los Nosecuantos (rock y pop). Otros músicos de la región son Shakira y Juanes (Colombia), Israel Brito (Ecuador) y Los Kjarkas (Bolivia).

Lectura

José Cardona-López, un colombiano radicado en los Estados Unidos, es profesor de literatura hispanoamericana en la Texas A&M International University. Ha dictado cursos de creación literaria en la Escuela Española de Middlebury College y ha publicado varias obras literarias, incluyendo la novela *Sueños para una siesta* (1986), los volúmenes de cuentos *La puerta del espejo* (1983), *Todo es adrede* (1993), *Siete y tres nueve* (2003) y el libro de investigaciones *Teoría y práctica de la nouvelle* (2003). Su cuento «El candidato» trata de un personaje político que se preocupa más por su imagen y por su individualidad que por el trabajo que realizaría si fuera elegido.

Antes de leer

A. **Para comentar** En grupos de tres, contesten las siguientes preguntas.

1. ¿Han escuchado Uds. alguna vez un buen discurso político u otro muy aburrido? ¿Qué características se asocian con un buen discurso político?
2. ¿Conocen a un político / una mujer político a quien admiran? ¿Por qué lo/la admiran? Si no conocen a ninguno, en su opinión, ¿cómo debe ser un buen político / una buena mujer político?
3. Muchas veces durante las campañas políticas, el público se cansa de la retórica de los candidatos porque sabe que no puede contar con sus promesas. ¿Qué opinan Uds. de la siguiente afirmación?

   «Las palabras son baratas, pero la acción cuesta.»

B. **Acercándose al tema** Lea el título de la ficha y las nueve palabras asociadas con los candidatos. Con un compañero / una compañera, decida si los espacios en blanco requieren un sustantivo, un verbo o un adjetivo. Luego, escoja la palabra apropiada de la ficha para completar las oraciones.

El candidato		
la campaña	el ensayo[1]	el pecho[2]
eliminar	esconderse	inaugurar
entumecido/a[3]	obsesionado/a	ubicuo/a

[1]*rehearsal* [2]*chest* [3]*numb*

1. Aicardo Umaña inició su candidatura a la presidencia de la república con una _________ para eliminar el déficit, pavimentar calles y repartir[1] juguetes en diciembre.
2. En sus discursos, Aicardo constantemente usa la palabra **yo** (*Yo* soy tal, *yo* haré esto, *yo* prometo, etcétera) y empuja[2] con vigor el índice[3] derecho contra su _________ cuando dice el «yo».
3. Una vez, en un discurso de 90 minutos para _________ una exposición, el narrador le contó 87 yoes. La mano del candidato terminó _________.
4. El narrador concluye que su manera de señalarse[4] a sí mismo cuando pronuncia el «yo» es un movimiento que ha requerido mucho _________.
5. El narrador está _________ con contar el número de veces que Aicardo dice «yo» en cada discurso que da.
6. Cuando asiste a los discursos de Aicardo, el narrador _________ detrás de un árbol para que el candidato no lo vea.
7. En todas las fotos que salen en la prensa, se ve ese _________ dedo fusilándole el pecho,[5] y la boca abierta como una O mayúscula.[6]

[1]*give out* [2]*pushes* [3]*index finger* [4]*pointing* [5]fusilándole... *shooting into his chest* [6]*upper case*

El candidato

Después de no verlo por casi quince años, ahora Aicardo Umaña se ha convertido en candidato a la presidencia de la república. Su ascenso hasta la candidatura lo inició con campañas para pavimentar calles de barrios y periféricos de la capital y para repartir juguetes en diciembre. Fue diputado,[1] más tarde senador, y en algunas reuniones internacionales presentó ponencias para que el país pudiera salir del subdesarrollo. Ahora, por la televisión promete, cito:[2] «eliminar

VOCABULARIO

VOCABULARIO

[1]*(congressional) delegate* [2]*(I) quote*

VOCABULARIO

el déficit en nuestra balanza de pagos y de paso rescatar al país de las pezuñas de apátridas noches infaustas», fin de cita.[3]

Recuerdo que él tenía vena de candidato para todo, de líder. En el colegio ayudó a organizar el voluntariado infantil de la Cruz Roja y el cuerpo de los *Boy Scouts*. En cada izado[4] de la bandera a cargo de nuestro curso era el animador, el orador y el declamador de turno. Aicardo es abogado y en Francia estudió política internacional. Luego que el doctor Severo Umaña dejó la embajada, le costeó a Aicardo, su hijo, un viaje de seis años por todos los países de Europa. ¡Cómo hubiera sido de bueno encontrármelo en Roma! Hubiéramos[5] bebido vino entre las ruinas del Foro y después él hubiera[6] dicho un discurso lleno de floripondios junto a algo que tocó César Augusto, mientras dos gatos y yo lo escuchábamos. Bueno, por lo menos nos habría sobrado risa.[7]

VOCABULARIO

VOCABULARIO

VERIFICAR ¿Quién(es)? ¿Dónde? ¿Qué pasó?

Durante estos dos últimos años he seguido paso a paso su carrera de candidato presidencial, pero me he tomado el cuidado de no presentármele,* de no dejarme ver de él. Lo he visto por la televisión haciendo su campaña. Con esa sonrisa de foto de cumpleaños[V] instalada en su cara robusta, dice: «Yo soy tal, yo haré esto, yo prometo, yo haré lo otro, hasta yo podría, seré yo quien, si yo hubiera sido escuchado, yo dije». Y empuja con vigor el índice derecho contra su pecho cuando dice el yo.[V]

VISUALIZAR

VISUALIZAR

He concluido que su manera de señalarse a sí mismo cuando pronuncia el yo es un movimiento que ha requerido mucho ensayo. Me lo imagino todas las mañanas ante el espejo,[8] en práctica de su única gimnasia digital. Antes que diga el yo, su mano derecha ya está empuñada[9] y el índice

VOCABULARIO

[3]fin... *end quote* [4]*raising* [5]Habríamos [6]habría [7]nos... *there would have been extra laughter to go around* [8]*mirror* [9]*in a fist*

*In this context **presentármele** means: «presentarme ante él».

VISUALIZAR

VOCABULARIO

dispuesto a disparársele.[10] Llega el yo y es como el instante cero para los cohetes espaciales en Houston:[v] el índice de Aicardo va directo al esternón.[11] De acuerdo con la cantidad de yoes que diga en su intervención, su mano derecha permanecerá empuñada o no todo el tiempo. Una ocasión, en un discurso de noventa minutos para inaugurar una exposición internacional de cañas para saxofones altos le conté ochenta y siete yoes. Creo que ese día su mano terminó entumecida.

VISUALIZAR

VOCABULARIO VISUALIZAR

Cuando lo entrevistan por la radio no puedo mirarle su mano derecha con el índice tieso,[12] pero alcanzo a escuchar el ruido seco y afelpado[13] de la punta digital sobre la corbata, a la altura del esternón. En las plazas públicas, que es donde estoy más cerca de él, su mano permanece por horas a la intemperie[14] de la tarde y de mis ojos. No hago más que mirarla y contar los yoes que él dice. A veces mi conteo adquiere el ritmo del corazón del atleta que está a punto de culminar alguna prueba de fondo, y debo contar a pares con el fin de no quedarme atrás. Por el temor a que él de pronto perciba mi mirada y entonces responda mirándome, siempre me escondo detrás de un árbol[v] o me hago en el marco de una puerta. A decir verdad, le temo más a los ojos de Rosita, su esposa. Mientras él habla, ella está a su lado con un ramo de flores. Sonríe, estira el cuello y gira la cabeza como un periscopio.[v] En casa le dirá a Aicardo que allá estaba Fulanito de Tal o Sutanito de Cual.[15] Además, como no es mucha la gente que asiste a las plazas, cada vez debo mantenerme más escondido.

VERIFICAR ¿Quién(es)? ¿Dónde? ¿Qué hacía?

VISUALIZAR

VISUALIZAR

VISUALIZAR

La campaña electoral está por terminarse y Aicardo ha llegado a la completa punta de su publicidad. A diario la prensa lo muestra en grandes fotos y posando de mil maneras, menos su índice y su boca. Ese dedo está siempre fusilándole el pecho[v] y la boca abierta como una O mayúscula, subrayando la vocal del consabido[16] yo.

En las fotos está de *smoking*[v] [17] en un lujoso salón y brinda con champaña, de sport y casco amarillo carga un niño y mira una obra que construyen, de saco y corbata en una conferencia o en una mesa redonda, todo de blanco en un campo de golf, en traje de baño en la piscina de su casa.[v] Precisamente en la última foto que le vi estaba asomado al borde de su piscina. Acababa de terminar la braceada,[18] el cabello chorreaba mucha agua. Tenía la boca abierta, como haciendo un gesto de vencedor. Los brazos en palanca para levantar el cuerpo, la pierna izquierda ya sobre el borde. El índice derecho estaba recto y dirigido hacia arriba, en actitud bélica. ¡Cómo me reí de ese dedo! Me reí hasta cuando miré su pecho. Recordé que siendo jóvenes, los dos fuimos muchas veces a balnearios[19]

[10]*shoot at him* [11]*sternum* [12]*taut* [13]*velvety* [14]a… al aire libre [15]Fulanito… *What's-his-name or So-and-so* [16]*aforementioned* [17]*tuxedo* [18]*breast stroke* [19]*spas*

VOCABULARIO

VISUALIZAR

y que jamás le vi un lunar[20] grande en el pecho. Seguí mirándole el pecho, observándolo con mucho detalle. Vi una mancha redonda, oscura, un bajo relieve sobre el esternón. Esa mancha era nada menos que un hueco profundo en la piel que a lo mejor le llegaba hasta la espalda.[V]

[20]*mole*

VERIFICAR

¿Quién(es)? ¿Dónde? ¿Qué pasó?

Después de leer

A. Comprensión Conteste las siguientes preguntas, según el cuento.

1. ¿Quién es Aicardo Umaña? ¿Qué relación tiene con el narrador?
2. ¿De qué manera se preparó Aicardo Umaña para ser candidato presidencial?
3. Cuando Aicardo estaba en Europa, ¿se encontró con el narrador en Roma? ¿Cómo lo sabe Ud.?
4. ¿Qué movimiento hace Aicardo que le fascina al narrador?
5. ¿Con qué palabra que dice el protagonista corresponde ese movimiento?
6. ¿Qué papel desempeña la esposa del candidato?
7. ¿Cuáles son algunas de las fotos del candidato que el narrador describe?
8. ¿Qué ve en la foto del candidato sin camisa cuando este salía de la piscina? ¿Entiende Ud. la relación entre el hueco que ve en la foto y el gesto frecuente de Aicardo?

PASADO

HIPÓTESIS

B. Como si fuera Dios

Paso 1 En parejas, completen el siguiente relato inquietante con la forma apropiada del pretérito o del imperfecto y, en el caso de una situación contraria a la realidad, con el pasado de subjuntivo.

Durante la campaña electoral, Aicardo siempre ________[1] (circular) por las calles dando la mano a todos y besando a los bebés como si ________[2] (ser) la persona más importante del mundo. Un día, cuando ________[3] (pararse) enfrente de un edificio estatal para dar su discurso habitual, un grupo de indígenas ________[4] (empezar) a gritarle. Aicardo ________[5] (tratar) de seguir con su discurso como si no los ________[6] (escuchar), pero no ________[7] (ser) posible porque de repente ________[8] (llegar) cientos de personas en una manifestación contra su candidatura. Los indígenas ________[9] (caminar) hacia Aicardo como si ________[10] (avanzar) hacia un enemigo de guerra. En ese momento, Aicardo ________[11] (sentirse) como si no ________[12] (tener) ningún aliado en este mundo.

Paso 2 En parejas, hablen de qué harían si fueran Aicardo después de haber experimentado esa situación tan inquietante.

Paso 3 En parejas, piensen en una situación polémica en su universidad, ciudad o país. Describan a una de las personas involucradas en esa controversia, usando oraciones con **como si.** Utilicen distintos verbos.

MODELO: El nuevo presidente del gobierno estudiantil presentaba sus ideas como si fuera la persona más brillante del mundo.

C. ¿Los líderes nacen o se hacen?

Paso 1 ¿Por qué y para qué entran las personas en la política? Ponga las siguientes razones en orden del 1 (la más importante) al 9 (la menos importante). Después, comparta sus respuestas con un compañero / una compañera.

_____ para ayudar a las personas de pocos recursos
_____ para cambiar el mundo
_____ para combatir las injusticias
_____ para relacionarse con personas famosas
_____ para pasar a la historia
_____ por dinero
_____ por poder
_____ por fama
_____ por responsabilidad cívica

Paso 2 ¿Qué hacen las personas para prepararse para una carrera política? Complete las siguientes oraciones con un compañero / una compañera.

1. Estudian...
2. Trabajan en...
3. Participan en organizaciones como...
4. Se inscriben en...
5. Hacen de voluntarios en...
6. Tratan de conocer a...

Paso 3 Ahora vuelvan a considerar los **Pasos 1** y **2** pensando en la situación de Aicardo Umaña. ¿Por qué y para qué entró en la política? ¿Qué hizo para prepararse?

Paso 4 ¿Qué le parece el estilo de Aicardo Umaña? Imagínese que Ud. es experto/a en publicidad y va a ayudar a Aicardo a mejorar su imagen pública. Dele recomendaciones concretas sobre cómo cambiar su mensaje y su estilo para causar mejor impresión en los ciudadanos de su país.

D. Para discutir En grupos de tres, contesten las siguientes preguntas. Luego, compartan sus respuestas con el resto de la clase.

1. ¿Qué promesas hace Aicardo Umaña como candidato presidencial? ¿Cuáles son algunas de las promesas que hacen los candidatos políticos en este país?
2. ¿Cree Ud. que los candidatos tienen la intención de cumplir con sus promesas? En general, ¿son confiables (*trustworthy*) los políticos? Explique sus respuestas.
3. Cuando Ud. votó por primera vez, ¿cómo decidió por quién votar? ¿Cuáles eran los criterios más importantes para Ud.?
4. ¿Cuáles son las cualidades personales y profesionales que Ud. busca en un líder político / una líder política? ¿Cuánto pesa en su decisión su carisma, su habilidad oratoria, su edad, su experiencia, su esposo/a?
5. ¿Cuáles son las cuestiones sociales o políticas que más influyen en su voto? Explique por qué estos temas son importantes para Ud.

¡A escribir!

A. Lluvia de ideas En grupos pequeños, hagan una lista de los problemas actuales que les parezcan urgentes a nivel local, nacional e internacional.

B. Composición: Persuación Escriba un discurso (*speech*) como si fuera un escritor / una escritora de discursos para el presidente / la presidenta de su universidad, dirigido a los estudiantes que se gradúan de la universidad este año. Describa algunos de los problemas actuales que van a enfrentar en el mundo real y hábleles de cómo pueden involucrarse en la política, explicándoles por qué vale la pena participar activamente en ella.

1. escoger un título inspirador
2. escribir un párrafo introductorio sobre el mundo que van a enfrentar
3. describir las posibles causas de los problemas
4. darles una idea de cómo pueden participar y resolver esos problemas
5. escribir una conclusión

C. Diálogo En grupos de tres, lean el discurso de sus compañeros y luego decidan cuál de los tres es más apropiado y se acerca más a la personalidad y filosofía del presidente / de la presidenta de su universidad.

Hablando del tema

Antes de empezar a conversar con sus compañeros de clase sobre los siguientes temas, prepare una ficha para la conversación, otra para el debate y otra para la reacción ante la cita.

A. Conversación: Problemas actuales Revise las expresiones de **Para conversar mejor.** Luego, en parejas o grupos de tres, contesten las siguientes preguntas.

Para conversar mejor

Debe... / Tiene que...	Me molesta(n) (que...)
En mi caso...	Me preocupo que...
Es evidente que...	No creo que...
Francamente...	No me gusta (que...)

- ¿Cuáles son los problemas actuales más graves?
- En su opinión, ¿hay alguna situación social o política actual que sea la más urgente?
- ¿Qué les gustaría que hiciera el gobierno para solucionar los problemas actuales? ¿Qué les molesta en cuanto a cómo el gobierno de este país maneja estos problemas ahora?
- ¿En qué circunstancias se volverían Uds. revolucionarios/as? ¿Qué harían?

B. Debate: Cómo cambiar el mundo Revise las expresiones de **Para debatir mejor.** Después, prepare tres argumentos a favor y tres en contra de emular a un revolucionario como el Che Guevara.* Luego, presente sus argumentos en un debate. No sabrá qué lado tendrá que defender.

Para debatir mejor

A FAVOR	EN CONTRA
Así es.	De ninguna manera.
Exacto.	Lo siento, pero…
Podría ser.	No sabes lo que dices.
Tienes razón.	Temo que estés equivocado/a.

«Para muchos, el Che Guevara es un héroe, un icono, un mito y hasta un santo por haber sido un defensor feroz de la gente pobre. Es admirable seguir ejemplos de héroes revolucionarios como el Che, quien fue un visionario y dedicó su vida a cambiar el mundo y ayudar a los demás. Uno debe estar dispuesto a morir por una causa en la que cree firmemente.»

«No podemos respetar o idolatrar a nadie que haya matado a otros en el nombre de la justicia. La glorificación de una persona violenta no debe ser la inspiración de nadie. Si busca una fuente de inspiración para cambiar el mundo, debe estudiar la vida de Gandhi o de Martin Luther King, Jr. En comparación, el Che es una desgracia.»

*El Che Guevara nació en la Argentina pero se hizo famoso a nivel mundial por su liderazgo en movimientos revolucionarios marxistas. Junto con Fidel Castro ayudó a realizar la Revolución cubana (ver Nota histórica, página 65) y después salió para llevar la revolución marxista a otros países. Después de su muerte en Bolivia, llegó a ser un símbolo popular para la contracultura revolucionaria. Su lucha por la justicia para las masas ha sido retratada en películas como *Diarios de motocicleta* y *Che.*

C. **Reacción: La globalización** Revise las expresiones de **Para reaccionar mejor.** Luego, reaccione ante la siguiente cita. Añada razones que apoyen sus opiniones.

Para reaccionar mejor

Creo/Opino/Supongo que…	Es posible que…
Es horrible que…	Es una desgracia que…
Es normal que…	¡Qué vergüenza!

«La globalización es una de las manifestaciones más positivas del progreso; la gente de los países en vías de desarrollo debe aceptar que sus tradiciones tienen que ceder a los conocimientos avanzados del mundo desarrollado.»

CAPÍTULO 6

Hacia el porvenir:

Un mundo más verde y conectado

Un sueño virtual

Punto clave

FUTURO

Temas centrales

- predicciones para el futuro
- la tecnología
- el ambientalismo

Zona de enfoque

- Centroamérica

En este capítulo, Ud. va a explorar el tema del mundo del futuro.

Preguntas para considerar

- ¿Cuáles son los problemas más graves del medio ambiente y cómo se resolverán en el siglo XXI?
- ¿Habrá más gente comprometida con el ambientalismo en el futuro?
- ¿Se considera Ud. optimista o pesimista ante los problemas mundiales?
- ¿Qué innovaciones tecnológicas cambiarán la vida para siempre?
- ¿Cuáles son las ventajas y desventajas del acceso constante a la tecnología?
- La escena que se ve en esta página representa a una niña guatemalteca obsesionada con el Internet. ¿Cómo cambiarán las comunidades aisladas del mundo con el acceso omnipresente al Internet?

MULTIMEDIA

La historia

Preparativos

Soñando con las vacaciones

Situación: Sara, Diego y Javier hablan sobre sus planes para escaparse a Nicaragua juntos antes de que termine el año y todos se vayan a distintos lugares. Pasarán una semana en Finca Esperanza Verde, una reserva natural privada que ofrece programas de turismo ecológico. Lea el diálogo y preste especial atención al uso del vocabulario nuevo, que está **en negrita.**

DIEGO: Ya está todo. Tenemos reservaciones en Esperanza Verde por siete días. Yo pasaré unos días en Guatemala antes para comprar artesanías y, cuando termine, los veré en Managua.

JAVIER: ¡Chévere! Es increíble que hayamos podido arreglar esto tan fácilmente.

SARA: Más **asombroso** aún es que todos estén dispuestos a quedarse en un lugar tan remoto sin acceso al Internet.

JAVIER: En realidad es **inimaginable** que tú, Diego, entre todos, estés desconectado por siete días sin **chatear, mandar mensajes de texto** o meterte a Facebook.

DIEGO: Será difícil, pero me viene bien el desafío.

SARA: Pues para mí será fácil. Ya que terminé y entregué la tesis, tengo ganas de desconectarme completamente.

DIEGO: Fran me dijo que la finca es alucinante. Es parte de un proyecto internacional de **desarrollo sostenible.** Podremos ver su cafetal, que **cultiva** café bajo sombra, aprender todo lo que hacen para **proteger el medio ambiente** allí, hacer caminatas y montar a caballo por **el bosque lluvioso.**

JAVIER: ¿Cuánto hace que no montas a caballo?

DIEGO: Hace mucho. Les **aseguro** que Sergio y yo ya tenemos planes de montar a caballo todos los días.

SARA: Será un viaje genial y aprenderemos un montón. Pero **me pregunto** si, al volver, podremos resistir a la tentación de escribir un artículo o **un blog** sobre el turismo responsable.

DIEGO: Pues me imagino que la experiencia nos **impactará** mucho. Y si queremos **tomar en serio** nuestra responsabilidad ecológica, haremos algo para compartir esta experiencia.

JAVIER: El gran desafío será relajarnos y absorber todo nuestro entorno sin pensar en lo que haremos cuando volvamos.

SARA: Desafío aceptado.

ACTIVIDADES

A. Detective Busque en el diálogo ejemplos de las siguientes metas comunicativas: Narración en el pasado (P), Reacciones y recomendaciones (R), Hablar del futuro (F) y Hablar de los gustos (G). Subraye cada palabra o frase que represente una (o una combinación) de estas metas comunicativas. Luego, escriba al margen la(s) letra(s) que corresponde(n) a cada ejemplo subrayado (P, R, F o G).

MODELOS: Pues para mí será fácil. (F)
Fran me dijo que la finca es alucinante. (P)

B. Comprensión Conteste las siguientes preguntas, según el diálogo.

1. ¿Por qué pasarán los amigos una semana en Nicaragua?
2. ¿Dónde se quedarán?
3. ¿Qué inconveniente tiene ese lugar?
4. ¿Qué les interesa a los amigos de ese lugar?
5. ¿Qué piensa que los cinco amigos harán cuando vuelvan de este viaje?

C. Reacciones y recomendaciones Complete las siguientes oraciones sobre el diálogo, utilizando un conector en cada oración.

MODELO: A Javier le sorprende que...
A Javier le sorprende que hayan podido arreglar el viaje tan fácilmente porque los cinco siempre están tan ocupados con su trabajo y sus estudios.

1. Es bueno que Diego...
2. Es interesante que Esperanza Verde...
3. Es obvio que los cinco amigos...
4. Qué bueno que en Nicaragua...

Conectores

aunque
en cambio
para que + *subjuntivo*
por lo tanto
porque
puesto que
sin embargo
ya que

D. Diálogo En parejas, preparen un diálogo entre Francisco y Diego en el que Diego le exprese que se siente un poco nervioso de estar desconectado por tanto tiempo. Fran le asegura que la tienda está en buenas manos y que no pasará nada malo en una semana. Presenten el diálogo a la clase.

Vocabulario del tema

Acciones para hablar del futuro

adivinar	to guess, divine
aportar	to contribute
asegurar	to assure
enfrentar	to face, confront
implementar	to implement
predecir (*like* **decir**)*	to predict
preguntarse	to wonder, ask oneself
tener un impacto	to impact

Para describir el futuro

asombroso/a	astonishing
desastroso/a	disastrous
disponible	available
ingenioso/a	ingenious
inimaginable	unimaginable
innovador(a)	innovative
insalubre	unhealthy
pacífico/a	peaceful
peligroso/a	dangerous
provechoso/a	helpful, beneficial
renovable	renewable
sano/a	healthy
sostenible	sustainable

COGNADOS: **catastrófico/a, grave, humanitario/a**

Acciones para hablar del medio ambiente

acabarse	to run out, use up
amenazar	to threaten
cultivar	to grow, cultivate
empeorar	to worsen
(mal)gastar	to use (waste)
prohibir	to forbid
proteger	to protect
reciclar	to recycle
sobrevivir	to survive
tomar en serio	to take seriously

¿Por qué es chistosa esta tira cómica? ¿Qué nos revela del futuro?

Para hablar de la responsabilidad ecológica

el ambientalismo	environmentalism
el bosque lluvioso	rain forest
el calentamiento global	global warming
la capa de ozono	ozone layer
el comercio justo	fair trade
la contaminación	pollution
la deforestación	deforestation
el desarrollo sostenible	sustainable development
el dióxido de carbono	carbon dioxide
el efecto invernadero	greenhouse effect
la energía solar	solar energy
la escasez	lack, scarcity
los hábitos de consumo	habits of consumption
el reciclaje	recycling
la sobrepoblación	overpopulation

Para describir a la gente que piensa en verde

comprometido/a	committed
consciente	aware
minimalista	minimalist

*__Predecir__ is like __decir__ except in the future and conditional: **predeciré, predecirás, predecirá,...; predeciría, predecirías, predeciría,....**

respetuoso/a	respectful

Para hablar de la tecnología

el aparato	apparatus, gadget
el avance	advance
la computadora portátil	laptop
la conexión inalámbrica	wireless connection
el enlace	link
el salón de charla	chat room
el teléfono móvil o celular	cell phone
el teletrabajo	telecommuting
bajar	to download
bloguear	to blog
chatear	to chat
escribir un mensaje de texto	to text
navegar	to browse
teclear	to type

COGNADOS: **el ciberespacio, el Internet, la página Web, la realidad virtual, la tecnología digital, las videoconferencias**

ACTIVIDADES

A. ¿Se realizará antes del 2050?

Indique si Ud. cree que las siguientes predicciones se realizarán o no para el año 2050. Explique por qué sí o por qué no.

		SÍ	NO
1.	Habrá más conciencia sobre los efectos de los hábitos de consumo en el medio ambiente.	☐	☐
2.	El 25 por ciento de la población hará su trabajo por medio del teletrabajo.	☐	☐
3.	Dejaremos de usar papel y todas las comunicaciones serán por aparatos tecnológicos.	☐	☐
4.	El 50 por ciento de los productos en el mercado internacional será de comercio justo.	☐	☐
5.	Toda la comida insalubre dejará de ser popular.	☐	☐
6.	No tendremos que teclear porque nuestros pensamientos aparecerán en la pantalla por telepatía.	☐	☐
7.	Los que hayan hecho inversiones en las compañías de reciclaje serán ricos.	☐	☐
8.	La deforestación y las emisiones de dióxido de carbono empeorarán el calentamiento global.	☐	☐
9.	El costo de una computadora portátil bajará a 100 dólares.	☐	☐
10.	Para recibir fondos federales, las universidades tendrán que implementar medidas para proteger el medio ambiente y requerir una clase de ecología para todos.	☐	☐
11.	Todo el mundo podrá tomar clases virtuales gratis en Harvard o en cualquier universidad.	☐	☐
12.	Para evitar la sobrepoblación, se prohibirá que las parejas tengan más de un hijo / una hija.	☐	☐

B. Me pregunto cómo sería la vida si.... En la opinión de las siguientes personas, ¿cómo sería la vida si pasara lo siguiente? En parejas, completen las oraciones con diferentes adjetivos de la siguiente lista. Luego, añadan el derivado de otro adjetivo de la lista para describir las emociones de las personas afectadas. Sigan las indicaciones del número 1 como modelo.

Para describir las emociones, utilice adjetivos que terminan en **-ado** o **-ido: alucinado/a, emocionado/a, sorprendido/a,** etc.

alarmante	desastroso/a	intrigante
alucinante	emocionante	preocupante
asombroso/a	fascinante	relajante
degradante	frustrante	repugnante
deprimente	horripilante	sorprendente

1. Una persona muy extrovertida: Si el teletrabajo reemplazara el trabajo de la oficina, *la vida sería* **deprimente.** *Yo me sentiría* **frustrada** *porque...*
2. Un corredor de maratones: Si la contaminación fuera tan grave que fuera difícil respirar...
3. Un ambientalista: Si se acabara el petróleo...
4. Un adolescente adicto al Internet: Si mis padres me amenazaran con desconectar la conexión inalámbrica por un mes...
5. Una persona innovadora: Si el gobierno invirtiera más dinero en los avances tecnológicos...
6. Una médica: Si todos tomaran en serio el problema de la comida insalubre...
7. Un ecologista comprometido: Si el gobierno proveyera más fondos para enfrentar el calentamiento global...
8. Una estudiante consumista: Si mi nueva compañera de cuarto fuera una minimalista radical...
9. Unas adolescentes: Si cerraran todos los centros comerciales y sólo pudiéramos hacer compras a través del Internet...

C. Universidad EARTH ¿Qué tan verde es tu universidad?

Paso 1 Mire la descripción de una universidad en Costa Rica dedicada al ambientalismo. Después, contesten en parejas las preguntas que siguen.

Creada en 1990, **Universidad EARTH,** localizada en Costa Rica, ofrece una educación universitaria en ciencias agrícolas y recursos naturales para contribuir al desarrollo sostenible de los trópicos. Su modelo educacional se basa en cuatro principios fundamentales: el compromiso social, la consciencia ambiental, una mentalidad empresarial y el desarrollo de valores humanos. Estudiantes de todas partes del mundo estudian con profesores y agricultores locales para aprender a ser líderes en desarrollo sostenible en sus propios países. El énfasis es promover el desarrollo sin explotar los ecosistemas frágiles de las zonas tropicales.

- Muestra de cursos ofrecidos: Producción de cultivos tropicales; El ser humano y el desarrollo del Trópico; Ética y pensamiento crítico; Economía, política y ambiente; Sistemas alimentarios y economía mundial.

1. Si hubiera más universidades como esta, ¿serían populares entre sus amigos?
2. ¿Por qué es importante ofrecer cursos en ética y pensamiento crítico en un programa de ciencias agrícolas y recursos naturales?

Paso 2 Indiquen si en su universidad se realizan las siguientes prácticas «verdes».

_____ reciclar papel
_____ invertir en proyectos de energía renovable
_____ reciclar botellas y latas
_____ prestar bicicletas para el transporte en el campus o la ciudad
_____ prometer tener emisiones neutras de carbono
_____ comprar productos locales
_____ cultivar parte de la comida que se sirve en la universidad
_____ usar energía solar
_____ ofrecer una especialidad en estudios del medio ambiente
_____ ¿?

Paso 3 En grupos de tres, escriban una carta al presidente / a la presidenta de su universidad exigiendo que la universidad adopte tres prácticas verdes específicas (use **Es urgente que…, Es esencial que…,** etc.). Después de cada demanda, explique cómo estas prácticas beneficiarán a la universidad en el futuro.

D. **Preguntas personales** En parejas, contesten las siguientes preguntas, utilizando el vocabulario nuevo. Mientras escuchen a su compañero/a, reaccionen con algunas de las expresiones de **Para conversar mejor.**

Para conversar mejor

¿En serio?
Yo también.
Sería horripilante.
Estoy de acuerdo.
Es verdad.
Tienes razón.
¿Tú crees?
Me sorprende que creas eso.
Puede ser.
Sería fenomenal.
¡Qué chévere/guay/padre!
¡Qué pena!
¡Qué bueno!

1. ¿Cuánto tiempo pasa al día pegado/a a un aparato electrónico? ¿Qué aparato usa más? ¿Siente una necesidad o una responsabilidad de estar conectado/a constantemente? ¿Cómo se sentiría si tuviera que pasar una semana en un lugar sin conexión inalámbrica?
2. ¿Por qué cree Ud. que Facebook y aplicaciones parecidas, como Twitter, son tan populares?
3. En su opinión, ¿cuál ha sido el avance tecnológico más importante durante su vida? ¿De qué manera ha cambiado la vida de los seres humanos? ¿Cuál será la novedad más importante en el futuro?
4. ¿Cómo participa Ud. en los esfuerzos «verdes»? ¿Qué hacen organizaciones como Greenpeace para promover el ambientalismo?

(*continúa*)

5. ¿Son populares en su universidad los productos de comercio justo? ¿Presta Ud. atención al origen de los productos que usa? ¿Qué productos de comercio justo compra Ud.? ¿Hay productos que no compre o lugares donde prefiera no comprar porque sabe que a esos negocios no les importa el comercio justo?
6. ¿Cuáles serán las profesiones más necesarias en el futuro? ¿Qué impacto social o global tendrán esas profesiones? ¿Cree Ud. que su especialización académica le prepara bien para tener un trabajo impactante cuando se gradúe? ¿Cómo podrá usar sus estudios y su futura profesión para tener un impacto en la sociedad?

E. **Problemas repentinos** Entre todos, revisen los siguientes problemas y hagan una lista de palabras nuevas de este capítulo y de los capítulos anteriores que los ayuden a conversar con facilidad sobre cada problema repentino. Después, en parejas, preparen un diálogo espontáneo sobre cada problema.

1. Un estudiante frustrado / una estudiante frustrada tiene sólo un semestre más para graduarse. Habla con su consejero/a sobre su especialización académica (use su propia especialización). Cree que sus clases no le han preparado para una profesión futura. El/La estudiante sugiere hacer una pasantía[1] con una organización local donde podrá ganar experiencia práctica y a la vez recibir crédito. El consejero / La consejera es muy inflexible. Le explica que no cree que sea útil tal pasantía y que además, está seguro/a que la universidad no le daría crédito.
2. Un(a) estudiante quiere convencer al director / a la directora de servicios alimenticios[2] de su universidad de que sólo use productos de comercio justo. Al director / A la directora le preocupan los precios altos de dichos productos.

[1]*internship* [2]servicios... *food services*

NOTA CULTURAL • El Internet en el mundo hispano

Hay muchas iniciativas para cerrar la brecha digital en Centroamérica. Un ejemplo es Enlace Quiché, empezado por USAID en 2000 y ahora operado de manera independiente en Guatemala. El proyecto entrena a gente indígena en zonas rurales a usar computadoras y el Internet. En Panamá, el gobierno ha abierto Infoplazas, centros comunitarios con acceso al Internet, programas educativos e información a bajo costo para todos los ciudadanos. En cada vez más zonas rurales de Latinoamérica los niños se han beneficiado del proyecto «Un portátil por niño,» cuya meta es distribuir una computadora portátil a todos los niños y asegurar acceso al Internet en las zonas más remotas.

Además de iniciativas masivas, en más y más ciudades y pueblos se encuentran cibercafés y tiendas pequeñas desde donde uno puede mandar mensajes por correo electrónico, buscar información a través del Internet o hablar por Skype con seres queridos en otras partes del mundo.

El Internet también sirve como foro para proveerle información a un público internacional. Por ejemplo, organizaciones como la Fundación Rigoberta Menchú, fundada por la indígena guatemalteca que ganó el Premio Nobel en 1992, elaboran páginas Web para informar al mundo sobre sus actividades y sobre injusticias cometidas en contra de la gente indígena de Guatemala. Por otra parte, el Internet puede ser una buena fuente para comprar y vender productos de comercio justo. PEOPLink, por ejemplo, lleva computadoras y cámaras de vídeo a los pueblos y les enseña a los artistas a vender sus productos directamente al público por medio del Internet.

Preguntas

1. ¿Considera Ud. que el acceso a la tecnología debe ser un derecho humano? ¿Por qué?
2. ¿Cómo cambiaría la vida de los niños en zonas rurales si todos tuvieran acceso a una computadora portátil y una conexión inalámbrica?

Actividad

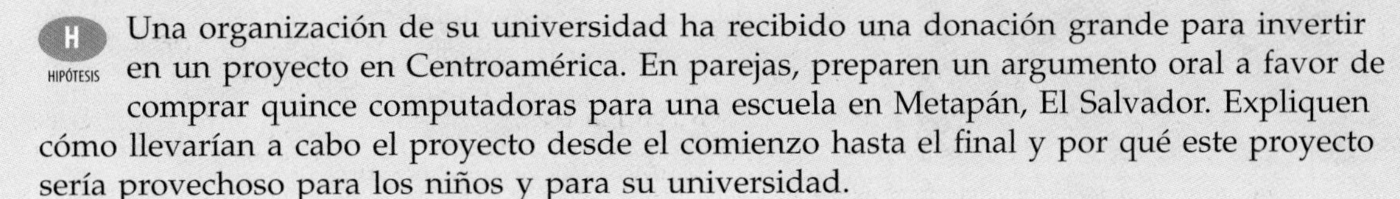

H HIPÓTESIS Una organización de su universidad ha recibido una donación grande para invertir en un proyecto en Centroamérica. En parejas, preparen un argumento oral a favor de comprar quince computadoras para una escuela en Metapán, El Salvador. Expliquen cómo llevarían a cabo el proyecto desde el comienzo hasta el final y por qué este proyecto sería provechoso para los niños y para su universidad.

Puntos clave

Hablar del futuro

En esta sección del capítulo, Ud. va a practicar la meta comunicativa **Hablar del futuro.** Para hacerlo bien, hay que utilizar las estructuras gramaticales (los puntos clave) de la siguiente tabla que pertenecen a la meta comunicativa. Antes de continuar, estudie las explicaciones de estas estructuras gramaticales en las páginas 228–232.

LA META COMUNICATIVA DE ESTE CAPÍTULO		
ICONO	META COMUNICATIVA	PUNTOS CLAVE
F FUTURO	Hablar del futuro	• el futuro • el subjuntivo en cláusulas adverbiales

PRUEBA DIAGNÓSTICA

Una artesana guatemalteca

Diego quiere colaborar con una organización de comercio justo para buscar nuevas artesanías para su tienda. Diego y Laura conversan sobre el viaje que él hará a Guatemala antes de su viaje a Nicaragua. Complete su diálogo con la forma correcta de los verbos que están entre paréntesis. **¡OJO!** El diálogo habla del futuro e incluye conjeturas e hipótesis que emplean conjugaciones en el futuro.

DIEGO: Cuando Martín y yo _____ [1] (llegar) a Guatemala el lunes, _____ [2] (reunirse) con un grupo de artesanos mayas.

LAURA: ¡Qué interesante! ¿Has estudiado el maya quiché para que _____ [3] (comunicarse) con la gente indígena?

DIEGO: Creo que los líderes _____ [4] (ser) bilingües. De todas maneras, con tal de que yo _____ [5] (mantener) la mente abierta y les _____ [6] (demostrar) que respeto su cultura, seguramente _____ [7] (llevarse, nosotros) bien. Trabajar directamente con los artesanos me _____ [8] (asegurar) que reciban una compensación justa por su trabajo.

LAURA: ¿Qué tipos de artesanía _____ [9] (importar) para la tienda?

DIEGO: A menos que _____ [10] (haber) problemas en la aduana, _____ [11] (traer, yo) máscaras, tejidos y objetos de plata y jade. En cuanto _____ [12] (regresar, nosotros), tú, Javi, Sergio y Sara _____ [13] (saber) todos los detalles.

LAURA: ¡_____ [14] (Venir, tú) con muchas aventuras que contar!

Expresiones útiles

Conjunciones A SPACE* (siempre llevan el subjuntivo)

Antes de que	*before*
Sin que	*without*
Para que	*so that*
A menos que	*unless*
Con tal de que	*provided that*
En caso de que	*in case*

Conjunciones THE CD* (pueden llevar el indicativo o subjuntivo)

Tan pronto como	*as soon as*
Hasta que	*until*
En cuanto	*as soon as*
Cuando	*when*
Despúes de que	*after*

*__A SPACE__ and **THE CD** are mnemonic devices. They are created from the first letter of each of the conjunctions in these lists. See pp. 230–232 of the **Explicación gramatical** section in the green pages for more information about these conjunctions.

ACTIVIDADES

FUTURO

Las siguientes actividades le darán la oportunidad de practicar las metas comunicativas. Habrá un énfasis particular en hablar del futuro utilizando las cláusulas adverbiales y el subjuntivo.

A. Las bolas de cristal

Paso 1 En parejas, consulten su bola de cristal y predigan lo que le pasará a nuestro planeta. Conjuguen el verbo que está entre paréntesis y completen las oraciones con sus predicciones.

1. Cuando _______ (eliminarse) las emisiones de dióxido de carbono...
2. En cuanto _______ (invertirse) en más proyectos de energía renovable...
3. A menos que nosotros _______ (proteger) los océanos...
4. Sin que los agricultores _______ (cultivar) más productos orgánicos...

Paso 2 Ahora, en parejas, hagan predicciones sobre el futuro de los siguientes temas para el año 2050. ¿En qué se parecerán a su estado actual? ¿En qué serán diferentes?

1. la apariencia física de los jóvenes
2. la familia
3. el romance
4. el ocio
5. la gente indígena
6. la política
7. la tecnología
8. el medio ambiente

Paso 3 Ahora, escriba tres predicciones sobre su propio futuro. Puede hablar de su apariencia física cuando sea mayor, su futura vida amorosa; su familia, trabajo, diversiones, etcétera. Puede basar sus predicciones en algo que Ud. espera que se realice o en unos sueños locos. Luego, comparta sus predicciones con un compañero / una compañera. Su compañero/a reaccionará ante sus predicciones, utilizando frases como **No creo que..., Es posible que..., Dudo que..., Supongo que....**

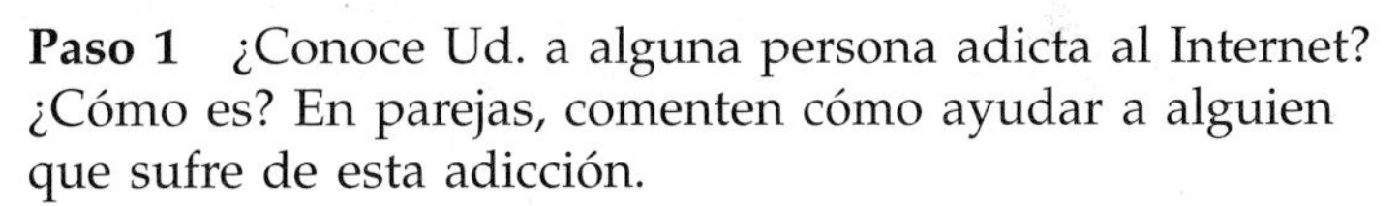

B. ¿Adicto/a al Internet?

Paso 1 ¿Conoce Ud. a alguna persona adicta al Internet? ¿Cómo es? En parejas, comenten cómo ayudar a alguien que sufre de esta adicción.

Paso 2 En parejas, lean los siguientes trozos de noticias tomados de un periódico hispano. Luego, completen las oraciones con la forma correcta de los verbos que están entre paréntesis. Expliquen por qué se usa la conjugación en cada caso.

1. Netahólicos Anónimos, un grupo en línea que tiene un programa de doce pasos muy similar a los doce pasos de Alcohólicos Anónimos, ofrece esta oración de la serenidad: «Concédeme la serenidad de saber cuándo desconectarme».

a. En caso de que una persona adicta al Internet _______ (necesitar) ayuda para resistir a la tentación de conectarse, hay una oración que puede darle la fuerza necesaria.
b. Tan pronto como la persona adicta al Internet _______ (pronunciar) la oración de la serenidad, pudo desconectarse y salir de la casa.
c. Cuando las personas adictas _______ (asistir) a las reuniones de gente que sufre de los mismos problemas, se sienten apoyadas y comprendidas.

2. Algunos de los síntomas de un netahólico / una netahólica: Cuando no está en línea, exhibe agitación psicomotriz (ciberataques), tiene sueños o fantasías relacionados con el Internet o exhibe movimientos involuntarios de teclear con los dedos.

   a. Cuando Alfonso _______ (estar) en línea por más de cuatro horas, empieza a sufrir de agitaciones psicomotrices.
   b. Hasta que no _______ (admitir) que es adicto al Internet, Alfonso seguirá teniendo estos síntomas sin remedio.
   c. Tan pronto como su esposa _______ (reconocer) que Alfonso sufría de ciberataques, llamó a un psicólogo para concertar una cita.

Paso 3 En parejas, imagínense que Ud. y su compañero/a son psicólogos especializados / psicólogas especializadas en el tratamiento de las adicciones. Han decidido tratar a Julio, un netahólico de 17 años, con hipnosis para cambiar varios aspectos de su comportamiento peligroso. Terminen las siguientes oraciones para decirle a Julio qué hará o qué le pasará en cuanto se despierte de la hipnosis.

1. Julio, la próxima vez que _______ (querer) prender la computadora...
2. A menos que _______ (tener) que hacer investigaciones para las tareas...
3. No _______ (jugar) a videojuegos a menos que...
4. Cuando _______ (despertarse) de esta hipnosis...

Paso 4 En grupos de tres, contesten las siguientes preguntas.

1. ¿Es Ud. adicto/a al Internet? ¿Cómo lo sabe?
2. ¿Qué aparato o aplicación podría dejar de usar? ¿Cuál sería imposible dejar de usar? Explique.

C. Hacer de voluntario/a

Paso 1 Lea los siguientes anuncios sobre oportunidades para dedicar su tiempo, conocimiento, empatía, creatividad y generosidad a los demás.

¡Más allá de la playa!
Pasa el verano haciendo de voluntario en el bosque lluvioso de Costa Rica.

- Investigaciones sobre los pájaros, monos y tortugas costarricenses
- Identificación de orquídeas
- Proyectos de ecoturismo
- Colaboración en el desarrollo de agricultura orgánica

«Aprendimos tanto de la naturaleza y de la generosidad de la gente. Esta experiencia cambió cómo entendemos nuestro lugar en el mundo. ¡Gracias, Costa Rica!»

Claudia, Albany, NY, EE UU

¡Tu grano de arena* para un futuro mejor!

Ven a Antigua a trabajar con niños guatemaltecos.

- Dar clases de español básico a niños de primaria
- Atender a los niños de un orfanato
- Dar clases de arte a adolescentes
- Ofrecer instrucción en baloncesto

«Los niños son increíbles. Me enseñaron a ver el mundo con ojos diferentes. Ha sido una experiencia alucinante.»

Gabriel, Reno, NV, EE UU

Paso 2 Imagínense que Ud. y un compañero / una compañera han decidido participar en estos programas. Uno/a de Uds. (estudiante A) irá a Costa Rica; el otro / la otra (estudiante B) irá a Guatemala. Háganse las siguientes preguntas y sean creativos/as en sus respuestas.

PREGUNTAS PARA ESTUDIANTE A

1. Cuando _______ (estar) en Costa Rica, ¿en cuál de los cuatro proyectos trabajarás?
2. Para que _______ (no haber) problemas de comunicación con tus colegas costarricenses, ¿qué harás para mejorar tu español?
3. Antes de que _______ (empezar) el programa, ¿qué harás para estar en buena condicion física?
4. Tan pronto como _______ (terminar) el proyecto, ¿volverás directamente a casa o viajarás?

PREGUNTAS PARA ESTUDIANTE B

1. Antes de que _______ (ir) a Guatemala, ¿qué tienes que hacer?
2. Con tal de que la agencia te _______ (permitir) escoger el grupo con el que quieres trabajar, ¿con qué edad estarás más cómodo/a?
3. En caso de que _______ (tener) que dar clases de arte, ¿qué materias llevarás de casa para estar preparado/a?
4. En cuanto _______ (llegar) a Antigua, ¿qué harás para integrarte en la cultura guatemalteca?

Paso 3 Si tuviera que preparar una página Web para hacer propaganda para un viaje de trabajo voluntario, ¿qué incluiría en la página? Escriba una sección de una página Web publicitando uno de los lugares aquí anunciados. Incluya cinco actividades que el viajero / la viajera hará cuando llegue.

---

*La expresión **aportar tu grano de arena** quiere decir *to do your part* (*to contribute your grain of sand*). Se usa para referirse a un proyecto grande al que todos contribuyen un poco para realizarlo: Si todos **aportamos nuestro grano de arena....**

D. Una universidad para el futuro

Paso 1 Lea el siguiente párrafo sobre la Universidad para la Paz.

La Universidad para la Paz fue fundada en 1980 bajo el auspicio de la ONU. Ofrece un programa universitario para personas interesadas en promover y obtener la paz mundial. Su objetivo principal es: «promover entre todos los seres humanos un espíritu de entendimiento, tolerancia y coexistencia pacífica, estimular la cooperación entre los pueblos y ayudar a disminuir los obstáculos y amenazas a la paz y el progreso mundiales». La sede está en Costa Rica, país conocido por su compromiso con la paz y la democracia, y hay academias e instituciones afiliadas en muchos otros países.

MUESTRA DE CURSOS OFRECIDOS

- La ley internacional y los derechos humanos
- Los recursos naturales y el desarrollo sostenible
- El género y la paz
- La paz en la educación
- Los niños, la juventud y los conflictos armados
- La psicología de la violencia y la paz

Paso 2 En grupos de cuatro, contesten las siguientes preguntas, según el párrafo.

1. ¿Cuál de los seis cursos sería el más interesante para Uds.?
2. Si tuvieran la oportunidad de estudiar un semestre en esta universidad u otra similar, ¿lo harían? Expliquen.
3. ¿Se ofrecen en su universidad especialidades como las que ofrece la Universidad para la Paz? ¿Cuáles son?
4. Si pudiera crear una nueva especialidad en su universidad que fuera innovadora y que estuviera dedicada a la formación de profesionales para las próximas décadas, ¿qué tipo de programa sería? ¿En qué se enfocaría? ¿Qué impacto tendría esta especialización en la sociedad del futuro?

Paso 3 En parejas, hagan el papel de un(a) estudiante que empezará a estudiar en la Universidad para la Paz el próximo año. Terminen sus pensamientos respecto a sus expectativas sobre el futuro.

1. Tan pronto como _______ (llegar) a la universidad,...
2. Antes de que _______ (terminar) mis estudios,...
3. En cuanto yo _______ (graduarse),...
4. Después de que mis compañeros y yo _______ (hacer) una pasantía en la ONU, _______ (estar) preparados para...
5. Cuando _______ (obtener) mi licenciatura,...

E. Esperanza

Paso 1 En grupos de tres, hablen de las iniciativas que están en la página siguiente. Usen las siguientes frases u otras parecidas para expresar sus reacciones ante las iniciativas, hacer hipótesis y hablar del futuro.

Es alentador que...	Si pudiera,...	Si yo fuera...
Creo que...	Cuando haya...	Es increíble que...
Me alegro de que...	Espero que...	No dudo que...

La selva costarricense

1. **Ecología en Costa Rica** Los avances que se han hecho en este país para proteger sus recursos naturales y para apoyar a sus cafetaleros[1] han sido impresionantes. Hoy en día, Costa Rica es el país con el mayor porcentaje de tierra protegida en el mundo. Sus cafetaleros ahora reciben un precio más justo por el cultivo sostenible de café porque los consumidores son más conscientes del concepto de comercio justo.
2. **La Fundación Rigoberta Menchú Tum** Cuando la indígena maya-quiché Rigoberta Menchú ganó el Premio Nobel de la Paz en 1992, fundó una organización para dedicar sus ganancias a ayudar a la gente indígena de su país natal, Guatemala, con iniciativas para la educación, los derechos humanos, el autodesarrollo y la participación ciudadana. Una parte de sus programas de educación busca proveer educación y asistencia tecnológica a comunidades rurales indígenas.

Rigoberta Menchú

Las artesanas de Comasagua

3. **Arte Comasagua** En 2001, un terremoto[2] desastroso dejó el pueblo de Comasagua, El Salvador, completamente destruido. Muchas familias se quedaron sin sus tierras, casas y trabajos. Como respuesta, un grupo de mujeres locales empezaron Arte Comasagua, un proyecto de artesanías. Las artesanas usan materiales locales y de bajo costo —flores y plantas secas— para crear hermosas tarjetas y cuadros para vender. Su meta es crear una artesanía ecológica que contribuya a la economía local y que las ayude a preservar a sus familias, su pueblo y su futuro.

[1]*coffee growers* [2]*earthquake*

Paso 2: Si Uds. fueran a donar dinero a una de estas inciativas, ¿a cuál donarían dinero? ¿Por qué? Y, si quisieran trabajar de voluntarios/as en una de las organizaciones, ¿en cuál trabajarían? Expliquen.

Rincón cultural

Lugares fascinantes:

Centroamérica

El Canal de Panamá

1. **El Canal de Panamá** La construcción de este inmenso canal empezó en 1904 y terminó diez años después. Además de ser una maravilla de la ingeniería moderna, el canal ofrece otros atractivos. Un visitante puede ver cómo pasan los barcos por las esclusas[1] de Miraflores, Pedro Miguel y Gatún. Al lado del canal, hay algunos jardines botánicos, un zoológico[2] y caminos ecológicos. En medio del canal, hay un lago artificial, creado por la presa[3] Gatún, que contiene la Isla Barro Colorado, un bosque lluvioso donde se encuentra el Instituto de Investigación Tropical Smithsonian.

Tikal, Guatemala

2. **Ruinas mayas en Guatemala, Honduras y El Salvador** La civilización maya, una de las más importantes en la historia del mundo, dejó huellas[4] impresionantes en Centroamérica. Los mayas construyeron templos, pirámides, plazas enormes y ciudades que hoy se pueden admirar y apreciar por su valor artístico y destreza arquitectónica. **Tikal,** Guatemala, es la ciudad mejor restaurada de todas las ruinas de la civilización maya. Hay tumbas de reyes, edificios ceremoniales, palacios residenciales y administrativos y una cancha para juegos de pelota. En **Copán,** Honduras, se encuentran extraordinarios ejemplos del talento innovador de los mayas, como las estelas,[5] que son nueve enormes esculturas verticales de piedra elaborada. También de gran interés son los jeroglíficos que decoran los monumentos de Copán. La Escalinata de los Jeroglíficos incluye el texto escrito más largo que se ha descubierto en todos los sitios mayas. Este texto conmemora eventos importantes durante el reinado de los doce primeros reyes de Copán. Luego, **Cerén,** en El Salvador, conocida como «La Pompeya de América», se encuentra en el Parque Arqueológico Joya de Cerén. La ciudad fue cubierta de cenizas[6] de un volcán por miles de años hasta que fue descubierta en el año 1976. Los interesados en la arqueología se sentirían privilegiados de caminar por las ruinas de Centroamérica.

[1]*locks* [2]*zoo* [3]*dam* [4]*traces* [5]monumentos [6]*ashes*

El Lago de Nicaragua

Tortugas en la playa del Parque Nacional Tortuguero

3. **El Lago de Nicaragua** Con una extensión de 8.157 kilómetros cuadrados, este es el lago más grande de Centroamérica y uno de los diez más grandes del mundo. También es el único lago de agua dulce[7] donde habitan tiburones.[8] En la parte sur del lago se encuentra un archipiélago de 38 islas que se conoce como «Solentiname». En 1965 el sacerdote católico y poeta Ernesto Cardenal estableció en Solentiname una vivienda colectiva para artistas, poetas y artesanos. Estos interactuaban y colaboraban con los más de 1.000 habitantes campesinos nativos de las islas. El proyecto se basaba en los principios de la justicia social y la colaboración comunitaria de la llamada «Teología de la Liberación».
4. **El Parque Nacional Tortuguero, Costa Rica** Santuario de flora y fauna, Tortuguero sirve de vivienda a siete especies de tortuga, tres tipos de mono, perezosos[9] y otros mamíferos y más de 300 especies de ave. También hay lagartos[10] de un metro de extensión que parecen pequeños dinosaurios. De pequeños, estos lagartos pueden correr sobre el agua, así que se les conoce como «lagartos de Jesucristo». Este es sólo uno de los muchos parques nacionales de Costa Rica dedicados a la conservación de la naturaleza y al ecoturismo.

[7]de... *freshwater* [8]*sharks* [9]*sloths* [10]*lizards*

¡Viaje conmigo a Centroamérica!

Vea el vídeo para saber lo que Santiago les mandó a Javier y Sara sobre su viaje a Centroamérica.

Video footage provided by

BBC Motion Gallery

ACTIVIDADES

A. En parejas, contesten las siguientes preguntas sobre los lugares fascinantes.

1. Además de la maravillosa ingeniería del canal mismo, ¿qué atracciones turísticas hay en el Canal de Panamá?
2. ¿Cuáles son tres de los sitios arqueológicos de la civilización maya? ¿Qué se puede apreciar en cada uno?

(*continúa*)

3. ¿Por qué a un arquitecto le interesaría visitar las ruinas?
4. ¿Qué animal especial se encuentra en el Lago de Nicaragua?
5. ¿Qué se estableció en Solentiname en 1965?
6. ¿Qué animal o animales le interesaría(n) ver si fuera al Parque Nacional Tortuguero?

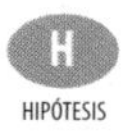

B. Localice los cuatro lugares fascinantes en el siguiente mapa de Centroamérica y ponga un número del 1 al 4 para indicar el grado de interés que Ud. tiene en visitar estos lugares. Turnándose con un compañero / una compañera, explique por qué a Ud. le interesa más el número 1 y por qué le interesa menos el número 4. Haga por lo menos tres comparaciones entre los dos lugares cuando presente su explicación.

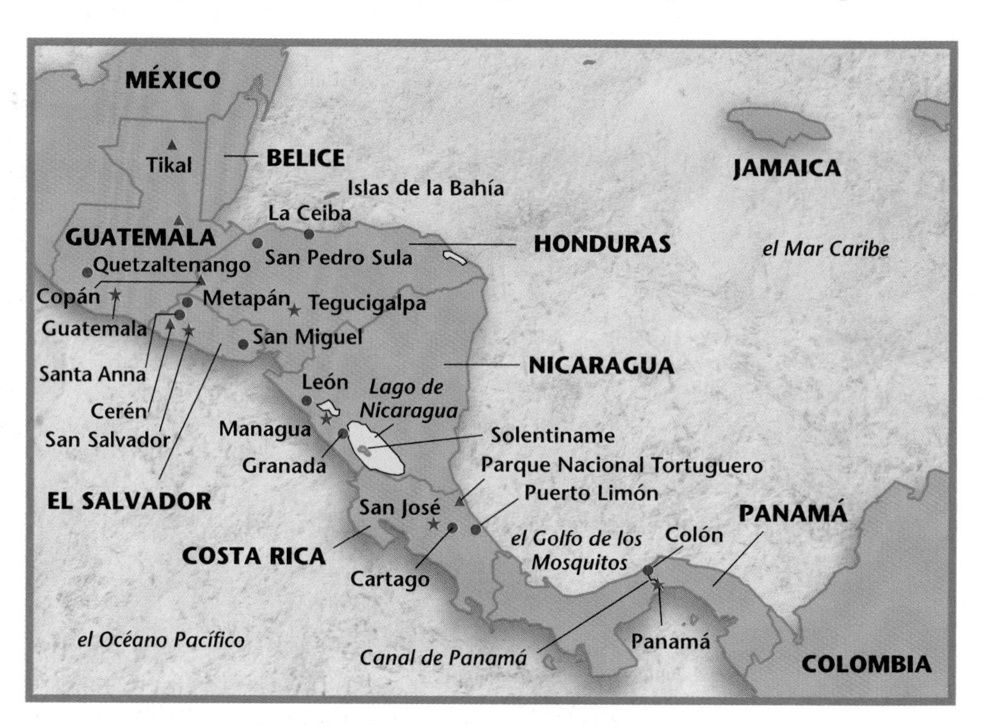

C. Ahora que ha leído sobre los lugares y ha visto el videoblog de Santiago, escriba una entrada en su blog sobre un viaje imaginario que Ud. haya hecho con unos amigos ecologistas a uno de los lugares fascinantes de Centroamérica. Siga el siguiente bosquejo.

MODELO: Acabamos de volver de ___________. El viaje fue ___________.

Nos quedamos en un eco-albergue fabuloso. Tenía…

El primer día… Otro día…

REACCIONAR

Nos encantó/encantaron… Nos molestó/molestaron…

R

RECOMENDAR

Para los que piensen ir a ___________, recomiendo que…

Si pudiera hacer de voluntario/a allí,…

Unas artistas hispanas:

Las indias kunas de Panamá y sus molas

Dos molas panameñas

A nivel mundial, los artistas más desconocidos y olvidados son los artesanos, los hombres y mujeres que trabajan en lo que se llama el «arte folclórico» o la artesanía. Aunque esta se considera arte «menor», ocupa un lugar muy importante en cualquier comunidad. Aporta mucho a la economía de una región y sirve para mantener las tradiciones, creencias y leyendas de cualquier cultura. Se puede decir que el trabajo de los artesanos sirve para unir el pasado, el presente y el futuro de un pueblo.

También es importante señalar que, mientras el mundo del arte formal suele estar dominado por los hombres, el mundo artesanal les brinda oportunidades a ambos sexos. Las indias kunas, por ejemplo, se han hecho famosas a nivel mundial por sus coloridas molas, telas bordadas de muchos colores brillantes que se aplican al frente y al dorso de sus blusas tradicionales. Los kunas habitan el archipiélago de Kuna Yala (o San Blas), un grupo de 300 islas en la costa noreste de Panamá. La sociedad es matrilineal y las molas forman la mayor parte del ingreso de cualquier familia.

Los diseños distintos de las molas se hacen con varias capas[1] de telas de diferentes colores. Las telas de encima se cortan y se cosen para revelar los colores de abajo. Los temas más típicos son mitológicos, religiosos, de animales, del mar, de personas o de diseños geométricos. Las kunas asocian la calidad de una mola con la simetría, el número de telas usadas, la complejidad del diseño y la perfección del cosido que debe ser casi invisible a simple vista.

Hoy es posible comprar molas en tiendas de artesanía en países desarrollados y aun por el Internet. Hay varias compañías de comercio justo que trabajan con las kunas para ayudarlas a vender sus molas. La globalización del mercado se demuestra hasta en los cambios de diseños. ¡Ahora se encuentran molas con diseños de elefantes y jirafas!

[1]*layers*

PREGUNTAS

En parejas, contesten las siguientes preguntas.

1. Miren las dos molas en esta sección. ¿Qué representan sus diseños? ¿Les gustan? ¿Por qué sí o por qué no?
2. ¿Por qué creen que las molas les interesan a los extranjeros?
3. ¿Por qué es raro que haya elefantes o jirafas en algunas molas?

ACTIVIDAD

COMPARAR

En otros países hay mujeres artesanas que también han creado artesanías muy valiosas, representativas de su cultura. Un ejemplo son las arpilleras (*burlap tapestries*) de Chile. En el Internet, busque imágenes de arpilleras chilenas y más ejemplos de molas de las indias kunas y compare las dos. ¿En qué se parecen y en qué se diferencian? Piense en los materiales, los colores, las imágenes y los temas representados.

La música guatemalteca

Una marimba, Antigua, Guatemala

La marimba es un xilofón largo, de madera, que se usa por toda Centroamérica y en las costas de Colombia y el Ecuador. Para la gente de Guatemala, el sonido de la marimba inspira un sentido de orgullo nacional y de nostalgia, especialmente entre los guatemaltecos exiliados. Probablemente la marimba llegó a esa zona a principios del siglo XVI, traída por esclavos africanos que sabían cómo hacerla y tocarla. Desde entonces, han aparecido tres tipos de marimba principales. La marimba de tecomate[1] es la más vieja y la más parecida a las marimbas que se encuentran en el sur de África. Otra es la marimba sencilla. Estas dos se usaban sobre todo para interpretar música religiosa. La tercera, que Ud. escuchará en la canción «Monseñor Mario Molina», es la marimba doble o cromática. Con esta, la marimba dejó de ser exclusividad de la Iglesia y empezó a usarse en ambientes seculares. Desde los años 70, la música de marimba es la forma musical más prestigiosa de Guatemala, hecho que se puede apreciar en las obras maestras ejecutadas en la llamada «marimba de concierto».

A consecuencia de la violencia de la guerra civil de los años 80, la marimba volvió a sus raíces espirituales como una manera de fortalecer las relaciones entre la Iglesia y las comunidades indígenas que sufrían bajo la opresión gubernamental y guerrillera.

[1]marimba... *gourd marimba*

ACTIVIDADES

A. **Antes de cantar** La canción «Monseñor Mario Molina» fue escrita por el Padre José Augustín Mateo Suar, un sacerdote de la iglesia del Quiché en Guatemala, para darle le bienvenida a un nuevo obispo a la diócesis en 2005. El grupo que toca la canción se compone de jóvenes músicos adolescentes. Tocan dos marimbas: una grande tocada por cuatro músicos y una tenor, tocada por tres músicos. Hay también un bajo, conchas de tortuga (*turtle shells*) y tambores. Conteste las siguientes preguntas.

1. ¿Qué tipo de vocabulario espera Ud. encontrar en una canción con la cual se celebra la llegada de un nuevo obispo?
2. ¿Conoce Ud. algunas canciones religiosas populares? ¿de qué tipo? ¿de qué tradición cultural vienen? ¿Por qué cree Ud. que la música es importante para muchas religiones?
3. ¿Prefiere oír música contemporánea en los servicios religiosos en vez de canciones tradicionales? Explique.
4. La marimba es un instrumento musical de las clases populares. ¿Qué efecto cree Ud. que tiene el uso de la marimba en los servicios religiosos dirigidos a la gente indígena en particular?

B. ¡A cantar! Escuche la canción «Monseñor Mario Molina» que se puede encontrar en el CD *Estampillas musicales.*

Monseñor Mario Molina

[*Coro*]
Hoy la iglesia del Quiché
se alegra con su pastor
Monseñor Mario Molina
que ha venido a guiar nuestro pueblo.
[*Se repite.*]

Gracias damos al Padre
por enviarnos un obispo
quien con el pueblo santificará
a la Iglesia. [*al coro*]

Auxilia[1] con tu gracia Padre
a tu hijo elegido
su ministerio sea edificar
a tu Iglesia. [*al coro*]

María, Madre de Dios
acompaña en la misión
a nuestro obispo en la construcción
del Reino. [*al coro*]

[1]Ayuda

C. Después de cantar En parejas, contesten las siguientes preguntas sobre la canción «Monseñor Mario Molina».

1. ¿Cuáles son las palabras clave que los/las ayudaron a entender el tema principal?
2. ¿Cómo se siente la gente con la llegada del Monseñor Mario Molina?
3. ¿Qué emociones evoca la canción en Uds.?

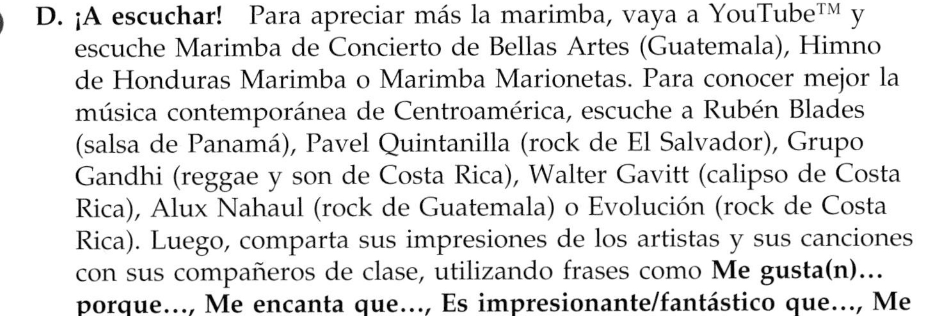

D. ¡A escuchar! Para apreciar más la marimba, vaya a YouTube™ y escuche Marimba de Concierto de Bellas Artes (Guatemala), Himno de Honduras Marimba o Marimba Marionetas. Para conocer mejor la música contemporánea de Centroamérica, escuche a Rubén Blades (salsa de Panamá), Pavel Quintanilla (rock de El Salvador), Grupo Gandhi (reggae y son de Costa Rica), Walter Gavitt (calipso de Costa Rica), Alux Nahaul (rock de Guatemala) o Evolución (rock de Costa Rica). Luego, comparta sus impresiones de los artistas y sus canciones con sus compañeros de clase, utilizando frases como **Me gusta(n)... porque..., Me encanta que..., Es impresionante/fantástico que..., Me sorprende que...** y **Es evidente que....**

Lectura

La escritora Gioconda Belli nació en Managua, Nicaragua, en 1948. Además de ser renombrada poeta, novelista y ensayista, ha estado siempre muy involucrada en la política de su país. Durante los años 60, trabajó con los Sandinistas, un movimiento revolucionario marxista que estuvo en el poder en Nicaragua de 1979 a 1990. Como escritora ha ganado un sinnúmero de premios, incluyendo el prestigioso premio literario de Casa de las Américas en 1978 por su colección de poemas, *Línea de fuego*. Sus numerosas publicaciones incluyen, además, *De la costilla de Eva* (poesía, 1987), *La mujer habitada* (novela, 1988) y *Waslala, Memorial al futuro* (novela, 1996). El poema que va a leer, «Los portadores de sueños», nos habla de la esperanza de los soñadores del mundo.

Antes de leer

A. Para comentar En grupos de tres, contesten las siguientes preguntas.

1. ¿Qué sueños tiene Ud. para su propio futuro?
2. ¿Qué sueños tiene en cuanto al futuro del mundo?
3. ¿Se siente optimista o pesimista cuando piensa en el futuro? ¿Por qué?
4. En febrero de 2009 entramos a la Época de Acuario. Según los astrólogos, esta época trae al mundo un período muy esperado de progreso en todo lo relacionado con la ciencia, la religión, el misticismo y el altruismo. Será un período de hermandad universal en el que veremos más compasión, altruismo y beneficencia. ¿Cuál es su reacción ante tales predicciones astrológicas?

B. Acercándose al tema Lea el título de la ficha y las nueve palabras asociadas con las predicciones. Con un compañero / una compañera, decidan si los espacios en blanco requieren un sustantivo, un verbo o un adjetivo. Luego, escoja la palabra apropiada de la ficha para completar las oraciones.

El futuro y las predicciones		
la catástrofe	la destrucción	el peligro
engendrar[1]	multiplicar	soñar
iluso/a[2]	compasivo/a	marcado/a

[1]*to father or to breed* [2]*naïve*

1. Todas las profecías dicen que el hombre va a causar su propia _________.
2. Pero siempre han existido los que _________ con la construcción de un mejor mundo.
3. Estos amantes de la vida venían al mundo _________ por el amor.
4. Son tan _________ que lloran por la muerte de un pajarito recién nacido.
5. Los portadores de profecías de _________ llamaron a los portadores de sueños románticos y pensadores _________ de utopías.
6. Pero los portadores de sueños hicieron el amor y _________ a nuevas generaciones que _________ sus sueños y los hacían correr por el mundo.
7. Los que buscan _________ en todas partes no tienen ojos para soñar.

Los portadores[1] de sueños

En todas las profecías
está escrita la destrucción del mundo.

Todas las profecías cuentan
que el hombre creará su propia destrucción.

Pero los siglos y la vida que siempre se renueva
VOCABULARIO engendraron[2] también una generación de amadores y soñadores,
hombres y mujeres que no soñaron con la destrucción del mundo,
sino con la construcción del mundo de las mariposas
y los ruiseñores.[3]

Desde pequeños venían marcados por el amor.
Detrás de su apariencia cotidiana
VOCABULARIO guardaban la ternura y el sol de medianoche.
Sus madres los encontraban llorando por un pájaro muerto[V]
VISUALIZAR y más tarde también los encontraron a muchos
muertos como pájaros.

VOCABULARIO Estos seres cohabitaron con mujeres traslúcidas
y las dejaron preñadas de miel y de hijos reverdecidos[4]
por un invierno de caricias.[5]

Así fue como proliferaron en el mundo los portadores de sueños,
atacados ferozmente por los portadores de profecías habladoras
de catástrofes.

VOCABULARIO Los llamaron ilusos, románticos, pensadores de utopías,
dijeron que sus palabras eran viejas
—y, en efecto, lo eran porque la memoria del paraíso es antigua
en el corazón del hombre—
los acumuladores de riquezas les temían
VOCABULARIO VISUALIZAR y lanzaban sus ejércitos[6] contra ellos,[V]
pero los portadores de sueños todas las noches hacían el amor
y seguía brotando su semilla del vientre[7] de ellas
que no sólo portaban sueños sino que los multiplicaban
y los hacían correr y hablar.
[...]

Son peligrosos —imprimían las grandes rotativas[8]
Son peligrosos —decían los presidentes en sus discursos
Son peligrosos —murmuraban los artífices de la guerra.[9]
[...]

[1]*bearers/carriers* [2]*gave birth to* [3]*nightingales* [4]las... *left them impregnated with honey and children who grew like grass* [5]*caresses* [6]*armies* [7]seguía... *their seed continued growing in the wombs* [8]*news pamphlets* [9]artífices... *architects of war*

(*continúa*)

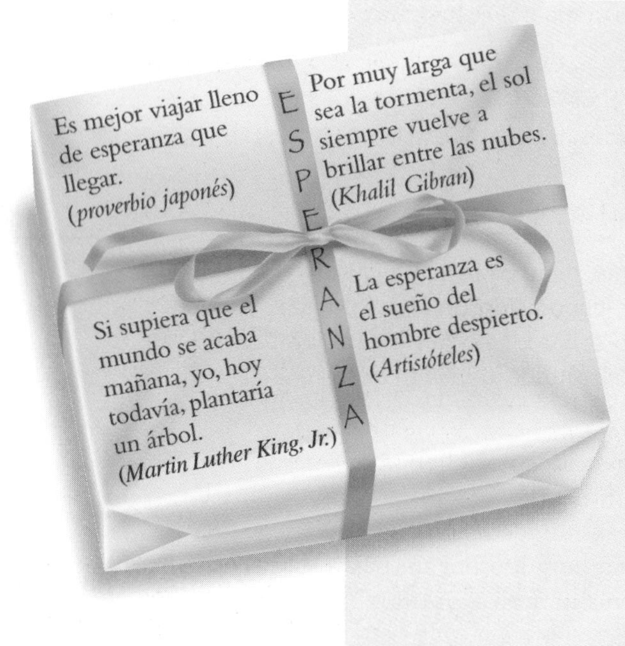

Los portadores de sueños conocían su poder
y por eso no se extrañaban[10]
Y también sabían que la vida los había
    engendrado
para protegerse de la muerte que anuncian las
    profecías
Y por eso defendían su vida aun con la muerte.
Y por eso cultivaban jardines de sueños
y los exportaban con grandes lazos[11] de colores
y los profetas de la oscuridad se pasaban noches
    y días enteros
vigilando[12] los pasajes y los caminos
buscando estos peligrosos cargamentos[13]
que nunca lograban atrapar[14]
porque el que no tiene ojos para soñar
no ve los sueños ni de día, ni de noche.

[10]no... *weren't surprised* [11]*ribbons* [12]*keeping watch over*
[13]*packages* [14]nunca... *they never managed to catch*

Después de leer

A. Comprensión

1. Según la voz poética, ¿qué dicen las profecías?
2. La voz poética encuentra la esperanza en cierto tipo de generación. ¿Cómo describe esa generación?
3. ¿Qué significa «las madres los encontraban llorando / por un pájaro muerto / y más tarde también los encontraron a muchos / muertos como pájaros»?
4. ¿Quiénes tienen miedo de los portadores de sueños? En su opinión, ¿por qué se sienten amenazados por ellos?
5. ¿Cómo reaccionan los portadores de sueños ante sus agresores?
6. ¿Por qué no pudieron encontrar los sueños los profetas de la oscuridad?
7. ¿Ud. se considera un portador / una portadora de sueños? ¿Por qué?

B. El lenguaje poético

Paso 1 Belli usó muchas imágenes e ideas muy concretas para expresar su mensaje en este poema. Indique los cinco sustantivos, cinco adjetivos y cinco verbos que Ud. cree que mejor expresan el mensaje central del poema.

Paso 2 Ahora, escoja el verso que, en su opinión, exprese mejor el mensaje central del poema. Con sus propias palabras, indique qué significa el verso y explique por qué lo escogió.

C. Los portadores de sueños versus los habladores de catástrofes

Paso 1 En parejas, llene los espacios en blanco con la forma apropiada del verbo que está entre parentesis.

Es normal que _________ (haber) diferentes maneras de ver la vida. Sería muy aburrido si todos _________ (enfrentar) los problemas diarios y mundiales con la misma actitud. Hay gente optimista que tan pronto como _________ (darse) cuenta de que una situación puede ser problemática, siempre _________ (buscar) lo positivo de la situación. Otros ven desastres por todos lados. Para ellos es muy importante _________ (tomar) en serio lo malo que ven a la vuelta de cada esquina.[1] A fin de cuentas, ¿qué _________ (pasar) si no estuvieran preparados? En realidad sería mejor si los optimistas _________ (ser) menos ingenuos en su optimismo y los pesimistas _________ (ver) la vida de una manera menos paranoica. ¿Es posible que _________ (cambiar)?

[1]a... *around every corner*

Paso 2 En grupos de tres, hablen de su propia actitud hacia los problemas cotidianos y los mundiales. ¿Son Uds. optimistas o pesimistas o algo entre los dos extremos? En su opinión, ¿hay más personas optimistas o pesimistas hoy en día? ¿Quiénes tienen más impacto en el mundo actualmente, los optimistas o los pesimistas?

Paso 3 Belli crea una imagen de sueños «exportados en lazos». Mire el «paquete de esperanza» en la página 188. ¿Cuál de las citas le inspira más a Ud.? ¿Por qué?

D. Para discutir Si Ud. fuera un «portador de sueños» / una «portadora de sueños», ¿qué sueños cultivaría? ¿Cómo cambiaría el mundo si se realizaran esos sueños?

E. Para futuras generaciones «Imagínate a toda la gente, viviendo la vida en paz» son algunas de las palabras que escribió John Lennon en su canción «Imagínate». ¿Puede imaginar ese mundo del que escribió Lennon? ¿Cómo quiere que sea el mundo que hereden sus hijos y nietos? Escriba una carta o un poema optimista a sus futuros hijos o nietos en que describa cómo será su mundo.

¡A escribir!

El Servicio Voluntario Universitario (SVU) en Nicaragua es parte del programa de Voluntarios de Naciones Unidas que les da a los estudiantes universitarios nicaragüenses la oportunidad de desarrollar sus destrezas profesionales y brindar sus aportes a proyectos que mejoran las condiciones de la vida humana. ¿Cree Ud. que a su universidad le interesaría ofrecer este tipo de oportunidad como parte integral de la formación de sus estudiantes? Explique.

A. **Lluvia de ideas** En grupos pequeños, hagan una lista de (1) los países o ciudades adonde posiblemente su universidad mandaría a sus estudiantes para hacer de voluntarios, (2) los proyectos que los estudiantes podrían realizar y (3) las acciones concretas que llevarían a cabo en este lugar.

B. **Composición: Una propuesta** Escoja un lugar, un proyecto y algunas de las acciones concretas que se apuntaron en la **Actividad A** para presentar a la administración de su universidad. Apoye la idea de ofrecer crédito universitario por esta labor.

    1. escoger un título en forma de una pregunta
    2. escribir un párrafo introductorio sobre el valor de trabajar como voluntario/a durante su carrera universitaria y el impacto que esto puede tener a nivel internacional
    3. describir un lugar ideal y un proyecto en particular que sirvan de programa piloto para esta iniciativa
    4. presentar las razones por las que cree que los estudiantes deben recibir crédito universitario por su labor
    5. escribir una conclusión

C. **Diálogo** En grupos de tres, lean las propuestas de sus compañeros y luego escojan la que sería más apropiada para el programa piloto de su universidad.

Hablando del tema

Antes de empezar a conversar con sus compañeros de clase sobre los siguientes temas, prepare una ficha para la conversación, otra para el debate y otra para la reacción ante la cita.

A. **Conversación: Conexiones globales** Revise las expresiones de **Para conversar mejor.** Luego, en parejas o en grupos de tres, contesten las siguientes preguntas.

Para conversar mejor

Creo/Opino/Supongo que...	Es possible que...
Dudo que...	Hay que tener en cuenta que...
Es evidente que...	No creo que...

- ¿Cuáles son los problemas mundiales que podemos resolver con la tecnología? Explique.
- ¿Cree que sería provechoso que las universidades obligaran a sus estudiantes a participar en un proyecto en el que propongan una idea innovadora para resolver un problema local, estatal o mundial? Explique.
- ¿Cree que todos los cursos universitarios deberían incluir un salón de «chatear» que requiera que los estudiantes tengan contacto con estudiantes de otros países para discutir los temas del curso? ¿Cuáles serían los beneficios de tal requisito?

B. Debate: Las clases virtuales Revise las expresiones de **Para debatir mejor.** Después, prepare tres argumentos a favor y tres en contra del valor de una licenciatura (*bachelor's degree*) virtual. Luego, presente sus argumentos en un debate. No sabrá qué lado tendrá de defender.

Para debatir mejor

A FAVOR	EN CONTRA
Eso es.	Eso no tiene sentido.
Estoy de acuerdo.	Lo siento, pero…
Muy bien dicho.	¿Hablas en serio?
No cabe duda.	Todo lo contrario.

«Una licenciatura obtenida a través de un programa virtual es tan valiosa como una licenciatura que se obtiene asistiendo a clases en vivo.»

«Nada puede reemplazar el contacto personal entre el estudiante y el profesor. Por eso la educación virtual nunca reemplazará la educación tradicional en el salón de clase.»

C. Reacción: El poder del dinero privado Revise las expresiones de **Para reaccionar mejor.** Luego, reaccione ante la siguiente cita. Añada razones que apoyen sus opiniones.

Para reaccionar mejor

Es alarmante que…
Es asombroso que…
Es evidente que…
Es inimaginable que…
Es probable que…
Es vergonzoso que…

«El sector privado es más efectivo en ofrecer ayuda económica y planificación para los cambios sociales que el sector gubernamental. Las iniciativas de la gente rica y poderosa como Shakira, Bill Gates, Carlos Slim Helu, Bono y Oprah Winfrey tienen más impacto mundial que las iniciativas políticas de los gobiernos.»

Explicación gramatical

LOS PUNTOS CLAVE

Descripción

The following grammar summaries on (A) agreement, (B) **ser** and **estar,** (C) past participles used as adjectives, and (D) uses and omission of articles will help you give more accurate descriptions in Spanish.

A. Agreement

Although you learned about subject/verb agreement and noun/adjective agreement when you first started to learn Spanish, you may still have problems with agreement (**concordancia**), especially when the person, place, or thing continues to be alluded to in a longer text. At this point, you are probably able to assign adjectives the correct gender when they are close to the noun they modify, but you may lose sight of the gender if the sentence continues. Note the following examples.

Incorrect: Las rosas amarillas que Javi le dio a Sara eran **bonitos.**
Correct: **Las rosas amarillas** que Javi le dio a Sara eran **bonitas.**

Remember that adjectives agree in number and gender with the nouns they modify. Adjectives ending in **-e** agree in number only (**un chico amable, una chica amable**). The plural is formed by adding **-s** to nouns and adjectives that end in a vowel (**la rosa roja, las rosas rojas**) and **-es** to nouns and adjectives that end in a consonant (**un joven alto, unos jóvenes altos**).

One roadblock to students' mastery of agreement is the existence of words that are not obviously masculine or feminine. The following lists contain some common nouns and rules that should help you.

1. Most nouns that end in **-a** or that refer to females are feminine.

   la brisa | la madre | la mujer | la reina

2. Most nouns that end in **-o** or that refer to males are masculine.

   el libro | el padre | el rey | el viento

3. Most nouns that end in **-ción, -sión, -d, -z, -ie, -is,** and **-umbre** are feminine.

   la actitud, la canción, la costumbre, la crisis
   la incertidumbre, la pensión, la realidad, la serie
   la superficie, la universidad, la virtud, la voz

4. Most nouns that end in **-l, -n, -r,** and **-s** are masculine.

   el amor, el árbol, el camión, el color
   el fin, el interés, el jamón, el lunar
   el mes, el papel, el perfil, el tenedor

5. Even though they end with **-a,** many words ending in **-ma, -pa,** and **-ta** are masculine.

el clima	el drama	el planeta	el programa
el cometa*	el idioma	el poema	el sistema
el diploma	el mapa	el problema	el tema

6. Feminine nouns that begin with a stressed **a-** or stressed **ha-** use masculine articles when they are singular, but feminine articles when they are plural. Remember that these feminine nouns always use feminine adjectives.

el agua fría	las aguas frías
un alma gemela	unas almas gemelas
un hacha larga	unas hachas largas

- Note that this rule applies only when the stress is on the first syllable, hence: **la atmósfera, la audición.**
- Also note that the word **arte** is generally masculine when it appears in the singular and feminine when it appears in the plural, hence: **el arte moderno, las artes gráficas.**

7. Some common words are shortened from their original feminine form. Although the shortened form ends in **-o,** the gender is still feminine.

la fotografía → la foto	la motocicleta → la moto

8. Many nouns ending in **-e** don't follow any specific gender rules. The gender of these nouns must be memorized. Most nouns ending in **-ante** or **-ente** that refer to a person can be masculine or feminine, depending upon the sex of the person to whom they refer.

el café	el/la estudiante
la gente	el/la gerente

9. Nouns and adjectives ending in **-ista** can be either masculine or feminine, depending on the gender of the person to whom they refer.

el/la artista	el presidente progresista
el/la dentista	la mujer realista
el/la periodista	

10. Finally, there are some nouns that do not follow any of the preceding rules. You will have to memorize their gender as you encounter them. Here are a few you may already know.

la cárcel	la mano	la miel	la sal

¡A practicar!

A. For each of the following words, indicate the number of the corresponding rule of gender found in the preceding explanation.

1. _____ el águila	7. _____ la foto	13. _____ el pan
2. _____ el archivo	8. _____ la luz	14. _____ el papel
3. _____ la crisis	9. _____ la mano	15. _____ la playa
4. _____ la cumbre	10. _____ la moto	16. _____ la voz
5. _____ el día	11. _____ la mujer	
6. _____ la flor	12. _____ la nariz	

*Note that **el cometa** means *comet,* but **la cometa** means *kite.*

B. Indicate the appropriate articles and adjectives for each of the following sentences.

1. _______ gente de mi barrio es muy _______. (simpático)
2. _______ aguas de los dos lagos son _______. (frío)
3. _______ fotos de mi novio, Francisco, son _______. (bonito)
4. _______ problema con _______ voz de Margarita es que es muy _______. (bajo)
5. _______ canciones que Leo canta son _______. (fabuloso)
6. _______ crisis con _______ clima en California es _______. (malo)
7. _______ nariz de Pepe, mi hermano menor, es muy _______. (largo)
8. _______ mapa de _______ ciudad que queremos visitar es _______. (pequeño)
9. _______ sol en las montañas es muy _______. (fuerte)
10. _______ árboles que están en _______ jardín son _______. (gigantesco)

B. Ser and estar

The irregular verbs **ser** and **estar** are used when describing people, places, and things. Here are some of the more common uses of **ser** and **estar.**

SER	ESTAR
1. to express inherent characteristics or the perceived norm with adjectives (I) Eva Perón **era** una mujer **elegante** y **sofisticada.** Ana **es** médica. 2. with **de** to indicate origin (O) José **es de** Costa Rica. 3. with **de** to indicate possession (PO) Las flores **son de** Camila. 4. to indicate time (T) and date (D) **Eran las 11:00** cuando Sara llegó. Mañana **es el 15 de septiembre.** 5. to express where an event takes place (E) ¿Dónde **es** el examen final? El concierto **es** en ese teatro.	1. to express the location of a physical entity (L) ¿**Dónde está** el bolígrafo? La foto **está en mi coche.** 2. to express a condition, such as health, mental state, or a change from the perceived norm (C) La profesora no puede hablar porque **está cansada.** Los niños **estaban** más animados ayer. Mariola, ¡**estás lindísima** hoy! 3. to form the progressive (P) El atleta **estaba sudando** (*sweating*) profusamente. María **está estudiando** con Pepe.

Note how the use of **ser** or **estar** in the following sentences changes their meaning.

1. La paella **es** muy rica. — *Paella is delicious. (It always is.)*
   La paella **está** muy rica. — *The paella tastes delicious. (this paella that I'm eating now)*
2. Horacio **es** nervioso. — *Horacio is nervous. (He is a nervous person.)*
   Héctor **está** nervioso. — *Héctor is nervous. (Something must have happened to make him nervous.)*

3. Susana **es** guapa. — *Susana is pretty. (She's a pretty woman.)*
   Lola **está** muy guapa. — *Lola looks very pretty. (She looks especially pretty today.)*
4. Ramón **es** aburrido. — *Ramón is boring. (He's a boring person.)*
   Pepe **está** aburrido. — *Pepe is bored. (right now)*
5. Paco **es** listo. — *Paco is smart. (He's an intelligent person.)*
   Juana **está** lista. — *Juana is ready. (She's prepared to begin/go.)*

¡A practicar!*

A. Select the correct word or phrase from those given to complete each of the following sentences.

1. La familia de Diego es ______.
   (en México, cerca de San Antonio, de México, tristes)
2. Los padres de Sergio estaban ______.
   (ricos, de San Francisco, norteamericanos, preocupados)
3. Laura creía que Sara era ______.
   (tímida, en otra tienda, llorando, con ella)
4. Sara estaba ______ cuando oyó las noticias.
   (joven, tomando un café, cruel, una trabajadora)
5. Javier es ______.
   (periodista, en Ruta Maya, frustrado, escribiendo un artículo)

B. Indicate the letter(s) (from the list of common uses of **ser** and **estar** at the beginning of this section) that explain(s) why **ser** or **estar** is used in each of the following sentences.

I = description of inherent characteristics	E = event
O = origin	L = location
PO = possession	C = description of state or condition
T = time	P = progressive
D = date	

1. ______ *Soy* de Miami. ¿Y tú?
2. ______ ¿*Está* pensando en mudarse a Puerto Rico?
3. ______ Su casa natal *está* en San Juan.
4. ______ Tengo que irme; ya *son* las 3:30.
5. ______ La reunión *es* en la casa de Cristina.
6. ______ *Estamos* preparados para el examen.
7. ______ *Era* la 1:00 cuando Laura llegó al laboratorio.
8. ______ Ellos *son* de Cuba, pero sus antepasados *eran* de España.
9. ______ La reunión *fue* en la oficina del presidente.
10. ______ *Es* una mujer muy lista y capaz.
11. ______ El coche rojo *es* de Diego.
12. ______ Marisol *estaba* muy contenta de oír la voz de su esposo.
13. ______ *Estuvo* estudiando durante tres horas.
14. ______ Los muebles antiguos *son* de sus abuelos.
15. ______ Hoy *es* el 30 de abril.

*There are more practice exercises in the *Online Learning Center* and the *Manual*.

DESCRIBIR

C. Fill in the blanks with the correct form of **ser** or **estar.**

Los cinco amigos viven en Austin, la capital de Texas. Austin _____[1] una ciudad de tamaño mediano, aunque _____[2] experimentando un gran crecimiento[a] en la población. Austin _____[3] conocido por su actividad en el campo de la música, por eso le gusta a Sergio vivir allí. Muchos de los conciertos _____[4] en la Calle Seis, que _____[5] muy cerca del centro de la ciudad. Uno de los lugares más tradicionales para ir a escuchar nueva música _____[6] el Continental Club. A veces toca allí un grupo de música cubana que se llama «Son Yuma». Bueno, en realidad los músicos de este grupo _____[7] estudiantes de los Estados Unidos. Pero los muchachos _____[8] muy dedicados; el año pasado fueron a Cuba a estudiar con músicos cubanos para perfeccionar su estilo. La chica que canta con ellos tiene una voz increíble. Ella _____[9] de Dallas, pero su español _____[10] tan bueno que parece _____[11] cubana. Este viernes, el grupo presentará un concierto de nueva música. El concierto _____[12] en el Club Palmeras, una salsateca importante. El club _____[13] de un primo de uno de los músicos. Los miembros del grupo _____[14] muy emocionados porque va a _____[15] un promotor musical de Nueva York para escucharlos. También _____[16] nerviosos, pero _____[17] seguro que todo saldrá bien.

[a]*growth*

C. Past participles used as adjectives

The past participle can be used as an adjective to modify a noun. This type of adjective is frequently used with **estar,** as it often describes the state or condition that results from an action or change. Remember that the rules of agreement apply.

- Regular past participles are formed by adding **-ado** to the stem of **-ar** verbs and **-ido** to the stem of **-er** and **-ir** verbs.

  Laura está **frustrada** con Sara. (frustrar)
  Diego y Sergio estaban **sorprendidos** porque había tanta gente en el café aquel día. (sorprender)
  Javier estaba **dormido** durante la reunión porque era **aburrida.** (dormir, aburrir)

- Some verbs have irregular past participles, whereas others simply add a written accent to maintain the appropriate stress.

COMMON IRREGULAR PAST PARTICIPLES		ADDED ACCENT
abrir: abierto	morir: muerto	caer: caído
cubrir: cubierto	poner: puesto	creer: creído
decir: dicho	resolver: resuelto	leer: leído
descubrir: descubierto	romper: roto	oír: oído
escribir: escrito	ver: visto	traer: traído
hacer: hecho	volver: vuelto	

¡A practicar!

Fill in the blanks with the appropriate form of the past participle of the verbs in parentheses.

Cuando Laura llegó a su laboratorio el domingo pasado, se llevó una sorpresa. La puerta, que normalmente está _____[1] (cerrar) con llave, estaba _____[2] (abrir). Con mucha precaución, Laura entró en el laboratorio y descubrió que todo estaba _____[3] (hacer) un desastre. Había muchas probetas[a] _____[4] (romper) y papeles _____[5] (tirar) por el piso, y algunos de los ratones de prueba estaban _____[6] (morir). Otras jaulas,[b] de algunos animales que se habían escapado, estaban _____ (abrir). Laura llamó inmediatamente a la policía. Era obvio que

[a]*test tubes* [b]*cages*

alguien había entrado en el laboratorio maliciosamente, tal vez con la intención de robar algo. Y qué lástima porque el trabajo de muchas personas estaba totalmente _______[8] (perder). Hasta hoy, el caso no está _______[9] (resolver) todavía.

D. Uses and omission of articles

DEFINITE ARTICLES

In Spanish, the definite article (**el/la/los/las**) is necessary in many cases in which no article is used in English. Although you will find exceptions, the following rules will serve as a general guideline to help you decide whether or not to use the definite article.

1. The definite article is needed before nouns that refer to concepts and abstract things and to nouns used in a general sense.

El amor nos ayuda a sobrevivir.	*Love helps us to survive.*
Los deportes son importantes para **la gente joven.**	*Sports are important for young people.*
El dinero puede causar problemas en vez de resolverlos.	*Money can cause problems instead of solving them.*

2. The definite article is used with nouns that refer to a general group.

La gente sin recursos necesita nuestra ayuda.	*People without resources need our help.*
Los inmigrantes han aportado mucho a nuestro país.	*Immigrants have contributed a lot to our country.*

3. The definite article is used for dates, seasons, meals, and hours.

Vamos a México **el 3 de enero** para pasar **el invierno** en la playa.	*We're going to Mexico on January third to spend the winter at the beach.*
Sirven **la cena** a eso de **las 8:00** de **la noche.**	*They serve dinner at about 8:00 P.M.*

4. The definite article is used in place of a possessive adjective for parts of the body and clothing.

Me puse **las sandalias** para ir a la playa.	*I put on my sandals to go to the beach.*
Rafael se lavó **la cara** con agua fría para despertarse.	*Rafael washed his face with cold water to wake up.*

5. The definite article precedes most professional titles or titles of respect, including **señor(a) (Sr[a].)** and **doctor(a) (Dr[a].)** when talking about people. The masculine plural article **los** is used with the singular surname when referring to a family.

La Sra. Romo fue a ver **al Dr.** Peña.	*Mrs. Romo went to see Dr. Peña.*
Los Rivera y **los Smith** son amigos.	*The Riveras and Smiths are friends.*

6. The definite article is used before names of sciences, skills, school subjects, and languages when they are the subjects of a sentence or the object of a preposition other than **de** or **en.** When languages are objects of a verb, the article is not used.

	El español es mi clase favorita, pero tengo problemas con **la conjugación** de los verbos.	*Spanish is my favorite class, but I have problems with verb conjugations.*
but	No estoy muy interesado en **química.**	*I'm not very interested in chemistry.*
	El libro de **alemán** cuesta más de 40 dólares.	*The German book costs more than $40.00.*
	Estoy tomando **historia, matemáticas** y **español.**	*I'm taking history, math, and Spanish.*

7. The definite article is used with **cama, cárcel, colegio, escuela, guerra, iglesia,** and **trabajo** when they are preceded by a preposition.

   Si vuelves de **la escuela** antes de las 3:30, todavía estaré en **la iglesia.** — *If you return from school before 3:30, I will still be in church.*

8. The masculine singular definite article **el** forms a contraction with the prepositions **de** and **a.** These are the only such contractions in Spanish.

   No encuentro las llaves **del coche.** — *I can't find the car keys.*
   but No encuentro las llaves **de la casa.** — *I can't find the house keys.*

   Ayer fui **al centro comercial** para comprar zapatos. — *Yesterday I went to the mall to buy shoes.*
   but Ayer fui **a la zapatería,** pero no me gustaron los precios de allí. — *Yesterday I went to the shoe store, but I didn't like the prices there.*

INDEFINITE ARTICLES

In Spanish, the indefinite article (**un/una/unos/unas**) is used less frequently than in English. Therefore, the rules in Spanish deal mostly with the omission of the article.

1. No indefinite article is used after the verb **ser** when referring to professions, nationalities, or political and religious affiliations. But whenever these items are modified by an adjective, the indefinite article must be used.

   No quiere ser **administradora.** — *She doesn't want to be an administrator.*
   Era republicano, pero ahora es **un demócrata apasionado.** — *He was a Republican, but now he's a fervent Democrat.*

2. No indefinite article is used before **otro/a, medio/a, cierto/a, mil, cien,** or **ciento.**

   No hay **otra manera** de hacer la receta excepto con **media libra** de tomates frescos. — *There's no other way to make the recipe except with a half pound of fresh tomatoes.*
   El libro cuesta **mil** ciento cincuenta **pesos.** — *The book costs one thousand one hundred fifty pesos.*

¡A practicar!

For the following narration, indicate the appropriate definite or indefinite article, according to the context of the story. **¡OJO!** In some cases, no article is required.

_____[1] primo de Sara es _____[2] maestro en _____[3] escuela secundaria cerca de _____[4] frontera[a] entre España y Portugal. Enseña _____[5] inglés y _____[6] matemáticas. En total tiene _____[7] cien estudiantes de _____[8] inglés y _____[9] ciento veinte estudiantes de _____[10] matemáticas.

_____[11] Sr. Garrudo es _____[12] jefe de estudios[b] de _____[13] secundaria e insiste en que _____[14] maestros lleguen _____[15] hora antes de que empiecen _____[16] clases para hablar sobre _____[17] mejor manera de ayudar a _____[18] estudiantes con _____[19] problemas de _____[20] aprendizaje.[c] Es _____[21] administrador comprensivo y dedicado a _____[22] desarrollo académico y psicológico de _____[23] estudiantes de su escuela. Él cree de todo corazón[d] que _____[24] dedicación, _____[25] paciencia y _____[26] amor son _____[27] componentes necesarios para asegurar[e] _____[28] éxito[f] de todos _____[29] estudiantes.

[a]*border* [b]jefe... *principal* [c]*learning* [d]de... *wholeheartedly* [e]*ensure* [f]*success*

Comparación

When describing people, places, things, emotions, and actions, we often compare them with others that are the same or different. In this section, you will review (A) comparisons of equality, (B) comparisons of inequality, (C) irregular comparative forms, and (D) superlatives.

A. Comparisons of equality

When you compare people, places, and things that are equal, use the following formulas.

1. **tan** + *adjective* + **como** (Note that the adjective always agrees with the noun it modifies.)

   Laura es **tan lista como** Sergio.
   Javi y Jacobo son **tan ambiciosos como** su padre.

2. **tan** + *adverb* + **como**

   Javier habla **tan rápidamente como** Sara.
   Laura duerme **tan profundamente como** Sara.

3. **tanto/a/os/as** + *noun* + **como** (Note that **tanto** agrees in number and gender with the noun it modifies.)

   Su tío tiene **tanto dinero como** su padre.
   Cristina ha traído **tantos regalos como** Diego.
   Marisol tiene **tantas amigas como** Sean.

4. *verb* + **tanto como**

   Felipe **gasta tanto como** yo.
   Jorge no **come tanto como** su hermano.

B. Comparisons of inequality

When you compare people, places, or things that are not equal, use the following formulas.

1. **más/menos** + *adjective, adverb,* or *noun* + **que**

   Marisol estaba **más contenta** con el Hotel Regina **que** tú.
   Uds. viajan **más frecuentemente que** nosotros.
   Este plan tiene **menos actividades que** el otro.

2. *verb* + **más/menos** + **que**

   Pablo siempre **paga menos que** Roberto.
   Por lo general, los europeos **fuman más que** los norteamericanos.

3. **más de/menos de** + *number*

   El viaje a Madrid le costará **menos de 1.000 dólares.**
   Hay **más de 55 personas** apuntadas (*signed up*) para esta excursión.

C. Irregular comparative forms

Some adjectives have an irregular comparative form.

mejor	*better*	mayor	*older; greater*
peor	*worse*	menor	*younger; lesser*

Esta clase es **mejor que** la del semestre pasado.
Carolina es **menor que** Sara pero **mayor que** Claudia.
Los efectos del terremoto (*earthquake*) son **peores que** los del huracán.

COMPARAR

D. Superlatives

Superlative comparisons rank one member of a group as the highest or lowest example of its kind. In general, superlatives are formed as follows.

definite article + *noun* + **más/menos** + *adjective* + **de**

Pancho es **el estudiante más entretenido** (*entertaining*) **de** todos.

¡OJO! Irregular forms precede the noun in this type of comparison. **Más/menos** is not used in these constructions.

Dormir en la playa es **la peor idea del** mundo porque hay muchos mosquitos.

¡A practicar!*

A. Write comparisons in complete sentences, using your imagination, the clues given, and the information from the following chart.

NOMBRE	EDAD	HERMANOS	SALARIO	COCHE
Javier	28	1	$2.000/mes	1990 Volkswagen
Laura	27	3	$1.200/mes	2004 Toyota Prius
Diego	32	3	$6.000/mes	Mercedes Benz

1. Laura **/** Diego **/** tener hermanos
2. Laura **/** Javier **/** joven
3. el coche de Javier **/** el coche de Laura **/** bueno
4. Diego **/** Javier **/** ganar dinero
5. Javier **/** Laura **/** rico
6. Laura **/** Diego **/** salir a comer
7. Javier **/** Diego **/** tomar el autobús

B. Translate the following sentences into Spanish.

1. Diego is the most serious of the five friends.
2. I think Austin is the most beautiful city in Texas.
3. Javier is the best person for giving advice.
4. Sara is the youngest one in her family.
5. That place is the best café in the city, but its bathrooms are the worst.

Narración en el pasado

PASADO

Narrating in the past requires that you know the past-tense verb forms and that you study and practice using the preterite, the imperfect, the present perfect, and the pluperfect tenses. To help you master this **meta comunicativa,** this section contains (A) a review of the verb forms for the preterite and imperfect; (B) hints for understanding the relationship and differences between them through the use of the **carne/columna** metaphor, an explanatory chart, and symbols to show how events take place in time and in relation to each other; (C) a list of verbs with different meanings in the preterite and imperfect; (D) a review of the present perfect and pluperfect tenses; and (E) **hace... que** constructions.

---

*There are more practice exercises in the *Online Learning Center* and the *Manual*.

A. Formation of the preterite and imperfect

1. Preterite forms

- Here is a review of preterite verb forms, including high-frequency irregular forms.

REGULAR PRETERITE FORMS						
HABLAR:	hablé	hablaste	habló	hablamos	hablasteis	hablaron
COMER:	comí	comiste	comió	comimos	comisteis	comieron
VIVIR:	viví	viviste	vivió	vivimos	vivisteis	vivieron
IRREGULAR PRETERITE FORMS						
DAR:	di	diste	dio	dimos	disteis	dieron
DECIR:	dije	dijiste	dijo	dijimos	dijisteis	dijeron
ESTAR:	estuve	estuviste	estuvo	estuvimos	estuvisteis	estuvieron
HACER:	hice	hiciste	hizo*	hicimos	hicisteis	hicieron
IR:†	fui	fuiste	fue	fuimos	fuisteis	fueron
PODER:	pude	pudiste	pudo	pudimos	pudisteis	pudieron
PONER:	puse	pusiste	puso	pusimos	pusisteis	pusieron
QUERER:	quise	quisiste	quiso	quisimos	quisisteis	quisieron
SABER:	supe	supiste	supo	supimos	supisteis	supieron
SER:†	fui	fuiste	fue	fuimos	fuisteis	fueron
TENER:	tuve	tuviste	tuvo	tuvimos	tuvisteis	tuvieron
TRAER:	traje	trajiste	trajo	trajimos	trajisteis	trajeron
VENIR:	vine	viniste	vino	vinimos	vinisteis	vinieron

- Verbs that end in **-car, -gar,** and **-zar** show a spelling change in the first-person singular of the preterite.

  buscar: busqué, buscaste, buscó,...
  pagar: pagué, pagaste, pagó,...
  empezar: empecé, empezaste, empezó,...

- An unstressed **-i-** between two vowels becomes **-y-** in the preterite.

  creer: creió → creyó
  creieron → creyeron

  leer: leió → leyó
  leieron → leyeron

- Although **-ar** and **-er** stem-changing verbs have no stem change in the preterite (**me acuesto → me acosté; pierde → perdió**), **-ir** stem-changing verbs do have a change in the preterite, but only in the third-person singular and plural. Thus, the stem vowels **e** and **o** change to **i** and **u,** respectively. You will notice in this text that some verbs are listed with two sets of letters in parentheses.

  conseguir (i, i) divertirse (ie, i) dormir (ue, u)

*The **-c-** in the preterite stem is replaced here with **-z-** to maintain the [s] sound ([θ] in Spain).
†Note that **ir** and **ser** share the same preterite forms. Context will determine meaning: **Mis tíos fueron a Londres para las vacaciones. Hace mucho tiempo que los dos fueron maestros.**

The first set of letters indicates a stem change in the present tense and the second set represents a change in both the preterite and the present participle.

PRETERITE FORMS OF STEM-CHANGING VERBS			
Verbs like PEDIR (i, i)		Verbs like DORMIR (ue, u)	
PRESENT	PRETERITE	PRESENT	PRETERITE
pido	pedí	duermo	dormí
pides	pediste	duermes	dormiste
pide	pidió	duerme	durmió
pedimos	pedimos	dormimos	dormimos
pedís	pedisteis	dormís	dormisteis
piden	pidieron	duermen	durmieron
PRESENT PARTICIPLE		PRESENT PARTICIPLE	
pidiendo		durmiendo	

2. Imperfect forms

- Here is a review of regular and irregular imperfect forms. Please note that there are only three irregular verbs in the imperfect.

REGULAR IMPERFECT FORMS						
HABLAR:	hablaba	hablabas	hablaba	hablábamos	hablabais	hablaban
COMER:	comía	comías	comía	comíamos	comíais	comían
VIVIR:	vivía	vivías	vivía	vivíamos	vivíais	vivían
IRREGULAR IMPERFECT FORMS						
IR:	iba	ibas	iba	íbamos	ibais	iban
SER:	era	eras	era	éramos	erais	eran
VER:	veía	veías	veía	veíamos	veíais	veían

B. Using the preterite and imperfect

A general rule of thumb to help you understand the distinction between the preterite and the imperfect is that the preterite is used to report events that were completed in the past. The focus may be on the beginning of an event (**Empezó a llorar.**), the end of an event (**Terminó de escribir el informe.**), or on the totality of an event from beginning to end (**Compró otro coche.**). On the other hand, when the focus is on an action that was in progress, with no concern for when it started or ended, the imperfect is used. Think of the preterite verbs as those that move the story line forward (the backbone of the story) and the imperfect as the descriptive filler (the flesh) used to enhance the listener's ability to picture more fully the circumstances of the past event being described. This distinction will be presented in three ways: (1) as a metaphor to guide you as you analyze and create past-tense discourse, (2) as a general explanation of when to use the preterite or the imperfect, and (3) as an explanation of how events take place in time.

1. The metaphor*

   The backbone/flesh metaphor can help you understand the relationship between the preterite and the imperfect. Think of the backbone (**la columna**) as the information that moves a story forward, a series of completed actions (preterite). As each event ends (represented with an **X**), a new event begins, which in turn moves the story forward in time. Notice that, in the events narrated below, each preterite verb moves the story line forward from the point of Santiago's waking up to the point of his leaving. The preterite is the backbone of the story.

Santiago se despertó temprano.	X	X	
Comió rápidamente.	X	X	
Salió corriendo de la casa.	X	X	backbone
Llegó a la oficina a las 8:00.	X	X	**(la columna)**
Firmó el documento.	X	X	
Salió para Lima.	X	X	

   Verbs in the imperfect do not introduce new events into the story and therefore do not move the story line forward. The imperfect stops the story line to fill in descriptive details or to "flesh out" the story. Hence the reference to the imperfect as the flesh (**la carne**) of the story. Note how the imperfect adds details.

FLESH (LA CARNE)	BACKBONE (LA COLUMNA)	FLESH (LA CARNE)
	Santiago se despertó temprano. X ↓	Era una mañana lluviosa.
	Comió rápidamente. X ↓	No tenía mucha hambre.
Quería llegar temprano.	Salió corriendo de la casa. X ↓	Estaba un poco nervioso.
	Llegó a la oficina a las 8:00. X ↓	Su jefe lo esperaba.
Temblaba un poco.	Firmó el documento. X ↓	Tenía que ser valiente.
	Salió para Lima.	

*This metaphor was devised and articulated by Dr. Ruth Westfall of the University of Texas at Austin.

Notice how the imperfect refers to a time specified by the preterite story line.

- At the time he woke up, it was a rainy morning.
- At the time of eating, he wasn't very hungry.
- He ran from his house because he wanted to arrive early. At the time of leaving, he was feeling a little nervous.
- At the time of his arrival at the office, his boss was waiting for him.
- He was shaking at the time of signing the document, but he had to be brave.
- Then he left for Lima.

This metaphor can be very helpful as you create your own stories in the past, and it is also helpful in analyzing existing texts in Spanish. Read the following narrative. On a separate sheet of paper, indicate the **columna** and the **carne** found in the narration, using the previous example as a model.

> El año pasado, Sara fue a Andalucía para pasar las vacaciones de primavera. Hacía muy buen tiempo. El sol brillaba[1] cada día. Primero, Sara paró en Granada, donde visitó la Alhambra. Era un lugar impresionante. Tenía vistas increíbles. Después, se marchó[2] a Sevilla para ver la famosa Semana Santa. Había flores por todas partes y las calles estaban llenas de gente de todas partes. Decidió entonces volver allí para hacer un reportaje para la emisora de radio.

[1]*was shining* [2]se... se fue

This metaphor can also be very useful when you are reading a text in Spanish. If you are confused about what happened in a particular passage, try focusing only on the preterite verbs, so you get the backbone of the story. Each verb in the preterite accounts for the forward movement of the narrative.

2. Usage chart

Here is a brief summary of some of the more common uses of the preterite and the imperfect.

PRETERITE X	IMPERFECT ~~~~~
completed action **Fui** al concierto. Me **puse** furiosa y **decidí** irme. El picnic **terminó** cuando **empezó** a llover.	*progression of an action with no focus on beginning or end* Lo **leía** con gran interés. **Dormía** tranquilamente. Mientras su padre **trabajaba,...**
completed actions in succession Se **levantó, comió** y **llamó** a Ana.	*habitual action* Siempre **comía** rápidamente.
completed action within a specific time period **Estudié** por dos horas anoche. **Vivió** cuatro años en Madrid.	*description of physical and emotional states, including past opinions and desires* El chico **era** alto y delgado. **Tenía** miedo de todo. **Quería** escaparse.
summary or reaction statement **Fue** un verano perfecto.	*background information such as time, weather, and age* **Eran** las 2:00 de la tarde y ya **hacía** frío. En 1978, ella **tenía** 13 años.

3. Uses of the preterite: expansion

   a. *Completed action.* Completed actions may refer to events that happened and ended quickly: ***Se sentó* en el sillón y *cerró* los ojos.** They may refer to the beginning or end of an action: ***Decidió* investigarlo. *Terminaron* la investigación.** Or they may refer to actions that started and ended in the past: ***Limpió* la casa entera.**

   b. *Completed actions in succession.* The preterite is used for a series of actions, in which one ended before the other began: ***Tomó* el desayuno, *limpió* la casa y *cortó* el césped** (*grass*). In this example, each action had a definite beginning and a definite end.

   c. *Completed action within a specific time period.* The preterite is used to describe an event that took place within a closed interval of time: **Diego *estudió* en Monterrey por cuatro años.** (He studied there during a closed interval of time—four years.)

   d. *Summary or reaction statement.* The preterite is also used in a summary statement or a reaction to a series of events packaged as a whole: **¿Qué tal la película? Me *encantó*. ¡*Fue* fenomenal!** (overall reaction to the movie as a whole); **¿Qué tal el viaje? *Fue* maravilloso.** (The whole trip was wonderful.)

4. Uses of the imperfect: expansion

   a. *Progression of an action with no focus on the beginning or end.* The imperfect is used to express what was in the process of happening at a given moment of the story in the past.

Elena **preparaba** la comida mientras su esposo **bañaba** a los niños.	*Elena was preparing the meal while her husband was bathing the children.* (beginning and end of both actions not specified)

   b. *Habitual action.* The imperfect is used to describe an activity that used to occur in the past when no definite length of time is mentioned.

Siempre **escuchaba** su música favorita en la sala.	*She always used to listen to her favorite music in the living room.* (habitual action)

   c. *Description of physical and emotional states, including past opinions and desires.* The imperfect is also used to describe characteristic states in the past.

Llevaba un traje elegante. **Estaba** guapísimo, pero **estaba** muy nervioso.	*He wore an elegant suit. He was looking extremely handsome, but he was very nervous.* (description of his physical and mental states)
Quería aprender más...	*He wanted to learn more . . .* (His desire was ongoing in the past.)

   d. *Background information such as time, weather, and age.* The imperfect is used to set the scene by giving background information.

Era una noche oscura.	*It was a dark night.* (background information)

- Note that the imperfect can also be used to refer to the future in a past statement.

Me dijo que **iba** a romper con Diego.	*She told me she was going to break up with Diego (in the near future).*
Afirmó que **venía** a la fiesta.	*He stated that he was coming to the party.*

5. How events take place in time

You may use the following symbols to help you remember the usage of the preterite and the imperfect in Spanish.

At a specific point in time **Decidió** mudarse. X	*Continuous, in progress* De niño, **tocaba** el piano.
Sequential **Hice** las tortillas, **cené** y **lavé** los platos. X X X	*Continuous, interrupted by another action* Me **bañaba** cuando **sonó** el teléfono.

¡A practicar!*

A. In this exercise you will work only with the four uses of the preterite listed in Section 3 (p. 207). Give the appropriate letter (a–d) for each verb in *magenta italics* to indicate which type of completed action is being expressed. Study the explanations again, if you wish.

1. Marisol y Sean *abrieron* _____ el café Ruta Maya en 1989.
2. El día que *inauguraron* _____ el café *fue* _____ fenomenal para ellos.
3. Todos sus amigos *llegaron* _____, *tomaron* _____ café y los *felicitaron* _____.
4. La madre de Marisol no *pudo* _____ asistir, pero *trató* _____ de llamarla durante todo el día.
5. En 1994, *celebraron* _____ el quinto aniversario del café; la madre de Marisol los *sorprendió* _____ y *llegó* _____ sin avisarlos.
6. *Fue* _____ una sorpresa muy especial.
7. ¡La celebración *duró* _____ tres días!

B. In this exercise you will work only with the four uses of the imperfect mentioned in Section 4 (p. 207). Give the appropriate letter (a–d) for each verb in *magenta italics* to indicate which type of ongoing activity or state is being described. Study the explanations again, if you wish.

1. El día de la apertura (*opening*) de Ruta Maya, Marisol *sentía* _____ un orgullo tan grande que no *podía* _____ contenerlo.
2. *Era* _____ un día perfecto. El sol *brillaba* _____, pero no *hacía* _____ demasiado calor.
3. Sean *limpiaba* _____ el nuevo bar mientras Marisol *preparaba* _____ las bebidas para la fiesta.
4. Marisol *llevaba* _____ un vestido nuevo y Sean le dijo que *estaba* _____ muy guapa.
5. Siempre *encendían* _____ unas velas especiales antes de cualquier ocasión importante.
6. Los dos *pensaban* _____ que su nuevo café *iba*† a ser un gran éxito.

C. Verbs with different meanings in the preterite and imperfect

The meanings of the following verbs change depending on whether they are used in the preterite or the imperfect.

---

*There are more practice exercises in the *Online Learning Center* and the *Manual*.

†Remember that the imperfect may be used to refer to the future in a past statement. None of the four uses of the imperfect as stated readily applies in this case.

	PRETERITE X	IMPERFECT ~~~~
conocer	*to meet* Por fin, los amigos **conocieron** a la madre de Javier. *Finally, the friends met Javier's mother.*	*to know, be acquainted with* Todos **conocían** la tienda de Diego. *Everyone was acquainted with Diego's store.*
saber	*to find out* **Supieron** la noticia. *They found out the news.*	*to know (facts)* **Sabían** que ella venía. *They knew that she was coming.*
poder	*to be able to (to try and to succeed)* **Pudieron** subir a la cima de la montaña. *They were able (tried and succeeded) to climb to the top of the mountain.*	*to be able to (no knowledge of attempt or success)* Dijo que **podía** bailar bien. *He said he could dance well.* (no indication of attempt or success, only of his self-declared ability)
no poder	*to try but fail* **No pudo** traducirlo. *He couldn't (tried but failed to) translate it.*	*to be incapable of* **No podía** traducirlo. *He wasn't capable of translating it.* (no indication of attempt or success)
querer	*to try (but ultimately not achieve)* **Quisimos** comprarlo. *We tried to buy it (but weren't able to for some reason).*	*to want* **Queríamos** comprarlo. *We wanted to buy it.*
no querer	*to refuse* **No quiso** terminar. *She refused to finish.*	*not to want* **No quería** terminar. *She didn't want to finish.*
tener	*to receive* **Tuvo** dos cartas hoy. *He received two letters today.*	*to have* **Tenía** mucho tiempo libre. *He had a lot of free time.*
tener que	*to have to (and to do)* Laura **tuvo que** ir al médico. *Laura had to go (and went) to the doctor.*	*to have the obligation to* Estaba preocupada porque **tenía que** estudiar. *She was worried because she had (the obligation) to study.*
costar	*to cost, be bought for* El suéter **costó** 150 pesos. *The sweater cost (and I bought it for) 150 pesos.*	*to cost, be available for* El abrigo **costaba** 500 pesos. *The coat cost (was priced at) 500 pesos.*

P
PASADO

¡A practicar!*

A. For the following sentences, indicate the use of each verb in *magenta italics*. Use **P** for preterite and **I** for imperfect, plus the letter explaining the usage (a–d from Section B, points 3 and 4 on p. 207) for each. Follow the model.

MODELO: Ayer *fue* un día fatal. → P:d

1. Sara *vivió* _____ en Salamanca de 1978 a 1995.
2. Antes *vivía* _____ en un pueblo cerca de Portugal.
3. Su apartamento en Salamanca *era* _____ pequeño pero muy acogedor (*cozy*).
4. Casi todos los días, *tomaba* _____ su cafecito en el bar de abajo.
5. Un día mientras *desayunaba* _____, *recibió* _____ la noticia de su beca (*scholarship*).
6. Cuando su hermana lo *supo* _____, *lloró* _____. Pero le *dijo* _____ que *quería* _____ lo mejor para ella.
7. Sara *fue* _____ a Madrid tres veces para arreglar sus papeles.
8. La última vez que *estuvo* _____ en Madrid, *había* _____ una larga cola y *tuvo* _____ que esperar mucho tiempo.
9. Desafortunadamente, *llevaba* _____ tacones altos (*high heels*).
10. *Fue* _____ un día horrible para ella.

B. Complete each blank with the appropriate preterite or imperfect form of the verb in parentheses.

Cuando Sergio ________[1] (ser) joven, ________[2] (ir) todos los veranos con su familia a México para visitar a la familia de su madre. Siempre le ________[3] (gustar) ver a sus primos, tíos y abuelos y pasar tiempo con ellos. Además, su abuela ________[4] (ser) una cocinera excelente y a Sergio le ________[5] (encantar) su comida. Una vez, cuando Sergio ________[6] (tener) 10 años, la familia entera ________[7] (ir) a pasar tres meses en Acapulco. Sus padres y sus tíos ________[8] (alquilar) una casa enorme cerca de la playa. Acapulco ________[9] (ser) una ciudad lindísima y/e ________[10] (hacer) muy buen tiempo, así que los primos ________[11] (poder) ir a la playa casi todos los días. Desafortunadamente, un día Sergio ________[12] (saber) que su otra abuela, la madre de su papá que ________[13] (vivir) en Boston, ________[14] (estar) enferma. El padre de Sergio ________[15] (tener) que ir a Boston urgentemente. Sergio ________[16] (querer) que su padre se quedara, pero también ________[17] (estar) preocupado por su abuelita. Cuando por fin Sergio y su madre ________[18] (estar) listos para salir, todos ________[19] (sentirse) tristes. A pesar de la enfermedad de su abuela paterna, Sergio lo ________[20] (pasar) muy bien ese verano. ________[21] (ser) unas vacaciones inolvidables.

D. The present perfect and pluperfect

1. Formation

The present perfect and pluperfect tenses are formed by combining the auxiliary verb **haber** and the past participle (for a review of past participles, see Section C of **Descripción** [p. 198]). In contrast to the past participle used as an adjective, the past participle in these tenses never changes in number or gender.

*There are more practice exercises in the *Online Learning Center* and the *Manual*.

PRESENT PERFECT		PLUPERFECT	
he vivido	hemos vivido	había hecho	habíamos hecho
has vivido	habéis vivido	habías hecho	habíais hecho
ha vivido	han vivido	había hecho	habían hecho

2. Usage

- The present perfect expresses an action that began in the past and has relevance to the present.

  ¡Qué sorpresa! Sara **ha terminado** el examen antes que los otros. Los padres de Sara **han decidido** ir a los Estados Unidos para pasar la Navidad con ella.

- On the other hand, the pluperfect expresses an action that had already happened before another action took place in the past.

  Javi nos dijo que **había trabajado** ocho días seguidos antes de tomar un descanso. Javier ya **había salido** de Ruta Maya cuando Sara llamó por él.

¡A practicar!*

A. Since the five friends in Austin met, some changes have occurred in their lives. Complete the following sentences with the appropriate present perfect form of the verb in parentheses.

1. Sergio __________ (conseguir) un contrato con Santana.
2. Javier __________ (romper) con su novia.
3. Laura no __________ (volver) a ver a Manuel en el Ecuador.
4. Diego __________ (tener) mucho éxito con Tesoros.

B. Complete the following sentences with the appropriate pluperfect form of the verb in parentheses to indicate that the actions took place before the change mentioned in **Actividad A.**

1. Antes de trabajar con Santana, Sergio __________ (trabajar) con grupos poco conocidos.
2. Antes de romper con su novia, Javier __________ (soñar) con tener relaciones duraderas.
3. Antes de volver a los Estados Unidos, Laura le __________ (prometer) a Manuel que volvería a Quito dentro de tres meses.
4. Antes de tener éxito en su negocio, Diego __________ (hacer) una inversión (*investment*) muy grande.

E. Hace... que

1. To express that an action *has been going on* over a period of time and is still going on, use the phrase **hace** + *period of time* + **que** + *present tense.*

   —¿Cuánto tiempo **hace que estudias** aquí? —*How long have you been studying here?*
   —**Hace dos años que estudio** aquí. —*I've been studying here for two years.*

2. To express how long *ago* something happened, use the **hace... que** construction with the *preterite.*

   Hace dos años que fui a Lima. *I went to Lima two years ago.*

*There are more practice exercises in the *Online Learning Center* and the *Manual*.

3. To express an action that *had been going on* prior to a past point in time, use the imperfect and **hacía** instead of **hace.**

Hacía cinco años que no la **veía** cuando decidió llamarla.	*He hadn't seen her for five years when he decided to call her.*

4. To express an action that *had already been completed* prior to a past point in time, use the pluperfect and **hacía** instead of **hace.**

No lo podía creer—**hacía 25 años que había llegado** a Caracas.	*She couldn't believe it—she had arrived in Caracas 25 years earlier.*

5. This type of construction may sometimes be used without the **que.**

—¿Cuánto tiempo **hace que estudias** aquí?	*—How long have you been studying here?*
—Hace dos años.	*—(I've been studying here for) Two years.*
Recibimos la revista **hace un mes.**	*We received the magazine a month ago.*

¡A practicar!

Translate the following sentences into Spanish.

1. I'm sorry! How long have you been waiting?
2. I've wanted to eat at this restaurant for a long time.
3. How long ago were you born?
4. Aura left for Buenos Aires six years ago and never returned.
5. Celia had been studying for six hours when Sergio called her.
6. Matías wasn't surprised; he had read about the problem three years earlier.

Reacciones y recomendaciones

When reacting to situations or making recommendations in Spanish, you will often need to use the subjunctive mood. To help you master the concepts of the subjunctive, this section contains a review of (A) present subjunctive forms, (B) past subjunctive forms, (C) the use of the subjunctive in noun clauses, and (D) formal and informal commands.

A. Formation of the present subjunctive

1. The present subjunctive is formed by dropping the **-o** from regular present-tense first-person singular indicative forms, then adding **-e** endings to **-ar** verbs and **-a** endings to **-er/-ir** verbs.

FORMATION OF THE PRESENT SUBJUNCTIVE					
AYUDAR ayudo → ayud-		LEER leo → le-		VIVIR vivo → viv-	
ayude	ayudemos	lea	leamos	viva	vivamos
ayudes	ayudéis	leas	leáis	vivas	viváis
ayude	ayuden	lea	lean	viva	vivan

2. Verbs that undergo spelling changes or that are irregular in the first-person singular indicative retain this irregularity throughout the present subjunctive.

   conocer: conozco → conozca, conozcas, conozca,...
   escoger: escojo → escoja, escojas, escoja,...
   salir: salgo → salga, salgas, salga,...

3. There are only six irregular verbs in the present subjunctive. Note that the first letters of the infinitives of these irregular verbs, taken together, spell out the word DISHES.

   dar: dé, des, dé, demos, deis, den
   ir: vaya, vayas, vaya, vayamos, vayáis, vayan
   saber: sepa, sepas, sepa, sepamos, sepáis, sepan
   haber: haya, hayas, haya, hayamos, hayáis, hayan
   estar: esté, estés, esté, estemos, estéis, estén
   ser: sea, seas, sea, seamos, seáis, sean

4. Stem-changing **-ar** and **-er** verbs do not undergo a stem change in the subjunctive for the **nosotros** and **vosotros** forms. Stem-changing **-ir** verbs, however, do retain a stem change for those forms.

   -ar: sentarse (ie) me siente, nos sentemos, os sentéis
   -er: volver (ue) vuelva, volvamos, volváis
   -ir: pedir (i, i) pida, pidamos, pidáis; sentir (ie, i) sienta, sintamos, sintáis; morir (ue, u) muera, muramos, muráis

B. Formation of the past subjunctive

1. The past subjunctive of all verbs is formed by dropping the **-ron** from the third-person plural preterite form* and replacing it with endings that include **-ra.**† Note the written accents on the first-person plural forms.

FORMATION OF THE PAST SUBJUNCTIVE					
AYUDAR ayudaron → ayuda-		COMER comieron → comie-		VIVIR vivieron → vivie-	
ayudara	ayudáramos	comiera	comiéramos	viviera	viviéramos
ayudaras	ayudarais	comieras	comierais	vivieras	vivierais
ayudara	ayudaran	comiera	comieran	viviera	vivieran

2. Some argue that there are *no* irregular verbs in the past subjunctive, because any irregularities come from the third-person plural preterite form, which is the basis for the past subjunctive stem.

   dormir: durmieron → durmiera, durmieras, durmiera,...
   leer: leyeron → leyera, leyeras, leyera,...
   sentir: sintieron → sintiera, sintieras, sintiera,...
   ser: fueron → fuera, fueras, fuera,...

*See the previous section, **Narración en el pasado,** for a review of preterite forms.

†An alternative ending that includes **-se** is also possible, but it's much less common. Here's an example of **escribir** conjugated in this manner: **escribieron** → **escribiese, escribieses, escribiese, escribiésemos, escribieseis, escribiesen.**

C. Using the subjunctive in noun clauses

Sentences that use the subjunctive have two clauses: an independent (main) clause and a dependent (subordinate) clause. The two clauses are generally separated by the connector **que.**

INDEPENDENT CLAUSE		DEPENDENT CLAUSE
Yo recomiendo +	**que**	+ ella tenga más paciencia.
I recommend +	(*that*)	+ *she have more patience.*

Note that in English the connector *that* is optional, whereas **que** is not.

1. Conditions for the use of subjunctive in Spanish

    - The two clauses must have different subjects.

      (**Yo**) Quiero que **ellos** lleguen temprano. — *I want them to arrive early.*

    - If there is no change of subject, use the infinitive in the dependent clause.

      Quiero llegar temprano. — *I want to arrive early.*

    - The verb in the independent clause must be in the indicative and express (W) willing/wish, (E) emotion, (I) impersonal expressions, (R) requests and recommendations, (D) doubt or denial, or (O) **ojalá** (*I wish* or *Here's hoping*). If the verb in the independent clause does *not* fall into any of the above WEIRDO categories, the verb in the dependent clause must be in the indicative (even if the two clauses have different subjects). Compare the following paired examples, also noting how the sequence of tenses comes into play.

Quiero que ellos **estén** contentos en su nueva casa.	(W: *wish expressed*)
Sé que ellos **están** contentos en su nueva casa.	(*certainty expressed*)
Recomiendo que Loli **tenga** su propio dormitorio.	(R: *recommendation expressed*)
Estoy seguro de que Loli **tiene** su propio dormitorio.	(*certainty expressed*)
Tenía miedo de que **hubiera** cucarachas en la cocina.	(E: *emotion expressed*)
Era cierto que **había** cucarachas en la cocina.	(*certainty expressed*)

    - Impersonal expressions or generalizations that express willing/wish, emotion, request, doubt, or denial are followed by an infinitive. When one of these generalizations is personalized (made to refer to a specific entity), however, it is followed by the subjunctive in the dependent clause.

Es necesario matar las cucarachas.	(*general*)
Es necesario que **Javier mate** las cucarachas.	(*personalized*)
Era horrible tener cucarachas en casa.	(*general*)
Era horrible que **yo tuviera** cucarachas en casa.	(*personalized*)

    - Here are some expressions that use the subjunctive.

      W: willing/wish; R: requests (these expressions indicate a direct or implicit command)

      (no) decir (*irreg.*) que (when **decir** means *to tell someone to do something*)
      (no) desear que
      (no) necesitar que
      (no) querer (*irreg.*) que
      (no) recomendar (ie) que
      (no) sugerir (ie, i) que

E: emotion; O: **ojalá**

(no) alegrarse de que	(no) sentir (ie, i) que
(no) esperar que	(no) temer (*to fear*) que
(no) es una lástima que	ojalá (que)
(no) gustar que	

I: impersonal expressions (indicate opinion or a subjective reaction)

más vale que (*it's better that*)	(no) es mejor que
(no) es bueno que	(no) es necesario que
(no) es difícil que	(no) es posible que
(no) es importante que	(no) es probable que
(no) es imposible que	(no) puede ser que
(no) es increíble que	

D: doubt or denial[*]

dudar (*to doubt*) que	no es evidente/obvio que
negar (ie)[†] (*to deny*) que	no estar seguro de que
no creer que	no es verdad que
no es cierto que	no pensar (ie) que

2. Sequence of tenses

   a. If the verb in the main clause is in the present and denotes what the speaker perceives to be an objective opinion, then the action in the subordinate clause is expressed by an indicative tense based on the appropriate time frame.

MAIN CLAUSE (OBJECTIVE OPINION)	SUBORDINATE CLAUSE (INDICATIVE)	TIME FRAME OF ACTION IN SUBORDINATE CLAUSE
Sé que	comprendías.	past
Creo que	has comprendido.	
Supongo que	comprendiste.	
Opino que	comprendes.	present
Pensamos que	vas a comprender.	future
Me parece que	comprenderás.	

[*]Note that in cases where certainty is expressed, the indicative is used: No estoy segura de **que Elena** tenga **razón, pero** es cierto **que ella** sabe **mucho.**

[†]With **no negar,** either the indicative or the subjunctive may be used, although the tendency is to use the subjunctive: No niego **que** sea **verdad.**

b. If the verb in the main clause is in the present and denotes a subjective comment from the WEIRDO list, then the action in the subordinate clause is expressed by a subjunctive tense based on the appropriate time frame.

MAIN CLAUSE (SUBJECTIVE OPINION *WEIRDO* LIST)	SUBORDINATE CLAUSE (SUBJUNCTIVE)	TIME FRAME OF ACTION IN SUBORDINATE CLAUSE
No creo que Me alegro de que Dudo que Es importante que	hayas comprendido. comprendieras.	past
	comprendas.	present or future

c. If the verb in the main clause is in the past and denotes what the speaker perceives to be an objective opinion, then the action in the subordinate clause is expressed by an indicative tense based on the appropriate time frame in relation to that of the main clause.

MAIN CLAUSE (OBJECTIVE OPINION)	SUBORDINATE CLAUSE (INDICATIVE)	TIME FRAME OF ACTION IN SUBORDINATE CLAUSE
Pensábamos que Sabía que Era obvio que	ya se habían ido.	previous
	lo quería.	simultaneous
	llegarían pronto.	subsequent

d. If the verb in the main clause is in the past and denotes a subjective comment from the WEIRDO list, then the action in the subordinate clause is expressed by a subjunctive tense based on the appropriate time frame in relation to that of the main clause.

MAIN CLAUSE (SUBJECTIVE OPINION *WEIRDO* LIST)	SUBORDINATE CLAUSE (SUBJUNCTIVE)	TIME FRAME OF ACTION IN SUBORDINATE CLAUSE
No creíamos que	hubieras comprendido.	previous
Temía que Era necesario que	comprendieras.	simultaneous or subsequent

¡A practicar!*

A. Complete the following sentences with the corresponding indicative, subjunctive, or infinitive forms.

1. Los profesores insisten en que Laura _______ (asistir) a la recepción.
2. Es ridículo que Diego _______ (comprar) otro coche caro.
3. Es imposible que Juanito no _______ (saber) leer ese libro.
4. Niegan que tú _______ (ser) extranjero.
5. Alguien me dice que Uds. no _______ (ser) hermanos.
6. ¿Te sorprende que tu hermano _______ (ser) mi enemigo?
7. Creemos que Bárbara _______ (ir) a la playa durante el verano.
8. Espero que todos _______ (traer) su cuaderno de ejercicios.
9. Es necesario que nosotros _______ (trabajar) por la noche.
10. Dudan que yo _______ (poder) resolver el problema.

B. Complete the following sentences according to the context of each situation.

1. Javier fuma dos cajetillas (*packs*) de cigarrillos cada día.
   Es horrible que…
   El médico recomienda que…
2. Sara nunca sale con sus amigos porque siempre está estudiando.
   Es triste que…
   Es evidente que…
3. La novia de Diego siempre coquetea con otros hombres.
   Sugiero que Diego…
   Es obvio que su novia…
   A Diego no le gusta que su novia…

C. Fill in the blanks with the appropriate form of the verb in *magenta italics.*

1. Javier *bebe* demasiado café.
   Sé que Javier _________ demasiado café.
   Es horrible que Javier _________ demasiado café.
2. Antes, Javier *tomaba* muchos licuados.
   Todos sabemos que antes Javier _________ muchos licuados.
   Era increíble que antes Javier _________ tantos licuados y que no engordara.
3. Laura siempre *recibe* notas muy altas.
   Estoy seguro/a de que Laura también _________ notas muy altas cuando tenía 10 años.
   Es fantástico que Laura _________ notas muy altas el año pasado.
4. Pero en su primera clase de quechua, Laura *sacó* C en una prueba.
   Después, su padre supo que Laura _________ C en su primera prueba de quechua.
   Él pensaba que era sorprendente que su hija _________ C en su primera prueba de quechua.
5. Cuando era joven, Sara *quería* ser cantante.
   Todos pensaban que era chistoso que Sara _________ ser cantante, ya que cantaba muy mal.
   De sus amigos actuales, sólo Sergio sabe que antes Sara _________ ser cantante.
6. Sergio *hizo* tres viajes para llevar el equipo de sonido al concierto.
   —¿Quién le pidió que _________ los viajes?
   —Los músicos. Después, estaban muy contentos de que Sergio _________ tantos viajes para ayudarlos.

*There are more practice exercises in the *Online Learning Center* and the *Manual.*

D. Commands

1. With few exceptions, the forms used for commands are exactly the same as those used for the present subjunctive. Only the affirmative **tú** commands and the affirmative **vosotros** commands are formed differently.
   - To form regular affirmative **tú** commands, use the third-person singular (present indicative) form of the verb.
   - Here are the eight irregular affirmative **tú** commands.

   decir → di　　ir → ve*　　salir → sal　　tener → ten
   hacer → haz　　poner → pon　　ser → sé†　　venir → ven

   - To form all affirmative **vosotros** commands, replace the final **-r** of the infinitive with **-d.**

COMMANDS				
	UD.	UDS.	TÚ	VOSOTROS
hablar	hable no hable	hablen no hablen	habla no hables	hablad no habléis
comer	coma no coma	coman no coman	come no comas	comed no comáis
dar	dé no dé	den no den	da no des	dad no deis
decir	diga no diga	digan no digan	di no digas	decid no digáis
ir	vaya no vaya	vayan no vayan	ve no vayas	id no vayáis

2. Pronouns (reflexive, indirect object, direct object) attach to the end of affirmative commands and precede the conjugated verb in negative commands. In the case of more than one pronoun, the order is always reflexive, indirect, direct (RID). (See the **Hablar de los gustos** section of these green pages [pp. 220–226] for more on the use of direct and indirect object pronouns.)
   - Written accents are added if attaching pronouns to affirmative commands moves the stress to the third-to-last syllable or further back. This is done to maintain the stress of the original affirmative command form.

*The affirmative informal command for **ir** has the same form as that of **ver: ve.** Context will determine meaning: **¡Ve a casa!**, **¡Ve esa película!**

†The informal command form of **ser** is the same as the first-person singular indicative form of **saber: sé.** Again, context will determine meaning.

- When attaching the reflexive pronoun **os** to an affirmative **vosotros** command, remove the **-d** of the command form before attaching the **os** pronoun. (EXCEPTION: **id** retains the **-d** when adding this pronoun.) Additionally, remember to add an accent to the **i** preceding the **os** pronoun in the case of the affirmative **vosotros** commands of reflexive **-ir** verbs.

COMMANDS WITH PRONOUNS				
	UD.	UDS.	TÚ	VOSOTROS
hacerlo	hágalo no lo haga	háganlo no lo hagan	hazlo no lo hagas	hacedlo no lo hagáis
dármela	démela no me la dé	dénmela no me la den	dámela no me la des	dádmela no me la deis
levantarse	levántese no se levante	levántense no se levanten	levántate no te levantes	levantaos no os levantéis
divertirse	diviértase no se divierta	diviértanse no se diviertan	diviértete no te diviertas	divertíos no os divirtáis
irse	váyase no se vaya	váyanse no se vayan	vete no te vayas	idos no os vayáis

3. To express suggestions and collective commands, such as *Let's leave, Let's speak, Let's not sing,* and so forth, use the present subjunctive **nosotros** form.
   - The one exception to this rule is the affirmative form of **ir.** Use **vamos,** not **vayamos.**
   - In the affirmative form of reflexive verbs, the final **-s** is dropped before attaching the pronoun **nos.**

NOSOTROS COMMANDS		
	AFFIRMATIVE	NEGATIVE
hablar	hablemos	no hablemos
ir	vamos	no vayamos
llamarlo	llamémoslo	no lo llamemos
levantarse	levantémonos	no nos levantemos
irse	vámonos	no nos vayamos

REACCIONAR R RECOMENDAR

¡A practicar!*

A. Provide the affirmative and negative forms of the **Ud., Uds., tú,** and **nosotros** commands of the following phrases, substituting the correct pronouns for any *magenta italicized* words according to the models.

MODELOS: hacer *la tarea* →
Hágala. No la haga.
Háganla. No la hagan.
Hazla. No la hagas.
Hagámosla. No la hagamos.

1. ponerse *los zapatos*
2. escribir *a los padres*
3. decir *la verdad*
4. leer *los capítulos*
5. irse de aquí

B. Translate the following commands.

1. Let's buy it. (**la alfombra**)
2. Let's sit down.
3. Bring it. (**la cerveza, tú**)
4. Play it. (**la guitarra, Ud.**)
5. Don't lose them. (**las llaves, Uds.**)
6. Let's not get up.
7. Wait for him. (**Ud.**)
8. Leave. (**tú**)
9. Don't do it. (**tú**)
10. Give it to them. (**la respuesta, Uds.**)

Hablar de los gustos

GUSTOS

Expressing likes and dislikes in Spanish can be confusing to English speakers, since the verb **gustar** is not used in the same way as other verbs you have learned. Indirect object pronouns are a necessary element in the construction with **gustar,** so before it is explained, we will review (A) direct object pronouns, (B) the personal **a,** (C) indirect object pronouns, and (D) double object pronouns. Then (E) **gustar** and similar verbs will be reviewed.

A. Direct object pronouns

1. A direct object receives the action of a verb and answers the questions *whom?* or *what?* in relation to that action. Note the direct objects in the following examples.

Consiguió **el aumento.**	*He got the raise.* (What *did he get?* **el aumento**)
No vi a **Sara** anoche.	*I didn't see Sara last night.* (Whom *did I not see?* **Sara**)

*There are more practice exercises in the *Online Learning Center* and the *Manual*.

2. A direct object pronoun, like a direct object noun, receives the action of the verb and answers the questions *whom?* or *what?* These pronouns take the place of their corresponding nouns to avoid unnecessary repetition. Here is a complete list of direct object pronouns in Spanish.

DIRECT OBJECT PRONOUNS			
me	*me*	nos	*us*
te	*you (fam., s.)*	os	*you (fam., pl., Sp.)*
lo/la	*you (form., s.)*	los/las	*you (form., pl.)*
lo	*him, it (m.)*	los	*them (m.)*
la	*her, it (f.)*	las	*them (f.)*

Third-person direct object pronouns should be used only after the direct object noun has been identified. That is, if it is already known that the conversation is about Sara, we can refer to her as *her* rather than say *Sara* each time she's mentioned.

3. Direct object pronouns are placed immediately before a conjugated verb.

(Consiguió **el aumento.**)	**Lo** consiguió ayer.
(No vi a **Sara** anoche.)	No **la** vi anoche.
(No he hecho **la tarea** todavía.)	No **la** he hecho* todavía.

There are only three exceptions to this rule. (See number 4.)

4. Direct object pronouns *may* be attached to an infinitive and to the progressive form, but *must* be attached to *affirmative* commands.

Debe conseguir**lo.** = **Lo** debe conseguir.
No quería ver**la** anoche. = No **la** quería ver anoche.
Está preparándo**lo.** = **Lo** está preparando.
Prepáre**lo.** *but* No **lo** prepare.

Remember that when you attach a pronoun to a progressive form or affirmative command, a written accent is used to keep the original stress of the word: prepar**a**ndo → prepar**á**ndolo.

5. The following verbs are commonly associated with direct objects and direct object pronouns.

admirar	conocer	invitar	querer
adorar	conseguir	llamar	ver
ayudar	escuchar†	mirar	visitar
buscar†	esperar†	necesitar	

*Remember that the two elements that make up perfect tenses (a form of **haber** and the past participle) can never be separated. Accordingly, any pronouns that accompany a perfect tense verb will always appear before the conjugated form of **haber.**

†Note that **buscar** means *to look for,* **escuchar** means *to listen to,* and **esperar** means *to wait for.* The *to* and *for* that are part of the expression in English are simply part of the verb itself in Spanish, so the object pronoun used with the verb is a direct object pronoun, not the pronoun object of a preposition.

B. The personal a

In Spanish, the word **a** precedes the direct object of a sentence when the direct object refers to a specific person or personified thing. Indefinite pronouns that refer to people, such as **alguien, nadie,** and **quien,** are also preceded by the personal **a.** There is no equivalent for the personal **a** in English. Note the following examples in which the personal **a** is used.

Sara buscó **a** Javier. (*a specific person*)
Perdí **a** mi perro en el mercado. (*an animal that is close to you*)
Tenemos que defender **a** nuestro país. (*a personification of one's country*)
¿**A** quién llamaste? (*the* whom *refers to a person*)
No llamé **a** nadie. (**alguien** *and* **nadie** *always take the personal* **a** *when they are direct objects*)
but Busco un tutor nuevo. (*No personal* **a** *is used since the direct object is not a specific person.*)

C. Indirect object pronouns

1. Like a direct object, an indirect object also receives the action of a verb, but it answers the questions *to whom?* or *for whom?* the action is performed.

Sergio **le** escribió a **Sara.**	*Sergio wrote to Sara.* (To whom *did Sergio write?* **a Sara**)
No **les** mandó el cheque.	*He didn't send them the check.* (To whom *did he not send the check?* **a ellos**)

2. Review the following chart of indirect object pronouns. Note that indirect object pronouns have the same form as direct object pronouns except in the third-person singular and plural, represented by **le** and **les,** respectively.

INDIRECT OBJECT PRONOUNS			
me	*to me, for me*	nos	*to us, for us*
te	*to you, for you (fam., s.)*	os	*to you, for you (fam., pl., Sp.)*
le	*to you, for you (form., s.)*	les	*to you, for you (form., pl.)*
le	*to him, for him*	les	*to them, for them (m.)*
le	*to her, for her*	les	*to them, for them (f.)*

3. The placement rules for indirect object pronouns are the same as those for direct object pronouns.

Laura **me** dio su número.
Laura va a dar**me** su número. = Laura **me** va a dar su número.
Laura está buscándo**me.** = Laura **me** está buscando.
Da**me** tu número. *but* No **me** des tu número.

4. Because **le** and **les** have several equivalents, their meaning is often clarified with the preposition **a** followed by a noun or pronoun. **¡OJO!** Although the clarifying noun or pronoun is often optional, indirect object pronouns are not.

Sergio **le** escribió (**a Sara**).	*Sergio wrote to Sara.*
Diego **les** prepara una buena sopa (**a Uds.**).	*Diego is preparing a good soup for you.*
Va a mandar**le** la receta (**a ella**).	*He's going to send her the recipe.*

5. When trying to figure out whether to use a direct or an indirect object pronoun, if you can answer the question *to whom* or *for whom,* you know that the indirect pronoun **le** or **les** is required.

I help her every day.	Do you say "I help to her" or "I help for her"? No, so you use the direct object pronoun **la,** which answers the question *whom do I help?* not *to whom do I help?:* **La** ayudo cada día.
I send him letters often.	Do you say "I send letters to him often"? Yes, so you use the indirect object pronoun **le,** which answers the question *to whom do I send letters?:* **Le** mando cartas a menudo.

6. The following verbs are commonly associated with indirect objects and indirect object pronouns.

dar	hablar	preguntar	regalar
decir	mandar	prestar	servir
escribir	ofrecer	prometer	traer
explicar	pedir	recomendar	

D. Double object pronouns

1. It is common to have both a direct and an indirect object pronoun in the same sentence. When this occurs, the indirect object pronoun always precedes the direct object pronoun. Remember the acronym (RID) (reflexive, indirect, direct) to help you recall the sequence of pronouns.

Sara **nos los** regaló.	*Sara gave them to us.*
Diego **me la** prestó.	*Diego lent it to me.*
Javi quiere dár**mela.**	*Javi wants to give it to me.*

2. When both the indirect and direct object pronouns begin with the letter *l* (such as **le lo** or **les la**), the indirect object pronoun always changes to **se.**

Laura **le** compró **unas galletas.** → Laura **se las** compró.
Estoy trayénd**oles los libros.** → Estoy trayéndo**selos.**

Because **se** can mean **le** or **les,** easily standing for any number of referents—*to him, to her, to you* (singular or plural), *to them*—it is often necessary to clarify its meaning by using **a** plus a noun or pronoun.

Laura **se las** compró **a Sara.**	*Laura bought them for Sara.*
Estoy trayéndo**selos a Uds.**	*I'm bringing them to you.*

¡A practicar!*

Identify the direct object (*whom?/what?*) and the indirect object (*to/for whom? to/for what?*) in the following sentences. Then translate the sentences into Spanish, replacing each object with the appropriate object pronoun.

1. Javier served the clients coffee.
2. Sara told Laura that she wouldn't be home until late.
3. Diego, show Mr. Galindo the paintings, please.
4. Sergio had to call the musicians and then listen to the CDs.
5. Laura was preparing a surprise dinner for Javier.

*There are more practice exercises in the *Online Learning Center* and the *Manual.*

6. Javier, thank (**agradecer**) Laura for the dinner.
7. Sara used to visit her uncle in Salamanca every Sunday.
8. Sergio can buy the flowers for us.
9. Javier and Diego won't tell me the truth.
10. Sara wanted to sing us a song with her horrible voice.

E. Gustar and similar verbs

1. As you have learned in your prior Spanish studies, **gustar** means *to please* or *to be pleasing.* Thus, the subject of sentences with **gustar** and similar verbs is the person or thing that is pleasing, not the person to whom it is pleasing. Sentences with **gustar** and similar verbs use the following formula.

INDIRECT OBJECT PRONOUN		+	*GUSTAR*	+	SUBJECT
me	nos		**gust**a		*infinitive* (comer)
te	os	+	**gust**a	+	(*article*) *singular noun* (el café)
le	les		**gust**an		(*article*) *plural noun* (los tacos)

¿**Te gusta** cantar? — *Is singing pleasing to you?* (*Do you like singing / to sing?*)

Les gustó mucho la película. — *The movie was very pleasing to them.* (*They liked the movie a lot.*)

Me gustan los libros de Stephen King. — *Stephen King's books are pleasing to me.* (*I like Stephen King's books.*)

2. Note that subject pronouns are not generally used before the **gustar** construction. The most frequent mistake that students make with this construction is to forget that the person to whom something is pleasing is not the subject of the sentence. Note the following examples.

   Incorrect: Ana le gustó el gato.
   Correct: **A** Ana le gustó el gato. (**El gato** is the subject of the sentence, not **Ana:** *The cat was pleasing to Ana.*)

   He likes those cookies. = A él **le gustan** esas galletas. (*Those cookies* [plural] *are pleasing to him* [**le**].)

   Sergio and Diego like fried fish. = A Sergio y a Diego **les gusta** el pescado frito. (*Fried fish* [singular] *is pleasing to them* [**les**].)

3. Here are some other verbs that use the same construction as **gustar.** Note that in all the examples the verb matches the person or thing that is interesting, delightful, fascinating, and so on.

VERBOS COMO *GUSTAR*	
aburrir (*to bore*)	Me aburren las películas lentas.
asustar (*to frighten*)	Le asustan las películas de horror a mi hermana.
caer bien/mal (*to like/dislike someone*)	El nuevo profesor me cae muy bien.
convenir (*to be beneficial / a good idea*)	Te conviene estudiar esta lección.
dar asco (*to disgust; to turn one's stomach*)	Me dan asco las cucarachas.
dar ganas de (*to give the urge*)	—Ver ese anuncio me da ganas de llamar por una pizza ahora mismo.
dar igual (*to be all the same; not to matter*)	—¿Quieres salir ahora? —Me da igual.
disgustar (*to dislike*)	—¡Fuchi! (*Yuck!*) Me disgusta la pizza.
encantar (*to delight*)	—Pues, a mí me encanta la pizza.
fascinar (*to fascinate*)	A Javi le fascina todo tipo de música.
fastidiar (*to annoy; to bother*)	Te fastidian las personas tacañas, ¿verdad?
importar (*to matter*)	A Juan Carlos no le importa el precio.
interesar (*to interest*)	¿Te interesan las noticias internacionales?
molestar (*to annoy; to bother*)	¿Te molesta si fumo?
preocupar (*to worry*)	Me preocupa que la profesora nos dé una prueba mañana.
sorprender (*to surprise*)	Nos sorprende su actitud tan liberal.

¡A practicar!*

A. Complete the following sentences with the appropriate indirect object pronoun and the correct form of the verb in parentheses.

1. ¿A ti _______ _______ (gustar: *preterite*) la comida que sirvió?
2. A mí _______ _______ (encantar: *imperfect*) mirar la tele con mis padres cuando era joven.
3. A Laura y a Sara _______ _______ (fascinar: *preterite*) la película *La lengua de las mariposas*.
4. A mi hermana _______ _______ (dar: *present*) asco la comida frita.
5. A sus abuelos _______ _______ (molestar: *present*) la música de sus nietos.

*There are more practice exercises in the *Online Learning Center* and the *Manual*.

B. Form complete sentences according to the model.

MODELO: mis vecinos / molestar / las fiestas que tenemos cada fin de semana →
A mis vecinos les molestan las fiestas que tenemos cada fin de semana.

1. yo / dar asco / los perritos calientes (*hot dogs*) con mostaza (*mustard*)
2. los profesores / fastidiar / los estudiantes que no estudian
3. mi amigo / fascinar / las películas violentas
4. nosotros / encantar / estudiar astrología
5. los niños pequeños / interesar / los dibujos animados
6. los jóvenes / molestar / las reglas de las residencias universitarias

Hacer hipótesis

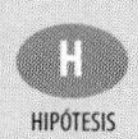

In this section, you will review how to express hypothetical situations. Hypothetical situations express what you or someone else would do given certain circumstances: *If I were president of the United States, I would first look for a diplomatic resolution to the conflict.* To form such hypothetical situations in Spanish, you will need to review (A) the past subjunctive, (B) the conditional, and (C) the various rules that govern the formation and use of hypothetical situations.

A. Past subjunctive and sequence of tenses

1. Past subjunctive

   For a review of the formation of the past subjunctive, see p. 213.

2. Sequence of tenses

   Remember that, if the main clause is in the past (and fits one of the WEIRDO categories), the subordinate clause will contain the past subjunctive. (See "Sequence of tenses" on pp. 215–216.)

   Es importante que los niños **duerman** la siesta.
   Era importante que los niños **durmieran** la siesta.

   La maestra **recomienda** que Luis **coma** algo antes de llegar a clase.
   La maestra **recomendó** que Luis **comiera** algo antes de llegar a clase.

   No le **gusta** que sus hijos **vivan** tan lejos.
   No le **gustaba** que sus hijos **vivieran** tan lejos.

B. The conditional

1. The conditional tense (*I would* go, I would speak,* and so on) of regular verbs is formed by adding the conditional endings to the entire infinitive of the verb. Note that the endings are the same for all **-ar, -er,** and **-ir** verbs. Here are some regular verbs in the conditional.

---

*When communicating the English idea of *would* in Spanish, you need to be careful. If *would* refers to a conditional action, often the result of a hypothetical situation, then use the conditional.

Iría **si no tuviera que trabajar.** — *I would go* if I didn't have to work.

However, if *would* refers to a habitual action that used to occur in the past, use the imperfect.

Iba **a la playa todos los días.** — *I would go* (I used to go) to the beach every day.

FORMATION OF THE CONDITIONAL					
VIAJAR		BEBER		DORMIR	
viajaría	viajaríamos	bebería	beberíamos	dormiría	dormiríamos
viajarías	viajaríais	beberías	beberíais	dormirías	dormiríais
viajaría	viajarían	bebería	beberían	dormiría	dormirían

2. Irregular verbs in the conditional have slightly different stems but take the same endings as regular ones. The twelve irregular verbs can be grouped into the following three categories.

SHORTENED STEMS

decir: dir- → diría, dirías, diría,...
hacer: har- → haría, harías, haría,...

-e- REMOVED FROM THE INFINITIVE

caber:* cabr- → cabría, cabrías, cabría,...
haber: habr- → habría, habrías, habría,...
poder: podr- → podría, podrías, podría,...
querer: querr- → querría, querrías, querría,...
saber: sabr- → sabría, sabrías, sabría,...

-dr- ADDED TO THE STEM

poner: pondr- → pondría, pondrías, pondría,...
salir: saldr- → saldría, saldrías, saldría,...
tener: tendr- → tendría, tendrías, tendría,...
valer: valdr- → valdría, valdrías, valdría,...
venir: vendr- → vendría, vendrías, vendría,...

C. Hypothesizing

1. A major component of expressing hypothetical situations is wondering "what if?". In this section, you will work with two types of *if* clauses: (1) those that represent a probable situation that is likely to happen or that represent a habitual action and (2) those that represent situations that are hypothetical or contrary to fact. Note the following examples.

   (1) Si estudio, recibiré una «A». (*there's still time for this to happen*) Si estoy preocupado, hablo con mi mejor amiga. (*habitual*)

   (2) Si **estuviera** en México, **visitaría** las ruinas mayas. (*I'm not in Mexico, so the statement is contrary to fact*)

***caber** = to fit

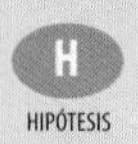

2. Here are some formulas that use *if* clauses.

   si + *present indicative* + *future* or *present* = probable or habitual

Si **tengo** tiempo, **iré** al cine contigo.	*If I have time, I will go to the movies with you.* (probable)
Si ella **toma** buenos apuntes, **saca** buenas notas.	*If she takes good notes, she gets good grades.* (habitual)

   si + *past subjunctive* + *conditional* = hypothetical (contrary to fact):

Si yo **fuera** Laura, no **iría** a Colombia.	*If I were Laura, I wouldn't go to Colombia.* (contrary to fact: I am not Laura)

3. To express hypothetical, contrary-to-fact situations about the past, use the following formula.

   si + *pluperfect subjunctive* + *conditional perfect* = hypothetical (contrary to fact)

Si yo **hubiera vivido** en el siglo XV, **habría sido** muy pobre.	*If I had lived in the 15th century, I would have been very poor.* (hypothetical, contrary to fact: I didn't live then)
Si **me hubiera casado** a los 17 años, no **habría terminado** mis estudios.	*If I had married at 17, I wouldn't have finished my studies.* (hypothetical, contrary to fact: I didn't get married)

¡A practicar!*

A. Complete the following sentences with the appropriate form of the verbs in parentheses. **¡OJO!** Not all sentences express hypothetical situations.

1. Si yo hablara mejor el español, ________ (conseguir) un puesto en el Perú.
2. Si mi jefe me pagara más dinero, ________ (trabajar: yo) más horas.
3. Si no tomo el desayuno, ________ (tener) poca energía.
4. Si pudiera cambiar de nombre, me ________ (poner) el nombre de ________.
5. Si viera un asesinato, ________ (llamar) a la policía.
6. Si yo ________ (ser) líder de este país, cambiaría muchas cosas.
7. Si ________ (lograr: yo) conseguir las entradas, te llamaré.
8. Si ________ (estar: yo) en Buenos Aires, iría a un bar de tango.

B. Change the following sentences to indicate that the situation is hypothetical. Then translate each sentence into English.

1. Si voy a España, visitaré el Museo del Prado en Madrid.
2. Si Luis tiene suficiente dinero, te mandará un boleto para ir a las Islas Galápagos.
3. Si estudio en Puerto Rico, asistiré a la Universidad Interamericana de San Germán.

Hablar del futuro

As you know, the **ir** + **a** + *infinitive* construction is often used to express future actions and states, usually with regard to the immediate future. Spanish also has a future tense with its own set of endings. In this section, you will review (A) the future tense, (B) another use of the future tense: the future of probability, and (C) talking about pending future actions by using the subjunctive in adverbial clauses.

---

*There are more practice exercises in the *Online Learning Center* and the *Manual*.

A. The future tense

1. The future tense, like the conditional (see the section on **Hacer hipótesis** [pp. 226–228]), is easy to form, adding future endings to the infinitive for regular forms.

FORMATION OF THE FUTURE					
ESCUCHAR		COMER		VIVIR	
escucharé	escucharemos	comeré	comeremos	viviré	viviremos
escucharás	escucharéis	comerás	comeréis	vivirás	viviréis
escuchará	escucharán	comerá	comerán	vivirá	vivirán

2. The same twelve verbs that are irregular in the conditional are also irregular in the future; their stems have the same irregularities as in the conditional, and their endings are regular.

SHORTENED STEMS

decir: dir- → diré, dirás, dirá,...
hacer: har- → haré, harás, hará,...

-e- REMOVED FROM THE INFINITIVE

caber: cabr- → cabré, cabrás, cabrá,...
haber: habr- → habré, habrás, habrá,...
poder: podr- → podré, podrás, podrá,...
querer: querr- → querré, querrás, querrá,...
saber: sabr- → sabré, sabrás, sabrá,...

-dr- ADDED TO THE STEM

poner: pondr- → pondré, pondrás, pondrá,...
salir: saldr- → saldré, saldrás, saldrá,...
tener: tendr- → tendré, tendrás, tendrá,...
valer: valdr- → valdré, valdrás, valdrá,...
venir: vendr- → vendré, vendrás, vendrá,...

B. The future of probability

The future can also be used to express probability or to conjecture about what is happening now. This can be tricky for speakers of English, because the English words and phrases used to indicate probability, such as *must, probably, wonder,* and so on, are not directly expressed in Spanish.

—¿Dónde **estará** Javi? — *—I wonder where Javi is. (Where could Javi be?)*

—Es lunes. **Estará** trabajando en Ruta Maya. — *—It's Monday. He's probably (must be) working at Ruta Maya.*

¡A practicar!*

A. Replace the **ir** + **a** + *infinitive* construction with the future in the following paragraph. **¡OJO!** Pay attention to pronoun placement.

Mamá, mañana tú *vas a despertarme*[1] temprano para que yo tenga tiempo de hacerlo todo bien. *Voy a ponerme*[2] un traje muy elegante para causarle una buena impresión a la entrevistadora. Cuando llegue a la oficina, *voy a saludarla*,[3] y ella me *va a decir*[4] que me siente. *Va a hacerme*[5] muchas preguntas sobre mis estudios y mi experiencia, y yo las *voy a contestar*[6] con cuidado y cortesía. No *voy a ponerme*[7] nerviosa. Cuando termine la entrevista, ella y yo *vamos a despedirnos*[8] cordialmente. ¡Estoy segura de que *van a llamarme*[9] muy pronto para ofrecerme el puesto!

B. Use the future of probability to make a conjecture about the following situations. Then translate the sentences into English.

1. Mario tiene el pelo canoso y muchas arrugas. ______ (Tener) por lo menos 70 años.
2. Alicia me dijo que llegaría a las 7:00, pero ya son las 7:30. ______ (Haber) mucho tráfico.
3. Pablo tiene un Rolls Royce y una casa en Boca Ratón. ______ (Ganar) mucho dinero.
4. La nueva película de mi primo ha sido un éxito maravilloso. ______ (Estar) muy contento.
5. Ricky Martin canta en inglés y español. ______ (Vender) muchos discos en el mercado internacional.

C. Using the subjunctive in adverbial clauses

It is important to remember that talking about future events often requires adverbial phrases (conjunctions) that refer to some pending time in the future or in the past. Here you will concentrate on two groups of frequently used conjunctions. The first group (A SPACE) denotes contingency, or actions that are contingent upon the completion of other actions, and the second group (THE CD) contains conjunctions of time. A SPACE conjunctions are always followed by the subjunctive (present or past). Use indicative after THE CD conjunctions if the action is habitual or completed (present or past indicative) and use subjunctive if the action is pending or has not yet materialized (present or past subjunctive).

A SPACE SUBJUNCTIVE	THE CD INDICATIVE OR SUBJUNCTIVE
antes de que	tan pronto como
sin que	hasta que
para que	en cuanto
a menos que	cuando
con tal (de) que	después de que
en caso de que	

*There are more practice exercises in the *Online Learning Center* and the *Manual*.

A SPACE (SUBJUNCTIVE)

Llámame **antes de que salgas** para el aeropuerto.
No voy a Jamaica este año **a menos que** me **den** más días de vacaciones.
Saldré contigo este viernes **con tal (de) que** no **vayamos** al cine.
No iba a aceptar el puesto **sin que** le **ofrecieran** más dinero.
El Sr. Mercado trabajaba mucho **para que** sus hijos **tuvieran** más oportunidades de las que él tenía.
Te di el número de teléfono **en caso de que** lo **necesitaras.**

THE CD (INDICATIVE OR SUBJUNCTIVE)

Juanito se pone triste **tan pronto como sale** su mamá. (*habitual in present: present indicative*)
Te llamo **tan pronto como llegue** mi esposo. (*pending in present: present subjunctive*)

Nuestro perro siempre comía **hasta que se enfermaba.** (*habitual in past: past indicative*)
Hasta que no pagara la multa (*fine*), no saldría de la cárcel. (*pending in past: past subjunctive*)

De niña, salía corriendo de la casa **en cuanto llegaba** su padre del trabajo. (*habitual in past: past indicative*)
Laura irá a Bolivia y Colombia **en cuanto tenga** suficiente dinero. (*pending in present: present subjunctive*)

Cuando llegó a Costa Rica, se fue al bosque lluvioso. (*completed action: past indicative*)
Nos sentiremos mucho más aliviados **cuando deje** de llover. (*pending in present: present subjunctive*)

Después de que Ema **salió** de la casa, su amiga Frida la llamó por teléfono. (*completed action: past indicative*)
Después de que aprendiera bien el español, le darían un aumento de sueldo. (*pending in past: past subjunctive*)

- Note that without the word **que,** the phrases **después de, antes de, para,** and **sin** become prepositions and are therefore followed by the infinitive.

Carmen vendrá **después de comer.**
Antes de tomar la pastilla, sugiero que llames al médico.
Para salir bien en el examen, debes estudiar más.
No vas a salir bien en este examen **sin estudiar.**

¡A practicar!*

Complete the following sentences with the appropriate form of the verb in parentheses. Then indicate whether the action is contingent (**CN**), pending or not completed (**P**), completed (**C**), or whether it denotes habitual behavior (**H**).

1. Iré a comprar las entradas antes de que ________ (llegar) mi hermano.
2. Hasta que no ________ (terminar) la tesis, Marta estaba muy nerviosa.
3. Marisa arregla su cuarto para que su madre ________ (estar) contenta.
4. Pensamos hacer caminatas (*to take long walks*) en las montañas a menos que ________ (llover) este fin de semana.
5. No me gusta viajar en avión cuando ________ (hacer) mal tiempo.
6. ¡Está bien! Iremos a Isla Mujeres con tal de que me ________ (ayudar: tú) con los niños.

*There are more practice exercises in the *Online Learning Center* and the *Manual.*

7. Te dejo un poco de dinero en caso de que los niños __________ (querer) merendar algo.
8. Cuando era joven, yo salía de casa sin que me __________ (ver) mis padres.
9. Joaquín siempre se baña antes de __________ (desayunar).
10. Cuando __________ (escuchar: yo) música clásica, me pongo muy relajado.
11. Llámeme tan pronto como __________ (saber: Ud.) algo, por favor.
12. Voy a estar en la biblioteca hasta que __________ (llegar: tú).
13. El otro día, después de que __________ (despedirse: nosotros), vi un accidente horrible.
14. Cuando __________ (mudarse: ella) a Nueva York el año pasado, no conocía a nadie.
15. Después de __________ (firmar) el contrato, Sergio se sintió emocionado.

Referencia de gramática

Los otros puntos gramaticales

A. Reflexive and reciprocal pronouns

1. Reflexive verbs usually express an action that one does to or for oneself. In English, this is understood but not always stated. Here are some of the more common reflexive verbs in Spanish.

acostarse (ue)	*to go to bed*	entristecerse (zc)	*to become sad*
afeitarse	*to shave*	levantarse	*to get up; to stand up*
alegrarse	*to become happy*	llamarse	*to be called*
asustarse	*to become afraid*	perderse (ie)	*to get lost*
bañarse	*to bathe*	ponerse (*irreg.*)	*to put on* (*clothing*)
deprimirse	*to get depressed*	preocuparse	*to become worried*
despertarse (ie)	*to wake up*	quitarse	*to take off* (*clothing*)
divertirse (ie, i)	*to have a good time*	reírse (i, i)	*to laugh*
ducharse	*to take a shower*	sentarse (ie)	*to sit down*
enfermarse	*to get sick*	vestirse (i, i)	*to get dressed*
enojarse	*to become angry*		

- Note that the reflexive pronouns attached to these infinitives change to correspond with the subject performing the action.

me baño	**nos** bañamos
te bañas	**os** bañáis
se baña	**se** bañan

- The placement of reflexive pronouns is the same as that of direct and indirect object pronouns. (See the discussion of direct object pronouns in the section on **Hablar de los gustos** [pp. 220–226].)

  Tienes que bañar**te** ahora. = **Te** tienes que bañar ahora.
  Los niños están bañándo**se.** = Los niños **se** están bañando.

2. The plural reflexive pronouns **nos, os,** and **se** can be used to express reciprocal actions that are expressed in English with *each other* or *one another.*

Nos queremos.	*We love each other.*
¿**Os** ayudáis?	*Do you help one another?*
Se admiran.	*They admire each other.*

3. Reflexive verbs may cease to be reflexive and instead take direct objects when the action is done to someone else.

acostar *to put (someone else) to bed* — acostarse *to go to bed*

A las 7:00 Marta **acuesta** a sus hijos.
Ella no **se acuesta** hasta las 11:30.

levantar *to raise, pick up; to lift* — levantarse *to get up; to stand up*

Rosa no puede **levantar** a su hijo porque es muy grande.
Rosa **se levanta** a las 7:00, pero no **nos levantamos** hasta las 8:00.

- Some verbs can also change their meaning when a reflexive pronoun is added.

dormir *to sleep* — dormirse *to fall asleep*

No **duermo** bien cuando bebo mucho.
Me duermo en clase cuando bebo mucho la noche anterior.

poner *to put, place; to turn on* — ponerse *to put on (clothing)*

Mi compañero de cuarto **pone** el aire acondicionado muy bajo.
Por eso tengo que **ponerme** un suéter aunque estamos en agosto.

¡A practicar!

Fill in the blanks with the correct forms of the appropriate verbs in parentheses.

Tengo una familia numerosa y todos tenemos un horario diferente. Yo ________[1] (acostarse/despertarse) a las 6:00 de la mañana y empiezo a ________[2] (ponerse/vestirse). Mi hermano, sin embargo, ya está despierto a esa hora y no puedo entrar en el baño porque él ________[3] (ducharse/sentarse). Él ________[4] (alegrarse/enojarse) si lo molesto. Mis hermanas gemelas, que ________[5] (llamarse/ponerse) Elena y Eloísa, son estudiantes de medicina. Cuando les toca el turno nocturno,[a] ellas llegan por la mañana y ________[6] (acostarse/levantarse) inmediatamente. Los demás ________[7] (divertirse/sentarse; nosotros) a la mesa para desayunar. Mis hermanos son muy cómicos y todos ________[8] (deprimirse/reírse; nosotros) un montón. Estoy segura de que tú no ________[9] (divertirse/entristecerse) tanto con tu familia como yo con la mía.

[a]les... *it's their turn to work the night shift*

B. Prepositions and verbs that take prepositions

1. The only verb form that can follow a preposition is the infinitive.

a	*to; at*	durante	*during*
antes de	*before*	en	*in; on; at*
con	*with*	hasta	*until*
de	*of; from*	para	*for; in order to*
después de	*after*	por	*for; because of*

¿Qué haces **para aprender** el vocabulario?
¿Lees **antes de dormir?**
¿Qué te gusta hacer **después de tomar** un examen?

2. Many verbs are accompanied by a preposition when preceding an infinitive (*inf.*) and/or a noun (*n.*). Here are some of the more common verbs of this type.

VERBS ACCOMPANIED BY A

acostumbrarse a + *inf.* or *n.*
adaptarse a + *inf.* or *n.*
animarse a + *inf.*
aprender a + *inf.*
ayudar a + *inf.*
comenzar (ie) a + *inf.*
dedicarse a + *inf.* or *n.*
empezar (ie) a + *inf.*
enseñar a + *inf.*
invitar a + *inf.* or *n.*
parecerse a + *n.*
volver (ue) a + *inf.** or *n.*

VERBS ACCOMPANIED BY CON

casarse con + *n.*
chocar con + *n.*
contar (ue) con + *inf.* or *n.*
cumplir con + *n.*
enfrentarse con + *n.*
soñar (ue) con + *inf.* or *n.*

VERBS ACCOMPANIED BY DE

acabar de + *inf.*
acordarse (ue) de + *inf.* or *n.*
aprovecharse de + *n.*
depender de + *n.*
despedirse (i, i) de + *n.*
disfrutar de + *n.*
divorciarse de + *n.*
enamorarse de + *n.*
encargarse de + *inf.* or *n.*
enterarse de + *n.*
olvidarse de + *inf.* or *n.*
tratar de + *inf.*

VERBS ACCOMPANIED BY EN

basarse en + *inf.* or *n.*
confiar en + *inf.* or *n.*
consistir en + *inf.* or *n.*
entrar en† + *n.*
fijarse en + *inf.* or *n.*
insistir en + *inf.*

VERBS ACCOMPANIED BY POR

disculparse por + *inf.* or *n.*
optar por + *inf.* or *n.*
preocuparse por + *inf.* or *n.*

3. Two verbs require **que** before an infinitive.

Hay que salir temprano.
Tiene que aumentar los sueldos.

---

*The phrase **volver a** + *infinitive* means *to do something again.*

Espero otros cinco minutos. Si no llega, vuelvo a llamarlo.
I'll wait another five minutes. If he doesn't arrive, I'll call him again.

†Some native speakers use the preposition **a** instead of **en** after the verb **entrar.**

¡A practicar!

Fill in the blanks with the appropriate preposition (**a, con, de, en**).

1. Javier y Jacobo se parecen mucho _____ su padre.
2. Durante todo el tiempo que pasó _____ el Ecuador, Laura nunca se animó _____ comer cuy (*guinea pig*).
3. La prima de Sara siempre había soñado _____ un hombre rico y guapo. El sábado pasado, se casó _____ el hombre _____ sus sueños.
4. La madre _____ Javier se preocupa _____ el bienestar (*welfare*) de su hijo.
5. Diego se fue sin despedirse _____ mí.
6. Las estadísticas se basan _____ unas encuestas telefónicas realizadas la semana pasada. Pero Sara no confía _____ las encuestas telefónicas.
7. Diego acaba _____ acordarse _____ que tiene que aumentar los sueldos _____ sus empleados.
8. Si Diego no empieza _____ cumplir _____ sus promesas, pronto su novia Cristina va a olvidarse _____ él y enamorarse _____ otro hombre.

C. Saber and conocer

1. **Saber** means *to know facts* or *pieces of information.* When followed by an infinitive, **saber** means *to know how to do something.*

No **saben** la dirección del jefe.	*They don't know the boss's address.*
¿**Sabes** usar esa máquina?	*Do you know how to use that machine?*

2. **Conocer** means *to know* or *to be acquainted* (*familiar*) *with* a person, place, or thing. It can also mean *to meet.* Note that the personal **a** is used before mention of a specific person.

Conocemos un café muy agradable.	*We know (are familiar with) a very pleasant café.*
¿Quieres **conocer** a mis padres?	*Do you want to meet my parents?*
No **conozco** a la dueña.	*I don't know the owner.*

¡A practicar!

Fill in the blanks with the appropriate form of the verb **saber** or **conocer.**

LIGIA: Oye, Kati, ¿ _______[1] un buen restaurante por aquí? Tengo ganas de salir a comer esta noche pero no _______[2] adónde ir.

KATI: ¡Claro que sí _______[3] un buen restaurante por aquí! Hay un restaurante argentino a tres calles en la esquina. _______[4] que no requieren reservación, pero creo que debes llegar temprano porque siempre hay gente esperando una mesa. _______[5] muy bien al dueño, don Mario. Si le dices que eres amiga mía, él te dará una de las mejores mesas. Don Mario _______[6] tratar muy bien a sus clientes especiales. Y si tienes la oportunidad, debes _______[7] al chef, Francisco. Es el hijo de don Mario, es bastante guapo, soltero y que yo _______,[8] no tiene novia.

D. Relative pronouns

Relative pronouns are used to join two simple sentences into one complex sentence. In the following example, the relative pronoun **que** replaces the repeated element in the second simple sentence (**El libro…**), thus forming one complex sentence.

> Diego necesita **el libro. El libro** tiene información sobre la artesanía boliviana.
> Diego necesita **el libro que** tiene información sobre la artesanía boliviana.

1. The pronoun **que** refers to things and people and expresses *that; which; who.*

Tengo el libro **que** querías.	*I have the book (that) you wanted.*
Es una persona **que** sabe mucho.	*He's a person who knows a lot.*

2. The pronoun **quien(es)** refers only to people, *may* be used in a nonrestrictive clause,* and *must* be used after a preposition or as an indirect object to express *who* or *whom.*†

Sara, **quien** es de España, vive en Austin.	*Sara, who is from Spain, lives in Austin.*
El chico **con quien** ella se quedaba es rico.	*The guy with whom she stayed is rich.*
El jefe, **a quien** no le gustan las fiestas, está allí.	*The boss, who doesn't like parties, is there.*

3. The pronouns **que** and **quien(es)** are the preferred choice in the Spanish-speaking world for informal speech. In writing and more formal speech situations, however, many native speakers prefer to use a set of compound relative pronouns after a preposition or to introduce a nonrestrictive clause. These compound relative pronouns are **el/la/los/las que** and **el/la/los/las cual(es)** and are used to express *that, which,* or *who/whom*. There is usually no semantic difference between the **que** or **cual** variants of these pronouns; the choice is a matter of personal preference.

Esa artesanía boliviana, **la que** buscaba Diego, es hermosa.	*Those Bolivian handicrafts, the ones that Diego was looking for, are beautiful.*
El cine **al cual** van está en el centro.	*The movie theater to which they are going is downtown.*

Additionally, the **el/la/los/las que** set can appear at the beginning of a sentence when the subject that the pronoun is replacing is already known or implied. In this case, these pronouns express *the one(s) that.*

La que me gustó más fue la falda verde.	*The one that I liked most was the green skirt.*

4. **Lo cual** refers to a concept or idea, will almost always appear in the middle of sentence, and expresses *which.*

El examen fue difícil, **lo cual** nos sorprendió.	*The exam was difficult, which surprised us.*

5. **Lo que** refers to a concept or idea. It is commonly used at the beginning of a sentence, but may also appear in the middle, to express *what* or *that which.*

Lo que no quiero es meterme en más líos.	*What I don't want is to get into more trouble.*
Eso es **lo que** te dije.	*That's what I told you.*

6. **Cuyo/a/os/as** is a possessive relative pronoun and is used like its English equivalent, *whose.* Note that it agrees in number and gender with the person or thing possessed.

El niño **cuyos** padres se marcharon está llorando.	*The child whose parents left is crying.*
La dueña **cuyo** negocio fracasó quiere empezar de nuevo.	*The owner whose business failed wants to start again.*

---

*A nonrestrictive clause is a clause embedded in a complex sentence and is usually set off by commas. These embedded elements represent afterthoughts or asides that can be removed without changing the fundamental meaning of the sentence. In nonrestrictive clauses that refer to people, either **que** or **quien(es)** may be used. However, many native speakers prefer to use **quien(es)** in all such cases.

†**Quien(es)** can be used as a direct object, but most native speakers omit the **a quien(es)** and introduce the embedded element with **que,** especially in informal speech. **La mujer a quien vimos en la tienda era muy alta.** → **La mujer que vimos en la tienda era muy alta.**

7. **Donde** can be used as a relative pronoun to express *where.*

Necesito trabajar en un lugar **donde** haya silencio absoluto.	*I need to work in a place where there is absolute silence.*

¡A practicar!

Fill in the blanks with the appropriate relative pronoun.

1. Javier, ______________ es puertorriqueño, es una persona ______________ sabe mucho.
2. ______________ Diego no quiere es que Cristina se enamore de otro hombre.
3. El Museo de Arte, ______________ tú buscabas, está cerrado hoy, pero hay otro museo ______________ te puede interesar.
4. El restaurante en ______________ pensaban almorzar sólo abre en la noche, así que fueron a una cafetería de ______________ había escuchado buenas cosas.
5. ¿Las canciones? ______________ más me gustaron eran las de *Los Lonely Boys.* ¿Los CDs? ______________ me prestaste están encima de la mesa.

E. Por and para

The Spanish prepositions **por** and **para** both mean *for.* Each has additional meanings, however, some of which are presented here.

1. Uses of **por**

by, by means of	Vamos **por tren.*** Debemos hablar **por teléfono** primero.
through, along	Caminamos **por el parque** y **por la playa.**
during, in (time of day)	Nunca estudio **por la mañana.**
because of, due to	Estoy nerviosa **por la entrevista.**
for = in exchange for	Piden $55 **por el libro.** Gracias **por todo.**
for the sake of	Quiero hacerlo **por ti.**
for = duration (often omitted)	Vivieron en España (**por**) **cuatro años.**
per	Hay dos premios **por** grupo.

- In addition, **por** is used in a number of phrases, some of which are included here.

por ejemplo	*for example*
por eso	*that's why, therefore*
por favor	*please*
por fin	*finally*
por lo general	*generally, in general*
por lo menos	*at least*
por si acaso	*just in case*
¡por supuesto!	*of course!*

2. Uses of **para**

in order to	Vienen a las 2:00 **para pintar** el cuarto.
for = destined for	El regalo es **para mi esposa.**
for = by (deadline, specified future time)	**Para mañana,** debe tenerlo listo.

*Many native speakers prefer using the preposition **en** instead of **por** with modes of transportation: **en avión, en bicicleta, en coche,** and so on.

for = toward, in the direction of	Salió **para Bolivia** ayer.
for = to be used for	Es **para guardar** la ropa.
for = as compared with others, in relation to others	**Para ellos,** no es importante. **Para (ser) tan joven,** es muy maduro.
for = in the employ of	Trabajan **para IBM** ahora.

¡A practicar!

Fill in the blanks with **por** or **para.**

_______[1] llevar una vida equilibrada, hago muchas cosas. _______[2] lo general, como bien y hago ejercicios _______[3] la mañana todos los días. A veces levanto pesas y a veces corro _______[4] el parque central de la ciudad. Tengo que decir que _______[5] la edad que tengo, me veo mucho más joven. El ejercicio no es tan importante _______[6] mis colegas de trabajo; _______[7] eso es que algunos ya están un poco gorditos. Bueno, ¡es _______[8] la falta de ejercicio y _______[9] lo mucho que comen! No es que yo quiera vivir _______[10] siempre; es que quiero estar aquí cuando mis hijos se casen y tengan sus propios hijos. Si me ofrecieran un millón de dólares _______[11] dejar la vida sana que tengo, _______[12] supuesto no lo aceptaría. La salud vale más que el oro.

F. Using the subjunctive in adjective clauses

An adjective clause describes a preceding noun. In the following example, the relative pronoun **que** introduces an adjective clause that describes what type of place the Ruta Maya café is.

El café Ruta Maya es un lugar **que atrae a gente diversa.**

Adjective clauses can also be introduced by **donde** if they describe a place, in the same way that the relative pronoun *where* is used in English.

Hay una mesa en Ruta Maya **donde siempre me siento.**

Note that the indicative (**atrae, siento**) is used in the adjective clause of the two preceding sentences. This is because the speaker is expressing an opinion or fact based on previous experience with the noun that each adjective clause describes (**un lugar** and **una mesa en Ruta Maya**). In the speaker's mind, the Ruta Maya café attracts a diverse mix of clients, and his or her special table exists.

1. When an adjective clause describes something of which the speaker has no prior knowledge (in other words, an unspecified or unknown person, place, or thing), the subjunctive is used in the adjective clause.

UNSPECIFIED OR UNKNOWN NOUN [−KNOWLEDGE] (SUBJUNCTIVE)	SPECIFIC OR KNOWN NOUN [+KNOWLEDGE] (INDICATIVE)
Necesito una clase que **empiece** antes de las 11:00.	Tengo una clase que **empieza** antes de las 11:00.
Buscamos un café que **sirva** café turco.	Buscamos el café que **sirve** café turco.
Busco un empleado* que **hable** español y chino.	Busco a la empleada* que **habla** español y chino.
Busco a alguien* que **juegue** al tenis bien.	Conozco a la persona* que **juega** bien.

*The personal **a** is not used with direct objects that refer to unspecified or unknown persons. However, remember that **alguien** and **nadie,** when used as direct objects, are always preceded by the personal **a.**

2. When the noun described by the adjective clause is part of a negative expression, the subjunctive is used in the adjective clause because, in effect, it is describing something that does not exist in the speaker's mind.

NEGATIVE EXPRESSION [−EXISTENCE] (SUBJUNCTIVE)	AFFIRMATIVE EXPRESSION [+EXISTENCE] (INDICATIVE)
No hay nadie en mi clase que **fume.**	Hay varios estudiantes en mi clase que **fuman.**
No conozco ningún hotel por aquí que **tenga** precios bajos.	Conozco un hotel por aquí que **tiene** precios bajos.

3. When a noun and the adjective clause describing it are part of a yes-or-no question, the subjunctive is used in the adjective clause because the speaker is uncertain whether the noun exists. (That's why the speaker is posing the question in the first place!) In answering such questions affirmatively, of course, the indicative is used; the subjunctive is used in answering them negatively.

YES-OR-NO QUESTION [−EXISTENCE] (SUBJUNCTIVE)	AFFIRMATIVE ANSWER [+EXISTENCE] (INDICATIVE)
¿Hay alguien aquí que **sepa** la dirección?	Sí, Marta la **sabe.**
¿Tienes un bolígrafo que me **prestes?**	Sí, aquí **tienes** uno.

YES-OR-NO QUESTION [−EXISTENCE] (SUBJUNCTIVE)	NEGATIVE ANSWER [+EXISTENCE] (SUBJUNCTIVE)
¿Hay una tienda por aquí donde **vendan** jamón serrano?	No, no hay ninguna tienda por aquí que **venda** jamón serrano.
¿Conoce Ud. a alguien que **hable** ruso?	No, no conozco a nadie que **hable** ruso.

¡A practicar!

Fill in the blanks with the appropriate form of the verbs in parentheses.

MAURA: ¿Hay un lugar en Austin donde la gente ________[1] (poder) relajarse y tomar café?
MIGUEL: Sí, Ruta Maya es un lugar donde la gente ________[2] (relajarse) y ________[3] (tomar) café todos los días.
MAURA: Pero busco un lugar que ________[4] (vender) café de comercio justo y donde ________[5] (haber) gente que ________[6] (hablar) español. ¿Existe un lugar así?

Diego necesita un empleado que ________[7] (saber) español y que ________[8] (ser) bueno para los negocios.

Desgraciadamente, Diego cree que no hay nadie que ________[9] (trabajar) tan bien como él. La verdad es que no hay nadie que ________[10] (cumplir) con sus expectativas (*expectations*).

Apéndice 1: ¡A practicar! Answer Key

Descripción

A. Agreement

A.

1. el águila, 6
2. el archivo, 2
3. la crisis, 3
4. la cumbre, 3
5. el día, 10
6. la flor, 10
7. la foto, 7
8. la luz, 3
9. la mano, 10
10. la moto, 7
11. la mujer, 1
12. la nariz, 3
13. el pan, 4
14. el papel, 4
15. la playa, 1
16. la voz, 3

B. 1. La, simpática 2. Las, frías 3. Las, bonitas 4. El, la, baja 5. Las, fabulosas 6. La, el, mala 7. La, larga 8. El, la, pequeño 9. El, fuerte 10. Los, el, gigantescos

B. **Ser** and **estar**

A. 1. de México 2. preocupados 3. tímida 4. tomando un café 5. periodista

B. 1. O 2. P 3. L 4. T 5. E 6. C 7. T 8. O, O 9. E 10. I 11. PO 12. C 13. P 14. PO 15. D

C. 1. es 2. está 3. es 4. son 5. está 6. es 7. son 8. son 9. es 10. es 11. ser 12. es/será 13. es 14. están 15. estar 16. están 17. es

C. Past participles used as adjectives

1. cerrada 2. abierta 3. hecho 4. rotas 5. tirados 6. muertos 7. abiertas 8. perdido 9. resuelto

D. Uses and omission of articles

1. El 2. – 3. una 4. la 5. – 6. – 7. – 8. – 9. – 10. – 11. El 12. el 13. la 14. los 15. una 16. las 17. la 18. los 19. – 20. – 21. un 22. al 23. los 24. la 25. la 26. el 27. los 28. el 29. los

Comparación

A. 1. Laura tiene tantos hermanos como Diego. 2. Laura es menor que Javier. 3. El coche de Javier es peor que el (coche) de Laura. 4. Diego gana más (dinero) que Javier. 5. Javier es más rico que Laura. 6. Laura sale a comer menos que Diego. 7. Javier toma el autobús más que Diego.

B. 1. Diego es el más serio de los cinco amigos. 2. Pienso que Austin es la ciudad más bella de Texas. 3. Javier es la mejor persona para dar consejos. 4. Sara es la menor de su familia. 5. Ese lugar es el mejor café de la ciudad, pero sus baños son los peores.

Narración en el pasado

B. Using the preterite and imperfect

A. 1. a 2. a, d 3. b, b, b 4. a, c 5. a, a, a 6. d 7. c

B. 1. c, c 2. d, d, d 3. a, a 4. c, c 5. b 6. c

C. Verbs with different meanings in the preterite and imperfect

A. 1. P:c 2. I:b 3. I:c 4. I:b 5. I:a, P:a 6. P:a, P:a; P:a, I:c 7. P:a 8. P:a, I:d, P:c 9. I:c 10. P:d

B. 1. era 2. iba 3. gustaba 4. era 5. encantaba 6. tenía 7. fue 8. alquilaron 9. era 10. hacía 11. pudieron 12. supo 13. vivía 14. estaba 15. tuvo 16. quería 17. estaba 18. estaban 19. se sentían 20. pasó 21. Fueron

D. The present perfect and pluperfect

A. 1. ha conseguido 2. ha roto 3. ha vuelto 4. ha tenido

B. 1. había trabajado 2. había soñado 3. había prometido 4. había hecho

E. Hace... que

1. ¡Lo siento! ¿Cuánto tiempo hace que esperas? 2. Hace mucho tiempo que quiero comer en este restaurante. 3. ¿Cuánto tiempo hace que naciste? 4. Aura salió para Buenos Aires hace seis años y nunca volvió. / Hace seis años que Aura salió para Buenos Aires y nunca volvió. 5. Hacía seis horas que Celia estudiaba cuando Sergio la llamó. 6. Matías no se sorprendió; hacía tres años que había leído del problema. /...había leído del problema hacía tres años.

Reacciones y recomendaciones

C. Using the subjunctive in noun clauses

A. 1. asista 2. compre 3. sepa 4. seas 5. son 6. sea 7. va 8. traigan 9. trabajemos 10. pueda

B. (*possible answers*) 1. ...fume tanto; ...deje de fumar 2. ...no se divierta; ...le gusta estudiar 3. ...rompa con ella; ...es muy extrovertida; ...hable con otros hombres

C. 1. bebe; beba 2. tomaba; tomara 3. recibía; recibiera 4. había sacado; hubiera sacado 5. quisiera; quería 6. hiciera; hubiera hecho

D. Commands

A. 1. Póngaselos. No se los ponga. / Pónganselos. No se los pongan. / Póntelos. No te los pongas. / Pongámonoslos. No nos los pongamos. 2. Escríbales. No les escriba. / Escríbanles. No les escriban. / Escríbeles. No les escribas. / Escribámosles. No les escribamos. 3. Dígala. No la diga. / Díganla. No la digan. / Dila. No la digas. / Digámosla. No la digamos. 4. Léalos. No los lea. / Léanlos. No los lean. / Léelos. No los leas. / Leámoslos. No los leamos. 5. Váyase de aquí. No se vaya de aquí. / Váyanse de aquí. No se vayan de aquí. / Vete de aquí. No te vayas de aquí. / Vámonos de aquí. No nos vayamos de aquí.

B. 1. Comprémosla. 2. Sentémonos. 3. Tráela. 4. Tóquela. 5. No las pierdan. 6. No nos levantemos. 7. Espérelo. 8. Sal. 9. No lo hagas. 10. Dénsela.

Hablar de los gustos

D. Double object pronouns

1. DO: coffee; IO: the clients; Javier se lo sirvió. 2. DO: that she wouldn't be home until late; IO: Laura; Sara se lo dijo. 3. DO: the paintings; IO: Mr. Galindo; Diego, muéstraselas, por favor. 4. DO: the musicians, the CDs; Sergio tuvo que llamarlos y escucharlos. 5. DO: a surprise dinner; IO: Javier; Laura se la estaba preparando / estaba preparándosela. 6. DO: the dinner; IO: Laura; Javier, agradécesela. 7. DO: her uncle; Sara lo visitaba en Salamanca todos los domingos. 8. DO: the flowers; IO: us; Sergio nos las puede comprar / puede comprárnoslas. 9. DO: the truth; IO: me; Javier y Diego no me la dirán. 10. DO: a song; IO: us; Sara nos la quería cantar / quería cantárnosla con su voz horrible.

E. Gustar and similar verbs

A. 1. te gustó 2. me encantaba 3. les fascinó 4. le da 5. les molesta

B. 1. (A mí) Me dan asco los perritos calientes con mostaza. 2. A los profesores les fastidian los estudiantes que no estudian. 3. A mi amigo le fascinan las películas violentas. 4. (A nosotros) Nos encanta estudiar astrología. 5. A los niños pequeños les interesan los dibujos animados. 6. A los jóvenes les molestan las reglas de las residencias universitarias.

Hacer hipótesis

A. 1. conseguiría 2. trabajaría 3. tendré (tengo) 4. pondría 5. llamaría 6. fuera 7. logro 8. estuviera

B. 1. Si fuera... visitaría (If I went to Spain, I would visit the Prado Museum in Madrid.) 2. Si Luis tuviera... te mandaría (If Luis had enough money, he would send you a ticket to . . .) 3. Si estudiara... asistiría (If I studied in Puerto Rico, I would attend the International University . . .)

Hablar del futuro

B. The future of probability

A. 1. me despertarás 2. Me pondré 3. la saludaré 4. dirá 5. Me hará 6. contestaré 7. me pondré 8. nos despediremos 9. me llamarán

B. 1. Tendrá... (He must be at least 70.) 2. Habrá... (There must be a lot of traffic.) 3. Ganará... (He must earn a lot of money.) 4. Estará... (He must be very happy.) 5. Venderá... (He must sell a lot of records on the international market.)

C. Using the subjunctive in adverbial clauses

1. llegue, CN 2. terminó, C 3. esté, CN 4. llueva, CN 5. hace, H 6. ayudes, CN 7. quieran, CN 8. vieran, CN 9. desayunar, H 10. escucho, H 11. sepa, P 12. llegues, P 13. nos despedimos, C 14. se mudó, C 15. firmar, C

Los otros puntos gramaticales

A. Reflexive and reciprocal pronouns

1. me despierto 2. vestirme 3. se ducha 4. se enoja 5. se llaman 6. se acuestan 7. nos sentamos 8. nos reímos 9. te diviertes

B. Prepositions and verbs that take prepositions

1. a 2. en, a 3. con, con, de 4. de, por 5. de 6. en, en 7. de, de, de 8. a, con, de, de

C. Saber and **conocer**

1. conoces 2. sé 3. conozco 4. Sé 5. Conozco 6. sabe 7. conocer 8. sepa

D. Relative pronouns

1. quien, que 2. Lo que 3. el cual / el que / que, que 4. el cual / el que / que, la cual / la que / que 5. Las que, Los que

E. Por and **para**

1. Para 2. Por 3. por 4. por 5. para 6. para 7. por 8. por 9. por 10. para 11. por 12. por

F. Using the subjunctive in adjective clauses

1. pueda 2. se relaja 3. toma 4. venda 5. haya 6. hable 7. sepa 8. sea 9. trabaje 10. cumpla

Apéndice 2: Conectores y palabras de transición

Secuencia de tiempo

primero	*first*
segundo	*second*
tercero	*third*
al mismo tiempo	*at the same time*
desde entonces	*from then on, since then*
después	*after*
durante	*during*
finalmente, al final	*finally, in the end*
luego	*then*
mientras	*while*
por último	*last of all*

Resultado

a causa de	*on account of*
por eso	*therefore, for that reason*
por esta razón	*for this reason, because*
por lo tanto	*therefore*

Concesión

a pesar de	*in spite of, despite*
por eso	*nevertheless*
por esta razón	*but*
por lo tanto	*nevertheless*

Contraste

al contrario	*on the contrary*
en cambio	*on the other hand, instead*
por otro lado	*on the other hand*
sino	*but (rather)*

Para añadir

además	*besides*
es más	*besides*
incluso	*even*
también	*also*

Opinión

Desde mi punto de vista...	*From my point of view...*
En mi opinión...	*In my opinion...*
Que yo sepa...	*As far as I know...*
Según...	*According to...*

Condición

a menos que	*unless*
con tal (de) que	*provided that*
para que	*so that*
puesto que	*since, given that*
tan pronto como	*as soon as*
ya que	*since, given that*

Conclusión

Así que...	*So...*
En conclusión...	*In conclusion...*
Para concluir...	*To conclude...*

Apéndice 3: Verb Charts

A. Regular Verbs: Simple Tenses

INFINITIVE PRESENT PARTICIPLE PAST PARTICIPLE	INDICATIVE					SUBJUNCTIVE		IMPERATIVE
	PRESENT	IMPERFECT	PRETERITE	FUTURE	CONDITIONAL	PRESENT	PAST	
hablar hablando hablado	hablo hablas habla hablamos habláis hablan	hablaba hablabas hablaba hablábamos hablabais hablaban	hablé hablaste habló hablamos hablasteis hablaron	hablaré hablarás hablará hablaremos hablaréis hablarán	hablaría hablarías hablaría hablaríamos hablaríais hablarían	hable hables hable hablemos habléis hablen	hablara hablaras hablara habláramos hablarais hablaran	habla / no hables hable hablemos hablad / no habléis hablen
comer comiendo comido	como comes come comemos coméis comen	comía comías comía comíamos comíais comían	comí comiste comió comimos comisteis comieron	comeré comerás comerá comeremos comeréis comerán	comería comerías comería comeríamos comeríais comerían	coma comas coma comamos comáis coman	comiera comieras comiera comiéramos comierais comieran	come / no comas coma comamos comed / no comáis coman
vivir viviendo vivido	vivo vives vive vivimos vivís viven	vivía vivías vivía vivíamos vivíais vivían	viví viviste vivió vivimos vivisteis vivieron	viviré vivirás vivirá viviremos viviréis vivirán	viviría vivirías viviría viviríamos viviríais vivirían	viva vivas viva vivamos viváis vivan	viviera vivieras viviera viviéramos vivierais vivieran	vive / no vivas viva vivamos vivid / no viváis vivan

B. Regular Verbs: Perfect Tenses

INDICATIVE										SUBJUNCTIVE			
PRESENT PERFECT		PLUPERFECT		PRETERITE PERFECT		FUTURE PERFECT		CONDITIONAL PERFECT		PRESENT PERFECT		PLUPERFECT	
he has ha hemos habéis han	hablado comido vivido	había habías había habíamos habíais habían	hablado comido vivido	hube hubiste hubo hubimos hubisteis hubieron	hablado comido vivido	habré habrás habrá habremos habréis habrán	hablado comido vivido	habría habrías habría habríamos habríais habrían	hablado comido vivido	haya hayas haya hayamos hayáis hayan	hablado comido vivido	hubiera hubieras hubiera hubiéramos hubierais hubieran	hablado comido vivido

C. Irregular Verbs

INFINITIVE PRESENT PARTICIPLE PAST PARTICIPLE	INDICATIVE					SUBJUNCTIVE		IMPERATIVE
	PRESENT	IMPERFECT	PRETERITE	FUTURE	CONDITIONAL	PRESENT	PAST	
andar andando andado	ando andas anda andamos andáis andan	andaba andabas andaba andábamos andabais andaban	anduve anduviste anduvo anduvimos anduvisteis anduvieron	andaré andarás andará andaremos andaréis andarán	andaría andarías andaria andaríamos andaríais andarían	ande andes ande andemos andéis anden	anduviera anduvieras anduviera anduviéramos anduvierais anduvieran	anda / no andes ande andemos andad / no andéis anden
caber cabiendo cabido	quepo cabes cabe cabemos cabéis caben	cabía cabías cabía cabíamos cabíais cabían	cupe cupiste cupo cupimos cupisteis cupieron	cabré cabrás cabrá cabremos cabréis cabrán	cabría cabrías cabría cabríamos cabríais cabrían	quepa quepas quepa quepamos quepáis quepan	cupiera cupieras cupiera cupiéramos cupierais cupieran	cabe / no quepas quepa quepamos cabed / no quepáis quepan
caer cayendo caído	caigo caes cae caemos caéis caen	caía caías caía caíamos caíais caían	caí caíste cayó caímos caísteis cayeron	caeré caerás caerá caeremos caeréis caerán	caería caerías caería caeríamos caeríais caerían	caiga caigas caiga caigamos caigáis caigan	cayera cayeras cayera cayéramos cayerais cayeran	cae / no caigas caiga caigamos caed / no caigáis caigan
dar dando dado	doy das da damos dais dan	daba dabas daba dábamos dabais daban	di diste dio dimos disteis dieron	daré darás dará daremos daréis darán	daría darías daria daríamos daríais darían	dé des dé demos deis den	diera dieras diera diéramos dierais dieran	da / no des dé demos dad / no deis den
decir diciendo dicho	digo dices dice decimos decís dicen	decía decías decía decíamos decíais decían	dije dijiste dijo dijimos dijisteis dijeron	diré dirás dirá diremos diréis dirán	diría dirías diría diríamos diríais dirían	diga digas diga digamos digáis digan	dijera dijeras dijera dijéramos dijerais dijeran	di / no digas diga digamos decid / no digáis digan
estar estando estado	estoy estás está estamos estáis están	estaba estabas estaba estábamos estabais estaban	estuve estuviste estuvo estuvimos estuvisteis estuvieron	estaré estarás estará estaremos estaréis estarán	estaría estarías estaría estaríamos estaríais estarían	esté estés esté estemos estéis estén	estuviera estuvieras estuviera estuviéramos estuvierais estuviera	está / no estés esté estemos estad / no estéis estén
haber habiendo habido	he has ha hemos habéis han	había habías había habíamos habíais habían	hube hubiste hubo hubimos hubisteis hubieron	habré habrás habrá habremos habréis habrán	habría habrías habría habríamos habríais habrían	haya hayas haya hayamos hayáis hayan	hubiera hubieras hubiera hubiéramos hubierais hubieran	

C. Irregular Verbs (continued)

INFINITIVE PRESENT PARTICIPLE PAST PARTICIPLE	INDICATIVE					SUBJUNCTIVE		IMPERATIVE
	PRESENT	IMPERFECT	PRETERITE	FUTURE	CONDITIONAL	PRESENT	PAST	
hacer haciendo hecho	hago haces hace hacemos hacéis hacen	hacía hacías hacía hacíamos hacíais hacían	hice hiciste hizo hicimos hicisteis hicieron	haré harás hará haremos haréis harán	haría harías haría haríamos haríais harían	haga hagas haga hagamos hagáis hagan	hiciera hicieras hiciera hiciéramos hicierais hicieran	haz / no hagas haga hagamos haced / no hagáis hagan
ir yendo ido	voy vas va vamos vais van	iba ibas iba íbamos ibais iban	fui fuiste fue fuimos fuisteis fueron	iré irás irá iremos iréis irán	iría irías iría iríamos iríais irían	vaya vayas vaya vayamos vayáis vayan	fuera fueras fuera fuéramos fuerais fueran	ve / no vayas vaya vayamos id / no vayáis vayan
oír oyendo oído	oigo oyes oye oímos oís oyen	oía oías oía oíamos oíais oían	oí oíste oyó oímos oísteis oyeron	oiré oirás oirá oiremos oiréis oirán	oiría oirías oiría oiríamos oiríais oirían	oiga oigas oiga oigamos oigáis oigan	oyera oyeras oyera oyéramos oyerais oyeran	oye / no oigas oiga oigamos oíd / no oigáis oigan
poder pudiendo podido	puedo puedes puede podemos podéis pueden	podía podías podía podíamos podíais podían	pude pudiste pudo pudimos pudisteis pudieron	podré podrás podrá podremos podréis podrán	podría podrías podría podríamos podríais podrían	pueda puedas pueda podamos podáis puedan	pudiera pudieras pudiera pudiéramos pudierais pudieran	
poner poniendo puesto	pongo pones pone ponemos ponéis ponen	ponía ponías ponía poníamos poníais ponían	puse pusiste puso pusimos pusisteis pusieron	pondré pondrás pondrá pondremos pondréis pondrán	pondría pondrías pondría pondríamos pondríais pondrían	ponga pongas ponga pongamos pongáis pongan	pusiera pusieras pusiera pusiéramos pusierais pusieran	pon / no pongas ponga pongamos poned / no pongáis pongan
predecir prediciendo predicho	predigo predices predice predecimos predecís predicen	predecía predecías predecía predecíamos predecíais predecían	predije predijiste predijo predijimos predijisteis predijeron	predeciré predecirás predecirá predeciremos predeciréis predecirán	predeciría predecirías predeciría predeciríamos predeciríais predecirían	prediga predigas prediga predigamos predigáis predigan	predijera predijeras predijera predijéramos predijerais predijeran	predice / no predigas prediga predigamos predecid / no predigáis predigan
querer queriendo querido	quiero quieres quiere queremos queréis quieren	quería querías quería queríamos queríais querían	quise quisiste quiso quisimos quisisteis quisieron	querré querrás querrá querremos querréis querrán	querría querrías querría querríamos querríais querrían	quiera quieras quiera queramos queráis quieran	quisiera quisieras quisiera quisiéramos quisierais quisieran	quiere / no quieras quiera queramos quered / no queráis quieran

C. Irregular Verbs (continued)

INFINITIVE PRESENT PARTICIPLE PAST PARTICIPLE	INDICATIVE					SUBJUNCTIVE		IMPERATIVE
	PRESENT	IMPERFECT	PRETERITE	FUTURE	CONDITIONAL	PRESENT	PAST	
saber sabiendo sabido	sé sabes sabe sabemos sabéis saben	sabía sabías sabía sabíamos sabíais sabían	supe supiste supo supimos supisteis supieron	sabré sabrás sabrá sabremos sabréis sabrán	sabría sabrías sabría sabríamos sabríais sabrían	sepa sepas sepa sepamos sepáis sepan	supiera supieras supiera supiéramos supierais supieran	sabe / no sepas sepa sepamos sabed / no sepáis sepan
salir saliendo salido	salgo sales sale salimos salís salen	salía salías salía salíamos salíais salían	salí saliste salió salimos salisteis salieron	saldré saldrás saldrá saldremos saldréis saldrán	saldría saldrías saldría saldríamos saldríais saldrían	salga salgas salga salgamos salgáis salgan	saliera salieras saliera saliéramos salierais salieran	sal / no salgas salga salgamos salid / no salgáis salgan
ser siendo sido	soy eres es somos sois son	era eras era éramos erais eran	fui fuiste fue fuimos fuisteis fueron	seré serás será seremos seréis serán	sería serías sería seríamos seríais serían	sea seas sea seamos seáis sean	fuera fueras fuera fuéramos fuerais fueran	sé / no seas sea seamos sed / no seáis sean
tener teniendo tenido	tengo tienes tiene tenemos tenéis tienen	tenía tenías tenía teníamos teníais tenían	tuve tuviste tuvo tuvimos tuvisteis tuvieron	tendré tendrás tendrá tendremos tendréis tendrán	tendría tendrías tendría tendríamos tendríais tendrían	tenga tengas tenga tengamos tengáis tengan	tuviera tuvieras tuviera tuviéramos tuvierais tuvieran	ten / no tengas tenga tengamos tened / no tengáis tengan
traer trayendo traído	traigo traes trae traemos traéis traen	traía traías traía traíamos traíais traían	traje trajiste trajo trajimos trajisteis trajeron	traeré traerás traerá traeremos traeréis traerán	traería traerías traería traeríamos traeríais traerían	traiga traigas traiga traigamos traigáis traigan	trajera trajeras trajera trajéramos trajerais trajeran	trae / no traigas traiga traigamos traed / no traigáis traigan
valer valiendo valido	valgo vales vale valemos valéis valen	valía valías valía valíamos valíais valían	valí valiste valió valimos valisteis valieron	valdré valdrás valdrá valdremos valdréis valdrán	valdría valdrías valdría valdríamos valdríais valdrían	valga valgas valga valgamos valgáis valgan	valiera valieras valiera valiéramos valierais valieran	vale / no valgas valga valgamos valed / no valgáis valgan
venir viniendo venido	vengo vienes viene venimos venís vienen	venía venías venía veníamos veníais venían	vine viniste vino vinimos vinisteis vinieron	vendré vendrás vendrá vendremos vendréis vendrán	vendría vendrías vendría vendríamos vendríais vendrían	venga vengas venga vengamos vengáis vengan	viniera vinieras viniera viniéramos vinierais vinieran	ven / no vengas venga vengamos venid / no vengáis vengan

C. Irregular Verbs (continued)

INFINITIVE PRESENT PARTICIPLE PAST PARTICIPLE	INDICATIVE					SUBJUNCTIVE		IMPERATIVE
	PRESENT	IMPERFECT	PRETERITE	FUTURE	CONDITIONAL	PRESENT	PAST	
ver viendo visto	veo ves ve vemos veis ven	veía veías veía veíamos veíais veían	vi viste vio vimos visteis vieron	veré verás verá veremos veréis verán	vería verías vería veríamos veríais verían	vea veas vea veamos veáis vean	viera vieras viera viéramos vierais vieran	ve / no veas vea veamos ved / no veáis vean

D. Stem-Changing and Spelling Change Verbs

INFINITIVE PRESENT PARTICIPLE PAST PARTICIPLE	INDICATIVE					SUBJUNCTIVE		IMPERATIVE
	PRESENT	IMPERFECT	PRETERITE	FUTURE	CONDITIONAL	PRESENT	PAST	
construir (y) construyendo construido	construyo construyes construye construimos construís construyen	construía construías construía construíamos construíais construían	construí construiste construyó construimos construisteis construyeron	construiré construirás construirá construiremos construiréis construirán	construiría construirías construiría construiríamos construiríais construirían	construya construyas construya construyamos construyáis construyan	construyera construyeras construyera construyéramos construyerais construyeran	construye / no construyas construya construyamos construid / no construyáis construyan
creer (y [*3rd-pers. pret.*]) creyendo creído	creo crees cree creemos creéis creen	creía creías creía creíamos creíais creían	creí creíste creyó creímos creísteis creyeron	creeré creerás creerá creeremos creeréis creerán	creería creerías creería creeríamos creeríais creerían	crea creas crea creamos creáis crean	creyera creyeras creyera creyéramos creyerais creyeran	cree / no creas crea creamos creed / no creáis crean
dormir (ue, u) durmiendo dormido	duermo duermes duerme dormimos dormís duermen	dormía dormías dormía dormíamos dormíais dormían	dormí dormiste durmió dormimos dormisteis durmieron	dormiré dormirás dormirá dormiremos dormiréis dormirán	dormiría dormirías dormiría dormiríamos dormiríais dormirían	duerma duermas duerma durmamos durmáis duerman	durmiera durmieras durmiera durmiéramos durmierais durmieran	duerme / no duermas duerma durmamos dormid / no durmáis duerman
pedir (i, i) pidiendo pedido	pido pides pide pedimos pedís piden	pedía pedías pedía pedíamos pedíais pedían	pedí pediste pidió pedimos pedisteis pidieron	pediré pedirás pedirá pediremos pediréis pedirán	pediría pedirías pediría pediríamos pediríais pedirían	pida pidas pida pidamos pidáis pidan	pidiera pidieras pidiera pidiéramos pidierais pidieran	pide / no pidas pida pidamos pedid / no pidáis pidan
pensar (ie) pensando pensado	pienso piensas piensa pensamos pensáis piensan	pensaba pensabas pensaba pensábamos pensabais pensaban	pensé pensaste pensó pensamos pensasteis pensaron	pensaré pensarás pensará pensaremos pensaréis pensarán	pensaría pensarías pensaría pensaríamos pensaríais pensarían	piense pienses piense pensemos penséis piensen	pensara pensaras pensara pensáramos pensarais pensaran	piensa / no pienses piense pensemos pensad / no penséis piensen

D. Stem-Changing and Spelling Change Verbs (continued)

INFINITIVE PRESENT PARTICIPLE PAST PARTICIPLE	INDICATIVE					SUBJUNCTIVE		IMPERATIVE
	PRESENT	IMPERFECT	PRETERITE	FUTURE	CONDITIONAL	PRESENT	PAST	
producir (zc, j) produciendo producido	produzco produces produce producimos producís producen	producía producías producía producíamos producíais producían	produje produjiste produjo produjimos produjisteis produjeron	produciré producirás producirá produciremos produciréis producirán	produciría producirías produciría produciríamos produciríais producirían	produzca produzcas produzca produzcamos produzcáis produzcan	produjera produjeras produjera produjéramos produjerais produjeran	produce / no produzcas produzca produzcamos producid / no produzcáis produzcan
reír (i, i) riendo reído	río ríes ríe reímos reís ríen	reía reías reía reíamos reíais reían	reí reíste rió reímos reísteis rieron	reiré reirás reirá reiremos reiréis reirán	reiría reirías reiría reiríamos reiríais reirían	ría rías ría riamos riáis rían	riera rieras riera riéramos rierais rieran	ríe / no rías ría riamos reíd / no riáis rían
seguir (i, i) (g) siguiendo seguido	sigo sigues sigue seguimos seguís siguen	seguía seguías seguía seguíamos seguíais seguían	seguí seguiste siguió seguimos seguisteis siguieron	seguiré seguirás seguirá seguiremos seguiréis seguirán	seguiría seguirías seguiría seguiríamos seguiríais seguirían	siga sigas siga sigamos sigáis sigan	siguiera siguieras siguiera siguiéramos siguierais siguieran	sigue / no sigas siga sigamos seguid / no sigáis sigan
sentir (ie, i) sintiendo sentido	siento sientes siente sentimos sentís sienten	sentía sentías sentía sentíamos sentíais sentían	sentí sentiste sintió sentimos sentisteis sintieron	sentiré sentirás sentirá sentiremos sentiréis sentirán	sentiría sentirías sentiría sentiríamos sentiríais sentirían	sienta sientas sienta sintamos sintáis sientan	sintiera sintieras sintiera sintiéramos sintierais sintieran	siente / no sientas sienta sintamos sentid / no sintáis sientan
volver (ue) volviendo vuelto	vuelvo vuelves vuelve volvemos volvéis vuelven	volvía volvías volvía volvíamos volvíais volvían	volví volviste volvió volvimos volvisteis volvieron	volveré volverás volverá volveremos volveréis volverán	volvería volverías volvería volveríamos volveríais volverían	vuelva vuelvas vuelva volvamos volváis vuelvan	volviera volvieras volviera volviéramos volvierais volvieran	vuelve / no vuelvas vuelva volvamos volved / no volváis vuelvan

Vocabulario español-inglés

This Spanish-English Vocabulary contains all the words that appear in the text, with the following exceptions: (1) most close or identical cognates that do not appear in the thematic vocabulary lists; (2) most conjugated verb forms; (3) most diminutives and augmentatives; (4) most adverbs ending in **-mente;** (5) days of the week, months of the year, basic colors, and most numbers; (6) subject, object, and demonstrative pronouns; (7) possessive and demonstrative adjectives; (8) glossed vocabulary from realia and authentic readings. Only meanings used in the text are given. Numbers following translations indicate the chapter in which that meaning of the word was presented as active vocabulary.

Words containing **ch** and **ll** are alphabetized according to the individual letters of these consonant clusters. For example, words beginning with **ch** are found within the letter **c.** Also, **n** precedes **ñ** in alphabetical order.

The gender of nouns is indicated, except for masculine nouns ending in **-o** and feminine nouns ending in **-a.** Stem changes and spelling changes are indicated for verbs: **dormir (ue, u); llegar (gu); traducir (zc, j).**

The following abbreviations are used in this vocabulary.

abbrev.	abbreviation	*m.*	masculine
adj.	adjective	*Mex.*	Mexico
adv.	adverb	*n.*	noun
C.A.	Central America	*pers.*	person
Ch.	Chile	*pl.*	plural
coll.	colloquial	*p.p.*	past participle
f.	feminine	*P.R.*	Puerto Rico
fig.	figurative	*prep.*	preposition
ger.	gerund	*pret.*	preterite
gram.	grammatical term	*pron.*	pronoun
inf.	infinitive	*s.*	singular
inv.	invariable	*Sp.*	Spain
irreg.	irregular	*subj.*	subjunctive
lit.	literal	*v.*	verb

A

abajo below; downstairs
abandonar to abandon
abierto/a (*p.p. of* **abrir**) open (2); opened; free
abismo abyss
abogado/a lawyer
abogar (gu) (por) to defend
abordar to undertake, tackle
abrazar (c) to hug (3); **abrazarse** to hug each other
abrazo hug
abrir (*p.p.* **abierto**) to open; **abrirse** to open up
absoluto/a absolute; **en absoluto** (not) at all; **no estoy de acuerdo en absoluto** I don't agree at all (3)
abstracto/a abstract
abuelo/a grandfather, grandmother; *pl.* grandparents
abundar to abound
aburrir to bore; **aburrirse** to get bored; **me aburre(n)** I'm bored by (4)
abuso abuse
acá (over) here

acabar to end; to finish, complete; to run out (6); **acabar con** to put an end to; **acabar de** + *inf.* to have just (*done something*)
académico/a academic
acantilado sewer
acaso *adv.* by chance
acceso access
accidente *m.* accident
acción *f.* action
aceite *m.* oil
acelerado/a *adj.* hurried
acento accent
aceptar to accept
acerca de about
acercarse (qu) (a) to approach
acero steel; **fábrica de acero** steel mill
acogido/a welcome
acomodado/a well-off
acompañar to accompany, go with
aconsejar to advise (3)
acontecimiento event
acordarse (ue) (de) to remember
acordeón *m.* accordion
acostumbrarse (a) to adjust (to) (2); to get accustomed, used to
actitud *f.* attitude
actividad *f.* activity
activismo activism
activista *n. m., f.* activist (5); *adj. m., f.* activist
activo/a active
acto act
actor *m.* actor
actriz *f.* (*pl.* **actrices**) actress
actuación *f.* behavior, conduct
actual present, current
actualidad *f.* present (*time*); **en la actualidad** currently
actualmente currently (5)
actualización *f.* updating
actuar (actúo) to behave, act
acudir (a) to go (to); to come (to)
acueducto aqueduct
acuerdo agreement; **(no) estar** (*irreg.*) **de acuerdo (con)** to (dis)agree (with) (2); **estoy completamente de acuerdo** I agree completely (3); **no estoy de acuerdo en absoluto** I don't agree at all (3); **ponerse** (*irreg.*) **de acuerdo** to agree, come to an agreement
acusar to accuse
adaptar to adjust; **adaptarse (a)** to adapt, adjust (to)
adecuado/a suitable
adelantar to advance
adelante *adv.* ahead, forward; **seguir (i, i) (g) adelante** to move/push forward
además besides (3); moreover; **además de** besides, in addition to
adepto/a adept
adicción *f.* addiction
adicional additional
adicto/a *n.* addict; *adj.* addicted
adiós good-bye
adivinación divination; guess
adivinar to guess (6)
adjetivo *gram.* adjective
adjuntar to enclose, attach
administración *f.* administration; **administración de empresas** business administration
admirable admirable
admiración *f.* admiration
admirador(a) admirer
admirar to admire
admitir to admit
adolescencia adolescence
adolescente *n. m., f.* adolescent
adonde (to) where; to which
¿adónde? (to) where?
adoptar to adopt
adoptivo/a adopted; **hijo adoptivo, hija adoptiva** adopted son, adopted daughter (2)
adorar to adore
adornado/a decorated
adquirir (ie) to acquire
adquisición *f.* acquisition
adquisitivo/a: poder (*m.*) **adquisitivo** purchasing power
adrenalina adrenaline
aduana *s.* customs
adulto/a *n., adj.* adult
adversario/a adversary
advertencia warning
advertir (ie, i) to warn, notify
aeropuerto airport
afectar to affect
afecto affection
afición *f.* pastime; inclination
aficionado/a fan, follower
afiliación *f.* affiliation
afirmar to declare
afirmación *f.* assertion; statement
afligir (j) to afflict; to grieve
afortunado/a fortunate
afrancesado/a taking on French characteristics
africano/a *n., adj.* African
afroamericano/a Afro-American
afrocubano/a Afro-Cuban
afrontar to confront
afroperuano/a Afro-Peruvian
afrouruguayo/a Afro-Uruguayan
afueras *pl.* suburbs; outskirts
agarrar to grab, seize, clutch
agencia agency
agente *m., f.* agent; **agente de viajes** travel agent
agitador(a) agitator
agobiado/a overwhelmed (4)
agotado/a exhausted (4)
agradable pleasant (1); agreeable
agradar to please
agradecer (zc) to thank
agrario/a agrarian
agregar (gu) to add
agresión *f.* provocation
agresividad *f.* aggression
agresivo/a aggressive
agrícola *adj. m., f.* agricultural
agricultor(a) farmer
agricultura agriculture
agrupación *f.* grouping
agruparse to group together
agua *f.* (*but* **el agua**) water; **agua dulce** freshwater; **agua potable** drinking water; **llave** (*f.*) **de agua** faucet
aguacate *m.* avocado
aguacero downpour
aguafiestas *s. m., f.* party pooper (4)
águila *f.* (*but* **el águila**) eagle
agujerado/a pierced; **orejas agujeradas** pierced ears
agujerearse to pierce
ahogar(se) (gu) to drown
ahora now; **ahora más que nunca** now more than ever; **ahora mismo** right now; **ahora que** now that; **ahora viene lo peor** now comes the worst part (3)
ahorrar to save (*money*)
aire *m.* air; **al aire libre** outdoors, in the open air
aislado/a isolated
ajo garlic
ajustar to adjust
alabanza praise
alabar to praise (2)
alameda park
alarmante alarming (5)
alarmista *n. m., f.* alarmist (5)
alba *f.* (*but* **el alba**) dawn
álbum *m.* album
alcahuete/a tattletale
alcanzar (c) to attain, reach (6); to catch up with
alcohol *m.* alcohol
alcohólico/a alcoholic
alegrarse (de) to be happy (about); **me alegro de que...** I'm glad that . . . (2)
alegre happy
alegría happiness
alejamiento estrangement
alejar to distance
alemán *m.* German (*language*)
alemán, alemana *n., adj.* German
Alemania Germany
alentador(a) encouraging
alfabetismo literacy
alfabetización *f.* instruction in reading and writing

alfombra rug
algo *pron.* something; *adv.* somewhat; **te voy a contar algo increíble (estupendo, ridículo) que le pasó a. . .** I'm going to tell you something incredible (wonderful, ridiculous) that happened to . . . (3)
algodón *m.* cotton
alguien *pron.* someone; **caerle** (*irreg.*) **bien/mal a alguien** to like/dislike someone (1); **dejar a alguien** to leave someone (3); **tomarle el pelo a alguien** to pull someone's leg (4)
algún, alguno/a *adj.* some; any; *pl.* some, a few; **algún día** some day; **alguna vez** ever (*with a question*); **de alguna manera** in some way; **en alguna parte** somewhere
aliado ally
aliar to become allies
alienar to alienate
alimentación *f.* nourishment (5)
alimentar (ie) to feed; to maintain
alimentario/a *adj.* food (related), nutritional
alimenticio/a *adj.* food; **servicios alimenticios** food services
alimento food, nourishment
aliviar to relieve (4)
allá there; **más allá de** beyond
allí there
alma *f.* (*but* **el alma**) soul; **alma gemela** soul mate (3)
almorzar (ue) (c) to eat lunch
almuerzo lunch
alpinismo mountain climbing
alquilado/a rented
alrededor *adv.* around; *n. m. pl.* surroundings
alternativo/a alternative
altitud *f.* altitude
alto/a tall; high; loud; **en lo alto de** on top of; **en voz alta** aloud
alterado/a upset
altruista *n. m., f.* altruist (5); *adj. m., f.* altruistic
altura height; altitude
alucinado/a amazed (3)
alucinante incredible (1); impressive (1); dazzling, amazing
aludir a to allude to
alumno/a student, pupil
ama (*f., but* **el ama**) *de casa* housewife
amable amiable, pleasant; kind
amador(a) lover
amanecer *m.* dawn
amante *n. m., f.* lover
amar to love
amargo/a bitter
amargura bitterness
amazónico/a Amazonian
ambición *f.* ambition
ambicioso/a ambitious
ambientalismo environmentalism (6)
ambiente *m. s.* surroundings; ambience; atmosphere; **medio ambiente** environment
ámbito field, sphere
ambos/as *pl.* both
amenaza threat
amenazante threatening
amenazar (c) to threaten (6)
América Latina Latin America
americanizarse (c) to become Americanized
americano/a American
amigo/a friend
amistad *f.* friendship (3)
amnistía amnesty
amor *m.* love; loved one; **amor libre** free love
amoroso/a amorous, loving; love
amplio/a broad, wide
amuleto amulet
amurallado/a walled
anagrama *m.* anagram
analfabetismo illiteracy (5)
analfabeto/a illiterate
análisis *m.* analysis
analizar (c) to analyze
anarquista *n. m., f.; adj.* anarchist
ancho/a wide
anciano/a old
andaluz(a) (*m. pl.* **andaluces**) Andalusian, of or pertaining to Andalusia in southern Spain
andar *irreg.* to walk
andinismo hiking
andino/a Andean, of or pertaining to the Andes Mountains
anfitrión, anfitriona host, hostess
ángel *m.* angel
angustiado/a distressed (4)
anillo ring
animación *f.* animation
animado/a lively, animated; in good spirits (4); **dibujo animado** (animated) cartoon
animalesco/a animal-like
animar to encourage, cheer up
ánimo energy; mind; **estado de ánimo** spirits, mood; **levantar el ánimo** to lift the spirits (4)
aniversario anniversary
anotar to make a note of
ansiedad *f.* anxiety
ansioso/a anxious
ante *prep.* before; in front of; in the presence of
anteayer yesterday
antemano: de antemano beforehand
antepasado/a ancestor (2)
anterior previous, former
antes *adv.* before, previously; **antes de que** + *subj.* before . . . (6)
antiaccidente anti-accident
antiguo/a old, old-fashioned; former
antropología anthropology
antropomórfico/a anthropomorphic
anual annual
anualmente yearly
anunciar to announce
anuncio advertisement; announcement
añadir to add
año year; **a los... años** at the age of . . . ; **año pasado** last year; **año que viene** next year; **cada año** every year; **los años veinte (treinta,...)** the twenties (thirties, ...); **primer año** first year; **tener** (*irreg.*)**... años** to be . . . years old
añorado/a yearned-for, desirable
apadrinar to sponsor
apagar (gu) to turn off
aparato apparatus, gadget
aparecer (zc) to appear
aparentemente apparently
apariencia appearance; **las apariencias engañan** looks deceive (1)
aparte *adj.* separate; **punto y aparte** (begin a) new paragraph
apasionado/a passionate (3)
apasionar to appeal deeply to
apatía apathy (5)
apegado/a devoted, attached to
apelativo name; nickname
apellido last name, family name
apenado/a pained, sad (3)
apenas hardly, barely
apetecer (zc) to please, appeal to; **me apetece(n)** I feel like (4)
aplatanado/a lethargic
aplicar (qu) (a) to apply (to)
apodo nickname
apoplejía: ataque (*m.*) **de apoplejía** stroke
aportación *f.* contribution
aportar to contribute (6)
aporte *m.* contribution
apóstol *m.* apostle
apoyar to support (*emotionally*) (2)
apoyo support, aid
apreciar to appreciate, value
aprecio appreciation
aprender to learn
apropiado/a appropriate
aprovechar(se) de to take advantage of (4)
aproximadamente approximately
apuesto/a neat, elegant, good-looking
apuntar to jot down, make a note of
apuntes *m. pl.* notes
árabe *n., adj. m., f.* Arab; *m.* Arabic (*language*)

aragonés, aragonesa Aragonese, of or pertaining to Aragon, in northern Spain
árbol *m.* tree
archifamoso/a world-famous
archipiélago archipelago
arco iris rainbow
arder to burn
área *f.* (*but* **el área**) area; field
arena sand
arenal *m.* large expanse of sand; quicksand
arete *m.* earring (1)
argentino/a *n., adj.* Argentine
argolla (wedding) ring
argumentar to argue (*debate*)
argumento argument
aristocracia aristocracy
Aristóteles Aristotle
arma *f.* (*but* **el arma**) weapon, arm
armado/a armed
armonía harmony (2)
arqueología archeology
arqueológico/a archeological
arqueólogo/a archeologist
arquitecto/a architect
arquitectónico/a architectural
arquitectura architecture
arreglarse to dress
arrestar to arrest
arriba above
arriesgar to risk
arrogancia arrogance
arrogante arrogant
arroyo stream
arroz *m.* (*pl.* **arroces**) rice
arruga wrinkle (1)
arruinar to ruin
arte *m., f.* art; **arte menor** minor art; **artes plásticas** three-dimensional art; **bellas artes** fine arts; **obra de arte** work of art
artefacto artifact
artesanal pertaining to handicrafts
artesanía craft, handicrafts
artesano/a artisan, craftsperson
artículo article; item
artista *m., f.* artist
artístico/a artistic
asado/a roast
ascendencia ancestry
ascenso ascent; promotion
asco: dar (*irreg.*) **asco** to disgust; **me da(n) asco** I'm disgusted by (4)
asediado/a battered
asegurar to insure; to assure (6)
asesinado/a assassinated, murdered
asesinato assassination, murder
asesoría advising
así *adv.* thus; that's how; in that way; like that; **así como** the same as, just as; **así pues** and so; **así que** therefore
asiático/a Asiatic, Asian
asignar to assign
asilo de ancianos assisted living facility
asimilación *f.* assimilation
asimilar to assimilate
asistencia attendance
asistir a to attend
asociación *f.* association
asociado/a associated; **estado libre asociado** commonwealth
asociarse con to associate oneself with
asomarse a to face
asombrado/a amazed, astonished
asombroso/a amazing, astonishing (6)
aspecto aspect; appearance; trait
aspirar to inhale
asqueado/a repulsed (3)
astilla splinter; **de tal palo, tal astilla** like father, like son
astillero shipyard
astronomía astronomy
astronómico/a astronomical
astrónomo/a astronomer
astuto/a astute, clever
asumir to assume, take
asunto matter
asustado/a frightened (3)
asustar to frighten; **asustarse** to become frightened
ataque *m.* attack; **ataque cardíaco** heart attack; **ataque de apoplejía** stroke; **ataque terrorista** terrorist attack
atemorizar (c) to frighten
atención *f.* attention; **prestar atención** to pay attention
atender (ie) a to take care of, tend to; to wait on
atentar to attempt; to make an attempt on
aterrorizar (c) to terrorize
atlántico/a: Océano Atlántico Atlantic Ocean
atleta *m., f.* athlete
atlético/a athletic
atmosférico/a atmospheric
atracción *f.* attraction
atractivo/a attractive
atraer (*like* **traer**) to attract (3); to draw
atrapado/a trapped
atrapar to *"grab"*, appeal to (*coll.*)
atrás *adv.* back, behind; **dejar atrás** to leave behind
atravesar (ie) to go through
atreverse to dare
atrevido/a daring (1)
atrocidad *f.* atrocity
aumentar to increase (4)
aumento increase
aun even
aún still, yet
aunque although, even though
auspiciado/a sponsored
autenticidad *f.* authenticity
auténtico/a authentic
autobiografía autobiography
autobús *m.* bus
autoestima self-esteem
automovilístico/a pertaining to automobiles
autonomía autonomy
autónomo/a autonomous
autor(a) author
autoridad *f.* authority
autorretrato self-portrait
avance *m.* advance (6)
avanzado/a advanced
avanzar (c) to advance (6)
avaricia greed
avenida avenue
aventura adventure
aventurero/a adventurous
avergonzado/a embarrassed (3)
averiguar (gü) to ascertain; to verify
aviación *f.* aviation
avión *m.* airplane; **avión secuestrado** hijacked airplane
avisar to inform; to warn
¡ay! oh!
ayer yesterday
aymara *m.* Aymara (*language and name of the indigenous tribe of Bolivia and Peru*)
ayuda help, assistance
ayudar to help
ayuntamiento city hall
azahar *m.* orange/lemon blossom
azteca *n., adj. m., f.* Aztec
azúcar *m.* sugar; **caña de azúcar** sugarcane
azucarero/a pertaining to sugar
azulejo tile

B

bacalao codfish
bachata *music and dance originating in Dominican Republic*
bahía bay
bailar to dance
bailarín, bailarina dancer
baile *m.* dance; (act of) dancing
bajar to come/go down; to get down; to lower; to download (6); **bajar del bus/tren** to get off the bus/train
bajo *prep.* under, beneath
bajo/a *adj.* short; low; **barrio bajo** slum
bala bullet
balada ballad
balancear to swing
balanza *s.* scales; balance; **balanza de pagos** budget
balboa *m.* *monetary unit of Panama*
balcón *m.* balcony
ballena whale
ballet *m.* ballet
baloncesto basketball

balsa *n.* raft
balsero/a *boat person from Cuba seeking refuge in the United States*
banco bank; bench
banda band
bandido/a bandit
baño bath; bathroom
bar *m.* bar
barato/a cheap; inexpensive
barba beard (1)
barbaridad *f.* gross remark; **¡qué barbaridad!** how awful! (1)
¡bárbaro! fantastic! (2)
barcelonés, barcelonesa person from Barcelona
barco boat
barquillo de helado ice-cream cone
barranca ravine, gorge
barrendero/a street sweeper
barriada district, neighborhood
barrio neighborhood; **barrio bajo** slum
barro mud
barroco/a Baroque
basar(se) en to base on
base *f.* base
básico/a basic
bastante *adj.* enough; quite a bit of; *adv.* rather; quite
basura garbage (6), trash
batalla battle; **campo de batalla** battlefield; **frente** (*f.*) **de batalla** battlefront
bebé *m., f.* baby
beber to drink
bebida drink
béisbol *m.* baseball
beisbolista *m., f.* baseball player
beisbolístico/a *adj.* pertaining to baseball
belleza beauty
bello/a beautiful; eloquent; **bellas artes** fine arts
beneficiar(se) to benefit
beneficio benefit; advantage
beneplácito blessing; approval, consent
benjamín, benjamina baby of the family (2)
besar to kiss (3); **besarse** to kiss each other
beso kiss
biblioteca library
bibliotecario/a librarian
bicicleta bicycle
bien *adv.* well **caerle** (*irreg.*) **bien a alguien** to like/dislike (someone) (1); **llevarse bien con** to get along well with; **lo pasé muy bien** I had a great time (4); **me cae(n) bien** I really like (*person or people*) (4); **pasarlo bien** to have a good time (4); **¡qué bien!** great! (2); **¡que lo pase/pases/pasen bien!** have a good time! (4)
bienestar *m.* well-being (4); **bienestar social** social welfare
bienvenida: dar (*irreg.*) **la bienvenida a** to welcome
bienvenido/a *adj.* welcome
bigote *m.* moustache (1)
bilingüe bilingual
biografía biography
biográfico/a biographical
biológico/a biological
bitácora log; blog
blanco/a: en blanco blank, empty
blando/a soft, tender
bledo: me importa un bledo I don't give a damn
bloguear to blog (6)
bloguero/a blogger
bloque *m.* block
blusa blouse
boca mouth
boda wedding
bodega warehouse
bola de cristal crystal ball
boleto ticket
boliche *m.* bowling alley
bolívar *m.* *monetary unit of Venezuela*
boliviano *monetary unit of Bolivia*
boliviano/a *n., adj.* Bolivian
bolso bag
bomba bomb
bombero firefighter; **mujer** (*f.*) **bombero** (female firefighter)
bombilla straw
bonito/a pretty
borbón *m.* bourbon
bordado/a embroidered
borde *m.* edge; verge; **al borde de** alongside
boricua *m., f.* Puerto Rican
borracho/a drunk
bosque *m.* forest; **bosque lluvioso** rain forest (6)
bosquejo outline; draft; sketch
bota boot
botánico/a botanical
botella bottle
Brasil *m.* Brazil
brasileño/a *n.* Brazilian
bravo/a: aguas bravas rough waters
brazo arm
brecha gap; **brecha cultural** culture gap; **brecha digital** (digital) information gap (6); **brecha generacional** generation gap (2); **brecha tecnológica** technology gap
breve brief
brillante brilliant; bright
brindar to offer; to toast
brochazo brushstroke
broma practical joke (4)
bromear to joke around (4)
bromista *n. m., f.* joker; *adj. m., f.* joking
bronce *m.* bronze
brujo/a sorcerer; warlock/witch
bruto/a stupid, brutish (1)
bucear to scuba dive
buen, bueno/a good; **buenos modales** good manners (2); **estar** (*irreg.*) **de buen humor** to be in a good mood **¡qué buena idea!** what a great idea! (3); **¡qué bueno!** how great! (4); **qué bueno que...** how great that . . . (2); **sacar (qu) buenas notas** to get good grades; **ser** (*irreg.*) **buena gente** to be a good person (1); **tener** (*irreg.*) **buena pinta** to have a good appearance (1)
buganvilla bougainvillea
bullicio din
buque *m.* ship; **buque de guerra** warship
Burdeos Bordeaux
burocrático/a bureaucratic
burujón *m.* pile (*Ch.*)
busca search
buscar (qu) to look for; to seek
búsqueda search

C

caballero gentleman
caballo horse; **montar a caballo** to ride/go horseback riding
cabaña cabin
cabello hair
caber *irreg.* to fit (on or into); **no cabe duda** no doubt about it
cabeza head; **dolor** (*m.*) **de cabeza** headache
cabo: llevar a cabo to carry out (5)
cada *inv.* each; every; **cada vez más** more and more
cadáver *m.* body, corpse
cadena chain
caducado/a expired
caer *irreg.* (*p.p.* **caído**) to fall; **caerle bien/mal a alguien** to like/dislike someone (1); **me cae(n) fenomenal** I really like (*person or people*) (4); **me cae(n) mal/fatal** I really don't like (*person or people*) (4)
café *m.* coffee; café, coffee shop
caído/a (*p.p. of* **caer**) *adj.* fallen; sagging
caja box
cajero/a cashier
cajón *m.* large box; crate
calabaza gourd
calamidad *f.* calamity
calavera skull
calcular to calculate
calentamiento global global warming (6)
calidad *f.* quality
caliente hot; **agua** (*f., but* **el agua**) **caliente** hot water
calificar (qu) to judge
callado/a quiet (1)

callar to silence; **callarse** to be quiet
calle *f.* street
callejón *m.* alleyway; **callejón sin salida** dead-end street
callejuela alleyway
calmar(se) to calm (oneself)
calor *m.* heat
calvo/a bald (1)
calzones *pl.* underpants
cama bed
cámara camera; chamber; **cámara de vídeo** video camera
cambiar to change
cambio change; **cambio de imagen** (*f.*) make-over; **a cambio** in exchange; **en cambio** on the other hand (3)
caminar to walk
caminata walk; **dar** (*irreg.*) **caminatas** to go on walks
camino trail; path (*fig.*)
campamento campground; campsite
campaña campaign (5)
campeonato championship
campesino/a *n.* farmer; *adj.* rural
campo area; field; countryside
canal *m.* canal
canario canary
cáncer *m.* cancer
canción *f.* song
candidato/a candidate
candidatura candidacy
candombe *m.* *dance of African origin*
canela cinnamon
canguro kangaroo
canoa canoe
canoso: pelo canoso gray hair (1)
cansado/a tired
cansar(se) to tire
cantante *m., f.* singer
cantar to sing
cantautor(a) singer-songwriter
cante (*m.*) **jondo** *Flamenco-style singing of Andalusian gypsy origin*
cantidad *f.* quantity
cañaveral *m.* sugarcane field/plantation
cañón *m.* canyon
capa de ozono ozone layer (6)
capacidad *f.* capacity; capability (6)
capaz *adj. m., f.* (*pl.* **capaces**) capable, able
capital *f.* capital (*city*); *m.* capital (*wealth*); *adj.* deadly
capitalismo capitalism
capitolio capitol
capítulo chapter
capricho whim
cápsula capsule
captar to capture; to grasp
capturado/a captured
cara face; **cara a cara** face-to-face; **¡qué cara tiene!** what nerve he/she has! (2); **tener** (*irreg.*) **mucha cara** to have a lot of nerve (1)
caracol: escalera de caracol spiral staircase
carácter *m.* character; nature
característica *n.* characteristic
característico/a *adj.* characteristic
caracterizar (c) to characterize
carbón *m.* coal
carcajadas: reírse (i, i) (me río) a carcajadas to laugh loudly (4)
cardíaco: ataque (*m.*) **cardíaco** heart attack
carga task; loading
cargar (gu) to carry; to load; to charge; **cargar(se) las pilas** to recharge one's batteries (4)
cargo job, position, office (*political*); **hacerse** (*irreg.*) **cargo de** to be put in charge of
Caribe *m.* Caribbean
caribeño/a *adj.* Caribbean
caricatura caricature, cartoon
caricaturista *m., f.* cartoonist
caridad *f.* charity
cariño affection
cariñoso/a affectionate (2)
carisma *m.* charisma
carne *f.* meat; **carne de vacuno/res** beef
caro/a expensive
carpeta folder, file
carrera career, profession; race (*sports*)
carro car
carta letter
cartearse to be a pen pal
cartel *m.* poster
cartelera billboard; **en cartelera** (currently playing) in movie theaters
cartón *m.* cartoon
cartonista *m., f.* cartoonist
cartuja monastery
casa house; **ama** (*f., but* **el ama**) *de casa* housewife
casado/a *n., adj.* married (person)
casamiento marriage, matrimony
casarse (con) to marry, get married (to) (3)
cascada waterfall
casco center; helmet
caseta booth
casi *inv.* almost
caso case, circumstance; question; **en caso de que** + *subj.* in case . . . (6); **hacer** (*irreg.*) **caso a** to pay attention to (2)
casona big rambling house
castellano Spanish (*language*)
castigar (gu) to punish (2)
castigo punishment
castillo castle
catalán, catalana *n., adj.* Catalan, of or pertaining to Catalonia in northeastern Spain; *m.* Catalan (*language*)
Cataluña Catalonia
¡cataplún! crash! (3)
catarata waterfall
catástrofe *m.* catastrophe
catastrófico/a catastrophic (6)
catedral *f.* cathedral
catedrático/a university professor
categoría category
católico/a Catholic
causa cause; **a causa de** because of
causar to cause; to produce
cautela caution
cauteloso/a cautious (3)
cautivar to captivate
CD-ROM *m.* CD-ROM
cebador(a) *m., f.* person who prepares *mate*
ceder to cede, give away
ceiba ceiba, kapok tree
ceja eyebrow (1)
celda cell
celebración *f.* celebration
celebrar to celebrate
célebre *adj.* famous, renowned
celebridad *f.* celebrity
celos *m. pl.* jealousy
celoso/a jealous (3)
cementerio cemetery
cena dinner, supper
cenar to have dinner
ceniza ash
cenote *m.* *cavernous underwater rock formation (Mex., C.A.)*
centenar *m.* (one) hundred
centrar(se) to center, focus
centro center; downtown; heart (*of a town*); **centro comercial** shopping center
Centroamérica Central America
centroamericano/a *n., adj.* Central American
cerca de near, close to; **de cerca** close up
cercanía closeness
cercano/a *adj.* close
cerrar (ie) to close
cerro hill
certero/a: disparador(a) certero/a sharpshooter
certeza certainty
certificado certificate
cervantino/a Cervantine (of or pertaining to Cervantes)
cerveza beer
chachachá *m.* *dance that combines rhythms of rumba and mambo*
chamán, chamana indigenous doctor/healer
chapulín *m.* grasshopper
chaqueta jacket
charango *small, guitarlike instrument*
charco puddle; **cruzar (c) el charco** to cross the pond (*Atlantic Ocean*)
charlar to chat (4)

chasquillas *pl.* bangs
chatear to chat (6)
chévere awesome; **¡qué chévere!** (how) awesome! (1)
chibcha *m., f. member of an indigenous, pre-Columbian people of Colombia; m.* Chibcha (*language*)
chico/a boy, girl; young person
chilenizarse (c) to take on Chilean characteristics
chileno/a *n., adj.* Chilean
chino/a *n., adj.* Chinese
chirimoya *dark-skinned fruit with sweet white pulp*
chisme *m.* gossip (4); rumor
chismear to gossip
chispa spark
chiste *m.* joke (4)
chistoso/a funny (1); **¡qué chistoso!** how funny! (4)
chocante shocking (5)
chocar (qu) to crash; to clash
chofer *m., f.* chauffeur
choque *m.* shock; clash
choza hut
chueco/a crooked
cibercafé *m.* cybercafe (*coffeehouse with computers*)
ciberespacio cyberspace (6)
cicatriz *f.* (*pl.* **cicatrices**) scar (1)
ciclo cycle
ciego/a blind; **cita a ciegas** blind date
cien, ciento/a hundred; **por ciento** percent
ciencia science; **ciencia ficción** science fiction
científico/a *n.* scientist; *adj.* scientific
cierto/a true; certain (*thing*); **por cierto** indeed
cigarro cigar
cine *m.* cinema, movies; movie theater; **estrella de cine** movie star
cineasta *m., f.* filmmaker
cinematográfico/a cinematographic
circuito circuit
circular to circulate
círculo circle
circundar to surround
circunstancia circumstance
cita quote; appointment, date; **cita a ciegas** blind date
ciudad *f.* city
ciudadano/a citizen (5)
cívico/a civic
civil civil; **guerra civil** civil war
civilización *f.* civilization
clandestino/a clandestine
clarín *m.* bugle
claro/a clear; distinct
clase *f.* class; type; **compañero/a de clase** classmate
clásico/a classic
clasificar (qu) to classify
cláusula *gram.* clause
clave *f. inv.* key; **punto clave** key point
cliente *m., f.* client, customer
clientela *s.* customers, clientele
clima *m.* climate
clínica clinic
clónico/a clone
club *m.* club
cobre *m.* copper
coche *m.* car; **coche descapotable** convertible
cocina kitchen; cooking
cocinar to cook
cocinero/a cook
coco coconut
codo elbow (1); **hablar por los codos** to talk a lot (1)
coexistir to coexist
cofradía religious brotherhood
coger (j) to pick up
cognado cognate
cohabitar to cohabit
coincidencia coincidence
coincidir to coincide
colaborar (con) to collaborate (with) (5)
colapse *m.* collapse
colchón *m.* mattress
colección *f.* collection
colectivo/a collective
colega *m., f.* colleague
colegio primary or secondary school
colmo last straw (*coll.*); **¡esto es el colmo!** this is the last straw! (2)
colocado/a placed
colombiano/a *n., adj.* Colombian
colón *m. monetary unit of Costa Rica and El Salvador*
color *m.* color
colorido/a colorful
colosal colossal
columna column
comandante *m., f.* commander
combatir to fight, combat
combinación *f.* combination
combinar to combine
comedia comedy
comedor *m.* dining room
comentar to comment on
comentario commentary, remark
comentarista *m., f.* commentator
comenzar (ie) (c) to begin, start
comer to eat
comercial: centro comercial shopping center
comercio commerce; **comercio justo** fair trade (6)
cometer to commit; **cometer un fraude** to commit fraud
cómico/a comical, funny; **tira cómica** comic strip
comida food
comienzo beginning
comiquísimo/a hilarious (4)
comisura corner of mouth
comité *m.* committee
como like; as; **así como** the same as; **como es de imaginar** as you can imagine; **tal y como** such as; **tan... como** as . . . as; **tan pronto como** as soon as (6); **tanto/a/os/as... como** as much/many . . . as
cómo how; **¿cómo?** how? **¿cómo lo pasó?** how did it go? (4)
compañero/a partner, companion; **compañero/a de clase** classmate; **compañero/a de cuarto** roommate; **compañero/a de trabajo** co-worker
compañía company
comparación *f.* comparison
comparar to compare
compartir to share (2)
compás *m.* beat, rhythm; **al compás de** to the beat of
compasión *f.* compassion (6)
compasivo/a compassionate; understanding
compatriota *m., f.* compatriot
competencia competition
competición *f.* competition
complacer (zc) to satisfy
complejidad *f.* complexity
complejo *n., adj.* complex
complementario/a complementary
complemento directo/indirecto direct/indirect object
completamente completely; **estoy completamente de acuerdo** I agree completely (3)
completar to complete
completo/a complete; in its/their entirety; **por completo** completely; **se me olvidó por completo** I completely forgot (2)
complot *m.* conspiracy, plot
componente *m.* component
componer (*like* **poner**) to put together, create
comportamiento behavior (2)
comportarse to behave oneself
composición *f.* composition
compositor(a) composer
compra: ir (*irreg.*) **de compras** to go shopping
comprar to buy
comprender to understand
comprensión *f.* comprehension; understanding (2)
comprensivo/a understanding (2)
comprometido/a committed (6)

compromiso commitment (3)
compuesto/a (*p.p. of* **componer**) **de** made up of
computadora computer; **computadora portátil** laptop
común common, ordinary; **en común** in common, shared
comunicación *f.* communication
comunicado de prensa *n.* press release
comunicar (qu) to communicate; to convey; **comunicarse con** to get/keep in touch with
comunicativo/a communicative
comunidad *f.* community
comunismo communism
comunista *n., adj. m., f.* communist
comunitario/a *adj.* community (6)
con with; **con tal de que** provided that (6); **soñar (ue) con** to dream about (3)
concebido/a conceived
concentrarse to focus, concentrate
concepto concept
concha shell
conciencia conscience (6)
concientización *f.* conscientization, awareness
concierto concert
conciliar to reconcile
conclusión *f.* conclusion
concordancia agreement
concreto/a concrete
concursante *m., f.* contestant
concurso contest
condenado/a a condemned to
condición *f.* condition
condicional *gram.* conditional tense
condiscípulo/a classmate
conducir (zc) (j) to lead; to drive (*a vehicle*)
conectar(se) to connect
conector *m.* connector
conexión *f.* connection; **conexión inalámbrica** wireless connection (6)
confederación *f.* confederation
conferencia conference
confesar (ie) to confess
confiar (confío) en to trust in (3)
confirmación *f.* confirmation
conflicto conflict
conformarse con to be satisfied with
conforme *conj.* as
confrontación *f.* confrontation
confundido/a confused (3)
congénito/a congenital
congregar to gather; to bring together
congresista *m., f.* delegate
congreso conference
conjetura conjecture, guess
conjugación *f. gram.* conjugation
conjugar (ue) (gu) to conjugate
conjunción *f.* conjunction
conjunto group; **conjunto musical** band, musical group
conmigo with me
conmovedor(a) *adj.* moving (*emotionally*)
conmover (ue) to move (*emotionally*)
connotación *f.* connotation
cono cone; **Cono Sur** Southern Cone (*area comprising Argentina, Chile, Paraguay, and Uruguay*)
conocido/a (well) known
conocer (zc) to know; to meet; to become acquainted with; to be familiar with
conocimiento knowledge
conquistador(a) conqueror
conquistar to conquer
consciente aware
consecuencia consequence
conseguir (*like* **seguir**) to get, obtain; to achieve; to manage
consejero/a counselor; advisor
consejo (piece of) advice; counsel
conservación *f.* conservation
conservador(a) *adj.* conservative (2)
conservar to conserve
considerar to consider; to regard
consigo with him; with it; with them
consistente consistent; **de manera consistente** consistently
consistir en to consist of
constante *adj.* constant
constitución *f.* constitution
constitucional constitutional
constituir (y) to constitute
construcción *f.* construction
construir (y) to construct, build
consultar to consult
consumar to consummate (*marriage*)
consumidor(a) consumer
consumir to consume
consumismo consumerism (6)
contacto contact; **mantener** (*like* **tener**) **contacto** to maintain contact; **perder (ie) contacto** to lose contact
contagiar to infect
contagioso/a contagious
contaminación *f.* pollution (6)
contar (ue) to count; to tell, recount; **contar con** to count on (2); **te voy a contar algo increíble (estupendo, ridículo) que le pasó a…** I'm going to tell you something incredible (wonderful, ridiculous) that happened to . . . (3)
contemporáneo/a contemporary
contenedor *m.* container
contener (*like* **tener**) to contain
contento happy, contented; **estoy súper contento/a (de que)** I'm very happy (that) (2)
contestar to answer
contexto context
contigo with you
contiguo/a adjacent, next to
continente *m.* continent
continuación *f.* continuation; **a continuación** following, next
continuar (continúo) to continue
continuo/a uninterrupted
contra against; **en contra de** opposing, against
contracultura counterculture
contradictorio/a contradictory
contraer (*like* **traer**) **matrimonio** to get married
contrario opposite; **al/de lo contrario** on the contrary
contraste *m.* contrast; **en contraste** in contrast
contrato contract
contribución *f.* contribution
contribuir (y) to contribute
control *m.* control
controversia controversy
convencer (z) to convince
convencional conventional
convenir (*like* **venir**) to be agreeable, suit; **me conviene(n)** it's good (a good idea) for me (*to do something*) (4); it's to my advantage (*to do something*)
convento convent
conversación *f.* conversation
conversar to converse
convertir(se) (ie, i) en to change, turn into
convivir to live together; to spend time together
convulso/a filled with upheaval
cooperación *f.* cooperation
coordinación *f.* coordination
copa stemmed glass; glass; drink; **Copa Mundial** World Cup
copia *n.* copy
copiar to copy
coquetear to flirt (3)
coqueteo flirtation
coquetería flirtatiousness
coral *m.* coral
corazón *m.* heart
corbata necktie
cordillera mountain range
coreografía choreography
coro chorus
coronilla: estar (*irreg.*) **hasta la coronilla** to be fed up to here
correcto/a correct
correo mail; **correo electrónico** e-mail
correr to run
corresponder to correspond
correspondiente *adj.* corresponding
corresponsal *m., f.* news correspondent
corrida bullfight
corrido *type of popular Mexican song*
corriente *f.* current; *adj.* ordinary
corrupción *f.* corruption

cortar to cut
corte *f.* (royal) court; **corte** (*m.*) **de luz** blackout
cortejar to court
cortés *adj. m., f.* polite, courteous
cortesía courtesy
corto/a short
cosa thing
cosecha harvest
coser to sew
cosmopolita *adj. m., f.* cosmopolitan
costa coast
costar (ue) to cost
costarricense *n., adj.* Costa Rican
costear to pay for
costilla rib
costo cost
costoso/a expensive
costumbre *f.* custom
cotidiano/a everyday, daily
cotizado/a coveted, sought-after
creación *f.* creation
crear to create
creatividad *f.* creativity
creativo/a creative
crecer (zc) to grow (up)
crecimiento growth (6)
crédito credit
creencia belief
creer (y) (*p.p.* **creído**) to believe; to think, be of the opinion; **me sorprende que creas eso** I'm surprised that you think/believe that (3); **no lo puedo creer** I can't believe it (2); **¿tú crees?** you think so? (3); **yo creo que...** I think that . . . (3)
crepúsculo twilight
cresta Mohawk (*hairstyle*)
criar(se) (me crío) to bring up (2); to be raised (2)
crimen *m.* (*pl.* **crímenes**) crime
crío/a child
criollo/a Creole; **francés** (*m.*) **criollo** French Creole (*language*); **inglés** (*m.*) **criollo** English Creole (*language*)
crisis *f.* crisis (5)
cristal: bola de cristal crystal ball
cristalino/a crystalline; crystal-clear
cristiano/a *n., adj.* Christian
criterio criterion
crítica *n.* critique, review; criticism
criticar (qu) to criticize
crítico/a *adj.* critical; *n.* critic
crónica chronicle (*written account*)
crudo/a raw
cruz *f.* (*pl.* **cruces**) cross
cuadro painting; table, chart
cual *pron.* which, what, who
cuál *pron.* which (one), what (one), who; **¿cuál?** which (one)?, what (one)?, who?
cualidad *f.* quality
cualquier *adj. inv.* any
cualquiera *pron.* (*pl.* **cualesquiera**) anyone; whichever
cuán how
cuando when (6); **de vez en cuando** sometimes (3)
cuanto how much; **en cuanto** as soon as (6); **en cuanto a** as far as . . . is concerned (5)
cuánto/a how much; *pl.* how many; **¿cuánto/a?** how much?; *pl.* how many?
cuartel *m. s.* barracks
cuarto/a *adj.* fourth
cuarto room; **compañero/a de cuarto** roommate
cubano/a *n., adj.* Cuban
cubanoamericano/a Cuban-American
cubanochileno/a Cuban-Chilean
cubierto/a (*p.p. of* **cubrir**) covered
cubismo Cubism
cubrir (*p.p.* **cubierto**) to cover
cuenta bill; **darse** (*irreg.*) **cuenta de** to realize (1); **se dio cuenta de que...** he/she realized that . . . (3); **tener** (*irreg.*) **en cuenta** to take into account
cuento story
cuero leather, hide
cuerpo body; **Cuerpo de Paz** Peace Corps
cuestas: a cuestas on the shoulder
cuestión *f.* question, issue
cuestionar to question
cueva cave
cuidado care; careful; **tener** (*irreg.*) **cuidado** to be careful
cuidar to take care of (*someone, something*) (2)
culinario/a culinary
culpa fault; blame
cultivar to develop (6)
culto/a well educated (1)
cultura culture
cumbia *popular dance originating in Colombia*
cumpleaños *n. s.* birthday
cumplir to carry out, fulfill; to turn a year older
cuna cradle
cura cure
curandero/a healer
curar to cure (6)
curiosidad *f.* curiosity
curioso/a curious
cursar to study (*in a particular level of school*)
cursi tasteless; pretentious; corny (1)
cursiva: letra (*s.*) **cursiva** italics
curso course
curva curve
cúspide *f.* top
cuyo/a whose

D

dado/a given
daga dagger
dama lady
danza dance
dañino/a harmful (3)
daño harm; injury; **hacer** (*irreg.*) **daño** to hurt
dar *irreg.* to give; to give up; to present; to carry out; **dar a** to look out on; **dar asco** to disgust; **dar caminatas** to go on walks; **dar clases** to teach clases; **dar de comer** to feed; **dar la bienvenida** to welcome; **dar la mano** to give a hand (to someone), help out; **dar miedo** to frighten; **dar un ataque cardíaco** to give someone a heart attack; **dar una fiesta** to throw a party; **dar un salto** to jump; **darse cuenta de** to realize (1); **me da(n) asco** I'm disgusted by (4); **me da(n) ganas de** I feel like (4); **me da(n) igual** I don't care, it's all the same to me (4); **me da(n) lo mismo** I don't care (about) (4); **(no) dar tiempo** to (not) allow time; **¡No me digas!** Really?!; **se dio cuenta de que...** he/she realized that . . . (3)
datar de to date from
dato fact; item; *pl.* data, information
debajo de under, underneath
debate *m.* debate
debatir to debate
deber *m.* duty *v.* ought to, should, must; **deber de** + *inf.* ought to (*do something*)
debido/a a owing/due to; because of
década decade
decadencia decadence
decano/a dean
decente decent
decepcionado/a disappointed (2); **estoy decepcionado/a porque...** I'm disappointed because . . . (2)
decidir to decide
decir *irreg.* (*p.p.* **dicho**) to say; to tell; to pronounce; **es decir** that is to say; **pero, ¿qué dices?** but, what do you mean / are you saying? (3); **querer** (*irreg.*) **decir** to mean
decisión *f.* decision; **tomar una decisión** to make a decision
declaración *f.* statement
declarar to declare; to state; to express
decoración *f.* decoration
decorado/a decorated
dedicación *f.* dedication
dedicar (qu) to dedicate, devote; **dedicarse** to commit oneself
dedo finger
deducir (zc, j) to deduce

defender (ie) to defend
defensa defense
defensor(a) defender
definición *f.* definition
definitivo/a definitive
deforestación *f.* deforestation (6)
degradación *f.* deterioration
degradante degrading (1)
dejar to leave; to let, allow; to give up; **dejar a alguien** to leave someone (3); **dejar de** + *inf.* to stop (*doing something*); **dejar en paz** to leave alone; **dejar encargado/a** to leave (someone) in charge; **dejar huella** to leave a mark/trace; **dejar plantado/a** to stand (*someone*) up (3)
delante de in front of
delfín *m.* dolphin
delgado/a thin, slim
delicado/a delicate
delicioso/a delicious
delito crime; offense
demanda demand
demás: los/las demás others
demasiado/a *adj.* too much; *pl.* too many; *adv. m. s.* too, too much
democracia democracy
democrático/a democratic
demonio demon
demostración *f.* demonstration
demostrar (ue) to demonstrate
denominar to name
dentro de in, inside of, within
denunciar to denounce
depender (de) to depend (on)
deporte *m.* sport
deportista *m., f.* athlete
deportivo/a pertaining to sports
depresión *f.* depression
deprimente depressing (1)
deprimido/a depressed (3)
derecha: a la derecha on the right
derecho *n.* right; privilege; **derechos humanos** human rights (5); **reservarse el derecho** to reserve the right
derramarse to overflow
desacuerdo disagreement
desafiante challenging
desafiar (desafío) to challenge
desafío challenge
desagradable unpleasant
desairar to insult
desalojar to dislodge; to evict; to evacuate
desanimado/a dejected; bummed (4)
desaparecer (zc) to disappear
desarrollado/a developed (5)
desarrollar to develop (5)
desarrollo development; **desarrollo sostenible** sustainable development (6); **en vías de desarrollo** *adj.* developing (5)
desastre *m.* disaster; **desastre natural** natural disaster (6)
desastroso/a disastrous (6)
desayunar to have breakfast
descalzo/a barefoot
descansado/a rested (4)
descansar to rest
descanso rest
descapotable: coche (*m.*) **descapotable** convertible
descarga unloading
descendencia descent
descender (ie) to descend
descendiente *m., f.* descendent
descomponer (*like* **poner**) to break
desconocer (zc) not to know, be familiar with
desconocido/a stranger
describir (*p.p.* **descrito**) to describe
descripción *f.* description
descrito/a (*p.p. of* **describir**) described
descubierto/a (*p.p. of* **descubrir**) discovered
descubrimiento *n.* discovering
descubrir (*p.p.* **descubierto**) to discover
desde from; since; **desde entonces/luego** since then; **desde mi punto de vista...** from my point of view . . . (3); **desde pequeño/a** from when he (she, they, *etc.*) was/were small; **desde que** since
desear to want, desire
desempeñar to carry out; **desempeñar un papel** to play a role
desempleo unemployment
desencantado/a disillusioned, disappointed
deseo desire
desesperación *f.* desperation
desesperado/a desperate
desesperante infuriating
desesperanza desperation
desfilar por to file by, parade past
desfile *m.* parade
desgracia misfortune; **por desgracia** unfortunately
desgraciadamente unfortunately (5)
desierto *n.* desert
desierto/a *adj.* deserted
designado/a designated
desigual unequal
desigualdad *f.* inequality
desilusión *f.* disappointment (2)
desilusionado/a disappointed
desilusionante disappointing (5)
desleal disloyal, traitorous
desnudo/a naked
desnutrición *f.* malnutrition (5)
desobediencia disobedience
desorganización *f.* disorganization
despacho office
despedir (i, i) to fire; **despedirse** to say good-bye
desperdiciar to waste
despertar(se) (ie) to wake up
despierto/a *adj.* awake
despistado/a absent-minded (1)
desplazado/a displaced
desplomarse to collapse
despreciar to despise; to scorn
después *adv.* after, afterward (3); later (3); **después de que** after (6); **poco después** soon after
destacar(se) (qu) to stand out
destellar to sparkle
destreza ability, skill
destrozado/a crushed; shattered
destrozar (c) to destroy
desvanecer (zc) to fade away
desvelarse to stay awake all night (3)
desventaja disadvantage
detalle *m.* detail; **con detalle** in detail
detener (*like* **tener**) to put a stop to; **detenerse** to stop
deteriorarse to deteriorate
determinar to determine
detrás de behind, in back of
devastador(a) devastating
devastar to devastate
devoto/a devout
día *m.* day; **al día** up to date; per day; **al día siguiente** (on) the next day; **algún día** some day; **cada día** every day; **Día de San Valentín** Valentine's Day; **hoy (en) día** nowadays (5); **ponerse** (*irreg.*) **al día** to catch up; **todo el día** all day; **todos los días** every day
diablo devil
diálogo dialogue
diamante *m.* diamond
diametralmente totally
diario *n.* diary, journal; daily newspaper
diario/a *adj.* daily
dibujar to draw, sketch
dibujo drawing, sketch; **dibujo animado** (animated) cartoon
diccionario dictionary
dicho/a (*p.p. of* **decir**) said; aforementioned
dictadura dictatorship
dictar to dictate
diferencia difference; **a diferencia de** unlike
diferenciación *f.* differenciation
diferenciar to distinguish; **diferenciarse** to differ, differentiate
diferente different
difícil difficult, hard
dificultad *f.* difficulty
difundir to broadcast
digital: brecha digital information gap (6)

digitalizado/a digitized
dignidad *f.* dignity
dilema *m.* dilemma
dimensión *f.* dimension
diminutivo *gram.* diminutive
dinamitar to dynamite
dinero money
dinosaurio dinosaur
dios(a) god, goddess; **¡válgame Dios!** God help me!
dióxido de carbono carbon dioxide (6)
diplomacia diplomacy
diplomático/a diplomatic
diputado/a congressman/congresswoman
dirección *f.* address; direction; management
directivo/a: junta directiva board of directors
directo/a direct
director(a) director
dirigir (j) to direct; **dirigirse a** to address; to move toward
disciplina discipline
disco record
disco(teca) discotheque
discriminación *f.* discrimination
disculpa: mil (*m.*) **disculpas** a thousand pardons (2)
discurso speech
discusión *f.* debate; argument
discutir to argue (3); to debate
diseñador(a) designer
diseñar to design
diseño design
disfraz *m.* (*pl.* **disfraces**) disguise
disfrutar de to enjoy (4)
disfuncional dysfunctional (2)
disgustar to annoy, displease; **me disgusta(n)** I don't like (4)
disgusto disgust; displeasure
disidencia dissidence
disidente *m., f.* dissident
disminuir (y) to decrease (4), diminish
disparador(a) certero/a sharpshooter
disparar to shoot
dispersión *f.* dispersal, dispersion
disponer (*like* **poner**) to have available
disponible available (6)
disposición *f.* disposition
dispuesto/a (*p.p. of* **disponer**) willing (to) (4)
distancia distance; **a larga distancia** long-distance; **a unos pasos de distancia** a few steps away
distante distant
distinguirse to distinguish
distinto/a different, distinct
distraer (*like* **traer**) to distract
distribución *f.* distribution
distribuir (y) to distribute
distrito district
diversidad *f.* diversity (5)
diversión *f.* diversion
diverso/a diverse; *pl.* various
divertido/a fun, amusing, entertaining
divertirse (ie, i) to have a good time; to have fun; **¡qué se divierta / te diviertas / se diviertan!** have a good time! (4)
dividir to divide
divisas *pl.* hard currency
divorciado/a divorced
divorciarse (de) to get a divorce (from) (3)
divorcio *n.* divorce
doble double
doctor(a) doctor
doctorado doctorate
doctoral: tesis (*f.*) **doctoral** dissertation
doctorarse to receive a doctorate
documento document; **documento de identidad** proof of identity
dólar *m.* dollar
doler (ue) to hurt, ache; **me duele** it hurts
dolor *m.* pain; **dolor de cabeza** headache
doloroso/a painful
doméstico/a *adj.* household
dominante dominant
dominar to dominate
dominicano/a *n., adj.* Dominican, pertaining to the Dominican Republic
don, doña *title of respect used before a person's first name*
donación *f.* donation
donar to donate (5)
donativo donation
donjuán *m.* womanizer
dorado/a golden
dormido/a sleepy; asleep
dormir (ue, u) to sleep; **dormirse** to fall asleep
dormitorio bedroom
dorso: al dorso on the back
dotado/a endowed
dragón *m.* dragon
drama *m.* play
dramatizar (c) to act out, dramatize
ducha shower
ducharse to take a shower
duda doubt
dudar to doubt
dueño/a owner; proprietor
dulce *n. m.* candy, sweet; *adj.* sweet (1); gentle; **agua** (*f., but* **el agua**) **dulce** freshwater
dulzura sweetness
duplicar (qu) to duplicate; to double
duquesa duchess
duradero/a lasting (3)
durante during; for
durar to last, endure
duro *n.* cent
duro *adv.* hard
duro/a hard, difficult; harsh

E

echar to emit; to throw out; **echar de menos** to miss (*someone/something*); **echar un piropo** to make a flirtatious remark
ecléctico/a eclectic, diverse
ecológico/a ecological
economía economy
económico/a economic; concerning money
ecosistema *m.* ecosystem
ecoturismo ecotourism
ecuatoriano/a *n., adj.* Ecuadorian
ecuatorianoandino/a of or pertaining to the Andean region of Ecuador
edad *f.* age; **Edad de Oro** Golden Age; **Edad Media** Middle Ages
edificio building
editar to edit
editor(a) editor
educación *f.* education; **de mala educación** *adv.* rudely
educado/a *adj.* polite (1); **de manera educada** *adv.* politely
educar(se) (qu) to educate
educativo/a educational
efectividad *f.* effectiveness
efectivo/a effective; functional
efecto effect; **efecto invernadero** greenhouse effect (6); **en efecto** in fact
eficaz (*pl.* **eficaces**) effective
eficiente efficient
egipcio/a *adj.* Egyptian
egoísta *adj. m., f.* egotistical (5); selfish (2)
ejemplar exemplary; model
ejemplo example; **por ejemplo** for example
ejercer (z) to practice (*a profession*); to exert
ejercicio exercise; **hacer** (*irreg.*) **ejercicio** to exercise
ejército army; **Ejército Zapatista de Liberación Nacional** National Liberation Zapatist Army (*guerrilla forces in Chiapas, Mexico*)
ejecutor(a) executor
elaboración *f.* elaboration
elaborar to create; to work out (*details*)
elástico/a elastic; stretchy
elección *f.* election, choice
electoral *adj.* electoral, election
electrodoméstico appliance
electrónico/a electronic; **correo electrónico** electronic mail (e-mail)
elefante *m.* elephant
elegante elegant
elegir (i, i) (j) to elect (4); to choose
elemento element
eliminación *f.* elimination
eliminar to eliminate (6)

elitista *n., adj m., f.* elitist
embajador(a) ambassador
embargo: sin embargo nevertheless
emblemático/a emblematic
embustero/a liar
emigración *f.* emigration
emigrar to emigrate
emisora (radio) station
emitir to broadcast
emoción *f.* emotion
emocionado/a excited (3)
emocional emotional
emocionante exciting (1); touching
emocionar to move, make emotional; to excite; **emocionarse** to get excited; **me emociona(n)** I'm excited by (4)
empanada turnover, stuffed pastry
empapar to drench
empatía empathy (6)
empedrado/a: calle (*f.*) **empedrada** cobblestone street
empeorar to become, get worse (6)
empezar (ie) (c) to begin; **empezar a** + *inf.* to begin to (*do something*)
empinado/a steep
empleado/a employee
emplear to employ; to use
empresa business
empresarial managerial
empresario/a manager, director
emular to emulate
enamorado/a in love
enamorarse de to fall in love with (3)
encantador(a) charming (1)
encantar to charm, delight; **me encanta(n)** I love, really like (4)
encarcelado/a jailed, incarcerated
encargar (gu) (de) to put in charge (of); to order; **encargarse (de)** to take charge of
encender (ie) to light; **encenderse** to fire up; to start to glow
encima de above; **pasar por encima de** to go over one's head; **por encima** above
encontrar (ue) to find; **encontrarse** to be located; **encontrarse con** to meet up with, run into
encuentro meeting, encounter
encuesta survey, poll
enemigo/a enemy
energía energy
enfadado/a angry (3)
énfasis *m. inv.* emphasis; emphases
enfatizar (c) to emphasize, stress
enfermedad *f.* illness
enfermero/a nurse
enfermo/a ill, sick
enfocar(se) (en) to focus (on)
enfoque *m.* focus
enfrentamiento confrontation
enfrentar to face, confront (6)
enfrentarse (con) to be faced (with)
enfrente de facing; in front of
enganche *m.* hook; harness (*on horses*)
engañar to deceive; **las apariencias engañan** looks deceive (1)
engaño deceit
engominado/a slicked down
enigmático/a enigmatic
enjuagar (gu) to rinse
enlace *m.* link (6)
enmarcado/a framed
enmudecer (zc) to silence, hush
enojado/a angry (3)
enojar to anger, make angry; **enojarse** to get angry
enorme enormous
enriquecer (zc) to enrich (6)
ensayar to rehearse
ensayista *m., f.* essayist
ensayo essay; practice
enseñanza education; teaching
enseñar to teach; to show; **enseñar a** + *inf.* to teach to (*do something*)
ensimismado/a self-centered (2)
entender (ie) to understand
enterarse (de) to become informed (about) (5)
entero/a entire
enterrar (ie) to inter, bury
entonación *f.* intonation
entonces then; **desde entonces** since then
entrada entrance; (event) ticket
entrar (a/en) to enter
entre between; among; in; **entre paréntesis** in parentheses
entregado/a dedicated
entregar (gu) to deliver; to give over; to turn in
entrenar to train
entretener(se) (*like* **tener**) to entertain (oneself) (4)
entretenido/a entertaining (4)
entretenimiento entertainment
entrevista interview
entrevistado/a interviewee
entrevistador(a) interviewer
entrevistar to interview
entrometido/a meddlesome (2)
entumecido/a numb
entusiasmado/a enthusiastic (4)
entusiasmar to enthuse; **entusiasmarse** to get/become enthusiastic
entusiasmo enthusiasm
enumerar to list
enviar (envío) to send
envidioso/a envious (2)
épico/a epic
época era; period (*time*)
equilibrado/a balanced
equilibrio balance (3)
equinoccio equinox
equipo team
equivalente *m.* equivalent
equivocado/a wrong; mistaken
equivocarse (qu) to be wrong; to make a mistake; **perdón, me equivoqué** sorry, I made a mistake (2)
era age, era
erotismo eroticism
erradicar (qu) to erradicate
error *m.* error
escala ladder; **escala de valores** hierarchy of values
escalera staircase; **escalera de caracol** spiral staircase
escalofrío chill
escalón *m.* step, stair; rung
escandalizar (c) to scandalize
escándalo scandal
escandaloso/a scandalous
escandinavo/a *n., adj.* Scandinavian
escaparse (de) to escape; to slip away
escape *m.* escape; getaway
escarbar to dig
escena scene
escenario stage
escénico/a: miedo escénico stage fright
esclavo/a slave
esclusa lock (*canal*)
escoba broom
escoger (j) to choose, pick
esconder to hide
escondite *m.* hiding place
escotilla hatch
escribir (*p.p.* **escrito**) to write; **escribir un mensaje de texto** to text (6)
escrito/a (*p.p. of* **escribir**) written; **por escrito** in writing
escritor(a) writer
escritorio desk
escritura writing
escuchar to listen; **escucha lo que le sucedió a...** listen to what happened to . . . (3)
escudo shield
escuela school; **escuela primaria** elementary school; **escuela secundaria** high school
escultor(a) sculptor
escultura sculpture
esencia essence
esencial essential
esfuerzo effort (4); **hacer** (*irreg.*) **un esfuerzo** to make an effort
esnob *adj. m., f.* snobbish
esoterismo esoterism
espacial *adj.* space, pertaining to outer space
espacio space; **espacio en blanco** blank space
espalda back

espantoso/a frightening
español *m.* Spanish (*language*)
español(a) *n.* Spaniard; *adj.* Spanish
especial special; **en especial** especially
especializar(se) (c) (en) to major (in); to specialize (in)
especialmente especially
especie *f.* species; type
específico/a specific
espectacular spectacular
espectáculo show, performance (4)
espectador(a) spectator
especular to speculate
espejo mirror
esperanza hope (2)
esperar to wait; to wait for, await; to hope (for); to expect
espía *m., f.* spy
espiga ear or spike of a plant
espinoso/a thorny
espíritu *m.* spirit
espiritual spiritual
espiritualidad *f.* spirituality
espléndido/a splendid
espontáneo/a spontaneous
esposo/a husband, wife; spouse
esqueleto skeleton
esquí *m.* ski
esquiar (esquío) to ski
esquina corner
estabilidad *f.* stability (2)
estable *adj.* stable (2)
establecer (zc) to establish
establecimiento establishment
estación *f.* station
estacionamiento parking; parking lot
estadísticas *pl.* statistics
estado state; condition; **en buen estado físico** in good (physical) shape; **estado de ánimo** mood; **estado libre asociado** commonwealth
estadounidense *n. m., f.* United States citizen; *adj.* pertaining to the United States
estancado/a stagnant
estancia stay, visit
estar *irreg.* to be; **estar de buen/mal humor** to be in a good/bad mood (4); **estar de moda** to be in style; **estar pasado/a de moda** to be out of style; **estoy completamente de acuerdo** I agree completely (3); **estoy decepcionado/a porque...** I'm disappointed because . . . (2); **estoy orgulloso/a de que...** I'm proud that . . . (2); **estoy súper contento/a de que...** I'm super-happy that . . . (2); **(no) estoy de acuerdo** I (don't) agree (2); **no estoy de acuerdo en absoluto** I don't agree at all (3); **ya estoy harto/a de que...** I'm fed up already (that . . .) (2)
estatal *adj.* state, of or pertaining to the state
estatua statue
estereotipado/a stereotyped
estereotipo stereotype
estético/a aesthetic
estilizado/a stylized
estilo style; **estilo de baile** dance style; **estilo de música** musical style; **estilo de vida** lifestyle
estimado/a esteemed
estimar to estimate
estimular to stimulate
estómago stomach
estrategia strategy
estratégico/a strategic
estrechez *f.* (*pl.* **estrecheces**) closeness
estrecho/a narrow; close (*relationship between people or things*) (2)
estrella star; **estrella de cine** movie star
estreno debut
estrés *m.* stress
estresado/a stressed (out) (4)
estresante stressful
estricto/a strict (2)
estrofa stanza; verse
estructura structure
estructurar to structure
estudiante *m., f.* student; **residencia de estudiantes** student dormitory
estudiantil *adj.* student, pertaining to students
estudiantina *n. group of students who play traditional music together*
estudiar to study
estudio study; studio; **estudio de grabación** recording studio
estudioso/a studious
estupendo/a wonderful; **te voy a contar algo estupendo que le pasó a...** I'm going to tell you something wonderful that happened to . . . (3)
estupidez *f.* (*pl.* **estupideces**) stupidity
ETA *f.* (*abbrev. for* **Euskadi ta Askatasuna**) Basque Homeland and Freedom (*Basque separatist group in Spain*)
etapa stage
etcétera et cetera
eterno/a eternal
eternidad *f.* eternity
ético/a ethical
etnia ethnic group
etnicidad *f.* ethnicity
étnico/a ethnic
etnobiográfico/a ethnobiographical
eufemismo euphemism
euro *m. monetary unit in continental Europe* (*Sp.*)
Europa Europe
europeo/a European
evadir to avoid
evento event
evidencia evidence
evidente evident
evitar to avoid
evocar (qu) to evoke
evolución *f.* evolution
evolucionar to evolve
exacerbar to aggravate, exacerbate
exacto/a exact
exagerar to exaggerate
examen *m.* exam, test; **examen de ingreso** entrance exam
examinar to examine; to investigate
exasperado/a exasperated
excavación *f.* excavation
excavar to dig, excavate
excelente excellent
excentricidad *f.* eccentricity
excéntrico/a eccentric
excepción *f.* exception
excesivo/a excessive
exceso excess
exclamar to exclaim
exclusivo/a exclusive
exigente demanding (2)
exhalar to exhale
exhibición *f.* exhibition, exhibit
exiliarse to go into exile
existencia existence
existir to exist
éxito success; **tener** (*irreg.*) **éxito** to be successful (4)
exitoso/a successful (3)
exótico/a exotic
exotismo exoticism
expansión *f.* expansion
expansor (*m.*) **de oreja** ear (hole) expander
expectativa expectation (2)
experiencia experience
experimentar to experience; to experiment
experto/a expert
expirar to expire
explicación *f.* explanation
explicar (qu) to explain
exploración *f.* exploration
explorar to explore
explosión *f.* explosion
explotación *f.* exploitation (4)
explotar to exploit
exponer (*like* **poner**) to exhibit; to make public; to expound
exportación *f.* export
exposición *f.* exposition; exhibit
expresar to express
expresión *f.* expression
expuesto/a (*p.p. of* **exponer**) exposed; made public
expulsar to eject; to throw out, expel
expulsión *f.* expulsion
extender (ie) to extend; **extenderse** to become spread out

extensión *f.* extension
extenso/a extensive
extraer (*like* **traer**) to extract
extranjero/a *n.* foreigner; **en el extranjero** abroad; *adj.* foreign
extrañar to miss (*someone/something*) (2); to surprise
extraño/a strange
extraordinario/a extraordinary
extraterrestre *n. m., f.* extraterrestrial
extravagante extravagant
extremadamente extremely
extremista *n., adj. m., f.* extremist (5)
extremo *n.* extreme
extremo/a extreme
extrovertido/a extroverted
EZLN *m.* (*abbrev. for* **Ejército Zapatista de Liberación Nacional**) National Liberation Zapatist Army (*guerrilla forces in Chiapas, Mexico*)

F

fábrica factory
fabricado/a manufactured
fábula fable
fabuloso/a fabulous
facción *f.* faction
fachada façade
fácil easy
facilidad *f.* facility; **con facilidad** with ease
factible feasible
factor *m.* factor
facultad *f.* school (*of a university*)
falda skirt
fallecer (zc) to die
falso/a false
falta lack; absence; **hacer** (*irreg.*) **falta** to need
faltar to lack
fama fame; reputation
familia family
familiar *n. m.* family member; *adj.* pertaining to the family
famoso/a famous
fanático/a *n.* fan, fanatic; *adj.* fanatical
fantasía fantasy
fantasma *m.* ghost
fantástico/a fantastic
farmacéutico/a *n.* pharmacist; *adj.* pharmaceutical; **receta farmacéutica** prescription
farmacia pharmacy
fascinación *f.* fascination
fascinante fascinating
fascinar to fascinate; **me fascina(n)** I'm fascinated by (4)
fascista *m., f.* fascist
fastidiar to annoy, bother; **me fastidia(n)** I'm bothered by (4)
fatal unfortunate; awful; **me cae(n) fatal** I don't like (*a person / people*) (4); **me sentí fatal** I felt awful; **pasarlo fatal** to have a terrible time (4)
fauno faun, satyr
favor *m.* favor; **a favor de** in favor of; **por favor** please
favorito/a favorite
fax *m.* fax
fecha date
federación *f.* federation
federal *n. m., f.* representative of the government; *adj.* federal
felicidad *f.* happiness (6)
feliz (*pl.* **felices**) happy
femenino/a feminine
fenomenal phenomenal; **¡fenomenal!** great! (2); **me cae(n) fenomenal** I really like (*a person/people*) (4)
fenómeno phenomenon
feo/a ugly
feria fair
feroz (*pl.* **feroces**) ferocious; fierce
festival *m.* festival
ficción *f.* fiction; **ciencia ficción** science fiction
ficha index card
ficticio/a fictitious
fiel: ser to be faithful (3)
fiesta party; festival; holiday; **dar** (*irreg.*) **una fiesta** to throw a party
fiestero/a *n.* fun-loving person, party animal, partyer; *adj.* party-going
figura figure
fijarse en to pay attention to; to notice
fijo/a fixed, set, unchanging
fila line; row; **primera fila** front row
filantrópico/a philanthropic
filosofía philosophy
filósofo/a philosopher
filtro filter
fin *m.* end; objective; purpose; **en fin** in short; **fin de semana** weekend; **por fin** finally
final *m.* end; **al final** finally (3)
finalidad *f.* aim, purpose
finalista *m., f.* finalist
finalmente finally (3)
financiar to finance (5)
financiero/a financial
finca farm
fino/a fine; sensitive
firme firm, solid
físico/a physical; **apariencia física** physical appearance; **aspecto físico** physical appearance; **en buen estado físico** in good (physical) shape
flaco/a skinny
flamboyán *m.* *type of tree found in the Caribbean*
flamenco *type of Spanish dance and music*
flexibilidad *f.* flexibility
flor *f.* flower; **en flor** blooming
floripondio exuberant flower; corny speech
flotar to float
folclor (*m.*) folklore
folclórico/a folkloric
folleto brochure
fomentar to foment, foster
fondo bottom; background; rear; foundation; *pl.* funds, funding; **de fondo** background; **en el fondo** at heart; in the depths; **recaudar fondos** to raise money (5)
forjado/a: hierro forjado wrought iron
forma form; figure; way; shape
formación *f.* training; education; formation
formar to form; to make up; **formarse** to take shape; **formar parte de** to be/form a part of, comprise
formato format
formular to formulate
foro forum
fortaleza fortress
forzar (ue) (c) to force
fósil *n. m., adj.* fossil
foto(grafía) photo(graph); **sacar (qu) fotos** to take pictures
fracaso failure (3)
fragancia fragrance
frágil fragile
fragmento fragment
francamente frankly (5)
francés *n. m.* French (*language*); **francés criollo** French Creole (*language*)
francés, francesa *n.* French person; *adj.* French
franco/a frank
frase *f.* sentence; phrase
fraude *m.* fraud; **cometer un fraude** to commit fraud
frecuencia: con frecuencia frequently, often
frecuentar to frequent, hang out in
frecuente frequent
fregadero kitchen sink
frenos *pl.* brakes
frente *m.* front; **frente a** facing, opposite; opposing
fresa strawberry
fresco/a fresh
frigidez *f.* (*pl.* **frigideces**) frigidity
frijol *m.* bean
frío cold; **hacer** (*irreg.*) **frío** to be cold outside (*weather*)
frito/a (*p.p. of* **freír**) fried
frívolo/a frivolous
frondoso/a leafy
frontera border (6)
frustración *f.* frustration
frustrado/a frustrated

frustrante frustrating
fruta fruit
fruto fruit (*as part or name of a plant*); fruit (*product, result*)
fuego fire
fuente *f.* fountain; source
fuerte strong, powerful; forceful; harsh, sharp
fuerza strength; force; **a la fuerza** by force
fugitivo/a *adj.* fugitive
fumar to smoke
función *f.* function; event; duty
funcionar to function, work
fundación *f.* foundation
fundador(a) founder
fundar to found; to establish
funeraria funeral parlor
furioso/a furious
fusilamiento shooting
fusilar to execute; to kill with a firearm
fusión *f.* fusion
fusta riding crop
fútbol *m.* soccer
futuro *n.* future
futuro/a *adj.* future

G

gafas *f. pl.* (eye)glasses (1)
galantería compliment
galápago *sea turtle of the Galapagos Islands*
galería gallery
gallego/a *n.* Galician (*person*); *m.* Galician (*language*); *adj.* Galician, of or pertaining to Galicia in northwestern Spain
galleta cookie; cracker
gallina hen
galope *m.* gallop; **al galope** very fast
gana: darle (*irreg.*) **la gana** to feel like; **me da(n) ganas de** I feel like (4); **tener** (*irreg.*) **ganas de** + *inf.* to feel like (*doing something*)
ganado livestock
ganar to win; to earn; **ganarle** to beat; **ganarse la vida** to earn a living
garantía guarantee
garantizar (c) to guarantee
gardeliano/a *pertaining to Carlos Gardel*
garganta throat
gas *m.* gas (*not* gasoline)
gastar to spend; to use (6)
gasto expenditure; *pl.* expenses
gato cat
geiser *m.* geiser
gel *m.* gel
gelatinoso/a gelatinous
gemelo/a *n., adj.* twin (2); **alma** (*f., but* **el alma**) **gemela** soul mate (3)
gemido wail
generación *f.* generation
generacional: brecha generacional generation gap (2)
general: en general / por lo general in general, usually
generar to generate
genéricamente generically
género genre; type; *gram.* gender
generosidad *f.* generosity
generoso/a generous
genético/a genetic (6)
genial wonderful (3)
genio/a genius
gente *f. s.* people; **ser** (*irreg.*) **buena/mala gente** to be a good/bad person / good/bad people (1); **gente indígena** indigenous people (5)
geografía geography
geográfico/a geographical
geométrico/a geometrical
gerundio *gram.* gerund
gesticular to gesticulate
gesto gesture
gigantesco/a gigantic
girar to turn
gitano/a *n., adj.* gypsy
glaciar *m.* glacier
globalización *f.* globalization (6)
globalizado/a globalized
globo balloon
glorificación *f.* glorification
glorioso/a glorious
gobernador(a) governor
gobernar (ie) to govern
gobierno government
golondrina swallow (*bird*)
goloso/a *n.* sweet-tooth
golpe *m.* blow; **de golpe** suddenly (3); **golpe de estado** coup d'etat
golpear to hit
gordito/a chubby
gordo/a fat
gordura obesity
gótico/a Gothic
gráfico/a graphic
gozar (c) de to enjoy
grabación *f.* recording
grabado engraving
grabar to record
gracia charm; *pl.* thanks; **mil gracias** thanks a million (*lit.*, a thousand thanks); **tener** (*irreg.*) **gracia** to be charming
gracioso/a funny
grado degree; amount; level
gradualmente gradually
graduarse (me gradúo) to graduate
gramatical *adj.* grammar, grammatical
gran, grande great; big, large, huge
grandeza greatness
grano grain
grasiento/a greasy
gratis free
grato/a pleasant; **trance** (*m.*) **grato** pleasant moment
Grecia Greece
grifo faucet
gritar to shout
grito shriek; shout; **el último grito** the latest fad
grosería crudeness; swear word
grosero/a rude (1)
grupo group; **grupo musical** band, musical group
guagua *n. m., f..* baby (*Ch.*)
guapo/a handsome, attractive
guaracha *dance of Caribbean origin*
guaraní *m.* Guarani (*indigenous language of Paraguay*); *monetary unit of Paraguay*
guardaespaldas *m. s.* bodyguard
guardar to store; to keep, save; to maintain; **guardar silencio** to remain silent; **guardar un secreto** to keep a secret
guatemalteco/a *n., adj.* Guatemalan
guay: ¡qué guay! (how) awesome! (1)
guayaba guava
guayabera *typical silk or cotton dress shirt of the Caribbean*
gubernamental governmental
guerra war (5); **guerra civil** civil war
guerrillero/a guerrilla fighter
gueto ghetto
guía *m., f.* guide; *f.* guidebook
guiño: hacerle (*irreg.*) **guiños a** to wink at
guión *m.* script
guitarra guitar
guitarrista *m., f.* guitarist
gustar to please, be pleasing; to like; **gustar** + *inf.* to like to (*do something*); **no me gusta que...** I don't like it that . . . (2)
gusto pleasure; taste; **de mal gusto** in poor taste (4); **me da gusto** I am pleased (to)

H

habanera *dance of Afro-Cuban origin*
haber *irreg.* to have (auxiliary v.); **haber de** to have to, must **habrá** (it) will be / take place; **hay** there is/are; **hubo** (it) happened / took place
habilidad *f.* ability; skill
habitación *f.* room; bedroom
habitante *m., f.* inhabitant
habitar to dwell
hábitat *m.* habitat
hábito habit; **hábitos de consumo** habits of consumption (6)
habitualmente habitually
hablador(a) talkative (1)
hablar to speak; to talk; **hablar por los codos** to talk a lot; **¡ni hablar!** no way! (2)

hacer *irreg.* (*p.p.* **hecho**) to do; to make; to cause; **hace** + (*period of time*) (*period of time*) ago; **hacer** + *inf.* to make (*do something*); to have (*something done*); **hacer caso a** to pay attention to; **hacer daño** to hurt; **hacer de voluntario/a** to volunteer (5); **hacer ejercicio** to exercise; **hacer falta** to need; **hacer ruido** to make noise; **hacer saber** to inform; **hacer trabajos sueltos** to freelance; **hacer un esfuerzo** to make an effort; **hacer una pregunta** to ask a question; **hacer una sugerencia** to suggest; **hacer uso de** to make use of; **hacerle guiños a** to wink at; **hacerse** to become
hacia toward
halagado/a flattered (3)
halagar (gu) to compliment; to show appreciation; to flatter
halcón *m.* falcon; hawk
hambre *f.* (*but* **el hambre**) hunger (5); **tener** (*irreg.*) **hambre** to be hungry
harina flour
harto/a (de) fed up (with), sick of (3); **harto/a hasta las narices** fed up to here (4); **ya estoy harto/a (de que)** I'm fed up already (that) (2)
hasta *prep.* until; up to; as far as; *adv.* even; **estar** (*irreg.*) **hasta las narices con** (*f.*) to have had it up to here (one's nose) with something; **hasta mañana** see you tomorrow; **hasta muy tarde** until very late; **hasta que** until (6); **¿hasta qué punto?** to what point?
hazmerreír *m.* laughingstock
hecho *n.* fact; event; **de hecho** in fact (5); **el hecho de que** + *subj.* the fact that . . . (5)
hecho/a (*p.p. of* **hacer**) done; made
hectárea hectare
heladería ice cream parlor
helado ice cream
heredar to inherit (2)
hereje *m., f.* heretic
herencia inheritance
herida *n.* wound
herido/a hurt, injured
herir (ie, i) to injure, wound
hermanado/a matched with; similar to
hermanastro/a stepbrother, stepsister (2); *pl.* stepsiblings
hermandad *f.* brotherhood; fraternity; **hermandad de mujeres** sisterhood; sorority
hermano/a brother, sister; *pl.* siblings; **hermano/a mayor** older/oldest brother, sister; **medio hermano, media hermana** half brother, half sister (2)
hermoso/a beautiful
héroe *m.* hero
heroico/a heroic
heroína heroine
hervir (ie, i) to boil
hierba grass
hierro forjado wrought iron
hijo/a son, daughter; **hijo adoptivo, hija adoptiva** adopted son, adopted daughter (2); **hijo único, hija única** only child (2)
himno nacional national anthem
hipocresía hypocrisy
hipócrita *n. m., f.* hypocrite; *adj. m., f.* hypocritical
hipótesis *f. inv.* hypothesis; hypotheses
hipotético/a hypothetical
hispano/a *n., adj.* Hispanic
hispanohablante *n. m., f.* Spanish speaker; *adj.* Spanish-speaking
historia history; story
histórico/a historic; historical
hogar *m.* home
hoja leaf; blade (*of grass*)
hola hello
holgado/a baggy
hombre *m.* man; **hombre de negocios** businessman
homenaje *m.* tribute
homogeneizarse to homogenize
homogéneo/a homogeneous
honesto/a honest
honor *m.* honor
hora hour; **ser** (*irreg.*) **hora de** + *inf.* to be time to (*do something*)
horario schedule
horripilante horrifying (5)
horror: ¡qué horror! how terrible! (2)
horroroso/a hideous; terrifying
hospedar to lodge, board; to host
hospital *m.* hospital
hospitalidad *f.* hospitality
hostil hostile
hotel *m.* hotel
hoy today; **hoy (en) día** nowadays (5)
huelga strike (5)
huella mark; **dejar huella** to leave a mark
huésped *m., f.* guest
huevo egg
humanidad *f.* humanity
humanitario/a humanitarian (6); **ayuda humanitaria** humanitarian aid
humano/a *adj.* human, pertaining to humanity; **derechos humanos** human rights; **ser** (*m.*) **humano** human being
humear to smoke (*food*); to emit smoke
humedecido/a moistened
húmedo/a humid
humilde humble
humillación *f.* humiliation
humor *m.* mood; humor; **estar** (*irreg.*) **de buen/mal humor** to be in a good/bad mood (4); **sentido del humor** sense of humor
huracán *m.* hurricane (6)

I

icono icon
idea idea; **lluvia de ideas** brainstorm
idealista *adj. m., f.* idealistic (5)
idéntico/a identical
identidad *f.* identity; **documento de identidad** proof of identity
identificación *f.* identification
identificado/a: objeto volador/volante no identificado UFO
identificar (qu) to identify
ideología ideology
ideológico/a ideological
idilio romance
idioma *m.* language
idolatrar to worship, idolize
idóneo/a *adj.* ideal
iglesia church
ignorar to ignore
igual *adj.* equal; the same; similar; **igual que** the same as; **me da(n) igual** I don't care, it's all the same to me (4); **me es igual** I don't care (4)
ilegal illegal
ilegítimo/a illegitimate
ilusión *f.* illusion
iluso/a naive
ilustración *f.* illustration
ilustrador(a) illustrator
ilustrar to illustrate
imagen *f.* (*pl.* **imágenes**) image
imaginación *f.* imagination
imaginario/a imaginary
imaginarse to imagine; **como es de imaginar** as you can imagine; **¡imagínate!** imagine that! (3)
imbecilidad *f.* stupidity
imitar to imitate
impaciente impatient
impactar to impact (6)
impacto impact
imperativo *gram.* imperative, command
imperfecto *gram.* imperfect tense
imperio empire
implementar to implement (6)
implicar (qu) to imply
imponer (*like* **poner**) to impose
importación *f.* import
importancia importance
importante important
importar to matter; to be important; to import; **me importa tres narices / un pepino** I couldn't care less (2); **me**

importa un bledo I don't give a damn; **(no) me importa(n)** I (don't) care about (4)
imposibilitar to make impossible
imposible impossible
imposición *f.* imposition
impotente impotent
impregnado/a full of
imprescindible indispensable
impresión *f.* impression
impresionado/a impressed
impresionante impressive (5); **es impresionante que...** it's impressive/awesome that . . . (2)
impresionar to impress
impresionismo Impressionism
impreso/a *adj.* (*p.p. of* **imprimir**) printed, print
imprimir (*p.p.* **impreso/a**) to print
improvisación *f.* improvisation
improvisar to improvise
impuesto tax
impuesto/a (*p.p. of* **imponer**) imposed
impulso impulse
inaceptable unacceptable
inaguantable unbearable (6)
inapropiado/a inappropriate
inaugurar to open, inaugurate
inca *adj. m., f.* Incan
incansable tireless
incapacidad *f.* inability, incapability
incendio fire
incertidumbre *f.* uncertainty
incipiente incipient
inclinar(se) to tip; to bow; to be disposed (*in favor*)
incluir (y) to include
incluso/a including
incomodidad *f.* discomfort
incompetente incompetent
incompleto/a incomplete
incomprendido/a misunderstood
inconcebible unfathomable
inconsciente unconscious
inconveniente *m.* obstacle; drawback
incorporar to incorporate
increíble incredible; **te voy a contar algo increíble que le pasó a...** I'm going to tell you something incredible that happened to . . . (3)
incrementar to grow
indagar (gu) to investigate
independencia independence
independiente independent
independizarse (c) to become independent
indicación *f.* indication
indicar (qu) to indicate
indicativo *gram.* indicative mood
indicio indication
indiferencia indifference
indígena *n., adj. m., f.* native; **gente** (*f.*) **indígena** (*but* **los indígenas**) indigenous people (5)
indignado/a indignant
indio/a *n., adj.* Indian; pertaining to the indigenous tribes of the Americas
indirecto/a indirect
individualidad *f.* individuality
individualismo individualism
individuo *n.* individual
indomable indomitable
indudable certain
indulgente lenient
industria industry
industrialización *f.* industrialization
inesperado/a unexpected
inestable unstable
infancia infancy; childhood
infantil infantile; child (*adj.*); **mano** (*f.*) **de obra infantil** child labor
inferior *adv.* lower
infinitivo *gram.* infinitive
inflexible inflexible, unyielding
influencia influence
influir (y) (en) to influence, have an influence (on)
información *f.* information
informar to inform; to report
informática computer science (6)
informativo *n.* news report
ingeniería engineering
ingeniero/a engineer
ingenio wit, ingenuity
ingenioso/a ingenious (6)
Inglaterra England
inglés, inglesa *adj.* English; *m.* English (*language*); **inglés criollo** English Creole (*language*)
ingrato/a ungrateful
ingresar to join
ingreso entrance; *pl.* income; **examen** (*m.*) **de ingreso** entrance exam
inhabilidad *f.* inability
iniciar to initiate, begin
iniciativa initiative
inicio beginning, start
inimaginable unimaginable (6)
ininterrumpidamente uninterruptedly
injusticia injustice (5)
injusto/a unfair
inmediato/a immediate; **de inmediato** immediately
inmenso/a immense
inmerso/a immersed, submerged
inmigración *f.* immigration
inmigrante *m., f.* immigrant
inmigrar to immigrate
inminente imminent (6)
inmoral immoral
innovador(a) innovative (6)
inofensivo/a inoffensive
inolvidable unforgettable (3)
inquietante disturbing (5)
inquieto/a restless (2); uneasy
insalubre unhealthy (6)
insatisfacción *f.* dissatisfaction
inscribirse en to enroll in, join
insinuarse (me insinúo) to insinuate
insistir (en) to insist (on)
insoportable unbearable (2)
inspiración *f.* inspiration
inspirador(a) inspiring
inspirar to inspire
instalar to install
instintivamente instinctively
institución *f.* institution
instituto institute
instrucción *f.* instruction; teaching
instructor(a) instructor
instruir (y) to instruct
instrumento instrument
insultado/a insulted
insultar to insult
intergeneracional intergenerational
integrar to integrate; **integrarse** to become integrated
íntegro/a integral; honest
intelecto intellect
intelectual intellectual
inteligente intelligent
intención *f.* intention
intensidad *f.* intensity
intensificar (qu) to intensify
intenso/a intense
intentar to attempt, try
interacción *f.* interaction
interactuar (interactúo) to interact
intercambio *n.* exchange
interés *m.* interest; **tener** (*irreg.*) **interés** to be interested
interesante interesting
interesar to be interesting; **interesarse por** to be interested in; **(no) me interesa(n)** I'm (not) interested in (4)
interétnico/a interethnic
interferir (ie, i) to interfere
intergeneracional intergenerational
interior *n. m.* inside, interior (part); *adj.* interior, internal; inland; **paz** (*f.*) **interior** inner peace; **ropa interior** underwear
interminable interminable, endless
internacional international
Internet *m.* Internet (6)
interno/a internal
interpretación *f.* interpretation
interpretar to interpret; to decipher
interrogar (gu) to interrogate, question
interrogativo/a *gram.* interrogative
interrumpir to interrupt
intervención *f.* intervention
intervenir (*like* **venir**) to intervene

íntimo/a intimate; close-knit; close (*relationship between people*) (2)
intocable sacred, sacrosanct
intolerancia intolerance
intricado/a intricate
intrigante intriguing
intrigar (gu) to intrigue
introducción introduction
introductorio/a introductory
introvertido/a introverted
intuición *f.* intuition
inundación *f.* flood (6)
inundar to flood
inútil useless
invadir to invade
invasión *f.* invasion
invención *f.* invention
inventar to invent
inverosímil implausible, unlikely, unrealistic
inversión *f.* investment
invertir (ie, i) to invest (5)
investigación *f.* research; study; investigation
investigador(a) researcher
investigar (gu) to investigate; to (do) research
invierno winter
invitación *f.* invitation
invitado/a guest
invitar to invite
involucrado/a involved (2); implicated
involucrarse to get involved, involve oneself
ir *irreg.* to go; **ir** + *ger.* to proceed, continue to (*do something*); **ir a** + *inf.* to be going to (*do something*); **ir a la moda** to dress fashionably (1); **ir de compras** to go shopping; **ir de vacaciones** to go on vacation; **irse** to leave; to go away
iris: arco iris rainbow
ironía irony
irónico/a ironic
irremediablemente irremediably
irreversible nonreversible
isla island
itinerario itinerary

J

jacarandá *m.* jacaranda tree
jade *m.* jade
jamás never, (not) ever
Japón Japan
japonés, japonesa (*pl.* **japoneses**) Japanese
jarabe *m.* syrup
jardín *m.* garden
jardinero/a gardener
jazz *m.* jazz
jefe/a boss
jeroglífico/a *adj.* hieroglyphic
Jesucristo Jesus Christ; **lagarto de Jesucristo** Jesus lizard (*tropical lizard capable of running across the surface of water*)
jirafa giraffe
jondo/a: cante (*m.*) **jondo** *Flamenco-style singing of Andalusian gypsy origin*
jornada journey; episode; workday; **jornada radial** radio broadcast
jorobado/a hunchbacked
joven *n. m., f.* young man, young woman; *pl.* the young, young people, youth; *adj.* young
joya jewel
joyería jewelry
judería Jewish quarter (*neighborhood*)
judío/a Jewish
juego game; play; **juego de luz** play of light
juerguista *m., f.* partier
jugador(a) player (*sport, game*)
jugar (ue) (gu) to play; **jugar (ue) (gu) un papel** to play a role
juguete *m.* toy
juguetón, juguetona playful
junta directiva board of directors
juntar to join; to gather; **juntarse** to get together
junto a next to, near; **junto con** along with; **juntos/as** *pl.* together
jurado/a: tener (*irreg.*) **jurado/a** to have it in for
justicia justice
justo *adv.* just, exactly
justo/a *adj.* fair; **comercio justo** fair trade (6)
juvenil *adj.* children's, child
juventud *f.* youth (*period in life*)
juzgar (gu) to judge

K

kayac *m.* kayak; **navegar (gu) en kayac** to go kayaking
kilogramo kilogram
kilómetro kilometer

L

laberinto labyrinth
labio lip
labor *f.* labor; effort
laboralmente in terms of labor
lado side; **al lado de** next to; **de al lado** next-door; **por otro lado** on the other hand; **por un lado** on one hand
ladrillo brick
largometraje *m.* feature film
lagarto lizard; **lagarto de Jesucristo** Jesus lizard (*tropical lizard capable of running across the surface of water*)
lago lake
laguna lagoon; small lake
lamentar to regret (1)
lamparita de escritorio desk lamp
lancha *n.* launch (*small boat*)
languidez *f.* (*pl.* **languideces**) languor
lanzar (c) to throw
lápiz *m.* (*pl.* **lápices**) pencil
largo/a long; lengthy; **a larga distancia** long-distance; **a largo plazo** long-term; **a lo largo de** throughout
lascivia lasciviousness, lewdness
lástima pity, shame
lastimar(se) to injure (oneself)
lata *n.* can
latín *m.* Latin (*language*)
latino/a Latin; Latin American
Latinoamérica Latin America
latinoamericano/a *n., adj.* Latin American
lazo bond, tie
leal loyal
lealtad *f.* loyalty
lección *f.* lesson
leche *f.* milk
lechero/a milkman/milkmaid
lector(a) reader
lectura reading
leer (y) (*p.p.* **leído**) to read
legado legacy
legítimo/a legitimate
leído/a (*p.p. of* **leer**) read
lejano/a distant, remote; (from) far away
lejos *adv.* far; **de lejos** from afar
lema *m.* slogan, motto
lempira *m.* *monetary unit of Honduras*
lengua language; tongue; **lengua materna** native (mother) tongue; **no tener** (*irreg.*) **pelos en la lengua** to speak one's mind (1); **malas lenguas** gossips
lenguaje *m.* language, verbiage
lentamente slowly
lentes *m. pl.* (eye)glasses (1)
lentitud *f.* slowness
leña firewood
letra letter, character; lyrics; **de tu puño y letra** by/in your own hand
levantar to raise; to pick up; to lift; to hold upright; **levantar el ánimo** to lift the spirits (4); **levantarse** to get up; to stand up
ley *f.* law; **ley marcial** martial law
leyenda legend
liberación *f.* liberation; **Ejército Zapatista de Liberación Nacional** National Liberation Zapatist Army (*guerrilla forces in Chiapas, Mexico*)
libertador(a) liberator
libertad *f.* liberty
libra *n.* pound
librar to liberate

libre free; **al aire** (*m.*) **libre** in the open air, outdoors; **amor** (*m.*) **libre** free love; **estado libre asociado** commonwealth; **ratos** (*pl.*) **libres** free time (4); **tiempo libre** free time
librería bookstore
libro book
licencia license; **licencia de conducir** driver's license
licenciatura bachelor's degree
licor *m.* liqueur
líder *m., f.* leader (5)
liderazgo leadership
liga league; **Ligas Mayores** Major Leagues (*baseball*)
limitar to limit
límite *m.* limit; **situación** (*f.*) **límite** extreme situation
limón *m.* lemon
lindo/a pretty
línea line
lío complicated situation; mess; **meterse en líos** to get into trouble; **¡qué lío!** what a mess! (1)
liso/a straight (*hair*) (1); smooth (*hair*)
lista list
listo/a bright, clever; ready
literario/a literary
literatura literature
llamar to call; **llamarse** to be called, named
llamativo/a showy, flashy (1); catchy
llanas *pl.* plains
llave *f.* key
llegada arrival
llegar (gu) to arrive; to come; **llegar a** + *inf.* to come to (*do something*); to reach the point of (*doing something*); **llegar a mayores** to go further, become a big deal; **llegar a ser** (*v.*) to become
llenar to fill (in)
lleno/a full; filled; **de lleno** fully
llevar to take; to carry; to wear; to have; to lead; to induce; **llevar a cabo** to carry out (5); **llevarse bien/mal (con)** to get along well/poorly (with) (1)
llorar to cry
llover (ue) to rain
lluvia rain; **lluvia de ideas** brainstorm
lluvioso/a rainy; **bosque** (*m.*) **lluvioso** rain forest (6)
localizar (c) to locate, find; to place
loco/a crazy; **volver (ue) loco/a** to drive crazy; **volverse (ue) loco/a** to go crazy
locura foolish notion; insanity
lógico/a logical
lograr to achieve; **lograr** + *inf.* to succeed in (*doing something*)
logro accomplishment
lucha fight (5); struggle (5)
luchador(a) fighter
luchar to fight; to struggle
luciente shining
lucir (zc) to shine
luego then; later
lugar *m.* place; **en primer lugar** in the first place; **sin lugar a dudas** without a doubt; **tener** (*irreg.*) **lugar** to take place
lujo luxury; **permitirse el lujo** to allow oneself the luxury
luminoso/a shining; **Sendero Luminoso** Shining Path (*Peruvian guerrilla group*)
luna moon
lunar *m.* beauty mark, mole (1)
luto mourning
luz *f.* (*pl.* **luces**) light; **corte** (*m.*) **de luz** blackout; **juego de luz** play of light; **luz solar** sunlight

M

macabro/a macabre
machismo male chauvinism
madera wood
madrastra stepmother (2)
madre *f.* mother
madrépora reef-building coral
madrileño/a Madrilenian, of or pertaining to Madrid
madrugada early morning (4); dawn
madrugar (gu) to get up early (4)
madurar(se) to mature
madurez *f.* maturity
maestría Master's degree
maestro/a teacher
magia magic
mágico/a magic, magical
magnético/a magnetic
magnífico/a magnificent
maíz *m.* (*pl.* **maíces**) corn
majestuoso/a majestic
mal *adv.* badly, poorly; **caerle** (*irreg.*) **mal a alguien** to like/dislike someone (1); **llevarse mal (con)** to get along poorly (with) (1); **me cae(n) mal** I don't like (*a person/people*) (4); **pasarlo mal** to have a bad time (4)
malanga root vegetable
malcriado/a ill-mannered (2)
malentendido misunderstanding (2)
malestar *m.* malaise, indisposition
malgastar to waste (6)
malnutrición *f.* malnutrition
malo/a *adj.* bad; ill; **de mal gusto** in poor taste (4); **de mala educación** rudely; **estar** (*irreg.*) **de mal humor** to be in a bad mood (4); **mala suerte** bad luck; **malas lenguas** gossips; **malos modales** bad manners (2); **¡qué mala onda!** what a bummer! (1); **¡qué mala pata!** what bad luck! (1); **ser** (*irreg.*) **mala gente** to be a bad person / bad people (1); **tener** (*irreg.*) **mala pinta** to have a bad appearance (1)
maltrato maltreatment
mamá mom, ma, mama
mami *f.* mommy (*coll.*)
mamífero mammal
manantial *n. m., adj.* spring (*water*)
mandar to send; to command
mandato command
mando command, control
mandón, mandona bossy (2); domineering
manera way; manner; **de manera adecuada/agradable/directa/educada/eficaz/personal** adequately/pleasantly/directly/politely/effectively/personally; **¡de ninguna manera!** no way! (3); **¿de qué manera?** how?, in what way?; **de todas maneras** at any rate, anyway
maní *m.* (*pl.* **maníes**) peanut
maníaco/a manic; **depresión** (*f.*) **maníaca** manic depression
manifestación *f.* demonstration (5); display
manifestar (ie) to protest; to express, show
manipulador(a) manipulative
mano *f.* hand; **a mano** by hand; **dar** (*irreg.*) **la mano** to give a hand, help out; **echar una mano** to lend a hand; **mano de obra infantil** child labor
mantel *m.* tablecloth
mantener (*like* **tener**) to maintain, keep (2)
manual *m.* manual, workbook; *adj.* manual; **trabajo manual** manual labor
manzana apple
maoísta *adj. m., f.* Maoist
mapa *m.* map
máquina machine
mar *m.* sea; **nivel** (*m.*) **del mar** sea level
maratón *m.* (*pl.* **maratones**) marathon
maravilla marvel, wonder; **lo pasé de maravilla** I had a wonderful time (4)
maravilloso/a marvelous
marcado/a marked
marcha social scene; **poner** (*irreg.*) **en marcha** to start up, set in motion; **tener** (*irreg.*) **mucha marcha** to have a lively social scene (4)
marcharse to leave
marcial martial; **ley** (*f.*) **marcial** martial law
maremoto tidal wave, tsunami (6)
margen *m.* margin
marginar to marginalize, exclude
marido husband
marino/a marine, pertaining to the sea
mariposa butterfly; **mariposa monarca** monarch butterfly
marítimo/a maritime
mártir *m., f.* martyr

marxista *adj. m., f.* Marxist
más more; **cada vez más** more and more; **más allá de** beyond; **nadie más** nobody else; **nunca más** never again; **ya no puedo soportarlo/la más** I can't stand it/him/her anymore (2)
masaje *m.* massage
masas *pl.* masses, populace
máscara mask
mascota pet
masculino/a masculine
masivo/a massive
matar to kill
mate *m. glass or mug made to hold* mate; **yerba mate** *herbal tea typical of Argentina*
matemáticas *pl.* mathematics
matemático/a mathematician
materia subject (*school*)
maternidad *f.* maternity
materno/a maternal; **lengua materna** native (mother) tongue
matrimonio marriage; married couple; **contraer** (*like* **traer**) **matrimonio** to get married
mausoleo mausoleum
máximo/a maximum, greatest
maya *n., adj. m., f.* Mayan
mayor older; oldest; greater; greatest; elderly; **hermano/a mayor** older/oldest brother/sister; **llegar (gu) a mayores** to go further, become a big deal
mayoría majority
mayormente primarily
mecánico/a mechanic
mediado/a: a mediados de in the middle of
medianamente quite, fairly
medianoche *f.* midnight
mediante by means of
medicamento medicine
medicina medicine
médico/a *n.* physician, doctor; *adj.* medical; **seguro médico** health insurance
medieval *m., f.* medieval
medio *n.* middle; means; medium; **en medio de** in the middle of; **medio ambiente** environment; **por medio de** by means of
medio/a *adj.* middle; half; **clase** (*f.*) **media** middle-class; **Edad** (*f.*) **Media** Middle Ages; **media naranja** soulmate (3); **medio hermano, media hermana** half brother, half sister (2); **Oriente** (*m.*) **Medio** Middle East
mediocridad *f.* mediocrity
mediodía *m.* noon
meditación *f.* meditation
Mediterráneo Mediterranean
mediterráneo/a *adj.* Mediterranean
megaciudad *f.* mega-city
mejor better; best; **a lo mejor** perhaps
mejoramiento improvement
mejorar to improve, make better (4)
melodía melody
melodramático/a melodramatic
melón *m.* melon; cantaloupe
memoria memory
mencionar to mention
menor *n. m., f.* child; minor; *adj.* younger; youngest; less; lesser; least; **arte** (*m.*) **menor** minor art
menos less; least; **a menos que** + *subj.* unless . . . (6); **al menos** at least; **echar de menos** to miss (*someone/something*); **menos de** + *number* less than (*number*); **menos... que** less . . . than; **por lo menos** at least
mensaje *m.* message
mensual monthly
mente *f.* mind
mentir (ie, i) to lie
menudo: (muy) a menudo (very) often, frequently
mercadear to trade, deal
mercado market
mercadotecnia marketing
merced *f.* mercy
mercenario/a mercenary
merecer (zc) to deserve (3)
merengue *m. popular dance originating in the Dominican Republic*
mero/a mere
mes (*m.*) month
mesa table
mesero/a waiter, waitress
mestizo/a of mixed (indigenous and European) parentage
meta goal
metabolismo metabolism
metáfora metaphor
metal *m.* metal
meter to put; to insert; **meter la pata** to put one's foot in one's mouth (1); **meterse** to get involved; **meterse con alguien** to try something with someone; **meterse en líos** to get into trouble (3)
meticuloso/a meticulous
método method
metro meter; subway
metropolitano/a metropolitan
mexicano/a *n., adj.* Mexican
mexicanoamericano/a *n., adj.* Mexican-American
mezcla mixture
mezclar to mix
mezquita mosque
micrófono microphone
miedo fear; **dar** (*irreg.*) **miedo** to frighten; **tener** (*irreg.*) **miedo** to be afraid
miel (*f.*)**: luna de miel** honeymoon
miembro member
mientras while; whereas; **mientras tanto** meanwhile; **mientras que** while, as long as
mil *m.* (one) thousand; **mil disculpas/perdones** a thousand pardons (2)
milagroso/a miraculous
militante militant
militar *m.* soldier; *adj.* military
milla mile
millón *m.* (one) million
millonario/a millionaire
mimado/a spoiled (*child*) (2)
mimar to spoil
mina mine
mineral *m.* mineral
minero/a miner
minimalista minimalist (6)
mínimo *n.* minimum; **como mínimo** as a minimum
mínimo/a *adj.* minimal, small
ministerio secretariat, ministry
ministro/a cabinet member; secretary
minuto minute
mirada *n.* look, gaze; expression (*of eyes*)
mirar to look; to look at; to watch
miseria misery; pittance
misión *f.* mission
misiva missive
mismo/a same; very; himself; yourself; **ahora mismo** right now; **al mismo tiempo** at the same time (3); **hoy mismo** this very day; **lo mismo** the same thing; **me da(n) lo mismo** I don't care (about) (4)
misquito Misquito (*indigenous language of Nicaragua*)
misterioso/a mysterious
misticismo mysticism
mitad *f.* half
mito myth
mitológico/a mythological
moda style; **de moda** fashionable; **estar** (*irreg.*) **de moda** to be in style (1); **ir** (*irreg.*) **a la moda** to dress fashionably (1); **estar** (*irreg.*) **pasado/a de moda** to be out of style (1)
modales *m., pl.* behavior, mannerisms; manners; **buenos/malos modales** good/bad manners (2)
modelo model
módem *m.* modem
moderador(a) moderator
modernidad *f.* modernity
modernismo Modernism
modernización *f.* modernization
moderno/a modern
modificar (qu) to modify
modo mode, way; **de modo** + *adj.* in a . . . way
mofarse de to mock, make fun of
mojado/a wet

mola *handicraft layered with fabrics of several colors*
molestar to bother, annoy; **me molesta(n)** I'm bothered by (4); **molestarse** to get annoyed
momento moment
momia mummy
momificado/a mummified
momificar (qu) to mummify
monarca: mariposa monarca monarch butterfly
monarquía monarchy
moneda currency
monetario/a monetary
mono monkey
monólogo monologue
monótonamente monotonously
montaña mountain
montañismo mountain climbing
montar: montar a caballo to ride/go horseback riding; **montar broncas** to cause trouble; **montar en bicicleta** to ride a bicycle; **montarse en** to board/ride
monte *m.* mount
montevideano/a *n., adj.* of or pertaining to Montevideo, Uruguay
montón *m.* pile
monumento monument
moreno/a dark-skinned; brunet(te)
morir (ue, u) (*p.p.* **muerto**) to die
moro/a Moor
morro hill
mosaico mosaic
mostrar (ue) to show
motivado/a motivated
motivo motive, motivation
moto(cicleta) *f.* motorcycle
motociclista *m., f.* motorcyclist
motor *m.* motor
mover (ue) to move
movible flexible, moveable
movida nightlife
movimiento movement
muchacho/a boy, girl
muchedumbre *f.* crowd
mucho/a much, a lot of; *pl.* many, a lot of; **lo siento mucho** I'm very sorry (2); **muchas veces** often; **tener** (*irreg.*) **mucha cara** to have a lot of nerve (1); **para muchos** for many (people); **tener** (*irreg.*) **mucha marcha** to have a lively social scene (4)
mudanza *n.* move (*residence*)
mudarse to move (*residence*) (2)
mudéjar relating to the Muslim Arab people living in Christian Spain in the late Middle Ages
muebles *m. pl.* furniture
muerte *f.* death
muerto/a (*p.p. of* **morir**) *n.* dead, deceased person; *pl.* the dead; *adj.* dead
mujer *f.* woman; **hermandad** (*f.*) **de mujeres** sisterhood; sorority; **mujer bombero** female firefighter; **mujer de negocios** businesswoman; **mujer policía** female police officer; **mujer político** female politician
mujeriego womanizer
mula mule; **trabajar como una mula** to work like a dog (4)
mulato/a mulatto
multa *n.* fine, penalty
multigeneracional multigenerational
multinacional multinational
múltiple *adj.* multiple
mundial *adj.* world, pertaining to the world; global; **a nivel mundial** globally, world-wide
mundo world
muñeco/a doll; mannequin
mural *m.* mural
muralista *m., f.* muralist
muralla (city) wall
museo museum
música music
musical: grupo musical band, musical group
músico/a musician
musulmán, musulmana (*pl.* **musulmanes**) *adj., n.* Muslim
mutuo/a mutual
muy very

N

nácar *m.* mother-of-pearl
nacer (zc) to be born; to originate
nacimiento birth
nación *f.* nation
nacional national; **himno nacional** national anthem
nacionalidad *f.* nationality
nacionalista *adj. m., f.* nationalistic
nada *pron.* nothing, (not) anything; *adv.* not at all; **en/para nada** (not) at all; **ni nada** or anything (*coll.*); **no valer** (*irreg.*) **nada** to be worthless; **pero eso no fue nada** but that was nothing (3)
nadie nobody, (not) anybody; **nadie más** nobody else
napoleónico/a Napoleonic
naranja orange; **media naranja** soulmate (3)
naranjo orange tree
narcotráfico drug traffic (5); drug trafficking (5)
nariz *f.* (*pl.* **narices**) nose; **harto/a hasta las narices** to be fed up to here (4); **me importa tres narices** I couldn't care less (2)
narración *f.* narration
narrador(a) narrator
narrar to narrate; to tell
narrativo/a narrative
natal native; of birth
nativo/a *adj.* native
nativoamericano/a *adj.* Native American
natural natural; **desastre** (*m.*) **natural** natural disaster (6); **recurso natural** natural resource; **remedio natural** natural remedy
naturaleza nature
nave *f.* (space)ship
navegable navigable
navegar to browse (6)
necesario/a necessary
necesidad *f.* necessity
necesitar to need
negar(se) (ie) (gu) to deny; to refuse
negativo/a negative
negocio *n.* business; *pl.* business (*in general*); **de negocios** *adj.* business; **hombre** (*m.*) **de negocios** businessman; **mujer** (*f.*) **de negocios** businesswoman
negrita boldface
neoyorquino/a New Yorker
nervioso/a nervous
netamente purely
neutro/a neutral
nevado/a snowy, snow-capped
ni neither, (not) either; nor; (not) even; **¡ni hablar!** no way! (2); **ni nada** or anything (*coll.*); **ni… ni** neither . . . nor; **¡ni pensarlo!** don't even think about it!; **¡ni se te ocurra!** don't even think about it! (2); **¡ni soñarlo!** in your dreams! (2); **ni un duro** not even a cent
nicaragüense *n., adj. m., f.* Nicaraguan
nieto/a grandson, granddaughter; *pl.* grandchildren
ningún, ninguno/a *adj.* no; (not) any; *pron.* none, not one; **¡de ninguna manera!** no way! (3)
niñero/a babysitter
niño/a baby; little boy, little girl; **de niño/a** as a child
nivel *m.* level; **a nivel mundial** globally; **nivel del mar** sea level
Nobel: Premio Nobel Nobel Prize
nobiliario/a related to nobility
nobleza nobility
noche *f.* night; **de la noche** P.M.; **esta noche** tonight; **por la noche** at night
nocturnidad *f.* nocturnal character
nocturno/a *adj.* night, nocturnal; **vida nocturna** nightlife
nombrar to name; to identify (*by name*)
nombre *m.* name
noreste *adj.* northeastern
normalmente normally
norte *m.* north; *adj.* north, northern

norteamericano/a *n., adj.* North American, of or pertaining to Canada and the United States
nostálgico/a nostalgic (3); homesick (3)
nota note; grade; **sacar (qu) buenas notas** to get good grades
notar to notice; **notarse** to be noticeable, apparent
noticia news item; *pl.* news
notorio/a notorious
novedad *f.* new development (6)
novela novel
novelista *m., f.* novelist
noviazgo courtship (3)
novio/a boyfriend, girlfriend; bride, bridegroom
nube *f.* cloud
nuevamente (once) again
nuevo/a new; **de nuevo** again; **nuevo sol** *m. monetary unit of Peru*
numerado/a numbered
número number
numeroso/a numerous
nunca never, (not) ever; **más** + *adj.* + **que nunca** more . . . than ever; **nunca más** never again
nutrición *f.* nutrition
nutritivo/a nutritious
ñoñería nonsense

O

o or; **o... o** either . . . or
oaxaqueño/a of or pertaining to the state of Oaxaca, Mexico
obedecer (zc) to obey (2)
obediente obedient
objetivo objective
objeto object; **objeto volador no identificado** UFO
obligación *f.* obligation
obligar (gu) to obligate, require
obra work; **mano** (*f.*) **de obra infantil** child labor; **obra de arte** work of art; **obra de teatro** play
obrero/a laborer, worker
obsceno/a obscene
observación *f.* observation
observador(a) observative
observar to observe
observatorio observatory
obsesión *f.* obsession
obesesionado/a obsessed
obsesivo/a obsessive
obsoleto/a obsolete
obstante: no obstante nonetheless
obtener (*like* **tener**) to obtain
obvio/a obvious
ocasión *f.* occasion
occidental western
occidente *m.* west
océano ocean
ocio leisure time
ocultismo occultism
oculto/a hidden; secret
ocupar to occupy
ocurrir to happen, occur, take place; **ocurrirse** to occur to; **¡ni se te ocurra!** don't even think about it! (2)
odiar to hate (3)
oeste *m.* West; *adj.* western
ofender to offend
ofendido/a offended
ofensivo/a offensive
oferta *n.* offer
oficial official
oficina office
oficio occupation, profession
ofrecer (zc) to offer
ofrenda offering
oído inner ear
oír *irreg.* (*p.p.* **oído**) to hear; **¡oye!** hey!
ojalá (que) + *present subj./past subj.* let's hope that . . . / I wish that . . .
ojo eye; **¡ojo!** be careful!
olivo olive tree
olor *m.* odor; scent
oloroso/a fragrant
olvidar to forget; **olvidarse de** to forget about; **se me olvidó por completo** I totally forgot (2)
ombligo navel (1)
ómnibus *m.* bus
omnipresencia omnipresence
onda: ponerse (*irreg.*) **de onda** to get with it; **¡qué mala onda!** what a bummer!
ondulado/a wavy, curved
opción *f.* option
ópera opera
operación *f.* operation
opinar to think, have an opinion
opinión *f.* opinion; **en mi opinión...** in my opinion . . . (3)
oponerse (a) (*like* **poner**) to oppose
oportunidad *f.* opportunity
oportunista *adj. m., f.* opportunistic (5)
oportuno/a suitable, appropriate
opositor(a) opponent
opresivo/a oppressive
oprimido/a oppressed
optar por to opt for
optimismo optimism
optimista *adj. m., f.* optimistic (5)
opuesto/a (*p.p. of* **oponer**) opposite
oración *f.* sentence
órbita orbit
orca killer whale
orden *m.* order (*alphabetical, chronological, etc.*); **en orden** in order
ordenador *m.* computer
ordenar to order; to give an order
oreja ear (1)
orfanato orphanage
orgánico/a organic
organización *f.* organization
organizar (c) to organize
orgullo pride
orgulloso/a proud (2); **estoy orgulloso/a de que...** I'm proud that . . . (2)
oriental *adj.* eastern
orientar to orient
Oriente (*m.*) **Medio** Middle East
origen *m.* origin
originalidad *f.* originality
originar(se) to originate; to give rise to
orilla shore, bank
oro gold; **Edad** (*f.*) **de Oro** Golden Age
orquesta orquestra
orquídea orchid
oscuridad *f.* darkness
oscuro/a dark
otoño autumn
otorgar to award
otro/a *pron., adj.* other; another; *pl.* other people; **el uno al otro** to one another; **el uno en el otro** in one another; **otra vez** again; **por otra parte / otro lado** on the other hand
OVNI *m.* (*abbrev. for* **objeto volador no identificado**) UFO
oxígeno oxygen
¡oye! (*from* **oír**) hey!
ozono: capa de ozono ozone layer (6)

P

paciencia patience; **tener** (*irreg.*) **paciencia** to be patient
paciente *n. m., f.* patient
pacificar (qu) to pacify
pacífico/a peaceful (6)
pacifismo pacifism
pacifista *m., f.* pacifist
pacto pact
padecer (zc) (de) to suffer (from)
padrastro stepfather (2)
padre *m.* father; senior; *pl.* parents; **¡qué padre!** (how) awesome! (1)
¡paf! bang! (3)
pagar (gu) to pay, pay for
página page; **página Web** Web page (6)
pago pay, payment
país *m.* country, nation; **país en vías de desarrollo** developing country; **país desarrollado** developed country; **país primermundista** first-world country
paisaje *m.* landscape
paja straw; **colchón** (*m.*) **de paja** straw mattress
pájaro bird
palabra word
palacio palace
paleta palette

palma palm; palm tree/leaf
palmera palm tree
palo stick; **de tal palo, tal astilla** like father, like son
paloma pigeon, dove
pampas *pl.* plains
pan *m.* bread
Panamá *m.* Panama
panameño/a Panamanian
pandilla gang
panel (*m.*) **solar** solar panel
pánico panic
panorama *m.* panorama
pantalla screen
pantalones *m. pl.* pants
pantera panther; **Pantera Rosa** Pink Panther
panti *m. s.* stocking, panty hose, tights
papá *m.* papa, daddy
papel *m.* paper; role; **jugar (ue) (gu) un papel** to play a role; **papel protagónico** lead role
paquete *m.* package
par *m.* pair; couple; **un par de** a couple of
para for; to; in order to; by (*time, date*); **no es para tanto** it's not such a big deal (2); **para nada** (not) at all; **para que** + *subj.* so that . . . ; **para siempre** forever
parada parade (*P.R.*)
paraguas *m. s.* umbrella
paraguayo/a Paraguayan
paralelo/a parallel
paralizar (c) to paralyze
paranoico/a paranoid
parapente *m.* paragliding
parar to stop
parecer (zc) to seem, appear (1); to seem like; **parecerse a** to look like (1); **me parece fascinante que...** it seems fascinating to me that . . . ; **¿qué te/le/les parece?** what do you think (about)?
parecido/a similar
pared *f.* wall
paredón *m.* (*pl.* **paredones**) rock wall
pareja pair; couple; partner
paréntesis *m. inv.* parenthesis; parentheses; **entre paréntesis** in parentheses
pariente *n. m., f.* relative
parpadear to blink
parque *m.* park
parqueo parking (lot)
párrafo paragraph
parrillada grilled meat
parte *f.* part; portion **de todas partes** from everywhere; **en alguna parte** somewhere; **en otras partes** elsewhere; **formar parte de** to be part of; **gran parte de** much of; **la mayor parte de** the better part of; **por otra parte** on the other hand; **por parte de** on behalf of; **por todas partes** everywhere; **tercera parte** (one) third
participación *f.* participation
participante *m., f.* participant
participar to participate
participativo/a participative
participio *gram.* participle
particular particular; special
partida departure; **punto de partida** point of departure
partido game, match; political party, faction
partir: a partir de starting from; on the basis of
partitura musical score; (*fig.*) guidelines
pasado *n.* past; *gram.* past tense
pasado/a *adj.* past; last; **estar** (*irreg.*) **pasado/a de moda** to be out of style (1); **la semana pasada** last week
pasajero/a fleeting
pasar to pass, go by; to happen; to spend (*time*); **¿cómo lo pasó/pasaste/pasaron?** how was it? / did you have a good time? (4); **lo pasé muy bien / de maravilla / fatal** I had a great time/ a blast / a terrible time (4); **pasar a ser** to become; **pasar por** to go through; to pass over, to stop by; **pasar por encima de** to go over one's head; **pasar tiempo** to spend time; **pasarlo bien/mal** to have a good/bad time (4); **pasarlo de maravilla/fatal** to have a wonderful/terrible time; **pasarse la vida** to spend one's life; **¡qué lo pase/pases/pasen bien!** have a good time! (4); **¿qué pasa?** what's happening?; what's going on?
pasatiempo pastime
Pascua Easter
pasear to go for a walk
paseo stroll
pasión *f.* passion
pasionaria passion flower
paso step; **a unos pasos de distancia** a few steps away
pastelería confectionary shop
pastilla pill
pata foot (*of an animal or bird*); **meter la pata** to put one's foot in one's mouth; **qué mala pata!** what bad luck! (1)
paternidad *f.* paternity
paterno/a paternal
patilla sideburn (1)
patovica *m., f.* bouncer
patria homeland
patrimonio patrimony
patriótico/a patriotic
patrocinar to sponsor
patrón, patrona: santo patrón, santa patrona patron saint
pauta rule
payaso/a clown
paz *f.* (*pl.* **paces**) peace (5); **acuerdo de paz** peace agreement; **Cuerpo de Paz** Peace Corps; **dejar en paz** to leave alone; **paz interior** inner peace; **sentirse (ie, i) en paz** to feel at peace
peca freckle (1)
pecho chest
pedazo piece
pedir (i, i) to ask (for), request; **pedir perdón** to beg pardon; to ask forgiveness; **pedir permiso** to ask for permission
pegadizo/a catchy
pegar (gu) to hit, strike
peinado hairdo
pelea quarrel
pelear(se) to fight (2); to quarrel
película movie
peligro danger
peligroso/a dangerous (6)
pelirrojo/a *n.* redhead; *adj.* red-headed (1)
pelo hair (1); **corte** (*m.*) **de pelo** haircut, hairstyle; **no tener** (*irreg.*) **pelos en la lengua** to speak one's mind (1); **tomarle el pelo a alguien** to pull someone's leg (4)
pelota ball
peluca wig (1)
pena pity; shame; **¡qué pena!** what a shame!; **valer** (*irreg.*) **la pena** to be worth it (5)
pendiente *m.* earring (1)
pensamiento thought
pensar (ie) to think; to consider; **ni lo pienses** don't even think about it (2); **¡ni pensarlo!** don't even think about it!; **pensar de** to think of (*opinion*); **pensar en** to think about
peor worse; worst; **ahora viene lo peor** now comes the worst part (3)
pepino: me importa un pepino I couldn't care less (2)
pequeño/a little, small; young; brief; **de pequeño/a** as a child; **desde pequeño/a** from when he (she, they, *etc.*) was/were small
percepción *f.* perception
percibir to perceive; to sense
perder (ie) to lose; to miss; **perder el tiempo** to waste time; **perderse** to get lost
pérdida loss
perdido/a lost (3)
perdón *m.* pardon; **mil perdones** a thousand pardons (2); **pedir (i, i) perdón** to beg pardon; to ask forgiveness; **perdón, me equivoqué** sorry, I made a mistake (2)
perdonar to forgive
peregrino/a pilgrim

perezoso *n.* sloth (*animal*)
perfección *f.* perfection
perfeccionista *n., adj. m., f.* perfectionist
perfecto/a perfect
perfil *m.* profile
perfumar to perfume, scent
perfume *m.* perfume
periférico/a peripheral
periódico *n.* newspaper
periódico/a *adj* periodic
periodismo journalism
periodista *m., f.* journalist, reporter
periodístico/a journalistic
período period (*time*)
peripecias *pl.* adventures
perla pearl
permanecer (zc) to remain
permanentemente permanently
permiso permission; **pedir (i, i) permiso** to ask permission
permitir to permit, allow; **permitirse el lujo** to allow oneself the luxury
pero but; **pero, ¿qué dices?** but, what do you mean/are you saying? (3)
perpetuar to perpetuate
perseguir (*like* **seguir**) to follow, pursue
personaje *m.* character
personal *m.* personnel
personalidad *f.* personality
perspectiva perspective
persuadir to persuade
pertenecer (zc) to belong; to remain
perturbar to bother
peruano/a Peruvian
pesado/a tedious, annoying (1)
pésame *m. s.* condolences
pesar to weigh; to hinder; **a pesar de** in spite of
pescado fish; fishing
pescador(a) fisherman, fisherwoman
pescar (qu) to fish
pesimista *m., f.* pessimist (5)
pésimo/a awful, terrible (2)
peso weight; *monetary unit of several Latin American countries*
petrificado/a petrified
petróleo oil
pez *m.* (*pl.* **peces**) fish
picante hot (*spicy*)
picaresca guile, wits
pico (mountain) peak
pictórico/a pictorial
pie *m.* foot; base; **a pie** on foot; **a pie de** at the foot, bottom of; **de pie** standing
piedra stone
pierna leg
pieza piece
pila battery
pillar to catch
piloto/a pilot
pingüino penguin
pinta: tener (*irreg.*) **buena/mala pinta** to have a good/bad appearance (1)
pintar to paint
pintor(a) painter, artist
pintoresco/a picturesque
pintura *n.* painting
piña pineapple
pirámide *f.* pyramid
pirata *m., f.* pirate
piropear to compliment (*romantically*) (3)
piropo romantic compliment (3); flirtatious remark; **decir** (*irreg.*)**/echar un piropo** to make a flirtatious remark
piso floor; ground; story (*of a building*)
pista clue; hint, tip
pizarra chalkboard
placer *m.* pleasure
plan *m.* plan; program
planear to plan
planeta *m.* planet
planificar (qu) to plan
planta plant
plantado/a: dejar plantado/a to stand (*someone*) up
plascentero/a pleasant
plástico/a *adj.* plastic; **artes** (*f.*) **plásticas** three-dimensional art
plata silver
plátano plantain
plato plate; dish, entrée
playa beach
plaza plaza, town square
plazo: a largo plazo long-term
plegaria prayer
pluscuamperfecto *gram.* pluperfect tense
población *f.* population
poblado/a populated
pobre *n. m., f.* poor person; *pl.* the poor; *adj.* poor; **¡pobrecito/a!** poor thing! (3)
pobreza poverty (5)
poción *f.* potion
poco/a *adj.* little, few
poco *n.* little bit; small amount; **hace poco** a short time ago; **poco a poco** little by little; **unos pocos** a few; *adv.* little, poorly
poder *m.* power; authority
poder *v. irreg.* to be able, can; **no lo puedo creer** I can't believe it (2); **poder** + *inf.* to be able to (*do something*); **puede ser** it could be (6); **ya no puedo soportarlo/la más** I can't stand it/him/her anymore (2)
poderoso/a powerful
poema *m.* poem
poemario book of poems
poesía poetry
poeta *m., f.* poet
poético/a poetic
polémica *n.* controversy
polémico/a *adj.* controversial (5)
polerón (canguro) *m.* (*pl.* **polerones**) (pocketed) hoodie, hooded sweatshirt
policía *m.* police officer; *f.* the police; **mujer** (*f.*) **policía** female police officer
policíaco/a *adj.* police; detective; of or pertaining to police or detectives
policial *adj.* police; detective; of or pertaining to police or detectives
política *s.* politics (5); policy (5)
político *n.* politician; **mujer** (*f.*) **político** female politician
político/a *adj.* political; **ciencias políticas** *pl.* political science
pollada large party
pollo chicken
polo pole
polvo dust
ponencia presentation, report
poner *irreg.* (*p.p.* **puesto**) to put, place; to put on; to give (*a name, title, etc.*); to turn on; **poner a prueba** to put to the test; **poner en marcha** to set in motion; **poner fin** to end; **ponerse** + *adj.* to become; **ponerse** to put on (*clothing*); to wear; to get, become (3); **ponerse** + *inf.* to begin to (*do something*); **ponerse al día** to catch up (4); **ponerse de acuerdo** to come to an agreement; **ponerse de onda** to get with it; **ponerse rojo/a** to blush
pontificio/a pontifical, papal
popularidad *f.* popularity
por for; through; by; because of; around; about; out of; in order to; **de por medio** in between; **estar** (*irreg.*) **por** + *inf.* to be about to (*do something*); **hablar por los codos** to talk a lot; **hablar por teléfono** to talk on the telephone; **por** + *inf.* because of (*doing something*); **por ciento** percent; **por cierto** indeed; **por completo** completely; **por correo electrónico** by e-mail; **por desgracia** unfortunately; **por ejemplo** for example; **por encima de** above; **por eso** therefore; that's why; **por fin** finally; **por hora** per hour; **por la noche** at night; **por la tarde** in the afternoon; **por lo general** in general; **por lo menos** at least; **por lo tanto** therefore; **por medio de** by means of; **por otra parte / otro lado** on the other hand; **por parte de** on behalf of; **por primera vez** for the first time; **¿por qué?** why?; **por si acaso** just in case; **por suerte** luckily; **por supuesto** of course; **por todas partes** everywhere; **por última vez** for the last time; **por último** finally; **se me olvidó por completo** I totally forgot
porche *m.* porch
portador(a) carrier, bearer

portarse to behave (2)
porvenir *m.* future
posarse to land
poseer (y) (*p.p.* **poseído**) to have, possess
posesión *f.* possession
posgrado/a *n., adj.* graduate
posibilidad *f.* possibility
posible possible
posindustrial postindustrial
positivo/a positive
posponer (*like* **poner**) to postpone (4)
postal: tarjeta postal postcard
postre *m.* dessert
postularse to run for office (5)
potable: agua (*f., but* **el agua**) **potable** potable/drinking water
pozo *n.* well
práctica *n.* practice
practicar (qu) to practice
práctico/a practical
precario/a precarious
precedente *m.* precedent
precolombino/a pre-Columbian
precoz (*pl.* **precoces**) precocious
predecir (*like* **decir**) to predict (6)
predicción *f.* prediction
predilecto/a favorite
preferencia preference
preferido/a favorite
preferir (ie, i) to prefer
pregunta question; **hacer** (*irreg.*) **una pregunta** to ask a question
preguntar to ask (a question); **preguntarse** to wonder, ask oneself (6)
prehispánico/a pre-Hispanic
prejuicio prejudice (5)
preliminar preliminary
premio prize, award; **Premio Nobel** Nobel Prize
premisa premise
prenda item of clothing
prensa *n.* press; **comunicado de prensa** press release
preocupación *f.* worry
preocupante worrisome (1)
preocupar to worry; **me preocupa(n)** I'm worried about (4); **preocuparse (por)** to worry (about)
preparación *f.* preparation
preparar to prepare; **prepararse** to get ready
preparativo preparation
preponderancia preponderance
presa dam
presencia presence
presenciar to witness, see, watch
presentación *f.* presentation
presentar to present; to introduce; **presentarse** to appear; to introduce oneself
presente *adj.* present
preservar to preserve
presidencia presidency
presidencial presidential
presidente/a president
presión *f.* pressure
presionar to pressure
prestar to lend; **prestar atención a** to pay attention to
prestigio prestige
prestigioso/a prestigious
presumido/a conceited (1)
presunto/a supposed
pretender to strive for; to try
pretensión *f.* aim, hope
pretérito *gram.* preterite tense
prevenir (*like* **venir**) to prevent
primario/a: escuela primaria elementary school
primavera spring
primer, primero/a first; **a primera vista** at first sight (1); **en primer lugar** in the first place; **primera fila** front row
primermundista: país (*m.*) **primermundista** first-world country
primo/a cousin
princesa princess
principal main, principal; notable; **punto principal** main point
príncipe *m.* prince
principio beginning; **a principios de** at the beginning of; **al principio** at/in the beginning
prioridad *f.* priority
privado/a private
privatizar (c) to privatize
privilegiado/a privileged
probabilidad *f.* probability
probar (ue) to prove; to try, taste
problema *m.* problem
problemático/a problematic
procedente de (coming) from
procesión *f.* procession
proceso process
proclamar(se) to proclaim, announce
procurar(se) to get, obtain
producción *f.* production; output
producir (zc) (j) to produce
producto product
productor(a) *adj.* producing; *n.* producer
profesión *f.* profession
profesional professional
profesor(a) professor
profundo/a profound; deep
progenitor *m.* progenitor
programa *m.* program
programado/a planned
progresista *m., f.* progressive
progreso progress
prohibido/a prohibited
prohibir to forbid (6)
prolífico/a prolific
prólogo prologue
promedio *n.* average
promesa *n.* promise
prometedor(a) *adj.* promising
prometer to promise
prominente prominent
promoción *f.* promotion
promocionar to promote
promotor(a) promoter
promover (ue) to promote (5)
pronombre *m.* pronoun
pronto soon; **de pronto** suddenly; **tan pronto como** as soon as (6)
propiedad *f.* property
propio/a (one's) own
proponer (*like* **poner**) to propose
proporcionar to give
propósito objective
propuesta proposal
prosa prose
prosperidad *f.* prosperity
protagónico/a: papel (*m.*) **protagónico** main role
protagonista *m., f.* protagonist
protagonizar (c) to play a leading role in; to star in
protección *f.* protection (2)
protector(a) protective (2)
proteger (j) to protect (6)
protegido/a protected
protesta *n.* protest
protestar to protest
provechoso/a helpful, beneficial (6)
proveer (y) (*p.p.* **proveído**) to provide (6)
provincia province
provocador(a) provocative
provocar (qu) to provoke
próximo/a next; impending
proyección *f.* projection; transmission
proyecto project
prudente prudent
prueba: poner (*irreg.*) **a prueba** to put to the test
pseudónimo pseudonym
psicológico/a psychological
psicólogo/a psychologist
psiquiátrico/a psychiatric
publicación *f.* publication
publicar (qu) to publish
publicidad *f.* publicity
público *n.* audience; public; people
público/a *adj.* public
pudrirse to become rotten, decay
pueblo town, village; people; public
puente *m.* bridge
puerco pork
puerta door
puerto port
puertorriqueñidad *f.* quality of being Puerto Rican
puertorriqueño/a *n., adj.* Puerto Rican
puesta del sol sunset

puesto *n.* position, job
puesto/a (*p.p. of* **poner**) put on; placed; **puesto que** since
pulmón *m.* lung; **a todo pulmón** at the top of one's lungs
pulpo octopus
punta *n.* point
punto point; **al punto de** about to; to the point of; **desde mi punto de vista** from my point of view (3); **¿hasta qué punto?** to what point?; **punto de partida** point of departure; **punto de vista** point of view; **punto principal** main point; **punto y aparte** (begin a) new paragraph
puntual punctual
puñado handful
puño fist; **de tu puño y letra** by/in your own hand
puro/a pure

Q

que that; which; what; who; **el hecho de que** + *subj.* the fact that . . . (5); **¡que lo pase/pases/pasen bien!** have a good time! (4); **¡que se divierta / te diviertas / se diviertan!** have a good time! (4)
qué which; what; who; **¿qué?** which?; what?; who?; **¿de qué manera?** how?, in what way?; **¿hasta qué punto?** to what point?; **pero, ¿qué dices? but, what** do you mean / are you saying? (3); **¿por qué?** why?; **¡qué barbaridad!** how awful! (1); **¡qué bien!** (how) great! (2); **¡qué buena idea!** what a great idea!; **qué bueno que...** how great that . . . (2); **¡qué cara tiene!** what nerve he/she has! (2); **¡qué chévere/guay/padre!** (how) awesome! (1); **¡qué chistoso!** how funny! (4); **¡qué horror!** how awful! (2); **¡qué lío!** what a mess! (1); **¡qué mala onda!** what a bummer! (1); **¡qué mala pata!** what bad luck! (1); **¿qué pasa?** what's happening?, what's going on?; **¡qué pena!** what a shame!; **¡qué suerte!** what (good) luck! (1); **¿qué tal... ?** how was . . . ?; **¿qué te/le/les parece?** what do you think (about)?; **¡qué vergüenza!** how embarrassing! (1)
quechua *m.* Quechua (*language spoken by indigenous peoples of Bolivia, Ecuador, and Peru*)
quedar to be left; to remain; to be located; to be; **no quedarle otro remedio** to have no alternative; **quedar alucinado** to be amazed; **quedar cerca** to be close, near to; **quedar en** + *inf.* to agree on (*doing something*); **quedarse** to stay
quehacer *m.* chore, task
quejarse (de) to complain (about) (2)
quejón, quejona *n.* complainer, whiner; *adj.* complaining (2), whining
quemado/a burned out (4)
querer *irreg.* to love (3); to want; **querer decir** to mean; **te quiero rendido** I love you devotedly
querido/a dear, beloved
queso cheese
quetzal *m. monetary unit of Guatemala*
quiché of or pertaining to the Quiché group of the indigenous Maya of Mexico and Central America
quicio doorjamb; **sacar (qu) de quicio** to drive crazy (*fig.*)
quien who; whom
quién who; whom; **¿quién?** who? whom?
química chemistry
quintilla cinquain (*five-line stanza*)
quitar to take away; to remove; **quitarse** to take off
quizá(s) perhaps

R

rabioso/a furious (3)
racialmente racially
ración *f.* ration
racionalizar (c) to rationalize
racismo racism
radiante radiant
radio *m.* radio (*apparatus*); *f.* radio (*programming*)
raíz *f.* (*pl.* **raíces**) root (2)
rama branch
ramalazo lash
ramo bouquet
rana frog
rancho ranch
rápido *adv.* quickly
rápido/a rapid, quick
raro/a strange (1); odd; unusual
rascacielos *m. s.* skyscraper
rasgo trait, characteristic (1)
rato (short) time, period, while; **ratos libres** (*pl.*) free time (4)
raza race (*ethnic*); **raza humana** human race
razón *f.* reason; **con razón** with good reason; of course!; **por esta razón** for this reason; **sí, tienes razón** yes, you are right (3); **tienes razón** you are right (2); **tienes toda la razón** you're completely right (3)
razonable reasonable
reacción *f.* reaction
reaccionar to react
real royal; real
realidad *f.* reality
realismo realism
realista *n. m., f.* **realist;** *adj. m., f.* realistic
realizar (c) to accomplish; fulfill (a goal) (4); to achieve; to attain; to carry out; to produce; **realizarse** to take place; to come true; to be fulfilled
rebaja discount
rebelar to rebel
rebelde rebellious (2); rebel
rebeldía rebelliousness
recado message, note
recargar (gu) las pilas to recharge one's batteries
recaudar fondos to raise money (6)
receta farmacéutica prescription
rechazar (c) to reject (1)
rechazo rejection
recibir to receive; to welcome
reciclaje *m.* recycling (6)
reciclar to recycle (6)
recién recently, newly
reciente recent
recinto *s.* grounds
recipiente *m.* container
recitar to recite
reclamo complaint
reclutador(a) recruiter
reclutar to recruit
recoger (j) to pick up; to collect; to gather
recomendación *f.* recommendation
recomendar (ie) to recommend (3)
reconciliar to reconcile
reconocer (zc) to recognize
reconocimiento recognition
reconstrucción *f.* reconstruction
recordar (ue) to remember
recorrido *n.* journey
recrear to recreate
recreo recreation (4)
recuerdo memory; souvenir
recuperar to regain; **recuperarse** to recuperate
recurrir to resort, appeal, turn (to)
recurso resource (5); **recursos naturales** natural resources
red *f.* network
redacción *f.* revision
redescubrir (*like* **cubrir**) to rediscover
redondo/a round
reducido/a reduced
reemplazar (c) to replace (6)
reencuentro rediscovery
referencia reference
referirse (ie, i) a to refer to
reflejar to reflect
reflexión *f.* reflection
reflexionar to reflect on, ponder
reforma reform
reforzar (ue) (c) to reinforce
refrán *m.* saying, proverb
refrescarse (qu) to refresh oneself
regalar to give (*a gift*)

regalo gift
regañar to scold (2)
régimen *m.* (*pl.* **regímenes**) (political) regime
región *f.* region
registro registration, registry
regla rule; regulation
reglamento rule; regulation
regresar to return
regreso *n.* return
reír(se) (i, i) (me río) (*p.p.* **reído**) to laugh; **reírse a carcajadas** to laugh loudly (4)
relación *f.* relationship; connection
relacionado/a con related to
relajado/a relaxed (4)
relajamiento *n.* slackening, relaxing
relajante relaxing
relajarse to relax (4)
relatar to recount, tell
relativo/a *adj.* relative
relato story, narrative
relevancia relevance
religión *f.* religion
religioso/a religious
rellenar to fill, stuff
relucir (zc) to shine; **salir** (*irreg.*) **a relucir** to come to light
remediar to remedy
remedio remedy, cure; solution; **no quedarle otro remedio** to have no alternative
remordimiento remorse
renacimiento rebirth
rencor *m.* rancor; resentment
rendido/a surrendered; submissive; **te quiero rendido** I love you devotedly
rendir (i, i) to surrender; to produce, yield
renombrado/a renowned
renovable renewable (6)
renovado/a renewed (4)
renovar (ue) to renew
renunciar to renounce
reñir (i, i) to quarrel, argue; to berate
reparación *f.* repair
reparto distribution
repasar to review
repatriación *f.* repatriation
repente: de repente suddenly (3)
repentino/a sudden
repetir (i, i) to repeat
repleto/a con replete/filled with
réplica copy, replica
replicar (qu) to reply; to replicate
reportaje *m.* news report
reportero/a reporter
representante *n. m., f.* representative
representar to represent
representativo/a *adj.* representative
represión *f.* repression
reprimir to repress
reproducido/a reproduced
reproductor player (*media*)
república republic; **República Dominicana** Dominican Republic
republicano/a Republican
repugnante disgusting (1)
reputación *f.* reputation
requerir (ie, i) to require
requisito requisite, requirement
res *f.*: **carne** (*f.*) **de res** beef
resaca hangover (4)
resentimiento resentment (3)
reseña *n.* review (*art, film*)
reserva reserve
reservado/a reserved (1)
reservar to reserve; **reservarse el derecho** to reserve the right
residencia residence; **residencia de estudiantes** student dormitory
resistencia resistance
resistir to resist
resolución *f.* resolution
resolver (ue) to resolve (5)
respectivo/a respective
respecto: al respecto in regard to the matter; **con respecto a** with respect to
respetar to respect
respeto respect
respetuoso/a respectful (6)
respirar to breathe
responder to responder, answer
responsabilidad *f.* responsibility
respuesta answer, reply; response
restaurante *m.* restaurant
resto rest, remainder; *pl.* remains
restricción *f.* restriction
restrictivo/a restrictive
resuelto/a (*p.p. of* **resolver**) solved
resultado result
resultar to prove, turn out (to be); **resultar de** to stem from; **resultar en** to produce, result in
resumen *m.* summary
resurgir (j) to revive
resurrección *f.* resurrection; **Domingo de Resurrección** Easter Sunday
retar to challenge; to take on
retener (*like* **tener**) to retain, keep
retirar(se) to withdraw
retórica rhetoric
retratar to portray
retrato portrait
retrocohete *m.* retrorocket
reubicar (qu) to relocate
reunión *f.* meeting; gathering
reunirse (me reúno) (con) to get together (with) (4); to gather
revelación *f.* revelation
revelar to reveal; to disclose
revista magazine
revolución *f.* revolution
revolucionar to revolutionize
revolucionario/a revolutionary
rey *m.* king
rezar (c) to pray
rico/a rich; delicious; **los ricos** *n. pl.* the rich
ridiculizar (c) to ridicule
ridículo/a ridiculous; **te voy a contar algo ridículo que le pasó a...** I'm going to tell you something ridiculous that happened to . . . (3)
riesgo risk (3)
rima *n.* rhyme
riñón *m.* kidney
río river
riqueza wealth; richness
risa laughter (4)
ritmo rhythm
ritual *m.* ritual
rizado curly (*hair*) (1)
robar to steal; to rob
robótico/a robotic
rodar (ue) to film
rodeado/a surrounded
rodear to surround
rodilla knee; **de rodillas** on one's knees, kneeling
rogar (ue) (gu) to beg (3)
rojo/a: ponerse (*irreg.*) **rojo/a** to blush
rol *m.* role
romancero collection of ballads
románico/a Romanesque
romántico/a romantic; **vida romántica** love life
romper (*p.p.* **roto**) to break; to rip; to break through; **romper con** to break up with (3)
ropa clothing; **ropa interior** underwear
rosa *n.* rose
rostro face (1)
roto/a (*p.p. of* **romper**) broken
rubio/a blond(e)
rueda wheel
ruido noise
ruina *n.* ruin
ruiseñor *m.* nigtingale
ruta route, road
rutina routine

S

saber *irreg.* to know (*facts*); **hacer** (*irreg.*) **saber** to inform; **saber** + *inf.* to know how to (*do something*)
sabiduría wisdom
sabor *m.* flavor
saborear to savor
sabroso/a tasty, flavorful; juicy
sacabullas *m. s.* bouncer
sacar (qu) to obtain, get; to take out; **sacar adelante** to get off the ground (*fig.*); **sacar buenas notas** to get good

grades; **sacar de quicio** to drive crazy (*fig.*); **sacar dinero** to withdraw money; **sacar fotos** to take pictures
sacerdote *m.* priest
sacrificar (qu) to sacrifice
sacrificio sacrifice
sado: (masoquista) sadomasochist
saeta *short, fervent religious song (Sp.)*
sagrado/a sacred
sala living room; room; **sala de chat** chat room
salida exit; **callejón** (*m.*) **sin salida** dead-end street
salir *irreg.* to leave; to go out; to come out, emerge; to get out; to play, premier (*TV, film*); **salir con** to date (3); to go out with
salón *m.* (class)room; **salón de charla** chat room (6)
salsa *musical/dance genre that combines various Caribbean rhythms of African origin*
salsateca dancehall (with salsa music)
salsero/a pertaining to salsa music or dance
salto *n.* leap; **dar** (*irreg.*) **un salto** to jump
salud *f.* health (5)
saludar to greet
saludable healthy
salvadoreño/a *n., adj.* Salvadoran
salvar to save (*someone, something*) (5)
salvo que except
san, santo/a *n.* saint; *adj.* holy; **Día** (*m.*) **de San Valentín** Valentine's Day; **santo patrón, santa patrona** patron saint; **Semana Santa** Holy Week
sandía watermelon
sanfermines *m. pl. yearly festival in Pamplona, Spain*
sangre *f.* blood
sangriento/a bloody
sanguinario/a bloodthirsty
sanitario/a sanitary
sano/a healthy (6)
santuario sanctuary
sarcástico/a sarcastic
sargento sergeant
satánico/a satanic
satanismo Satanism
satírico/a satirical
satisfacer (*like* **hacer**) to satisfy
satisfecho/a (*p.p. of* **satisfacer**) satisfied (3)
sección *f.* section
seco/a dry
secreto/a *adj.* secret
sector *m.* sector
secuestrado/a kidnapped; hijacked; **avión** (*m.*) **secuestrado** hijacked airplane
secuestrar to kidnap; to hijack
secuestro kidnapping (5); hijacking (5)
secundaria: escuela secundaria high school
seda silk
sede *f.* headquarters; venue
seducir (zc) (j) to seduce
seductor(a) seductive
seguido/a por followed by
seguir (i, i) (g) to follow; to continue (being); **seguir** + *ger.* to keep doing something (4)
según according to
segundo/a second
seguramente surely (5)
seguridad *f.* security
seguro/a safe; sure, certain
selección *f.* selection
selva *n.* jungle
selvático/a *adj.* jungle
semana week; **esta semana** this week; **fin** (*m.*) **de semana** weekend; **la semana pasada** last week; **la semana que viene** next week; **Semana Santa** Holy Week
semanal weekly
semblante *m.* face, expression
sembrar (ie) to sow
semejante similar
semejanza similarity
semestre *m.* semester
semibendición *f.* partial blessing
semilla seed
senador(a) senator
sencillo/a simple; plain
senderista *m., f. member of the Sendero Luminoso guerrilla group*
sendero path; **Sendero Luminoso** Shining Path (*Peruvian guerrilla group*)
sensación *f.* sensation
sensible sensitive (1)
sentado/a seated; **estar** (*irreg.*) **sentado/a** to be sitting down
sentarse (ie) to sit
sentido meaning, sense; **¿en qué sentido?** in what way/sense?; **sentido del humor** sense of humor
sentimental emotional; sentimental
sentimiento feeling, emotion
sentir (ie, i) to feel; to be sorry; **lo siento mucho** I'm very sorry (2); **sentirse** to feel; **sentirse en paz** to feel at peace; **siento que** + *subj.* I'm sorry that . . . (2)
señal *f.* sign
señalar to indicate; to signal
señor (Sr.) *m.* Mister (Mr.); man
señora (Sra.) Mrs.; woman
señorita (Srta.) Miss; young woman
separación *f.* separation
separar to separate; **separarse** to separate (prior to divorce)
separatista *adj. m., f.* separatist
sepultar to inter, bury
sequía drought (6)
ser *m.* being; **ser humano** human being
ser *v. irreg.* to be; **llegar (gu) a ser** to become; **me es igual** I don't care; **pasar a ser** to become; **puede ser que** + *subj.* it could be that . . . ; **ser buena/mala gente** to be a good/bad person / good/bad people (1); **ya sea... o...** whether . . . or . . .
serenata *n.* serenade
serie *f.* series
serio/a serious; **en serio** seriously; **¿en serio?** really? (1)
serpiente *f.* snake
servicio service
servir (i, i) to serve; to be useful
sesión *f.* session
sevillana *music and dance from Seville, Spain*
sexista *adj. m., f.* sexist
sexualmente sexually
shakespeariano/a Shakespearian
SIDA *m.* (*abbrev. for* **síndrome** [*m.*] **de inmunodeficiencia adquirida**) AIDS (5)
siempre always; **para siempre** forever; **siempre y cuando** as long as
sierra mountain range
siesta *n.* nap
siglo century
significado meaning, significance
significar (qu) to mean
significativo/a significant
siguiente following; next; **al día siguiente** (on) the next day
silbar to whistle
silencio silence
silla chair
silvestre rustic
simbólico/a symbolic
simbolismo symbolism
simbolizar (c) to symbolize
símbolo symbol
simbología symbology
simpático/a likable; friendly; nice
simplón, simplona simplistic
sin without; **callejón** (*m.*) **sin salida** dead-end street; **sin duda** without a doubt; **sin embargo** however; **sin igual** unrivaled; **sin problema alguno** without any problem; **sin que** + *subj.* without . . . (6)
sinagoga synagogue
sincero/a sincere
sindicato union (*labor*)
sinnúmero countless number
sino rather
sinónimo/a synonymous
sinrazón *f.* craziness
síntesis *f.* synthesis
sirena siren
sirviente, sirvienta servant, maid
sistema *m.* system
sitio place; site
situación *f.* situation

situarse (me sitúo) to situate oneself; to be located
sobre above; over; on, upon; about; against; **sobre todo** above all
sobrepoblación *f.* overpopulation (6)
sobresaliente outstanding, distinguishing
sobrevivir to survive (6)
socialista *n., adj. m., f.* socialist
socialmente socially
sociedad *f.* society
sociológico/a sociological
sofá *m.* couch, sofa
sofisticado/a sophisticated
sol *m.* sun; **nuevo sol** *monetary unit of Peru;* **puesta del sol** sunset
solar: luz (*f.*) **solar** sunlight
soldadera *term for Mexican women who joined the Mexican Revolution as soldiers*
soldado soldier
soledad *f.* solitude, loneliness
solemne solemn
soler (ue) + *inf.* to tend to (*do something*)
solidaridad *f.* solidarity
solidario/a solidary; jointly responsible
solidarizar (c) to render jointly responsible
sólido/a solid
solista *m., f.* soloist
solitario/a solitary
solo/a alone
sólo only; **no sólo... sino (que)** not only . . . but also; **tan sólo** merely
soltero/a *n.* bachelor, single woman; *adj.* single (3)
solución *f.* solution
solucionar to solve; to resolve
sombrero hat
sombrío/a somber; gloomy; dark
someterse to submit oneself
sonar (ue) to sound; to ring (*telephone*); **suena padrísimo** it sounds awesome (*Mex.*)
sonido sound
sonora: banda sonora soundtrack
sonreír(se) (*like* **reír**) to smile (4)
sonsacar (qu) to pry out
soñador(a) dreamer
soñar (ue) to dream; **¡ni soñarlo!** in your dreams! (2); **soñar con** to dream about (3)
soplar to blow
soplón, soplona snitch
soportar to put up with, tolerate; **ya no puedo soportarlo/la más** I can't stand it/him/her anymore (2)
sorbete *m.* straw
sorprendente surprising
sorprender to surprise; **me sorprende que creas eso** it surprises me that you believe that (3); **sorprenderse** to be surprised
sorprendido/a surprised
sorpresa surprise
sorpresivo/a unexpected, surprising
sospechar to suspect
sospechoso/a *n.* suspect
sostener (*like* **tener**) to sustain
sostenible sustainable; **desarrollo sostenible** sustainable development (6)
soviético/a Soviet
suavidad *f.* gentleness
suavizar (c) to soften
subcomandante *m.* subcommander
subcontratación *f.* outsourcing
subcultura subculture
subdesarrollado/a underdeveloped; **país** (*m.*) **subdesarrollado** under-developed country
subdesarrollo underdevelopment (5)
subida rise
subir to raise; to climb, go up; **subirse a la cabeza** to go to one's head (*fig.*)
subjetivo/a subjective
subjuntivo *gram.* subjunctive mood
sublimar to sublimate
subrayar to underline
suburbio suburb
suceder to happen; to take place; **escucha lo que le sucedió a...** listen to what happened to . . . (3)
Sudamérica South America
sueco/a Swedish
suegro/a father-in-law / mother-in-law
sueldo salary
suelto/a (*p.p. of* **soltar**)**: trabajo suelto** odd job; freelance work
sueño dream; sleepiness; sleep
suerte *f.* luck; **¡qué suerte!** what (good) luck! (1)
suéter *m.* sweater
suficiente enough, sufficient
sufrimiento suffering
sufrir to suffer; to undergo
sugerencia suggestion
sugerir (ie, i) to suggest (3)
suicidarse to commit suicide
suizo/a Swiss
sujeto subject
sumo/a much, a lot
sumamente extremely
sumiso/a submissive (2)
súper super; **estoy súper contento/a (de que)** I'm very happy (that) (2)
superar to overcome; to surpass; to improve
superficie *f.* surface
superhéroe; superheroína superhero; superheroine
supermercado supermarket
superstición *f.* superstition
supersticioso/a superstitious
supervivencia survival
suponer (*like* **poner**) to suppose
supremo/a supreme
supuestamente supposedly
supuesto (*p.p. of* **suponer**) meant; **por supuesto** of course
sur *m.* South; *adj.* south, southern; **Cono Sur** Southern Cone (*area comprising Argentina, Chile, Paraguay and Uruguay*)
surco furrow
sureste *m.* southeast
surgir (j) to arise; to come up
surrealismo surrealism
surrealista *n. m., f.* surrealist
sustantivo *gram.* noun

T

tabla table; chart
tacaño/a stingy (1)
táctica tactic
tacto tact
tal such; such as; **con tal de que** + *subj.* provided that . . . (6); **de tal palo tal astilla** like father, like son; **¿qué tal... ?** how is/was . . . ?; **tal como** such as; **tal vez** perhaps
talento talent
talismán *m.* talisman
taller *m.* workshop
tamaño size
también also, too (3); **yo también / a mí también** me too
tambor *m.* drum
tampoco neither, (not) either; nor; **yo tampoco / a mí tampoco** me neither
tan *adv.* so; as; such; so much; **tan... como** as . . . as; **tan pronto como** as soon as (6); **tan sólo** merely
tango *ballroom dance of Argentine origin*
tanguista *m., f.* (*also* **tanguero/a**) tango dancer
tanto *n.* certain amount; *adv.* so much; as much; **mientras tanto** meanwhile; **no es para tanto** it's not such a big deal (2); **por lo tanto** therefore
tanto/a *pron., adj.* so much; as much; *pl.* so many; as many; **tanto/a/os/as... como** as much/many . . . as
tapa appetizer
tapar(se) to cover (oneself)
tapiz *m.* (*pl.* **tapices**) tapestry
tardanza delay; slowness
tardar(se) to be late; to take time
tarde *n. f.* afternoon; **de la tarde** in the afternoon
tarde *adv.* late; **tarde o temprano** sooner or later
tarea homework
tarjeta card; **tarjeta postal** postcard; **tarjeta virtual** virtual (electronic) card
tatuaje *m.* tattoo
taza cup, mug

teatral *adj.* theatrical; theater
teatro theater; **obra de teatro** play
techo ceiling, roof
técnica *n.* technique
técnico/a *adj.* technical; **asesoría técnica** technical consulting
tecnología technology
tecnológico/a technological
tejano/a Texan
tejerse to weave together
tejido fabric
tela fabric, cloth; canvas (*for painting*)
teleférico cable car
telefónico/a *adj.* telephone, phone
teléfono telephone; **hablar por teléfono** to talk on the telephone; **teléfono móvil o celular** cell phone (6)
telegrama *m.* telegram
telenovela soap opera
telerrealidad *f.* reality TV
telescopio telescope
teletrabajo telecommuting (6)
tele(visión) *f.* television (*programming*)
televisivo/a *adj.* television (*related*)
televisor *m.* television (set)
telón *m.* curtain (*stage*)
tema *m.* theme; topic
temer to fear; to be afraid; **(no) temer que** + *subj.* (not) to fear that . . .
temor *m.* fear
temperatura temperature
tempestuoso/a stormy (3)
temporada season (*sports, holidays*)
temprano/a early; **tarde o temprano** sooner or later
tendencia tendency, trend
tender (ie) to tend to, have a tendency to
tener *irreg.* to have; to receive; **no tener pelos en la lengua** to speak one's mind (1); **¡qué cara tiene!** what nerve he/she has! (2); **tienes razón** you are right (2); **tienes toda la razón** you are completely right (3); **tener buena/mala pinta** to have a good/bad appearance (1); **tener cuidado** to be careful; **tener en cuenta** to take into account; **tener éxito** to be successful (4); **tener ganas de** + *inf.* to feel like (*doing something*); **tener gracia** to be charming; **tener hambre** to be hungry; **tener interés** to be interested; **tener jurado/a** to have it in for; **tener lugar** to take place; **tener mucha cara** to have a lot of nerve (1); **tener mucha marcha** to have a lively social scene (4); **tener paciencia** to be patient; **tener que ver con** to have to do with; **tener... años** to be . . . years old
tensión *f.* tension
tenso/a tense (4)
tentación *f.* temptation
teñido/a dyed (1)
teología *f.* theology
teoría theory
teórico/a theoretical
terapia therapy
tercer, tercero/a third; **tercera parte** (one) third
tercio (one) third
terminación *f.* ending
terminar to finish; to end; to end up; **terminar** + *ger.* to end up (*doing something*); **terminar de** + *inf.* to finish (*doing something*)
término term, terminology
ternura tenderness
terral *m.* land
terraza terrace
terremoto earthquake (6)
terreno ground; terrain
terrestre *adj.* land
territorio territory
terror *m.* terror, horror
terrorismo terrorism (5)
terrorista *n., adj. m., f.* terrorist
tertulia gathering
tesis *f. inv.* thesis; theses
tesoro treasure
testarudo/a stubborn (1)
testigo witness
testimonio testimony
tibio/a mild; warm
tiburón *m.* shark
tiempo time; weather; *gram.* verb tense; **al mismo tiempo** at the same time (3); **los tiempos modernos** modern times; **no dar** (*irreg.*) **tiempo** to not have/allow enough time; **pasar tiempo** to spend time; **perder (ie) el tiempo** to waste time; **tiempo libre** free time
tienda *n.* store, shop
tierra ground; land; earth; homeland; **Tierra** Earth
tigre *m.* tiger
tijereteado/a choppy, shaggy (*hair*)
tildar to brand, label
timidez *f.* shyness
tímido/a shy (1)
tío/a uncle, aunt; *m. pl.* aunts and uncles
típico/a typical
tipo type, kind; **tipo/a** guy / woman
tiquismiquis picky (1)
tira cómica cartoon, comic strip
tirano tyrant
tirar to throw; **tirarse** to throw at each other
títere *m.* puppet
titubear to hesitate; to stammer; **sin titubear** without hesitating
titulado/a entitled
titular *m.* headline
título title
tocar (qu) to touch; to play (*music, instrument*); to touch, move (*emotionally*); **tocarle** + *inf.* to be (someone's) turn / luck to (*do something*)
todavía still; yet
todo everything; **ante/sobre todo** above all; **gracias por todo** thanks for everything
todo/a *adj.* all (of); (the) entire; *pl.* every; *adv.* completely; **a todo pulmón** at the top of one's lungs; **de todas maneras** at any rate, anyway; **de todas partes** from everywhere; **por todas partes** everywhere; **tener** (*irreg.*) **toda la razón** to be completely right; **toda la vida** (one's) whole life; **todo el día** all day; **todo el mundo** everybody; **todos los días** every day
todos everyone, everybody
tolerancia tolerance (5)
tomar to take; to drink; **tomar apuntes** to take notes; **tomar en cuenta** to take into account; **tomar en serio** to take seriously (6), **tomar medidas** to take steps/measures; **tomar una decisión** to make a decision; **tomarle el pelo a alguien** to pull someone's leg (*fig.*)
tomate *m.* tomato
tonelada ton
tontería foolishness, silly thing
tonto/a silly, stupid
torcido/a twisted
torear to bullfight
tornado tornado (6)
tornarse to turn, become
torero/a bullfighter
toro bull; **corrida de toros** bullfight
torre *f.* tower
torrente *m.* torrent
tortuga turtle
tortuguero/a pertaining to turtles
tortura torture
totalitario/a totalitarian
totalmente completely
trabajador(a) *n.* worker, laborer; *adj.* hard-working
trabajar to work; **trabajar como una mula** to work like a dog (4)
trabajo *n.* work; job; **compañero/a de trabajo** co-worker; **trabajo manual** manual labor; **trabajo suelto** odd job, freelance work
tradición *f.* tradition
tradicional traditional
traducir (zc) (j) to translate
traductor(a) translator
traer *irreg.* (*p.p.* **traído**) to bring
tragedia tragedy
trágico/a tragic

traicionar to betray
traje *m.* suit
trama plot
trance *m.* moment; **trance grato** pleasant moment
tranquilidad *f.* tranquility
tranquilizar (c) to calm; **tranquilizarse** to calm down
tranquilo/a tranquil, calm; quiet
transcurrir to take place; to elapse (*time*)
transcender (ie) transcend
transfondo background; undercurrent
transformar to change, transform
transmitir to broadcast
transporte *m.* transportation; **transporte público** public transportation
transposición *f.* transposition
tras *prep.* behind; after
trasladar(se) to move (*location*)
traslúcido/a translucent
traspasar to go beyond
tratamiento treatment (5)
tratar to treat; to deal with; **tratar de** to be about; **tratar de** + *inf.* to try to (*do something*) (4); **tratarse de** to be a question of; to be about
trato treatment (3)
través: a través de through; via
travesura mischief, prank
travieso/a mischievous, naughty (2)
trayectoria trajectory
trazar (c) to trace, draw
trébol *m.* clover
tremendo/a tremendous
tren *m.* train
tribu *f.* tribe
tribunal *m.* court
triplicar (qu) to triple
triste sad
tristeza sadness
triunfar to succeed, triumph
trompeta trumpet
tronco trunk
tropas *pl.* troops
tropezar (ie) to trip, stumble
trova verse, song
trovador *m.* troubadour
trozo piece
tumba tomb
tumbar to knock down
túnel *m.* tunnel
tuno *member of a* **tuna,** *or traditional student music group in Spain*
turismo tourism
turista *n. m., f.* tourist
turístico/a *adj.* tourist; **guía turística** tour guide
turnarse to take turns
tutear to address using the familiar form

U

ubicarse (qu) to be located
ubicuo/a ubiquitous, everywhere
último/a final, last; latest; **el último grito** the latest fad; **por último** finally
un, uno/a one; *pl.* some, a few; **a unos pasos de distancia** a few steps away; **el uno al otro** to one another; **el uno en el otro** in one another; **por un lado** on one hand; **una vez** once; **unas veces** sometimes; **unos pocos** a few
único/a only; unique; **hijo único, hija única** only child (2)
unidad *f.* unity (2)
unidireccional one-directional
unido/a close-knit (2)
unión *f.* union
unir to unite, hold together; to join, bring together; **unirse** to unite
unitario/a centralist
universalidad *f.* universality
universidad *f.* university
universitario/a *adj.* university, pertaining to a university
urbano/a urban
urbe *f.* major city
urgente urgent (5)
urgir (j) to be urgent; **me urge** it's urgent for me
uruguayo/a *n., adj.* Uruguayan
usar to use; to wear
uso *n.* use
útil useful
utilizar (c) to use, make use of
utópico/a utopian
uva grape

V

vaca cow
vacaciones *f. pl.* vacation; **ir** (*irreg.*) **de vacaciones** to go on vacation
vacío/a empty
vacuno: carne (*f.*) **de vacuno** beef
vago/a vague; lazy (1)
valenciano/a of or pertaining to Valencia
valentía bravery
Valentín: Día (*m.*) **de San Valentín** Valentine's Day
valer *irreg.* to be worth; **más vale** it's better; **no valer nada** to be worthless; **valer la pena** to be worth it (5); **¡válgame Dios!** God help me!
validez *f.* (*pl.* **valideces**) validity
valiente valiant, brave
valioso/a valuable
valor *m.* value; worth; *pl.* values (2)
valorar to value
valse *m.* waltz
vanguardia vanguard; avant-garde
vanidad *f.* vanity
vapor *m.* steam
variado/a varied
variante varying
variar (varío) to vary
variedad *f.* variety
varios/as several; various
vasco/a: País (*m.*) **Vasco** Basque Country
vascuence *m.* Basque (*language*)
vasija earthenware pot, container
vaso (drinking) glass
vecindario neighborhood, small housing complex
vecino/a neighbor
vegetación *f.* vegetation
vejez *f.* old age
vela candle; sail
velocidad *f.* speed; **a toda velocidad** quickly
vendedor(a) merchant, seller
vender to sell
venezolano/a *n., adj.* Venezuelan
venir *irreg.* to come; **ahora viene lo peor** now comes the worst part (3); **el mes (la semana,…) que viene** next month (week, *etc.*)
venta sale
ventaja advantage
ventana window
ventanal *m.* large window
ver *irreg.* (*p.p.* **visto**) to see; to look at, watch; to observe; **tener** (*irreg.*) **que ver con** to have to do with; **volver (ue) a ver** to see again
verano summer
veras: de veras really; **¿de veras?** really? (1)
verdad *f.* truth; **de verdad** really; truly; **¿de verdad?** really?; **¿verdad?** right?, isn't that so?
verdaderamente truly (5)
verdadero/a real; true; genuine
verdemar *m.* sea green (*color*)
verdura vegetable
vergonzoso/a embarrassing
vergüenza shame; **¡qué vergüenza!** how embarrassing! (1)
verificar (qu) to verify
versión *f.* version
verso verse; line of poetry
vestido *n.* dress
vestir (i, i) to dress; **vestirse** to get dressed; to dress (oneself)
vestuario *n.* costuming
vez *f.* (*pl.* **veces**) time; **a la vez** at the same time; **a veces** sometimes; **alguna vez** ever (*with a question*); once (*with a*

statement); **cada vez más** more and more; **de vez en cuando** sometimes (3); **en vez de** instead of; **esta vez** this time; **otra vez** again; **por primera vez** for the first time; **tal vez** perhaps; **última vez** last time; **una vez** once
vía: en vías de desarrollo *adj.* developing
viaducto viaduct
viajar to travel
viaje *m.* trip; **agente** (*m., f.*) **de viajes** travel agent
vibración *f.* vibration
vicepresidente, vicepresidenta vice president
víctima victim
victoria victory
vida life
vidente *adj.* clairvoyant
vídeo video; **cámara de vídeo** video camera
videojuego video game
viejo/a *n.* old person; *adj.* old; elderly
viento wind
vino wine
viñeta vignette
violar to violate (*law*)
violencia violence
violín *m.* violin
virgen *f.* virgin
virtual virtual; **realidad** (*f.*) **virtual** virtual reality (6); **tarjeta virtual** virtual (electronic) card
visibilidad *f.* visibility
visión *f.* vision
visionario/a visionary
visita *n.* visit
visitante *m., f.* visitor
visitar to visit
vista view; **a primera vista** at first sight (1); **desde mi punto de vista...** from my point of view . . . (3); **punto de vista** point of view
visto/a (*p.p. of* **ver**) seen
visualizar (c) to visualize
vitrinear to window-shop
vivir to live, live through
vivo/a alive, living; brilliant; **en vivo** live
vocabulario vocabulary
vocación *f.* vocation
volador(a) flying; **objeto volador no identificado** UFO
volar (ue) to fly
volcán *m.* volcano
volcánico/a volcanic
voluntariado *n.* volunteering
voluntario/a volunteer; **hacer** (*irreg.*) **de voluntario/a** to volunteer (5)
voluntarioso/a willful, stubborn
voluntarismo volunteerism
volver (ue) (*p.p.* **vuelto**) to return, go back; **volver a** + *inf.* to (*do something*) again; **volverse** to become; **volver loco/a** to drive crazy (2)
vómito vomit; *pl.* vomiting
votar to vote
voto *n.* vote
voz *f.* (*pl.* **voces**) voice; opinion; **en voz alta** aloud

W

Web: página Web Web page (6)

Y

ya now; already; right now; at that point; **ya estoy harto/a (de que)** I'm fed up already (that) (2); **ya no** no longer; **ya no puedo soportarlo/la más** I can't stand it/him/her anymore (2); **ya que** since
yacer *irreg.* to lie buried
yerba mate *herbal tea typical of Argentina*
yuca yucca, cassava
yucateca *m., f.* person of or from the Yucatan Peninsula

Z

zanahoria carrot
zapatero/a shoemaker
zapatilla slipper
zapatista *m., f.* member of the National Liberation Zapatist Army (*guerrilla forces in Chiapas, Mexico*); *adj.* Zapatist; **Ejército Zapatista de Liberación Nacional** National Liberation Zapatist Army (*guerrilla forces in Chiapas, Mexico*)
zapoteca *m., f.* Zapotec
zócalo town square, plaza (*Mex.*)
zona zone; region
zoo(lógico) zoo

Index

Note: The first index deals with grammar and broad vocabulary categories, and the second index treats cultural topics

I. GRAMMAR

II. CULTURAL TOPICS

Credits

Grateful acknowledgment is made for use of the following:

Realia: *Page 17* Tin-Glao, CartoonArts International / CWS © Tin-Glao, Cartoonists & Writers Syndicate, www.nytsyn.com/cartoons; *46* © PIB Copenhagen A/S; *78* Tin-Glao, CartoonArts International / CWS © Tin-Glao, Cartoonists & Writers Syndicate, www.nytsyn.com/cartoons; *90 Vanidades,* January 31, 1995; *126* © 2005 Maitena; *140* Cartoon by Aguaslimpias (Leonardo Feldrich); *143* Agencia EFE; *170* Tin-Glao, CartoonArts International / CWS © Tin-Glao, Cartoonists & Writers Syndicate, www.nytsyn.com/cartoons.

Readings: *Pages 24–25* Message from Joaquín Sorolla to his wife Clotilde; *37–38* Courtesy of Vanidades Continental; *39* ECOS, May 2004; *67–69* From "Entrevista: Benito Zambrano Director" by Mauricio Vicent in *El País,* 26 December 2003. Used by permission; *100–102* "Peregrina" by Arturo Ortega Morán. Used courtesy of Arturo Ortega Morán, independent writer and columnist; *130–133* From "Chile: Tribus urbanas, rostros que buscan una identidad" by Rebeca Rojas Rodríguez, RadioUChile, January 21, 2008; *159–162* "El candidato," © José Cardona-López. Reprinted by permission of the author; *189–190* From "Los portadores de sueños" by Gioconda Belli. Used courtesy of Gioconda Belli.

Photographs: All photographs of the five friends © Jill Braaten. *Page 14* © Heather Jarry; *19* Wire Image/Getty Images; *23* © Heather Jarry; *25 A Walk on the Beach,* 1909 (oil on canvas), Joaquín Sorolla y Bastida, (1863–1923)/Museo Sorolla, Madrid, Spain, Giraudon/Bridgeman Art Library; *26* (top) National Gallery of Art, Washington, D.C./A.K.G. Berlin/Superstock/© 2009 Estate of Pablo Picasso/Artists Rights Society (ARS), New York; *26* (bottom left to right) Getty Images, Despotovic Dusko/Corbis Sygma, AP/Wide World Photos; *29* © 2002 Pixtal; *30* (top) © Patrick Ward/Corbis; *30* (middle) © 2005 by Robert Frerck and Odyssey Productions, Inc.; *30* (bottom) © 2005 by Robert Frerck and Odyssey Productions, Inc.; *33* © Pixtal/age Fotostock; *34* © Hugh Sitton/Zefa/Corbis; *36* © Phillipe Halsman/Magnum Photos; *40* © The Granger Collection, New York; *43* © Heather Jarry; *52* © Heather Jarry; *55* (bottom) © Karen Dietrich/Studio Antillania; *57* (top) © Jacqueline Veissid/Jupiter Images; *57* (center right) © Hola Images/Corbis; *57* (bottom) © Alistair Berg/Digital Vision/Getty Images; *58* © 2005 by David Dudenhoefer and Odyssey Productions, Inc.; *59* (top) AP Photo/Andres Leighton; *59* (bottom) Alfredo Maiquez/Lonely Planet Images; *60* AP/Wide World Photos; *62* © Nick Quijano; *63* © Authors Image/Alamy; *68* © Warner Brothers/courtesy Everett Collection; *70* (top) © Warner Bros/Courtesy Everett Collection; *70* (bottom) © Warner Bros/Courtesy Everett Collection; *71* © Warner Bros/Courtesy Everett Collection; *75* © Heather Jarry; *85* © Thomas R. Fletcher/Alamy; *88* Courtesy of Sharon Foerster and Anne Lambright; *90* (left) © AP/Wide World Photos; *90* (right) © The Granger Collection, New York; *91* © Samuel Gerardo Valdés Montemayor; *92* (top) © Corbis; *92* (bottom) © George Golton/Photo Researchers; *93* Courtesy of API Academic Programs International; *95* (top) © The Granger Collection, New York; *95* (bottom) © La Calavera de la Catrina, 1913 (zinc etching) (b/w photo) by José Guadalupe Posada (1851–1913). Private Collection/Giraudon/The Bridgeman Art Library; *96* © Eliseo Fernandez/Reuters/Landov; *100* Courtesy of Michael Schuessler; *101* Courtesy of Michael Schuessler; *107* © Heather Jarry; *115* © Reuters/Bettmann/Corbis; *118* © 2005 by Robert Frerck and Odyssey Productions, Inc.; *119* (top) © Mark Peterson/Corbis; *119* (bottom) © Daniel Luna/AP Wide World Photo; *121* © F. Damm/zefa/Corbis; *122* (top) © AP Photo/Michigan State University; *122* (bottom) © STR/AFP/Getty Images; *123* © Russell Thompson/Archive Photos; *127* © Marcelo Hernandez/AP Wide World Photo; *137* © Heather Jarry; *146* © Aizar Raldes/AFP/Getty Images; *148* © Bonnie Hamre 1998–2005; *150* (top) © Eitan Abramovich/AFP/Getty Images; *150* (bottom) © Photo by Mark Wilson/Getty Images; *152* (top) © Steve Vidler/Superstock;

152 (bottom) © Jan Butchofsky-Houser/Corbis; *153* (top) © Luis Alberto Aldonza/age fotostock; *153* (middle) © Digital Vision; *155* © Gonzalo Endara Crow; *157* © Hideo Haga/HAGA The Image Works; *167* © Heather Jarry; *176* Courtesy of Lily Haham; *181* (top left) © Dr. Parvinder Sethi; *181* (top right) © Reuters/Corbis; *181* (bottom) Photo courtesy of Aid to Artisans. © 2009 Aid to Artisans; *182* (top) © Royalty-Free/Corbis; *182* (bottom) © Jan Butchofsky-Houser/Corbis; *183* (top) © Nik Wheeler/Corbis; *183* (middle) © Visual & Written SL/Alamy; *185* (top) © Kevin Schafer/Corbis; *185* (bottom) © Danny Lehman/Corbis; *186* © Bob Daemmrich/The Image Works; *188* © Oscar Elias/AISA/Everett Collection.

MÉXICO, AMÉRICA CENTRAL Y EL CARIBE
0 250 500 750 MILLAS
0 250 500 750 KILÓMETROS
ELEVACIÓN
METROS PIES
3050 10000
1525 5000
610 2000
305 1000
152.5 500
0 0
ESTADOS UNIDOS
MÉXICO
CUBA
BAHAMAS
JAMAICA
HAITÍ
REPÚBLICA DOMINICANA
PUERTO RICO
BELICE
GUATEMALA
HONDURAS
EL SALVADOR
NICARAGUA
COSTA RICA
PANAMÁ
COLOMBIA
VENEZUELA
OCÉANO ATLÁNTICO
OCÉANO PACÍFICO
Golfo de México
MAR CARIBE
Golfo de California
Baja California
Península de Yucatán
SIERRA MADRE OCCIDENTAL
SIERRA MADRE ORIENTAL
SIERRA MADRE DEL SUR
Río Grande
Río Misisipí
Trópico de Cáncer
Ecuador
Canal de Panamá
Santa Fe
Albuquerque
Phoenix
San Diego
Mexicali
Tijuana
Tucson
El Paso
Nogales
Ciudad Juárez
Hermosillo
Chihuahua
Dallas
Austin
San Antonio
Houston
Nuevo Laredo
Memphis
Atlanta
Mobile
Nueva Orleáns
San Agustín
Orlando
Tampa
Miami
Nassau
Monterrey
Durango
Mazatlán
Cabo San Lucas
Guadalajara
Guanajuato
México, D.F.
Puerto Vallarta
Cuernavaca
Puebla
Veracruz
Acapulco
Oaxaca
Mérida
Cozumel
Chichén Itzá
Campeche
Belmopán
Guatemala
Tegucigalpa
San Salvador
Managua
San José
Panamá
La Habana
Santiago de Cuba
Guantánamo
Port-au-Prince
Kingston
Santo Domingo
San Juan
Barranquilla
Cartagena
Maracaibo
Caracas
Mérida
Medellín
Cali
Bogotá
N
S
E
W

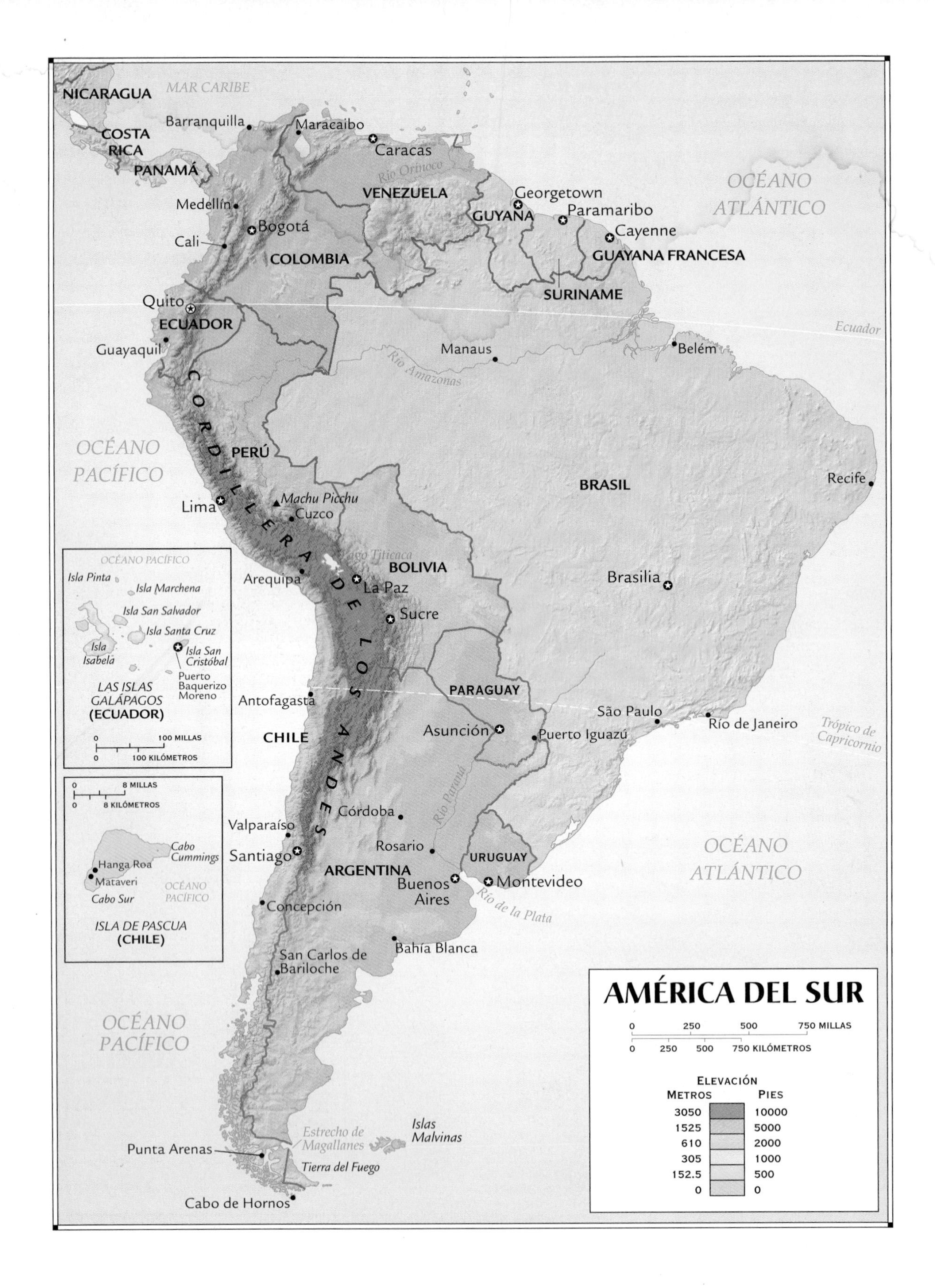

AMÉRICA DEL SUR
NICARAGUA
MAR CARIBE
COSTA RICA
PANAMÁ
Barranquilla
Maracaibo
Caracas
Río Orinoco
VENEZUELA
Georgetown
Paramaribo
Cayenne
GUYANA
GUAYANA FRANCESA
SURINAME
OCÉANO ATLÁNTICO
Medellín
Bogotá
Cali
COLOMBIA
Quito
ECUADOR
Guayaquil
Ecuador
Manaus
Belém
Río Amazonas
CORDILLERA DE LOS ANDES
OCÉANO PACÍFICO
PERÚ
Lima
Machu Picchu
Cuzco
BRASIL
Recife
Arequipa
La Paz
BOLIVIA
Sucre
Brasilia
OCÉANO PACÍFICO
Isla Pinta
Isla Marchena
Isla San Salvador
Isla Santa Cruz
Isla Isabela
Isla San Cristóbal
Puerto Baquerizo Moreno
LAS ISLAS GALÁPAGOS
(ECUADOR)
0 100 MILLAS
0 100 KILÓMETROS
Antofagasta
PARAGUAY
São Paulo
Río de Janeiro
Trópico de Capricornio
CHILE
Asunción
Puerto Iguazú
0 8 MILLAS
0 8 KILÓMETROS
Cabo Cummings
Hanga Roa
Mataveri
Cabo Sur
OCÉANO PACÍFICO
ISLA DE PASCUA
(CHILE)
Río Paraná
Córdoba
Valparaíso
Santiago
Rosario
URUGUAY
ARGENTINA
Buenos Aires
Montevideo
Río de la Plata
OCÉANO ATLÁNTICO
Concepción
Bahía Blanca
San Carlos de Bariloche
OCÉANO PACÍFICO
0 250 500 750 MILLAS
0 250 500 750 KILÓMETROS
ELEVACIÓN
METROS PIES
3050 10000
1525 5000
610 2000
305 1000
152.5 500
0 0
Estrecho de Magallanes
Islas Malvinas
Punta Arenas
Tierra del Fuego
Cabo de Hornos

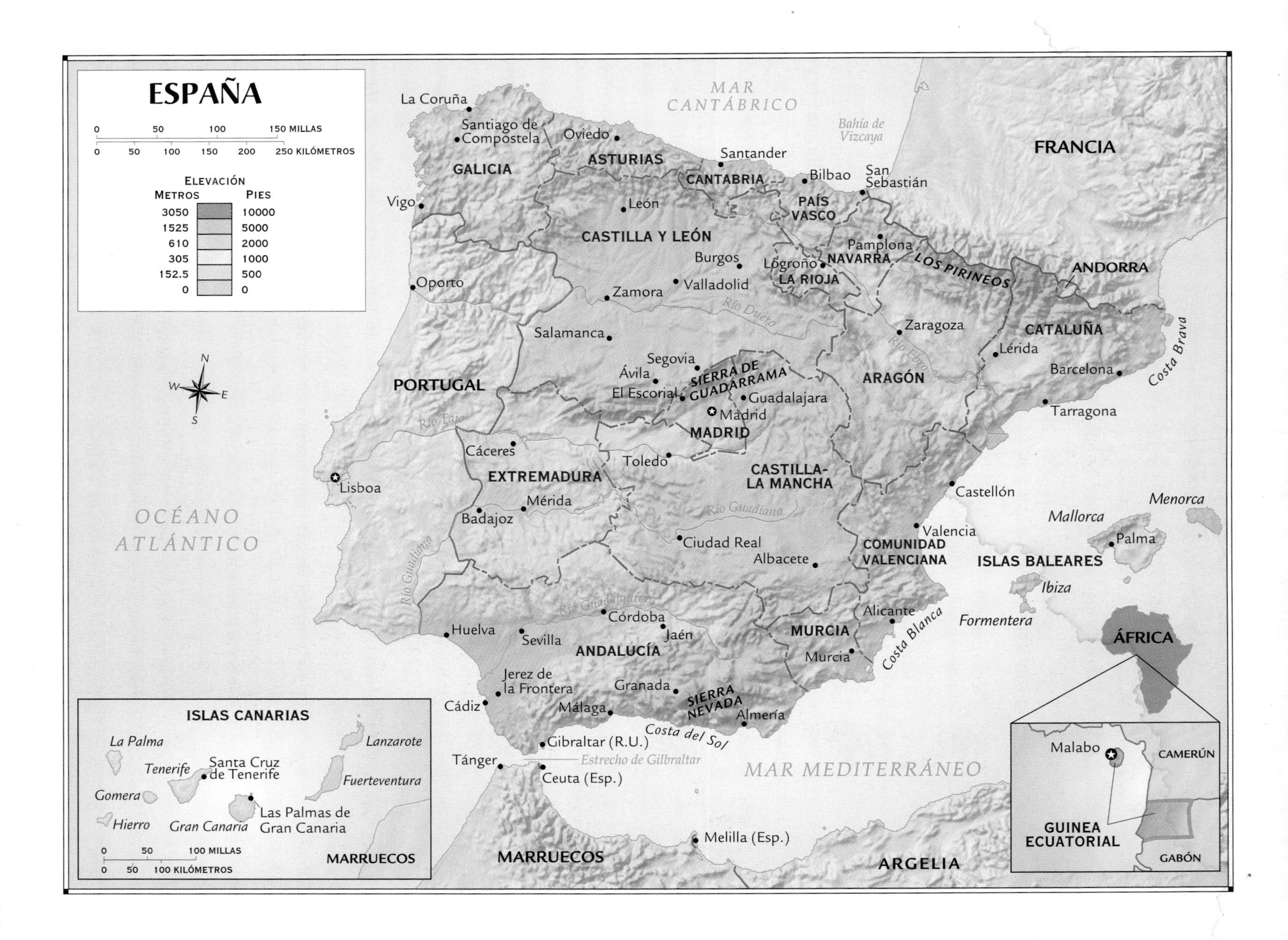

ESPAÑA
0 50 100 150 MILLAS
0 50 100 150 200 250 KILÓMETROS
ELEVACIÓN
METROS PIES
3050 10000
1525 5000
610 2000
305 1000
152.5 500
0 0
N E S W
OCÉANO ATLÁNTICO
MAR CANTÁBRICO
Bahía de Vizcaya
MAR MEDITERRÁNEO
FRANCIA
ANDORRA
PORTUGAL
MARRUECOS
ARGELIA
ÁFRICA
GALICIA
ASTURIAS
CANTABRIA
PAÍS VASCO
NAVARRA
LA RIOJA
CASTILLA Y LEÓN
ARAGÓN
CATALUÑA
MADRID
CASTILLA-LA MANCHA
COMUNIDAD VALENCIANA
EXTREMADURA
ANDALUCÍA
MURCIA
ISLAS BALEARES
LOS PIRINEOS
SIERRA DE GUADARRAMA
SIERRA NEVADA
Costa Brava
Costa Blanca
Costa del Sol
Estrecho de Gilbraltar
Río Ebro
Río Duero
Río Tajo
Río Guadiana
Río Guadalquivir
La Coruña
Santiago de Compostela
Vigo
Oporto
Lisboa
Oviedo
León
Santander
Bilbao
San Sebastián
Pamplona
Logroño
Burgos
Valladolid
Zamora
Salamanca
Segovia
Ávila
El Escorial
Madrid
Guadalajara
Toledo
Cáceres
Mérida
Badajoz
Ciudad Real
Albacete
Zaragoza
Lérida
Barcelona
Tarragona
Castellón
Valencia
Alicante
Murcia
Almería
Granada
Jaén
Córdoba
Sevilla
Huelva
Jerez de la Frontera
Cádiz
Málaga
Gibraltar (R.U.)
Ceuta (Esp.)
Tánger
Melilla (Esp.)
Mallorca
Menorca
Ibiza
Formentera
Palma
CAMERÚN
GABÓN
Malabo
GUINEA ECUATORIAL
ISLAS CANARIAS
La Palma
Tenerife
Gomera
Hierro
Gran Canaria
Lanzarote
Fuerteventura
Santa Cruz de Tenerife
Las Palmas de Gran Canaria
MARRUECOS
0 50 100 MILLAS
0 50 100 KILÓMETROS

Pistas calientes

(Hot Tips on the Seven Communicative Functions)

Descripción. Remember to use **ser** to describe physical and personality characteristics and **estar** to describe emotions. **Ser** is also used to talk about where events take place. Pay attention to agreement of nouns and adjectives: ***Una* clase aburrid*a*, *un* problema delicad*o*.**

Comparación. Remember that **más/menos... que** is used to compare things that are not the same and **tan/tanto... como** are used for things that are the same. When comparing equal nouns, be careful to pay attention to agreement: **Tiene *tantos problemas* como su hijo. Bebe *tanta cerveza* como sus amigos.**

Narración en el pasado. Remember that the preterite moves the story line forward in time and the imperfect fleshes out the story with descriptions and emotions: ***Fuimos* al campo el sábado. *Hacía* frío aquella noche, pero *llevábamos* mucha ropa y cuando *empezamos* a bailar, no *sentíamos* el frío.** When summarizing a past experience, use the preterite: **Fue una experiencia inolvidable.**

Reacciones y recomendaciones. Remember that subjective, reactive, or value judgment statements such as **Es fantástico que...** and **Es terrible que...** are followed by the subjunctive. The subjunctive is also required when making recommendations and suggestions, since the result of a recommendation is not in our control: **Es bueno que *tengan* / *hayan tenido* / *tuvieran* suficiente dinero. Ahora recomiendo que *empiecen* a ahorrar dinero para su próximo viaje.**

Hablar de los gustos. Remember that in sentences with **gustar**-type verbs, the thing liked is the grammatical subject, which therefore determines whether **gustar** is singular or plural. Don't forget that whoever likes the thing is the indirect object and must be preceded with **a: *A* Javi le gustan los museos. *A* los turistas les molesta el ruido.**

Hacer hipótesis. The conditional is easy to form. Just add **-ía, -ías, -ía, -íamos, -íais,** and **-ían** to the infinitive: **escucharía, comería, escribiría.** Remember that there are twelve irregular verbs for the conditional. In a purely hypothetical *if, then* sentence, remember to use the past subjunctive in the *if clause* (**Si supiera, Si pudiera...**) and the conditional for the result (**estaría furioso, llamaría a la policía**): **Si *estudiara* en México, mi español *mejoraría* mucho.**

Hablar del futuro. The future tense is easy to form. Just add **-é, -ás, -á, -emos, -éis,** and **-án** to the infinitive: **escucharé, comeré, escribiré**. Remember that the twelve verbs that are irregular in the conditional are also irregular in the future. Be aware of the use of subjunctive in many of the clauses that introduce future events: **Cuando *vaya*, irá al Prado. Tan pronto como *salgamos*, lo llamaremos.**